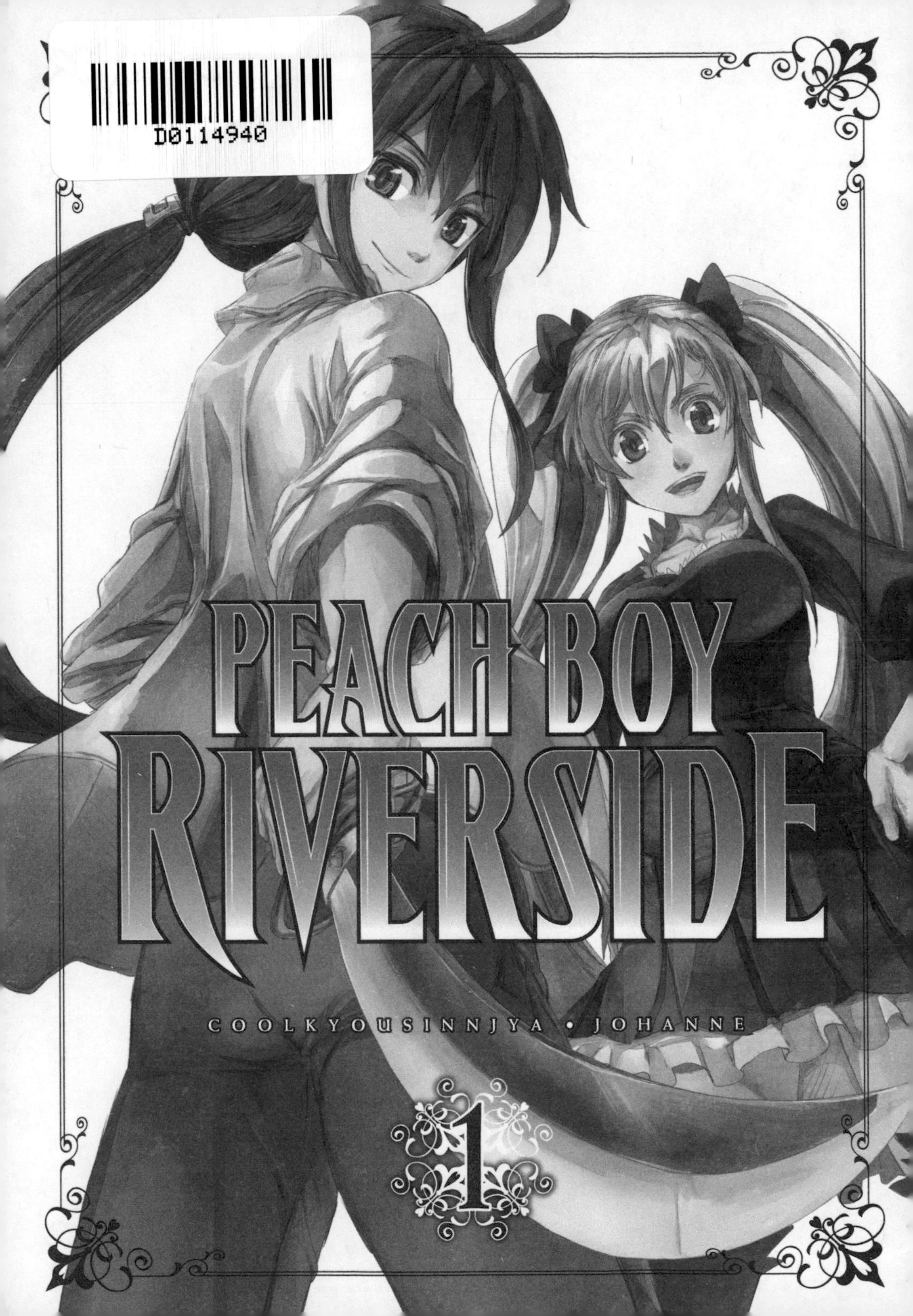
PEACH BOY
RIVERSIDE
COOLKYOUSINNJYA • JOHANNE
1

CONTENTS

CHAPTER 1:
THE PRINCESS AND THE IMPORTED PEACH

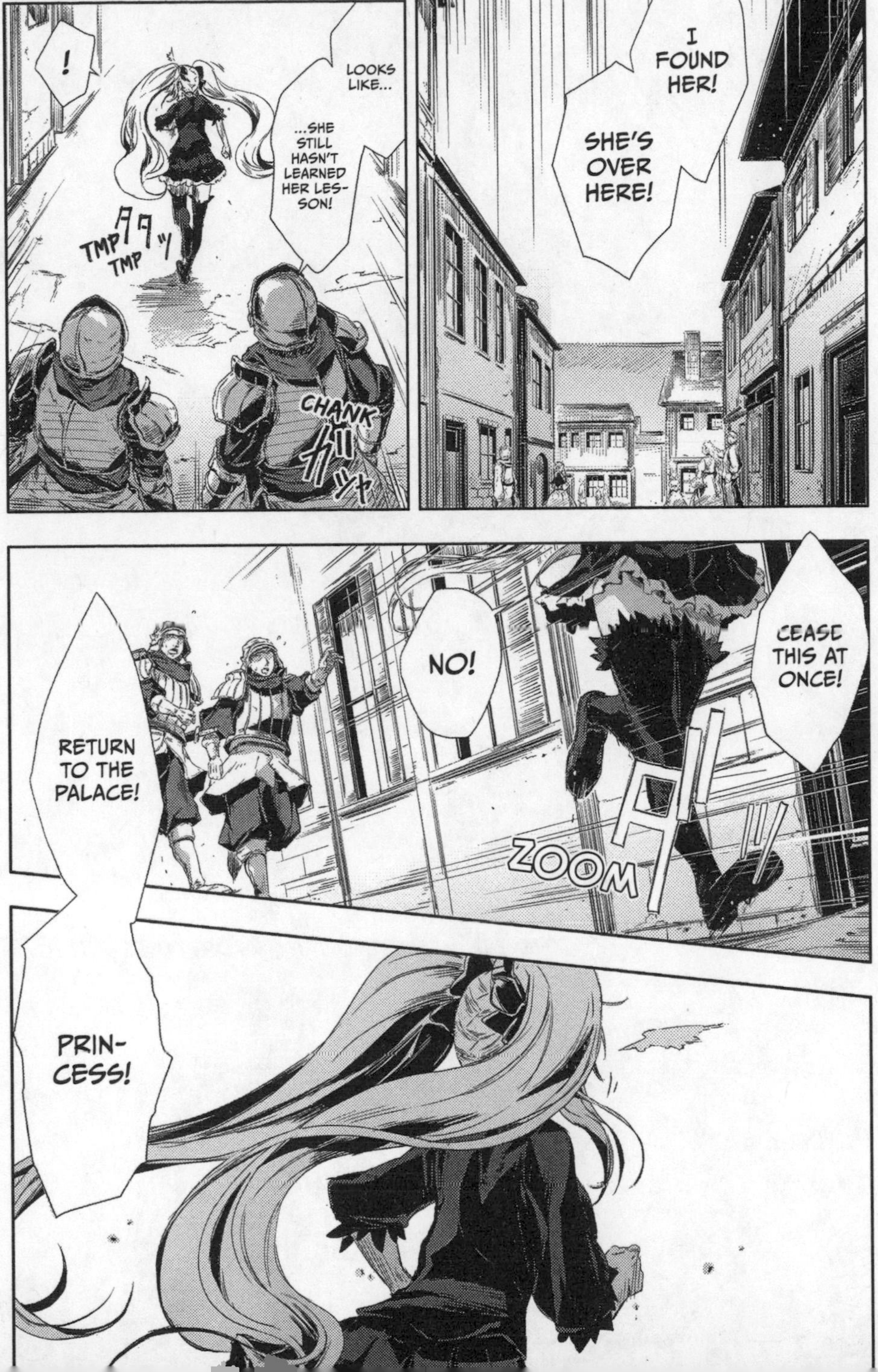
I FOUND HER!
SHE'S OVER HERE!
!
LOOKS LIKE...
...SHE STILL HASN'T LEARNED HER LES-SON!
TMP TMP
CHANK
CEASE THIS AT ONCE!
NO!
RETURN TO THE PALACE!
ZOOM
PRIN-CESS!

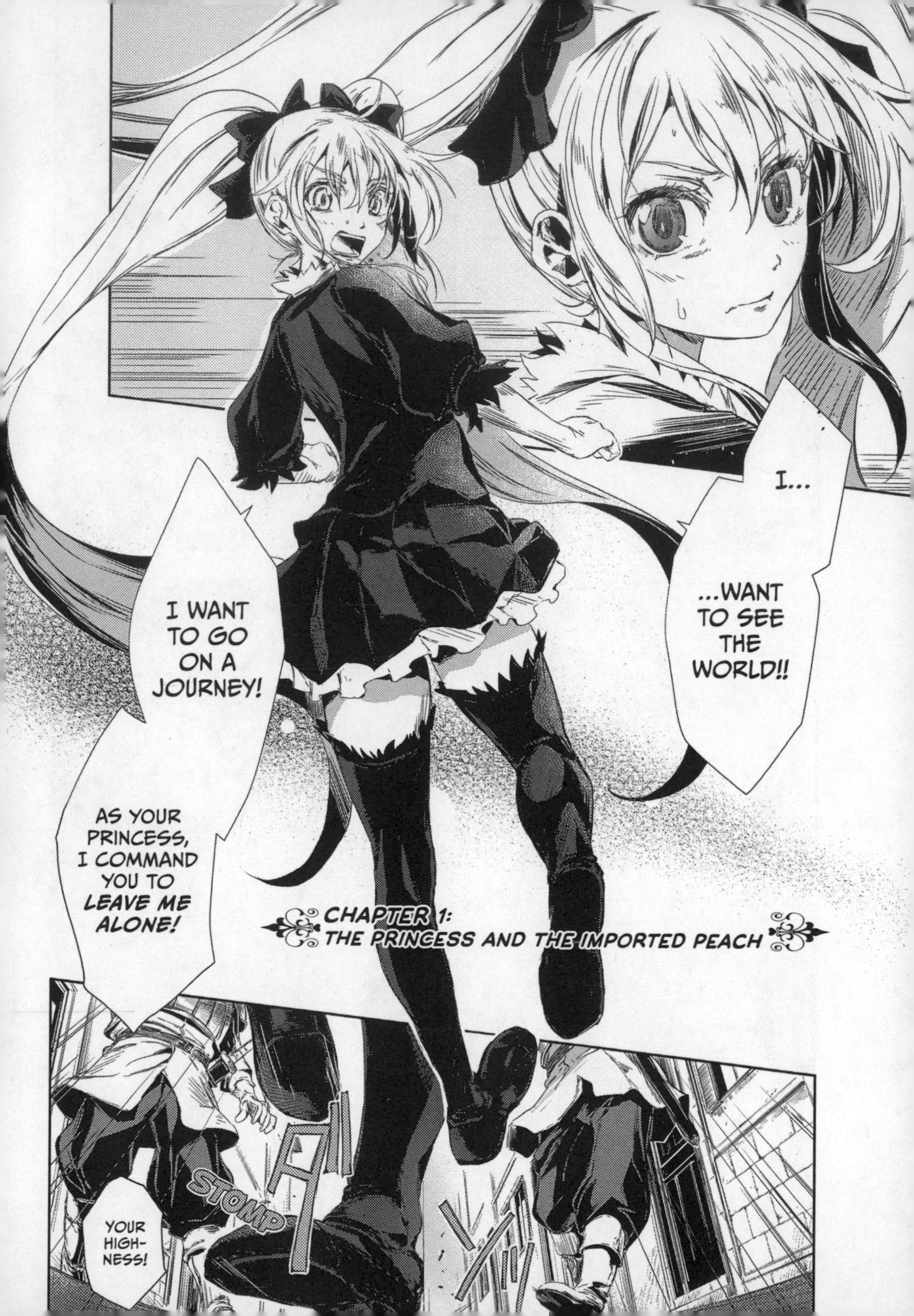
I...
...WANT TO SEE THE WORLD!!
I WANT TO GO ON A JOURNEY!
AS YOUR PRINCESS, I COMMAND YOU TO *LEAVE ME ALONE!*
CHAPTER 1: THE PRINCESS AND THE IMPORTED PEACH
STOMP
YOUR HIGH-NESS!

HERE ON THE WESTERN CONTINENT, MONSTERS ONCE RAN RAMPANT.
GRIPPED BY FEAR,
THE HUMANS CAME TOGETHER TO BUILD TALL CASTLES, DIG DEEPER MOATS,
AND RAISE ARMIES.
BUT THE MONSTERS WERE POWERFUL.
THE CONFLICT FELL INTO A STALEMATE.
IT WAS THEN...
...THAT A LONE TRAVELER...
...CAME PASSING THROUGH.
ANY-BODY HOME?

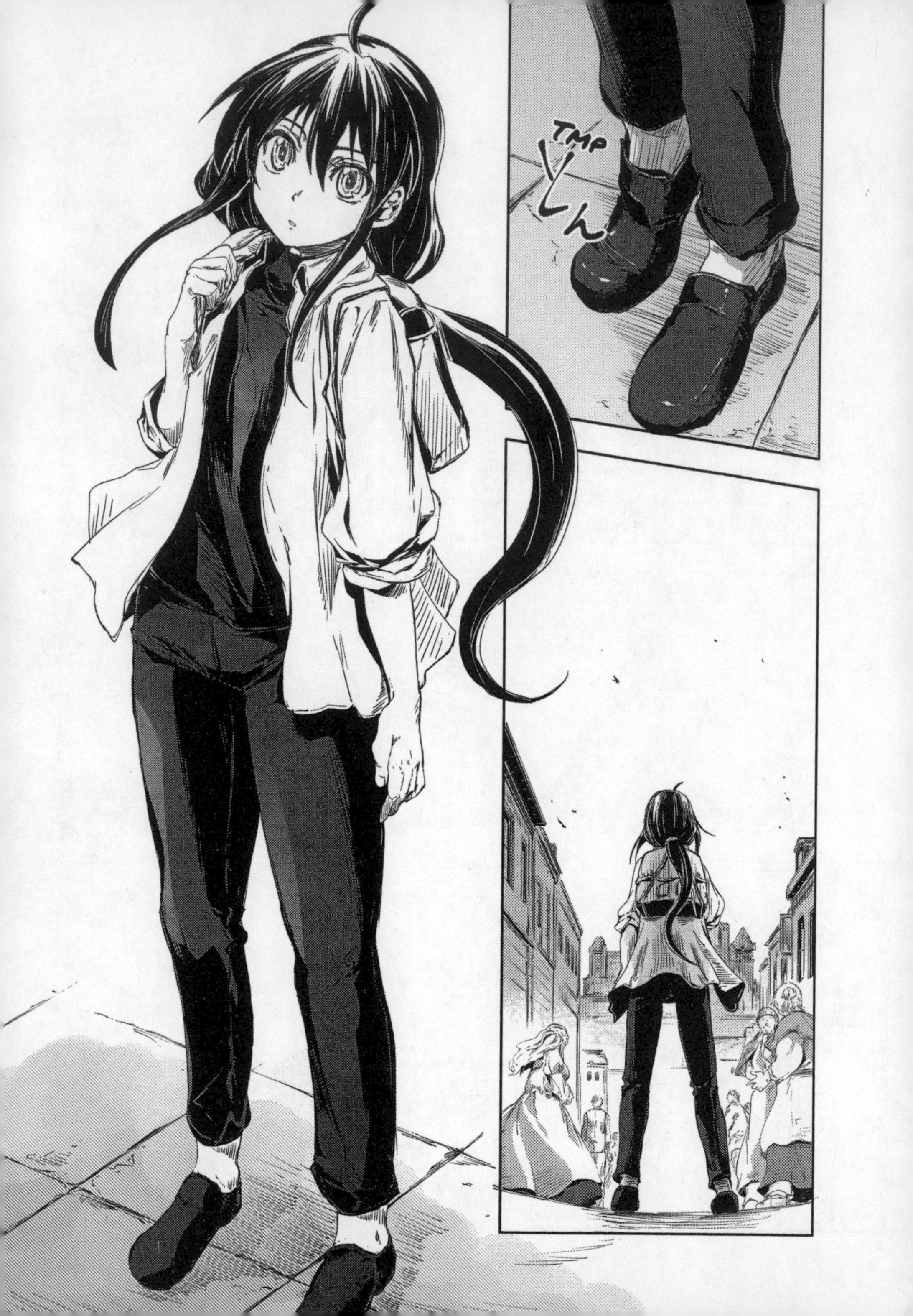
TMP

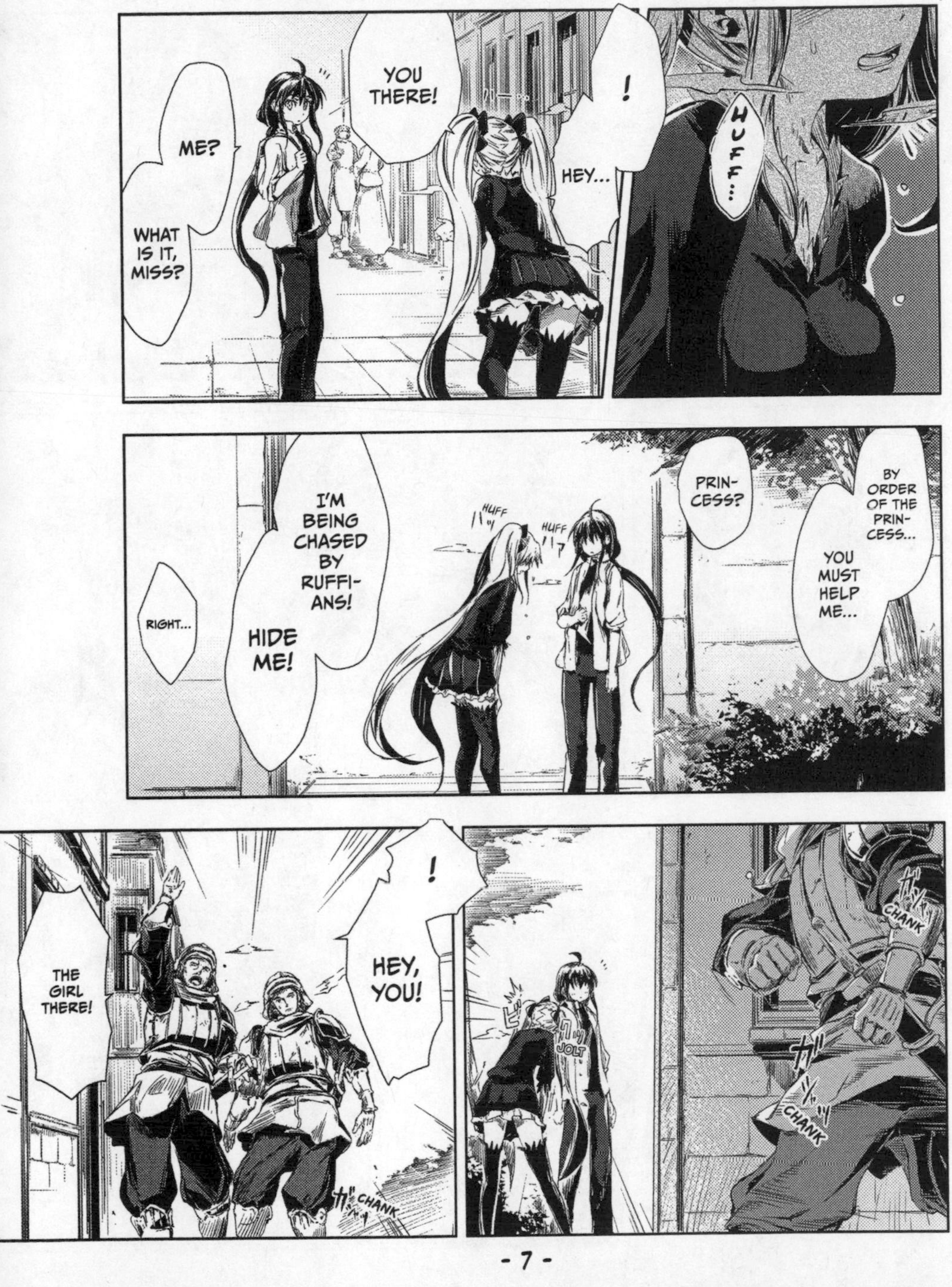
HUFF...
!
HEY...
YOU THERE!
ME?
WHAT IS IT, MISS?
BY ORDER OF THE PRINCESS...
YOU MUST HELP ME...
PRINCESS?
HUFF
HUFF
I'M BEING CHASED BY RUFFIANS!
HIDE ME!
RIGHT...
CHANK
CHANK
JOLT
!
HEY, YOU!
THE GIRL THERE!
CHANK

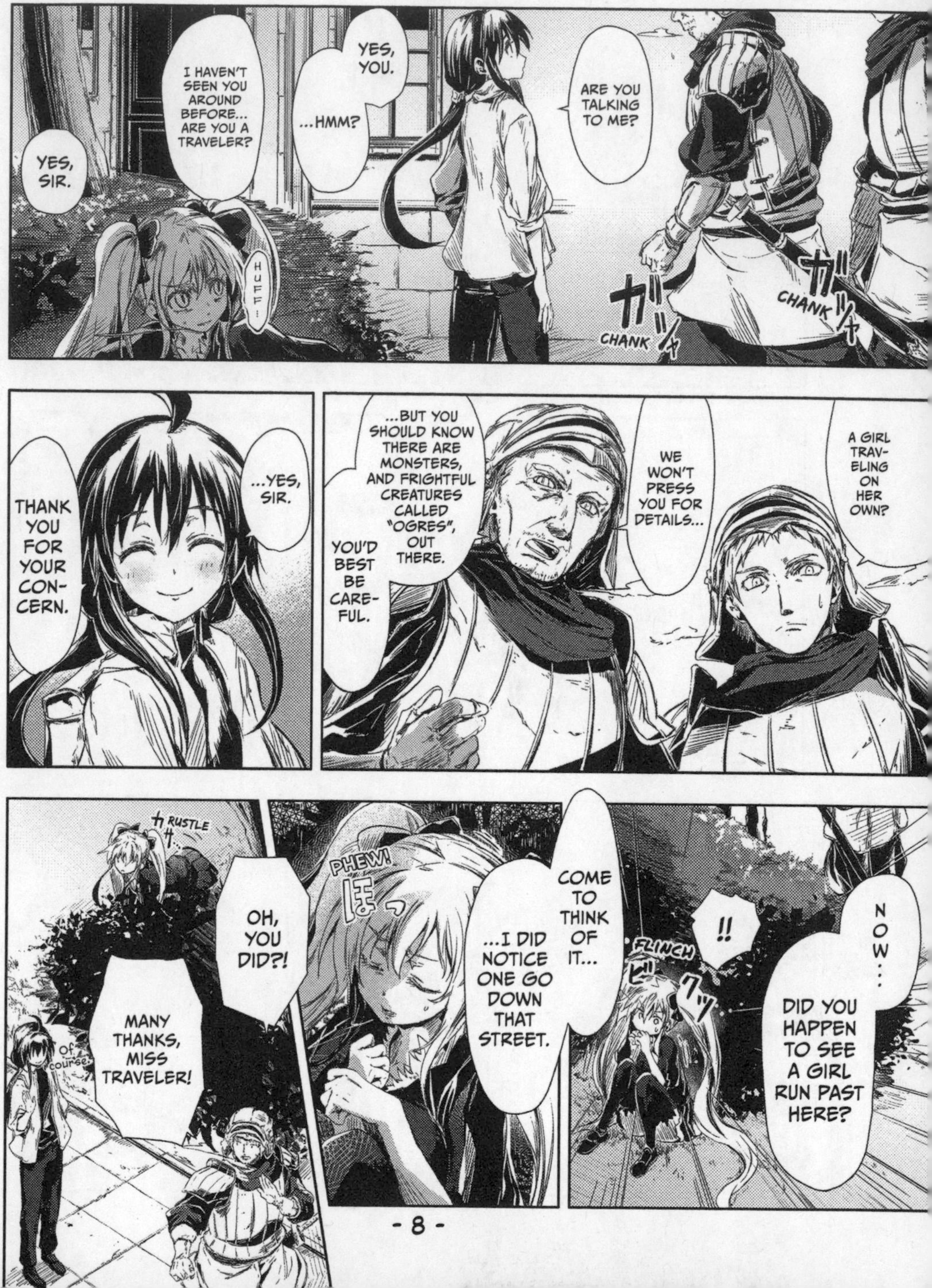
ARE YOU TALKING TO ME?
ガシャ CHANK
ガシャ CHANK
YES, YOU.
...HMM?
I HAVEN'T SEEN YOU AROUND BEFORE... ARE YOU A TRAVELER?
HUFF...
YES, SIR.
A GIRL TRAVELING ON HER OWN?
WE WON'T PRESS YOU FOR DETAILS...
...BUT YOU SHOULD KNOW THERE ARE MONSTERS, AND FRIGHTFUL CREATURES CALLED "OGRES", OUT THERE.
YOU'D BEST BE CAREFUL.
...YES, SIR.
THANK YOU FOR YOUR CONCERN.
NOW...
DID YOU HAPPEN TO SEE A GIRL RUN PAST HERE?
!!
ビクッ FLINCH
COME TO THINK OF IT...
...I DID NOTICE ONE GO DOWN THAT STREET.
ほっ PHEW!
OH, YOU DID?!
MANY THANKS, MISS TRAVELER!
RUSTLE
Of course.

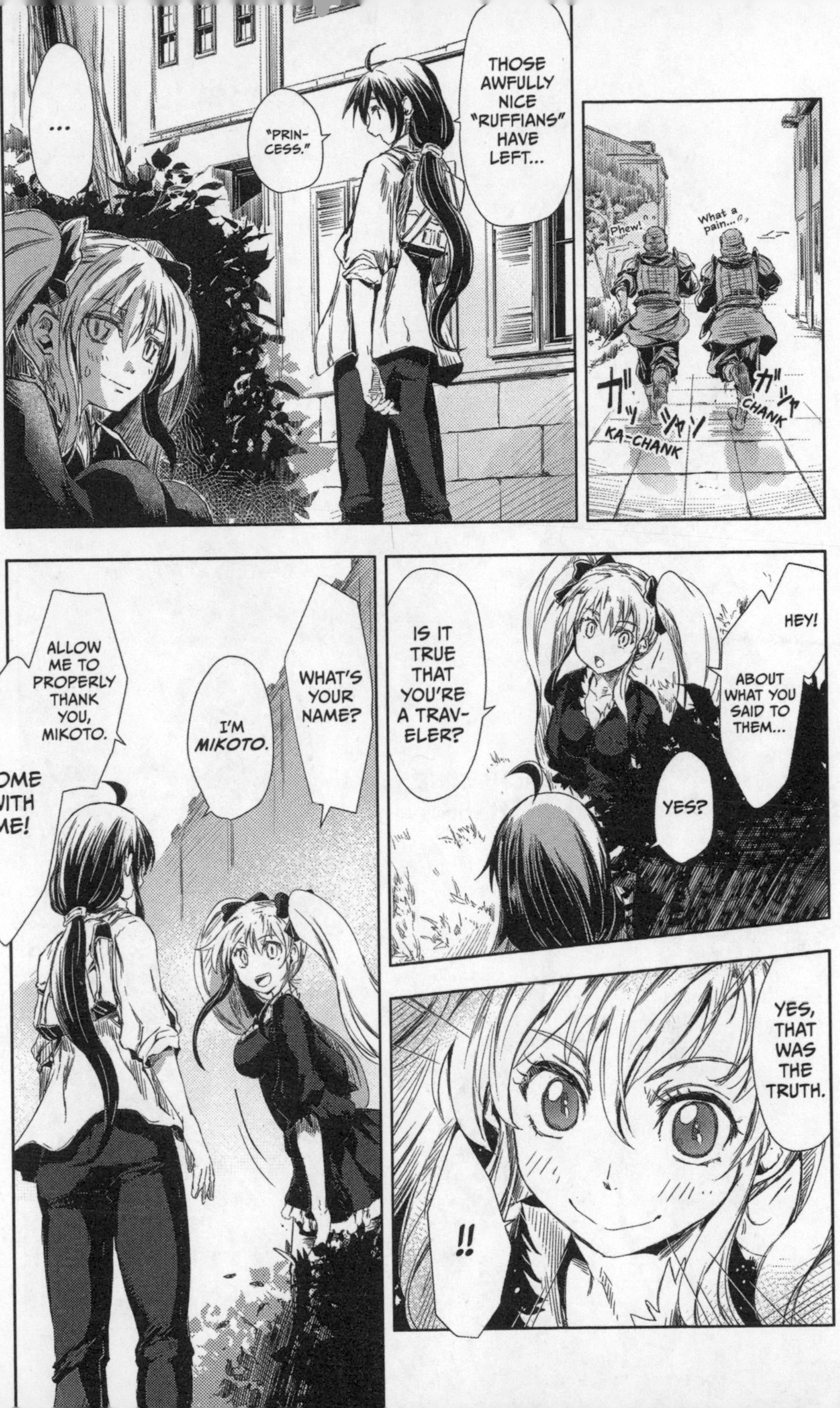

Phew!
What a pain...
ガッ
ジャン
KA-CHANK
ガシャ
CHANK
THOSE AWFULLY NICE "RUFFIANS" HAVE LEFT...
"PRIN-CESS."
...
HEY!
ABOUT WHAT YOU SAID TO THEM...
YES?
IS IT TRUE THAT YOU'RE A TRAV-ELER?
YES, THAT WAS THE TRUTH.
!!
WHAT'S YOUR NAME?
I'M MIKOTO.
ALLOW ME TO PROPERLY THANK YOU, MIKOTO.
COME WITH ME!

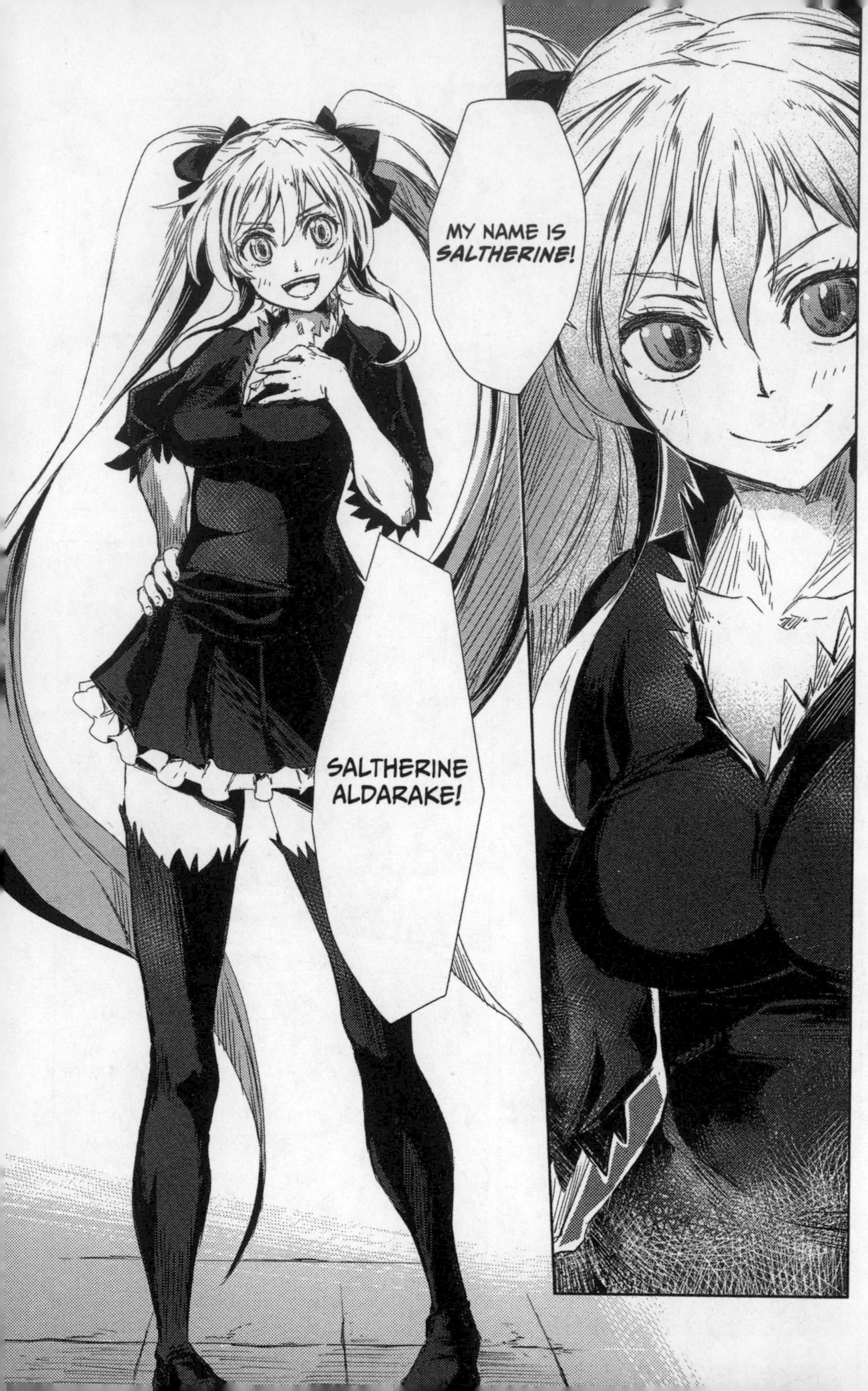
MY NAME IS SALTHERINE!
SALTHERINE ALDARAKE!

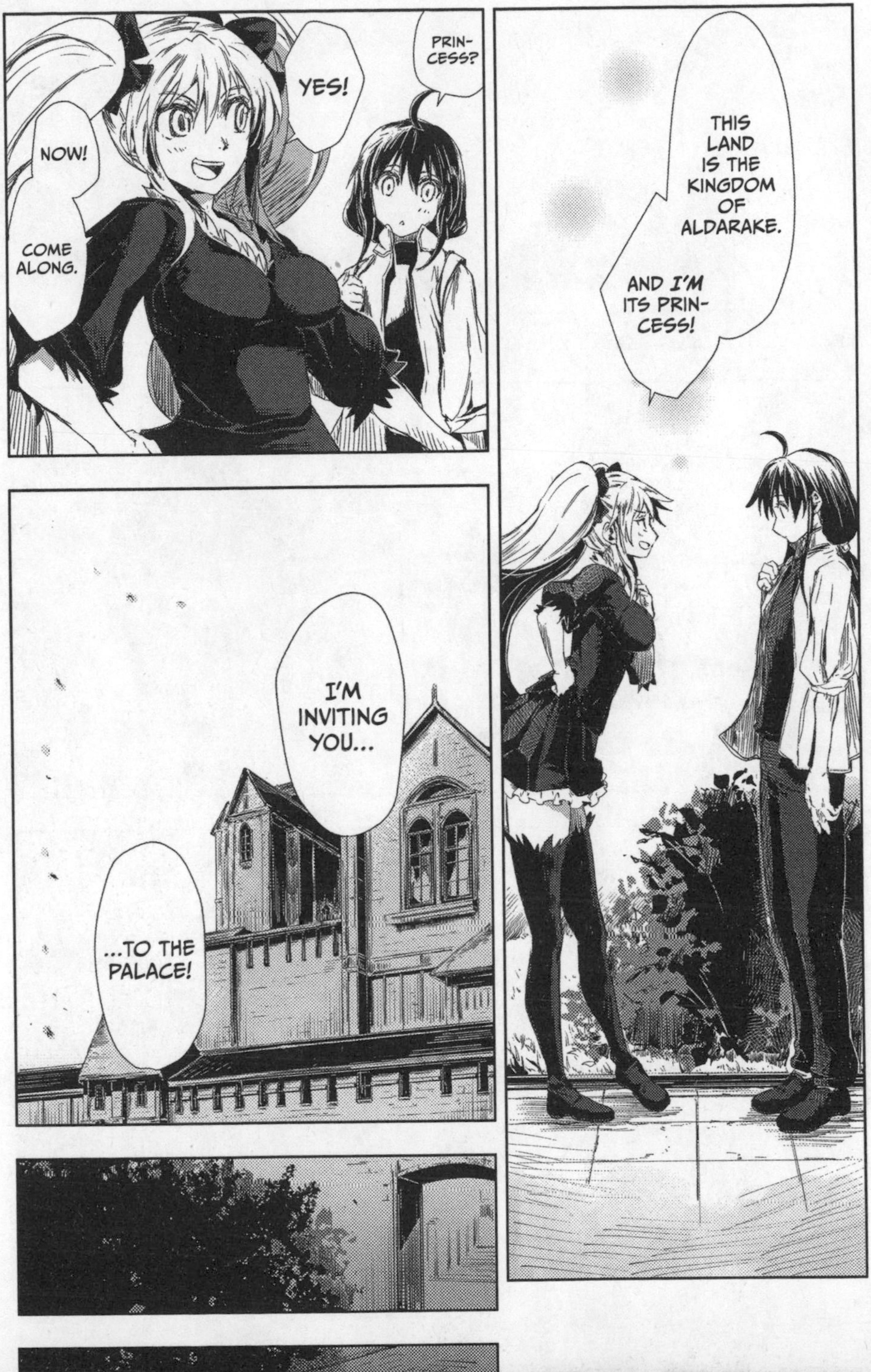
THIS LAND IS THE KINGDOM OF ALDARAKE.
AND *I'M* ITS PRINCESS!
PRINCESS?
YES!
NOW!
COME ALONG.
I'M INVITING YOU...
...TO THE PALACE!

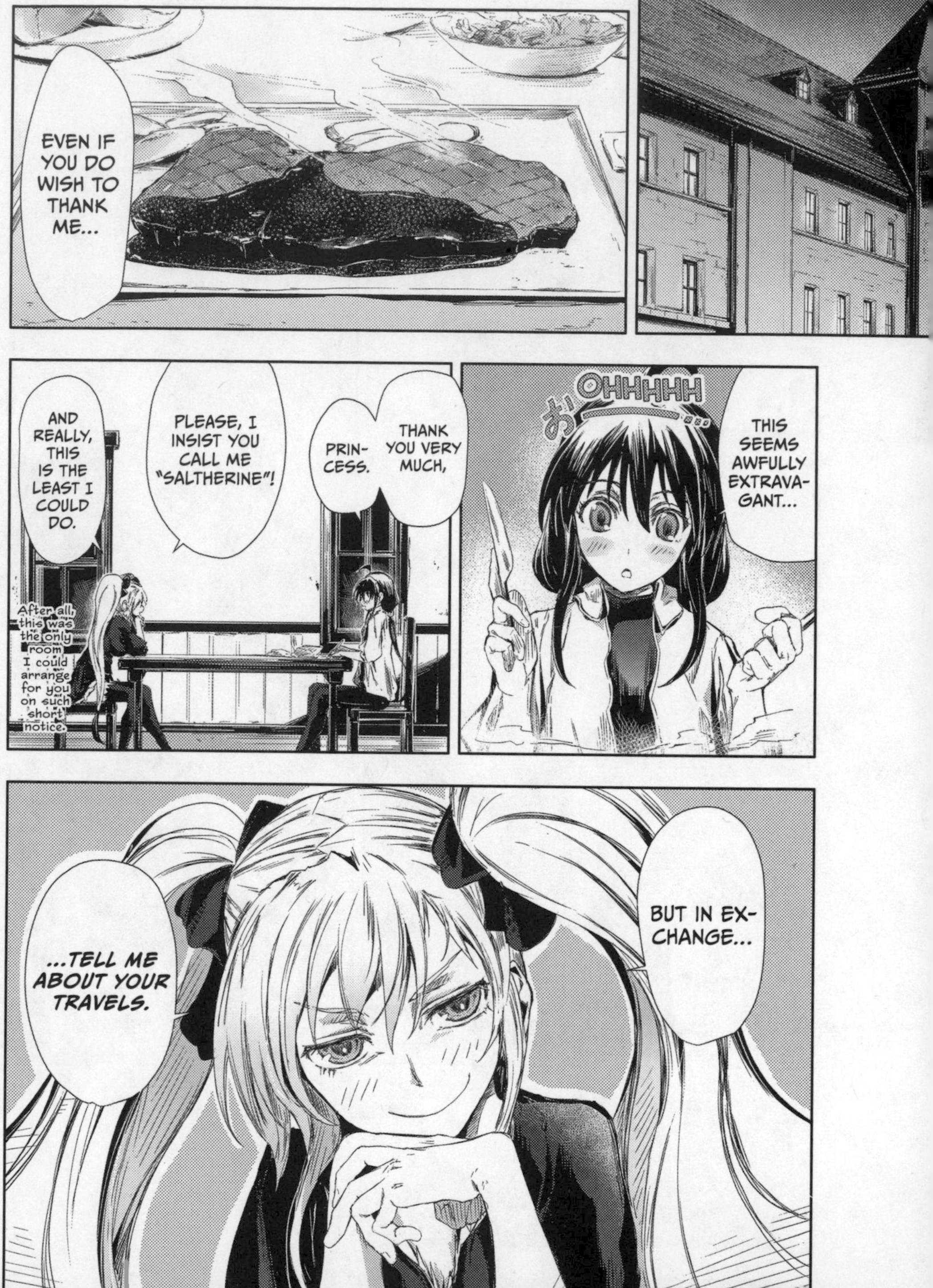
EVEN IF YOU DO WISH TO THANK ME...
お OHHHHH
THIS SEEMS AWFULLY EXTRAVA-GANT...
THANK YOU VERY MUCH,
PRIN-CESS.
PLEASE, I INSIST YOU CALL ME "SALTHERINE"!
AND REALLY, THIS IS THE LEAST I COULD DO.
After all, this was the only room I could arrange for you on such short notice.
BUT IN EX-CHANGE...
...TELL ME ABOUT YOUR TRAVELS.

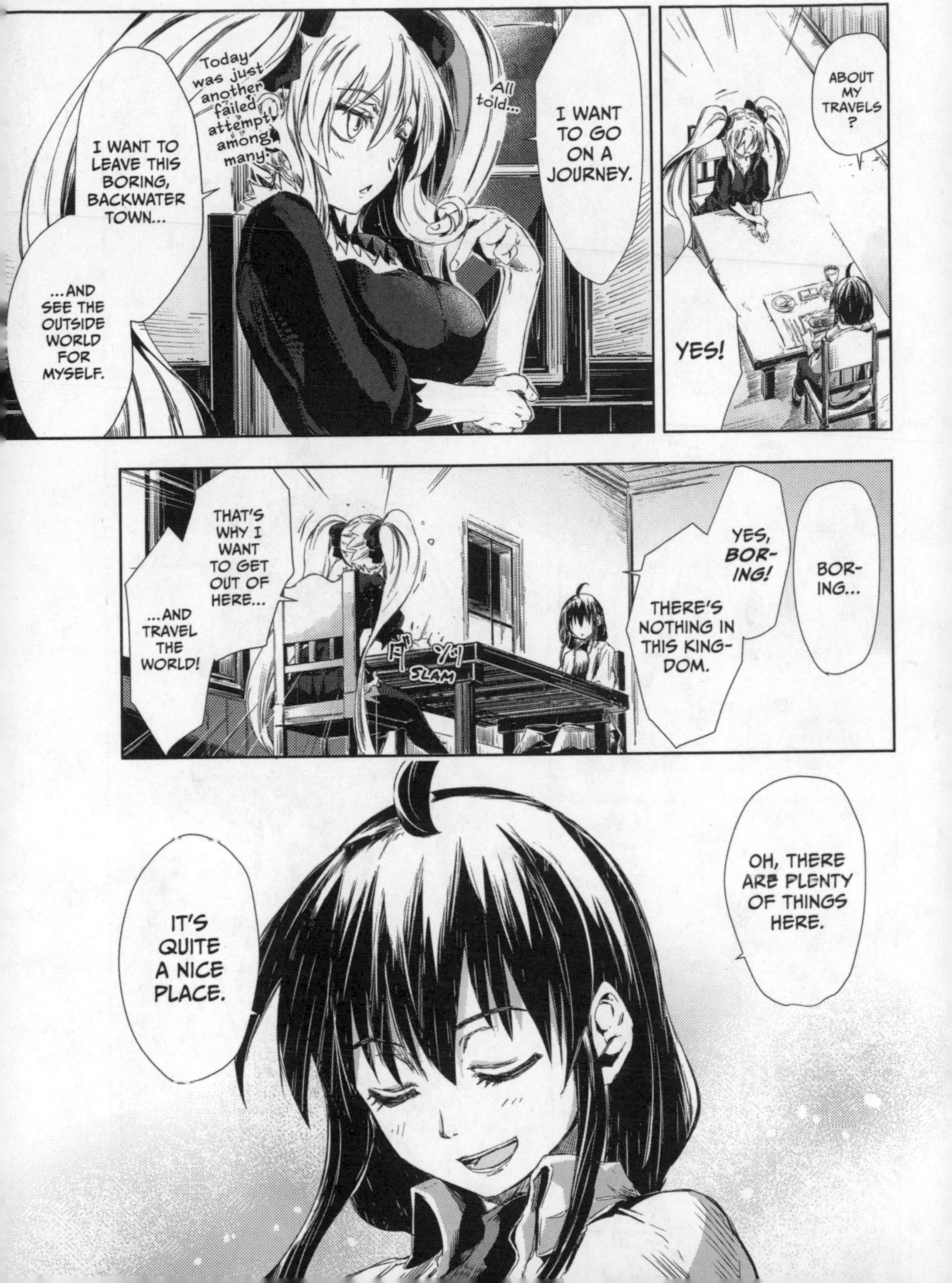
ABOUT MY TRAVELS?
YES!
I WANT TO GO ON A JOURNEY.
All told...
Today was just another failed attempt among many.
I WANT TO LEAVE THIS BORING, BACKWATER TOWN...
...AND SEE THE OUTSIDE WORLD FOR MYSELF.
BOR-ING...
YES, BOR-ING!
THERE'S NOTHING IN THIS KING-DOM.
SLAM
THAT'S WHY I WANT TO GET OUT OF HERE...
...AND TRAVEL THE WORLD!
OH, THERE ARE PLENTY OF THINGS HERE.
IT'S QUITE A NICE PLACE.

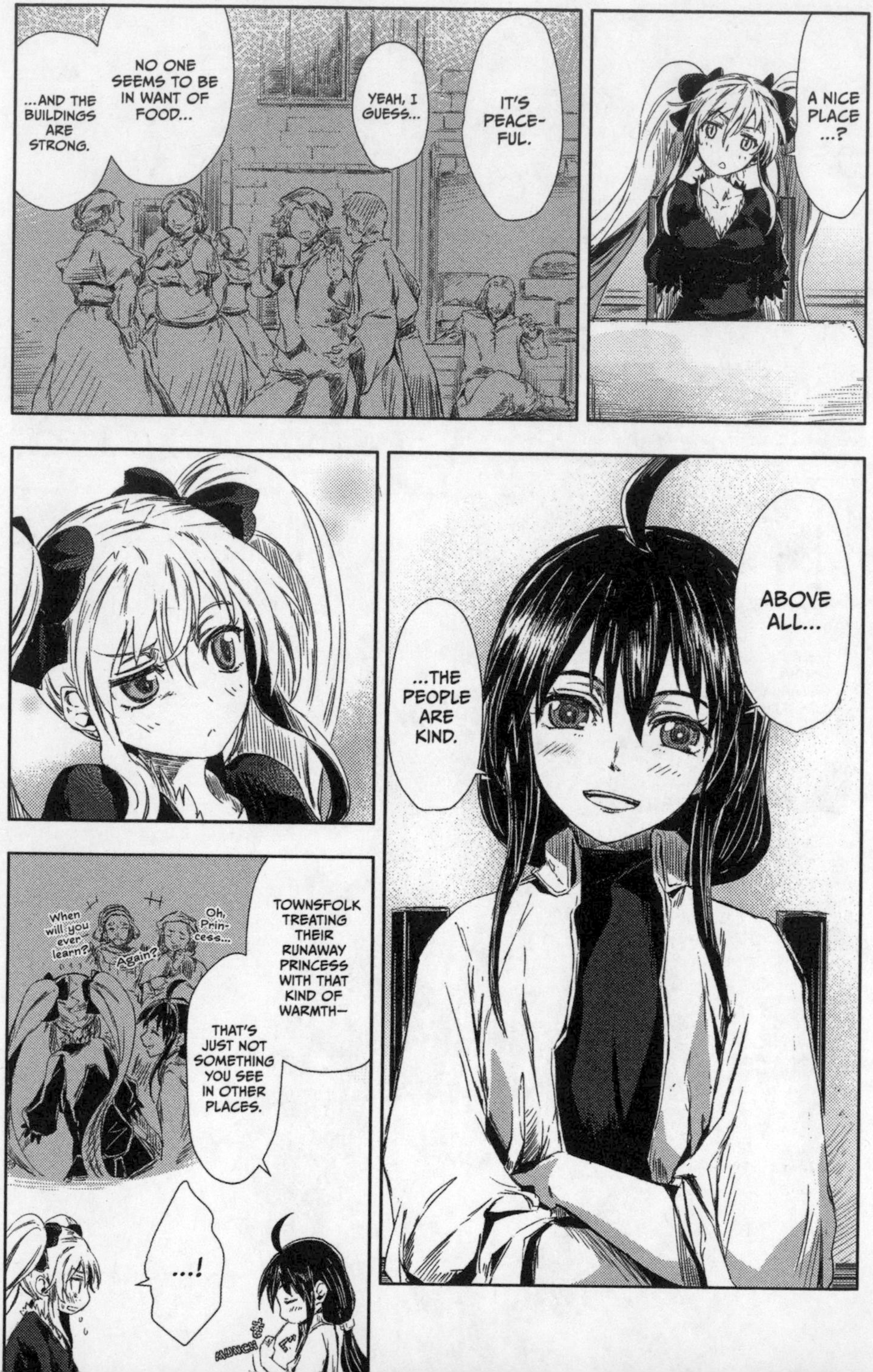
A NICE PLACE ...?
IT'S PEACE-FUL.
YEAH, I GUESS...
NO ONE SEEMS TO BE IN WANT OF FOOD...
...AND THE BUILDINGS ARE STRONG.
ABOVE ALL...
...THE PEOPLE ARE KIND.
TOWNSFOLK TREATING THEIR RUNAWAY PRINCESS WITH THAT KIND OF WARMTH—
THAT'S JUST NOT SOMETHING YOU SEE IN OTHER PLACES.
Oh, Prin-cess...
Again?
When will you ever learn?
...!

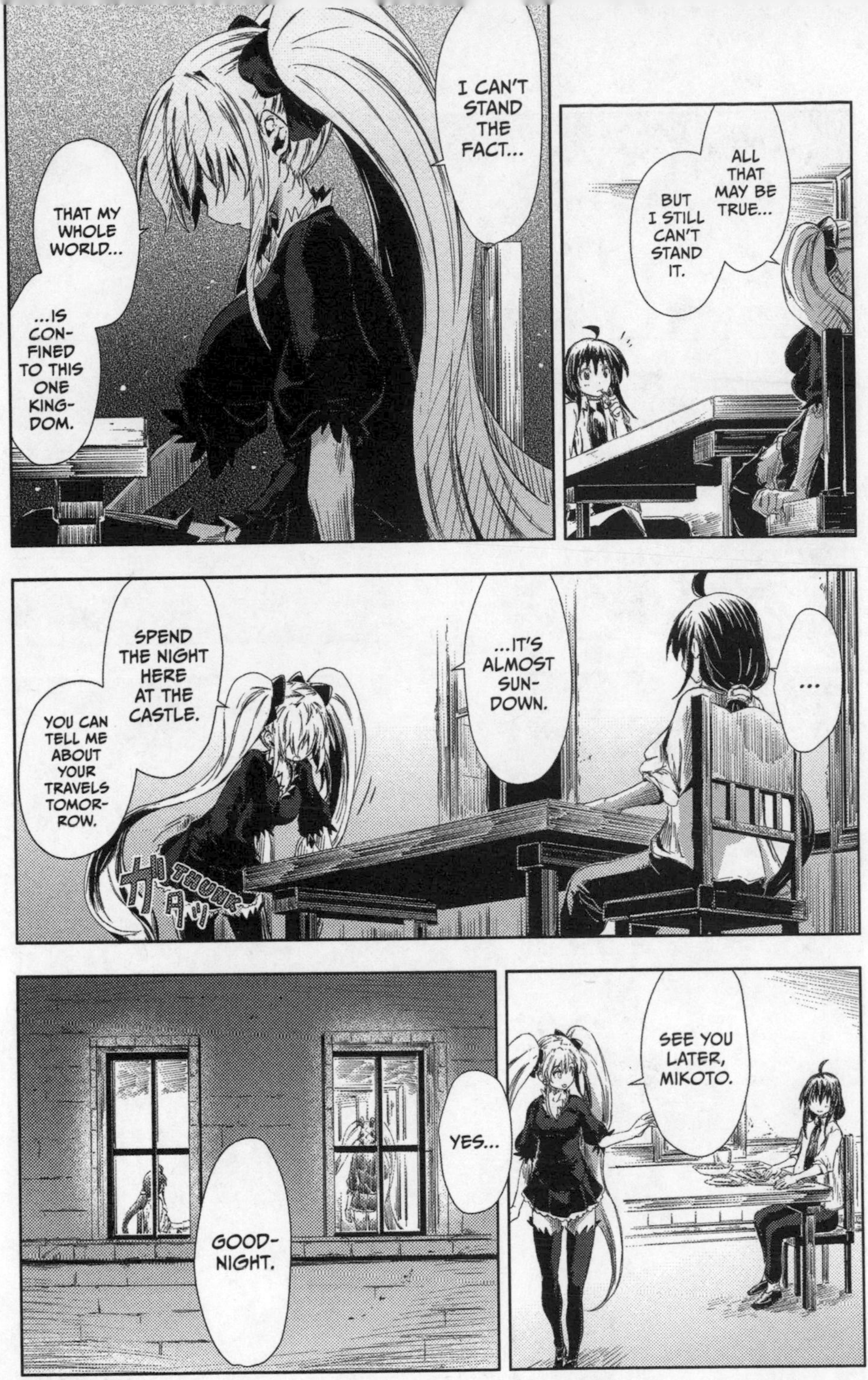
ALL THAT MAY BE TRUE...
BUT I STILL CAN'T STAND IT.
I CAN'T STAND THE FACT...
THAT MY WHOLE WORLD...
...IS CON-FINED TO THIS ONE KING-DOM.
...
...IT'S ALMOST SUN-DOWN.
SPEND THE NIGHT HERE AT THE CASTLE.
YOU CAN TELL ME ABOUT YOUR TRAVELS TOMOR-ROW.
ガタッ
THUNK
SEE YOU LATER, MIKOTO.
YES...
GOOD-NIGHT.

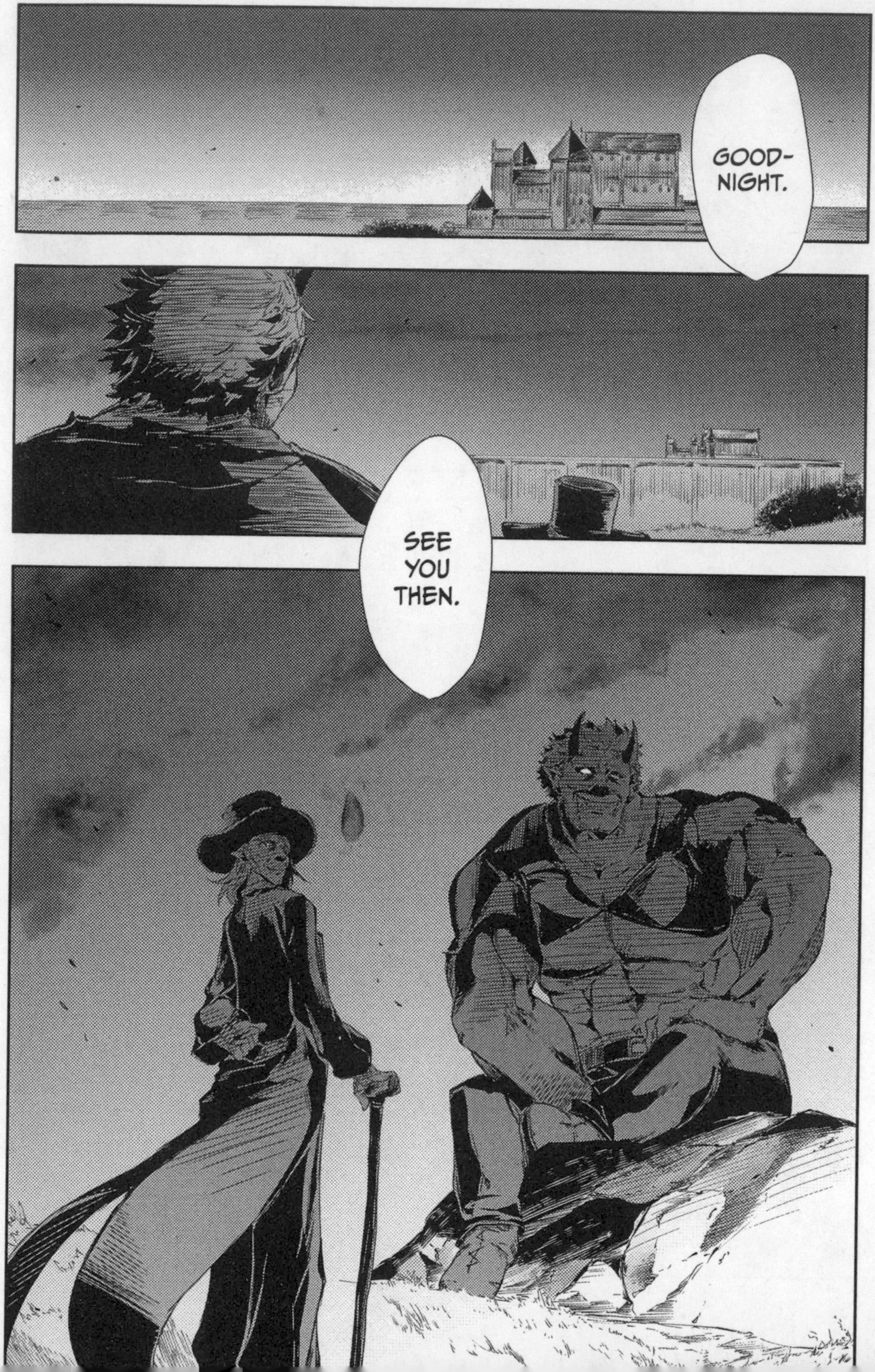
GOOD-NIGHT.
SEE YOU THEN.

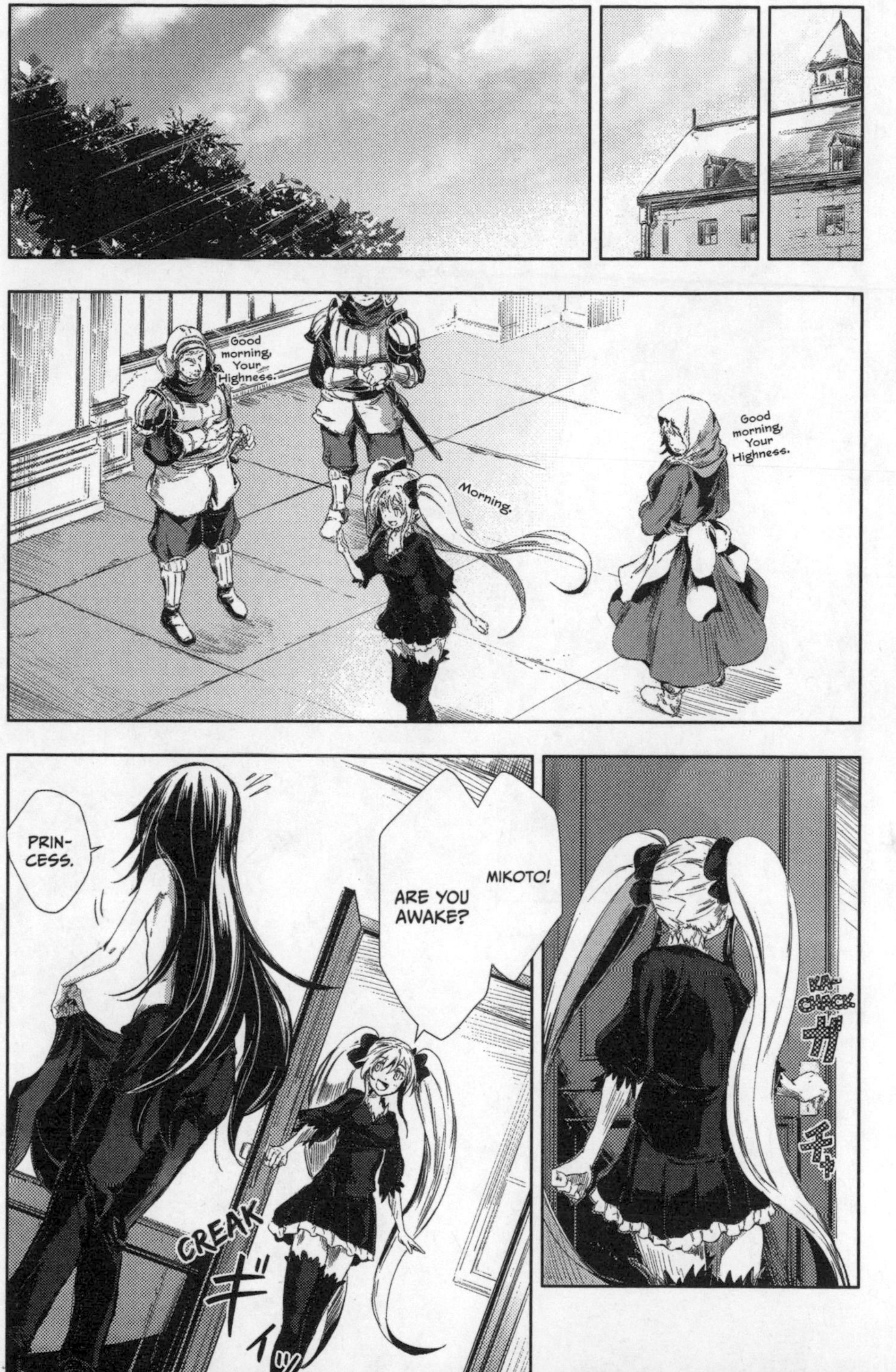
Good morning, Your Highness.
Morning.
Good morning, Your Highness.
KA-CHACK
ガチャ
MIKOTO! ARE YOU AWAKE?
PRIN-CESS.
CREAK
ギィッ

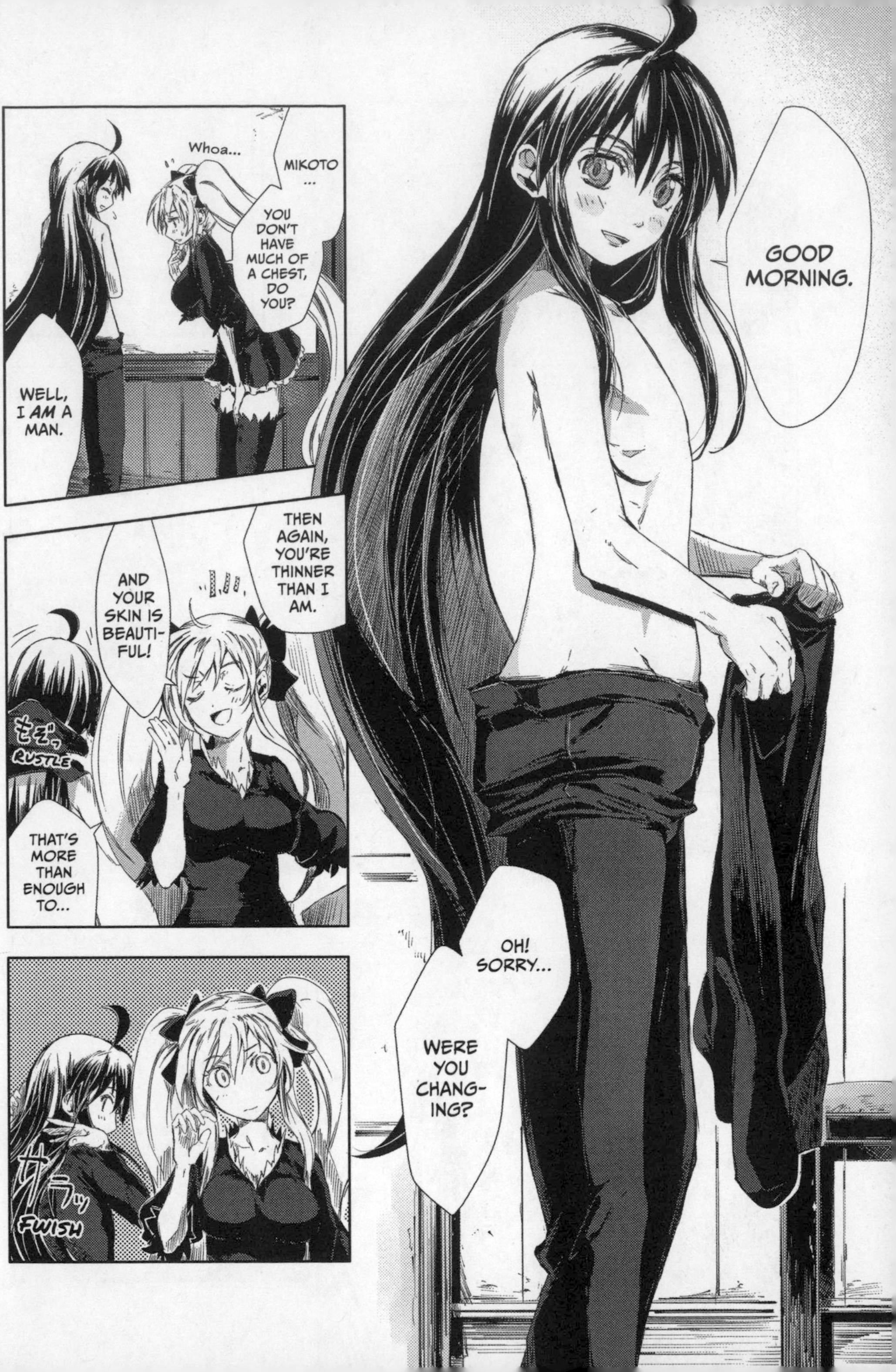
GOOD MORNING.
OH! SORRY...
WERE YOU CHANGING?
MIKOTO ...
Whoa...
YOU DON'T HAVE MUCH OF A CHEST, DO YOU?
WELL, I *AM* A MAN.
THEN AGAIN, YOU'RE THINNER THAN I AM.
AND YOUR SKIN IS BEAUTIFUL!
もぞっ
RUSTLE
THAT'S MORE THAN ENOUGH TO...
サラッ
FWISH

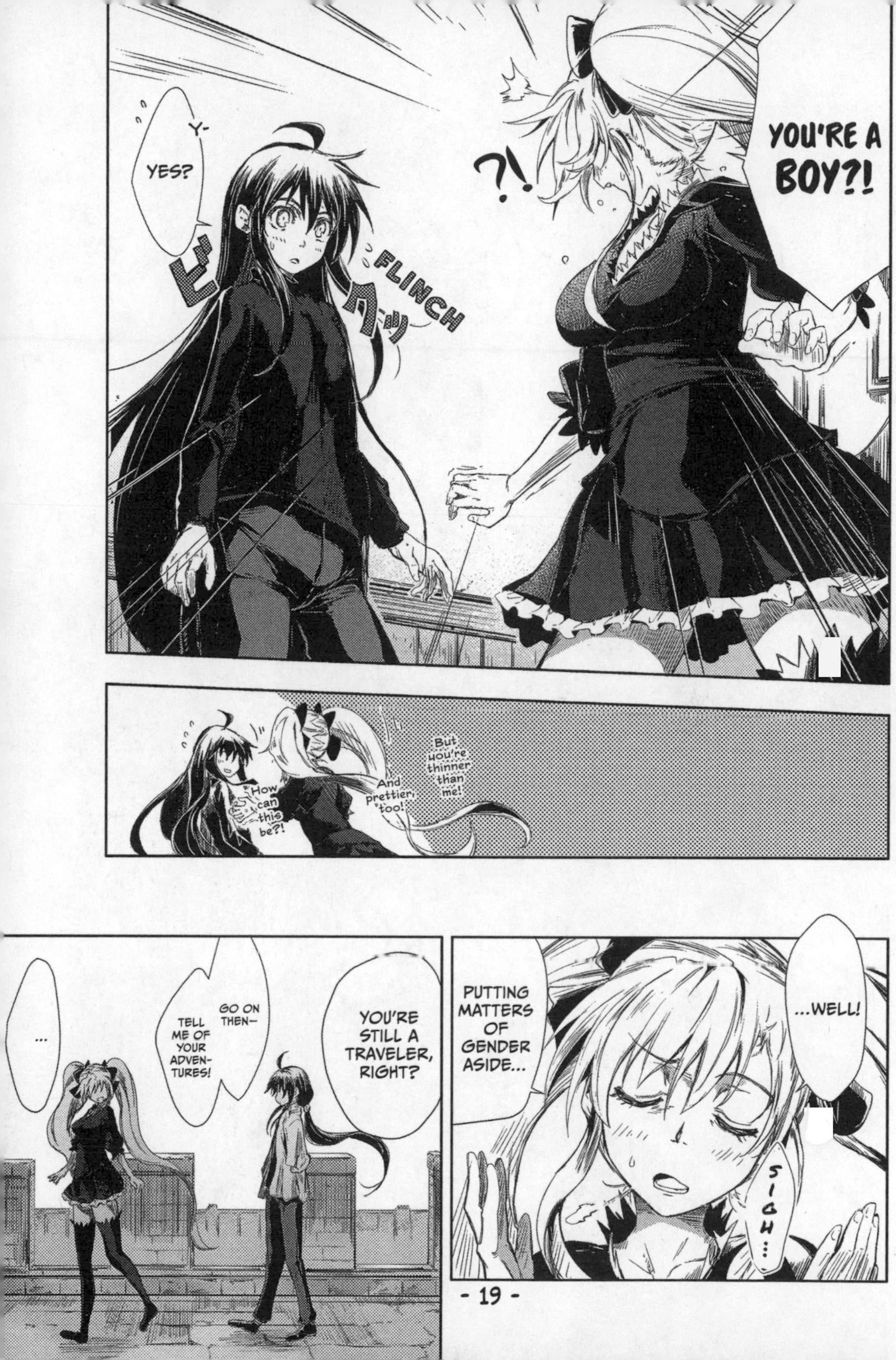
YOU'RE A BOY?!
?!
ビクッ
FLINCH
Y- YES?
But you're thinner than me!
And prettier, too!
How can this be?!
...WELL!
SIGH...
PUTTING MATTERS OF GENDER ASIDE...
YOU'RE STILL A TRAVELER, RIGHT?
GO ON THEN— TELL ME OF YOUR ADVENTURES!
...

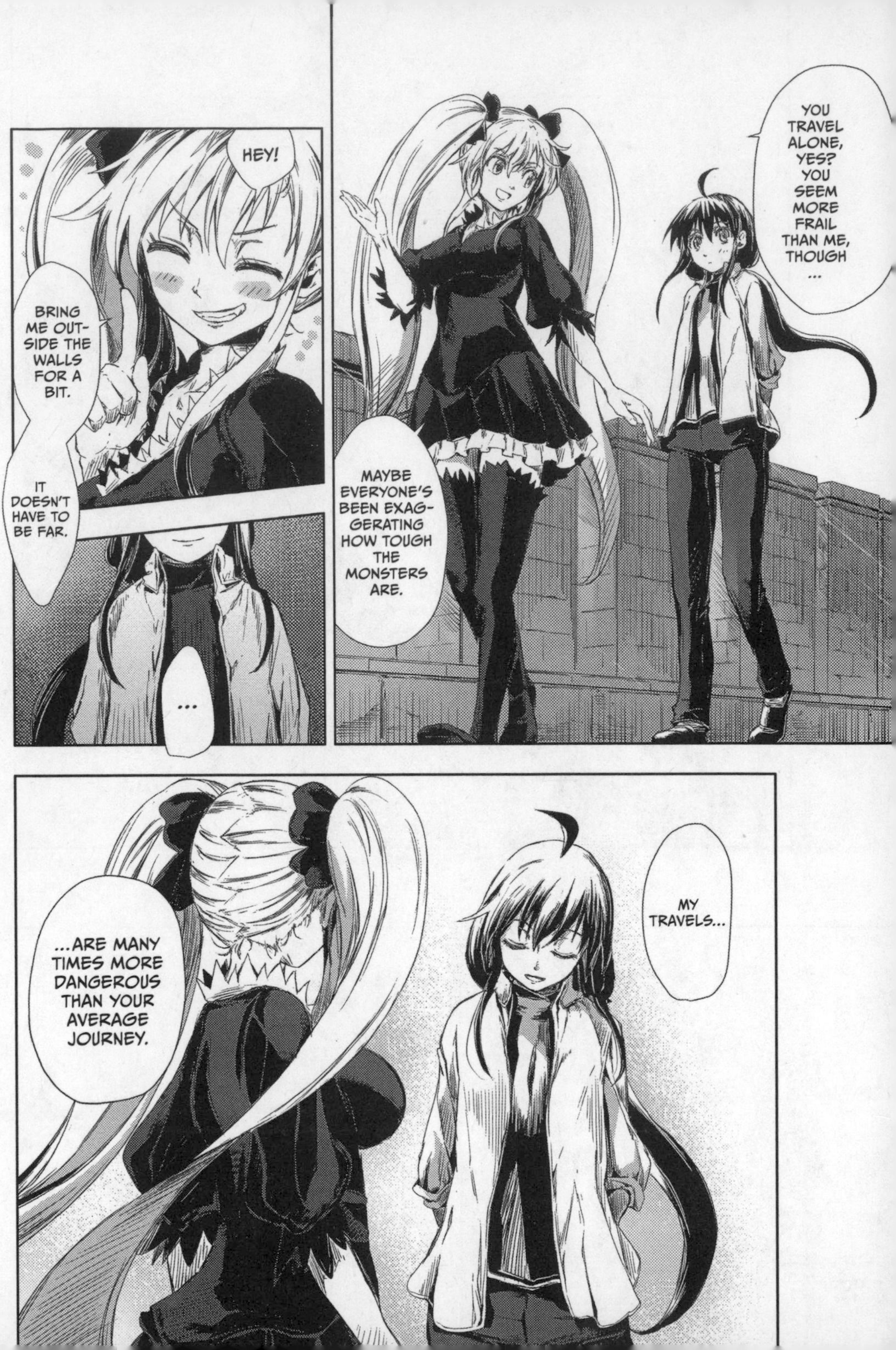
YOU TRAVEL ALONE, YES? YOU SEEM MORE FRAIL THAN ME, THOUGH ...
MAYBE EVERYONE'S BEEN EXAG-GERATING HOW TOUGH THE MONSTERS ARE.
HEY!
BRING ME OUT-SIDE THE WALLS FOR A BIT.
IT DOESN'T HAVE TO BE FAR.
...
MY TRAVELS...
...ARE MANY TIMES MORE DANGEROUS THAN YOUR AVERAGE JOURNEY.

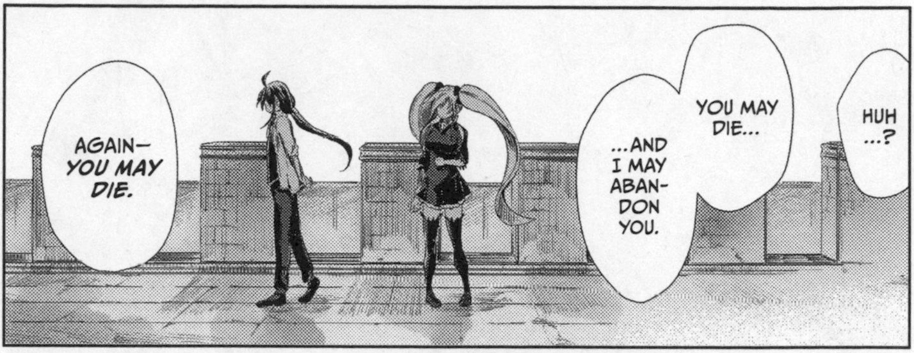
HUH ...?
YOU MAY DIE...
...AND I MAY ABAN-DON YOU.
AGAIN— YOU MAY DIE.

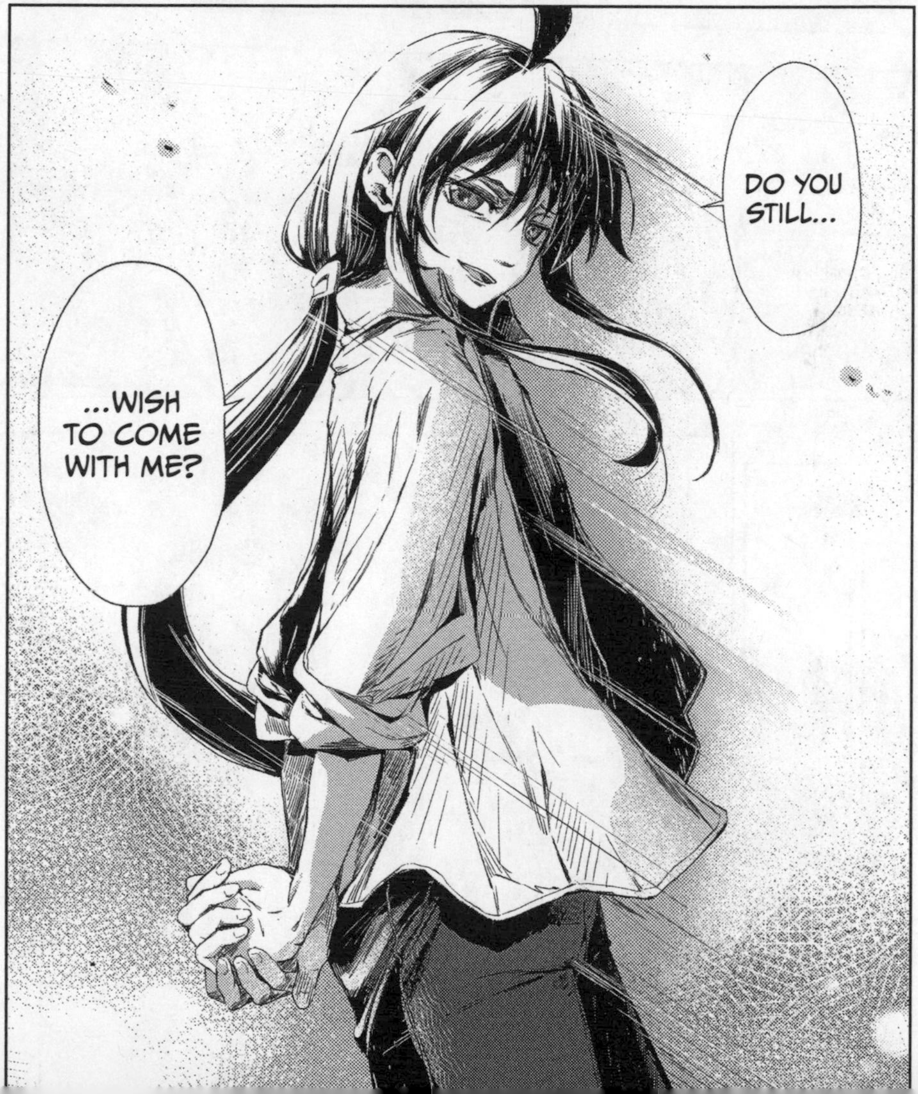
DO YOU STILL...
...WISH TO COME WITH ME?

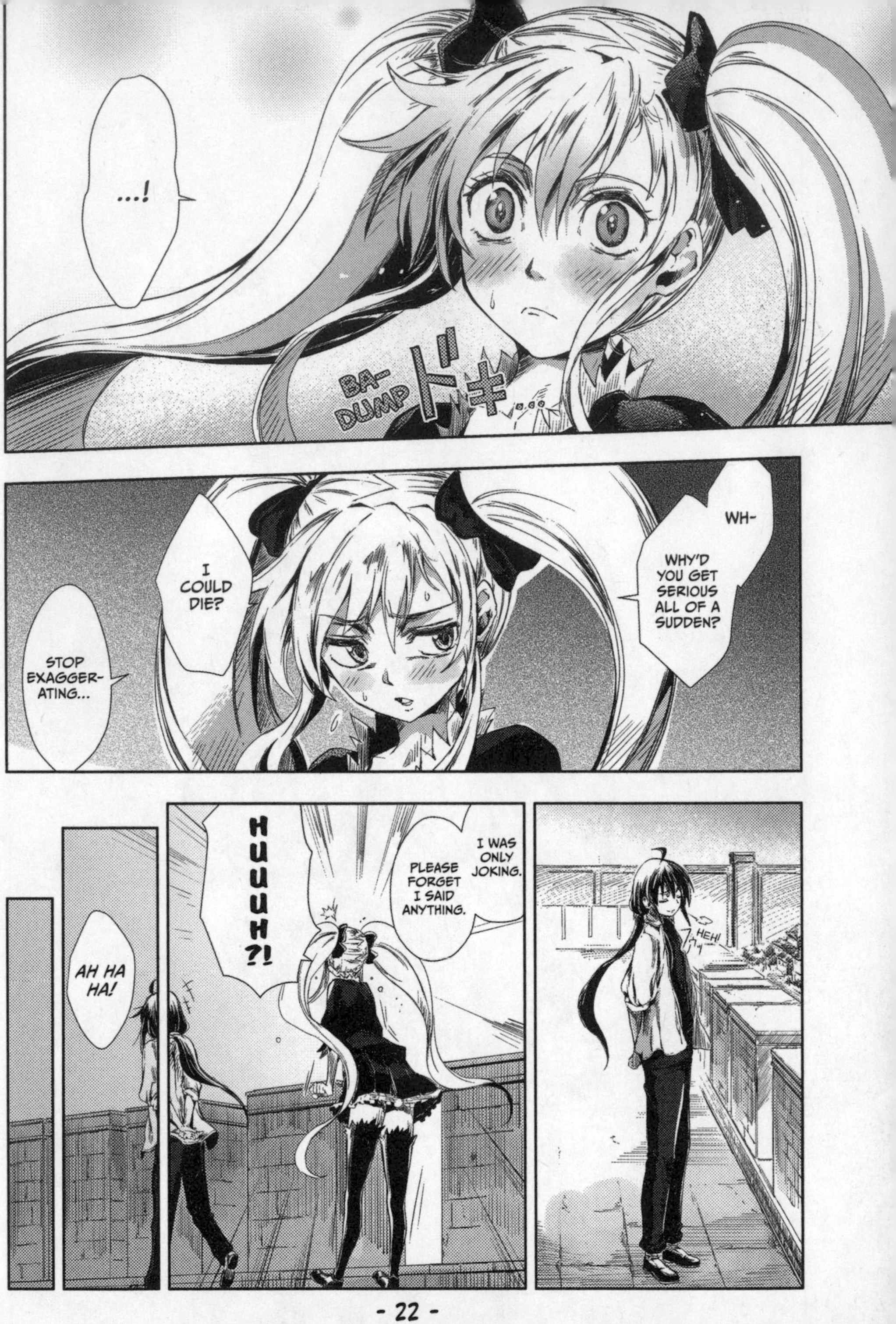
...!
BA-DUMP
ドキ
WH-
WHY'D YOU GET SERIOUS ALL OF A SUDDEN?
I COULD DIE?
STOP EXAGGERATING...
HEH!
I WAS ONLY JOKING.
PLEASE FORGET I SAID ANYTHING.
HUUUUH?!
AH HA HA!

NOW...

STATE YOUR BUSI-NESS.

I DON'T RECALL SUMMONING YOU HERE.

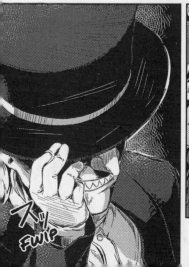

ズッ
FWIP

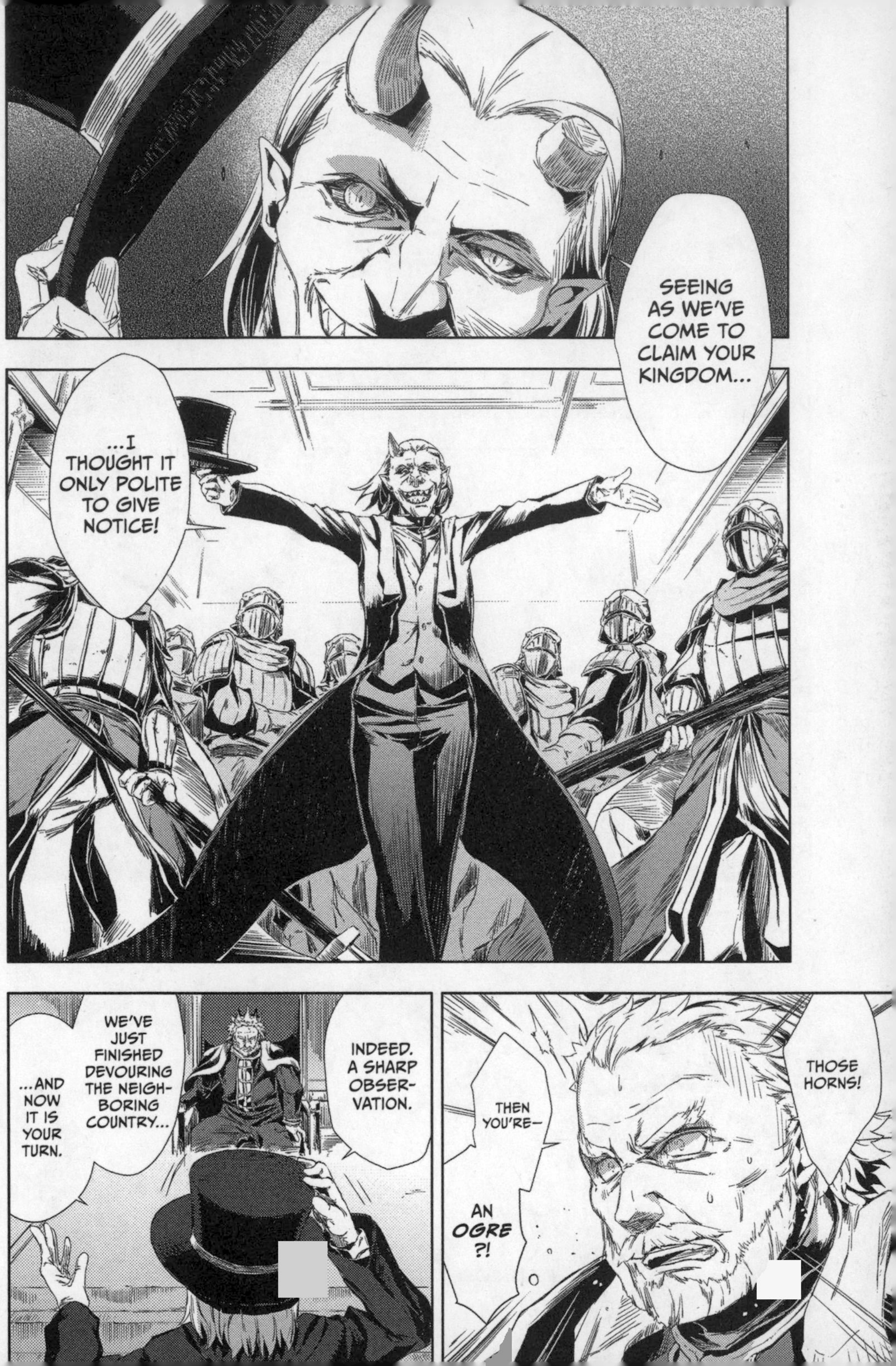
SEEING AS WE'VE COME TO CLAIM YOUR KINGDOM...
...I THOUGHT IT ONLY POLITE TO GIVE NOTICE!
THOSE HORNS!
THEN YOU'RE—
AN *OGRE*?!
INDEED. A SHARP OBSERVATION.
WE'VE JUST FINISHED DEVOURING THE NEIGH-BORING COUNTRY...
...AND NOW IT IS YOUR TURN.

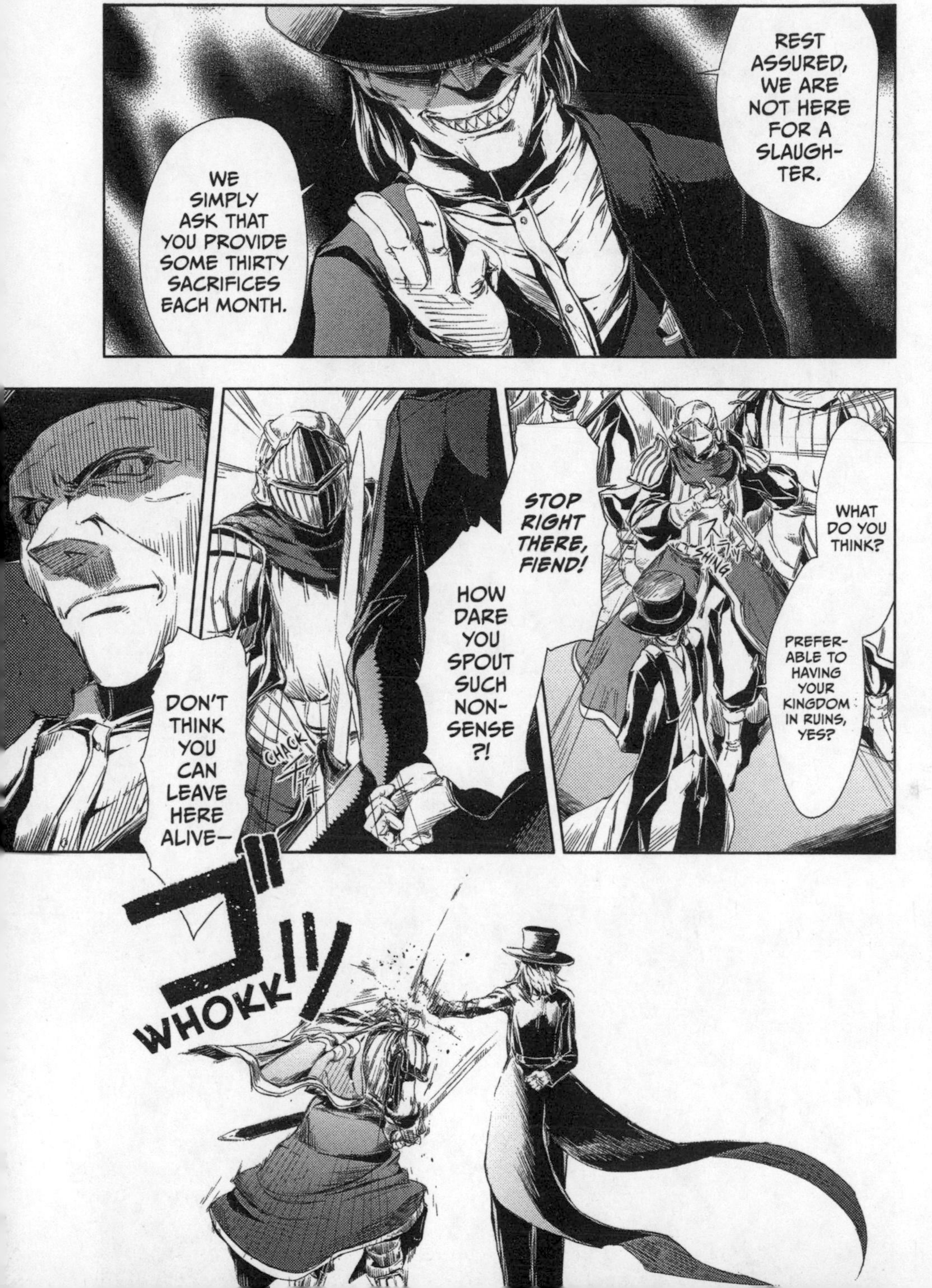
REST ASSURED, WE ARE NOT HERE FOR A SLAUGHTER.
WE SIMPLY ASK THAT YOU PROVIDE SOME THIRTY SACRIFICES EACH MONTH.
WHAT DO YOU THINK?
SHING
PREFERABLE TO HAVING YOUR KINGDOM IN RUINS, YES?
STOP RIGHT THERE, FIEND!
HOW DARE YOU SPOUT SUCH NON-SENSE?!
CHACK
DON'T THINK YOU CAN LEAVE HERE ALIVE—
WHOKK

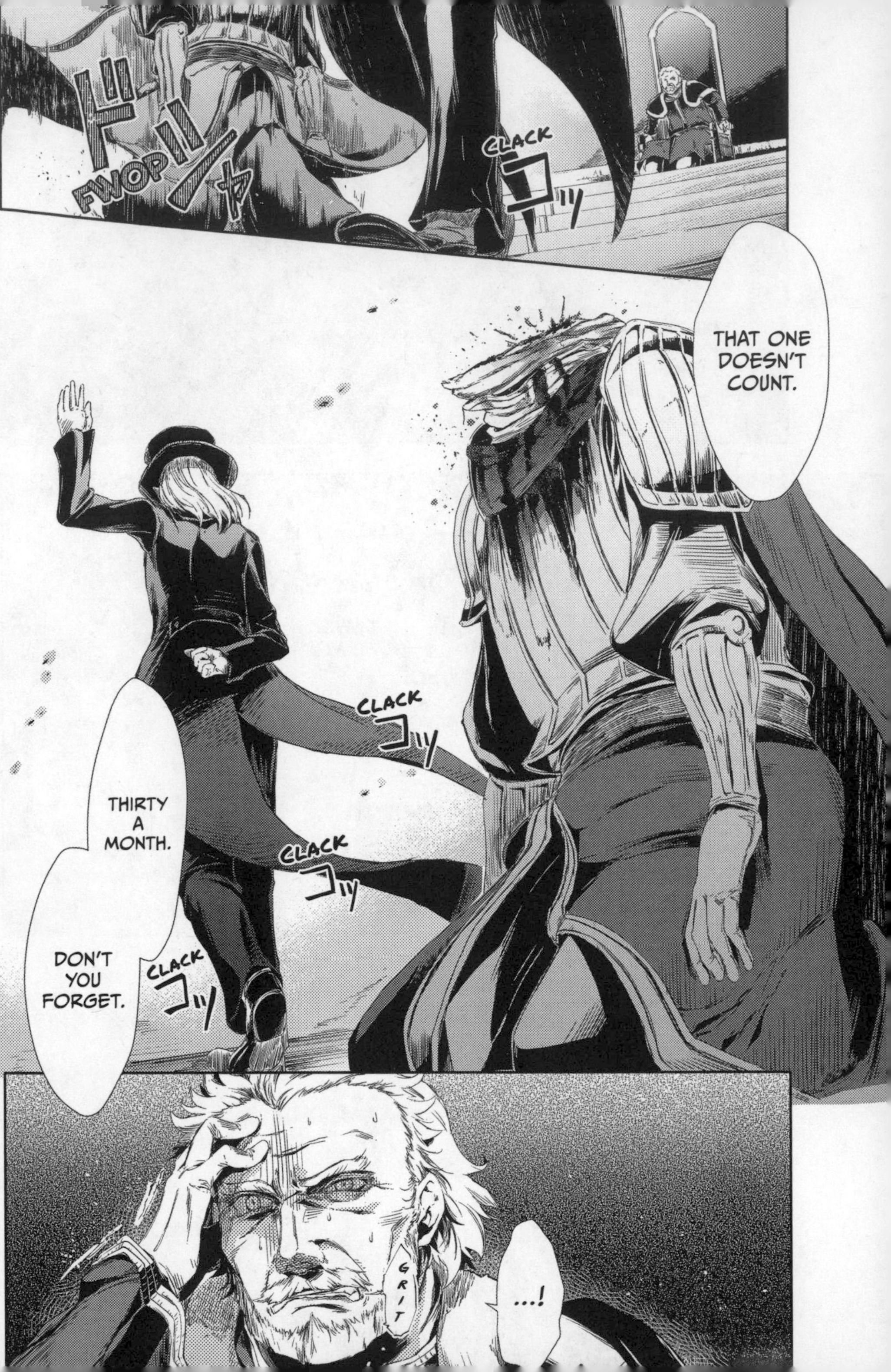
CLACK
コッ
FWOP
THAT ONE DOESN'T COUNT.
CLACK
コッ
THIRTY A MONTH.
CLACK
コッ
DON'T YOU FORGET.
CLACK
コッ
...!
GRIT

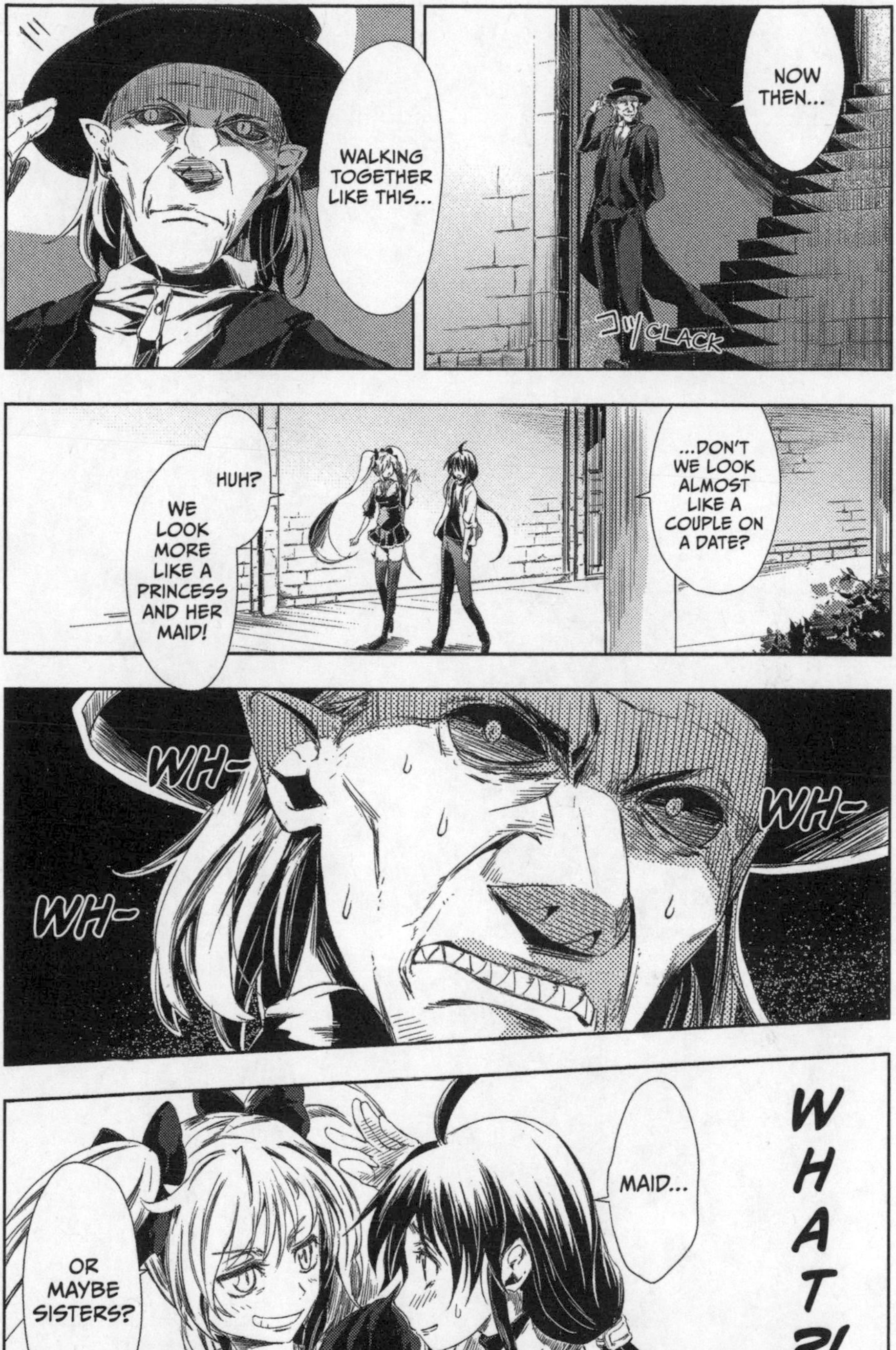
NOW THEN...
コツ/CLACK
WALKING TOGETHER LIKE THIS...
...DON'T WE LOOK ALMOST LIKE A COUPLE ON A DATE?
HUH?
WE LOOK MORE LIKE A PRINCESS AND HER MAID!
WH-
WH-
WH-
WHAT?!
MAID...
OR MAYBE SISTERS?

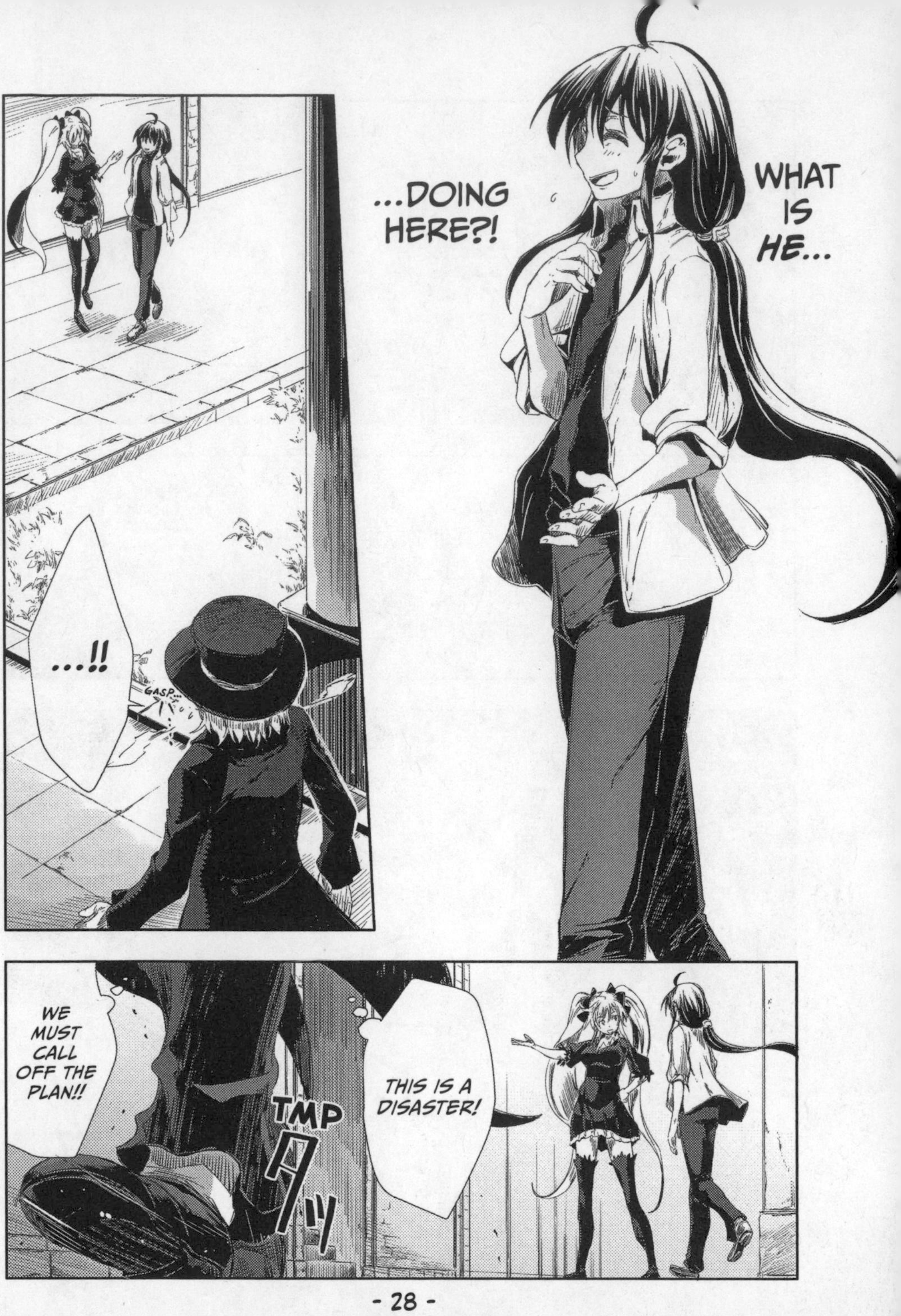
WHAT IS HE...
...DOING HERE?!
...!!
GASP...
THIS IS A DISASTER!
WE MUST CALL OFF THE PLAN!!
TMP
タッ

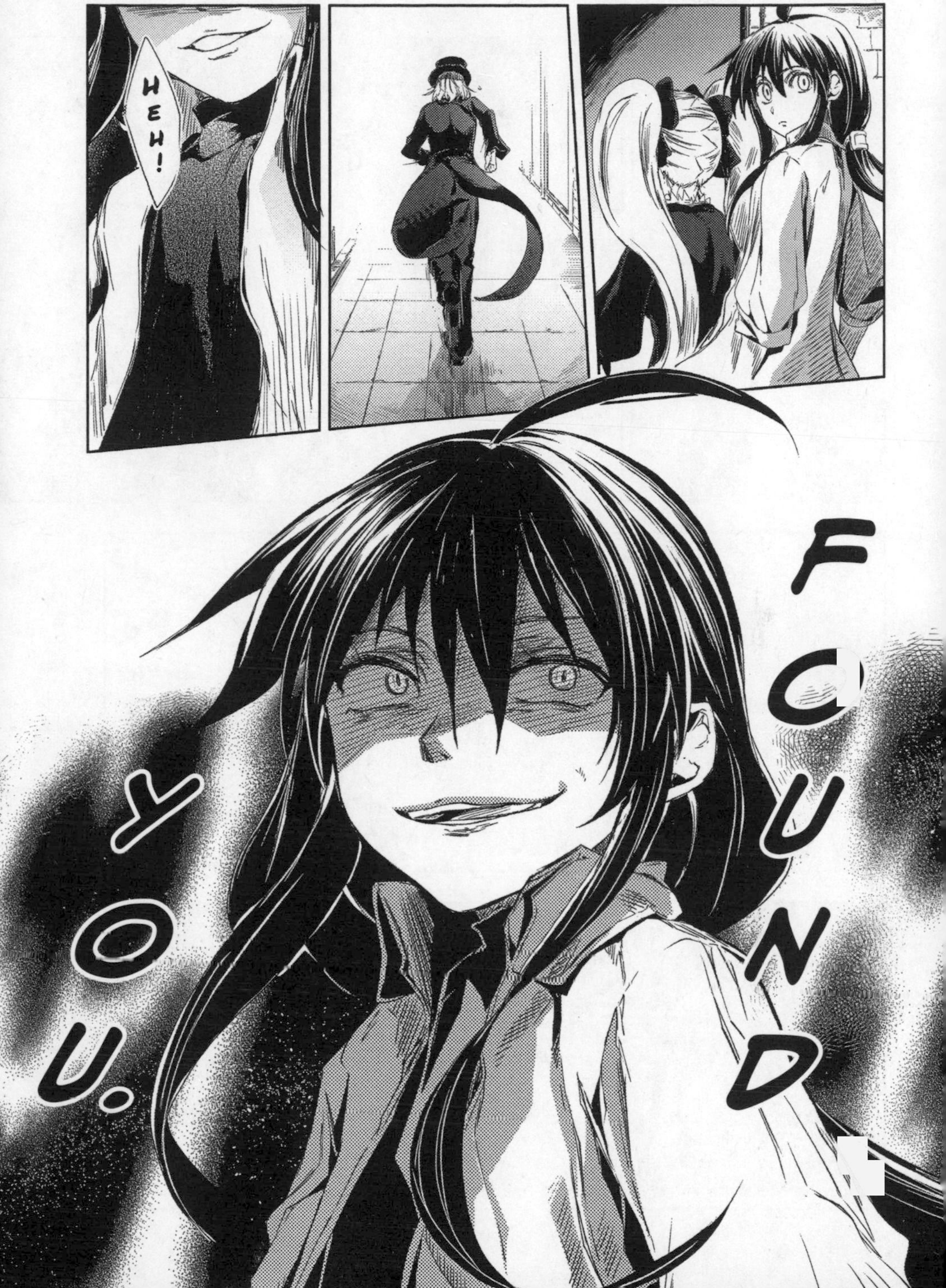
HEH!
FOUND YOU.

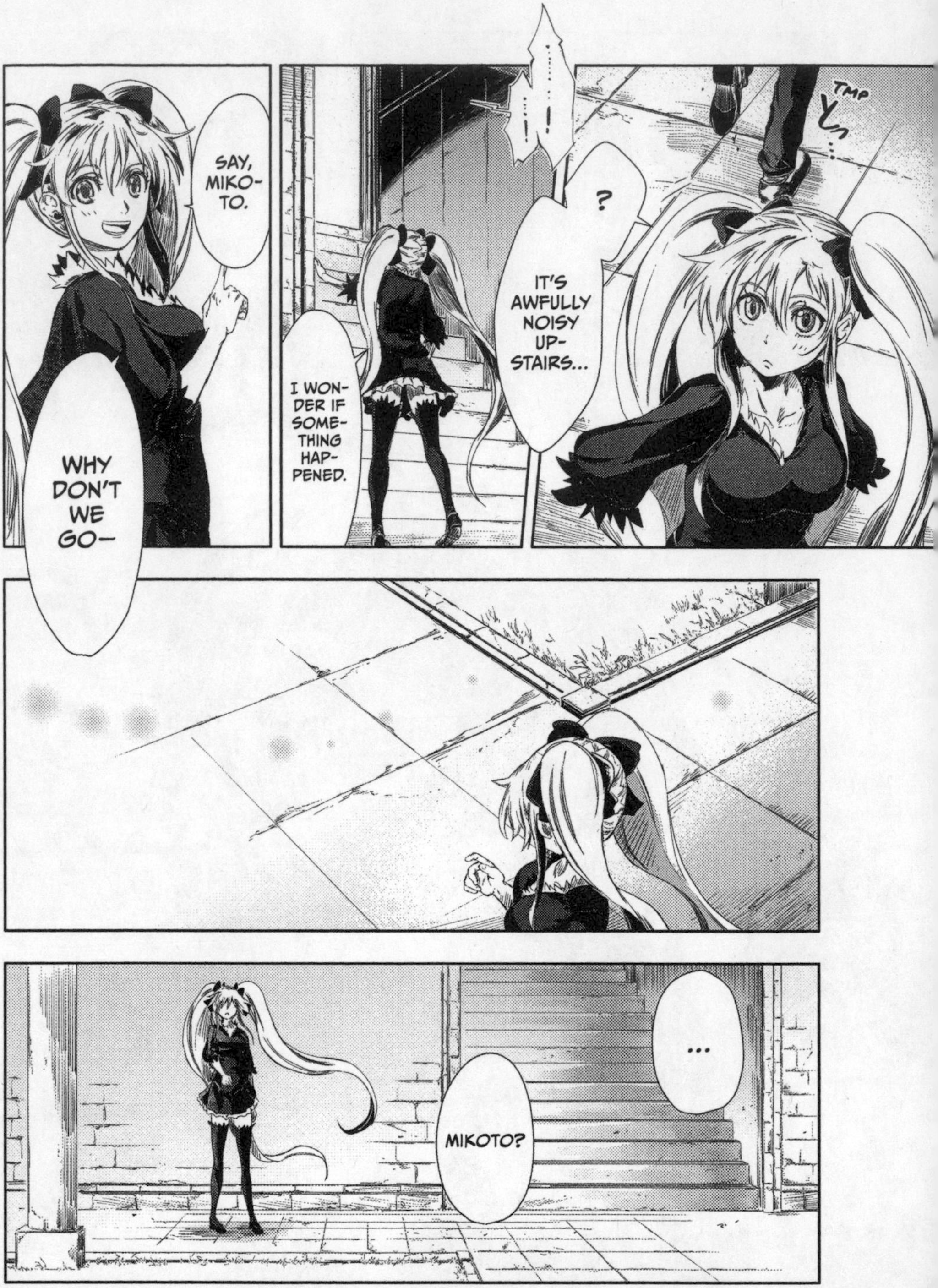
TMP
?
IT'S AWFULLY NOISY UP-STAIRS...
...!
I WONDER IF SOMETHING HAPPENED.
SAY, MIKO-TO.
WHY DON'T WE GO—
...
MIKOTO?

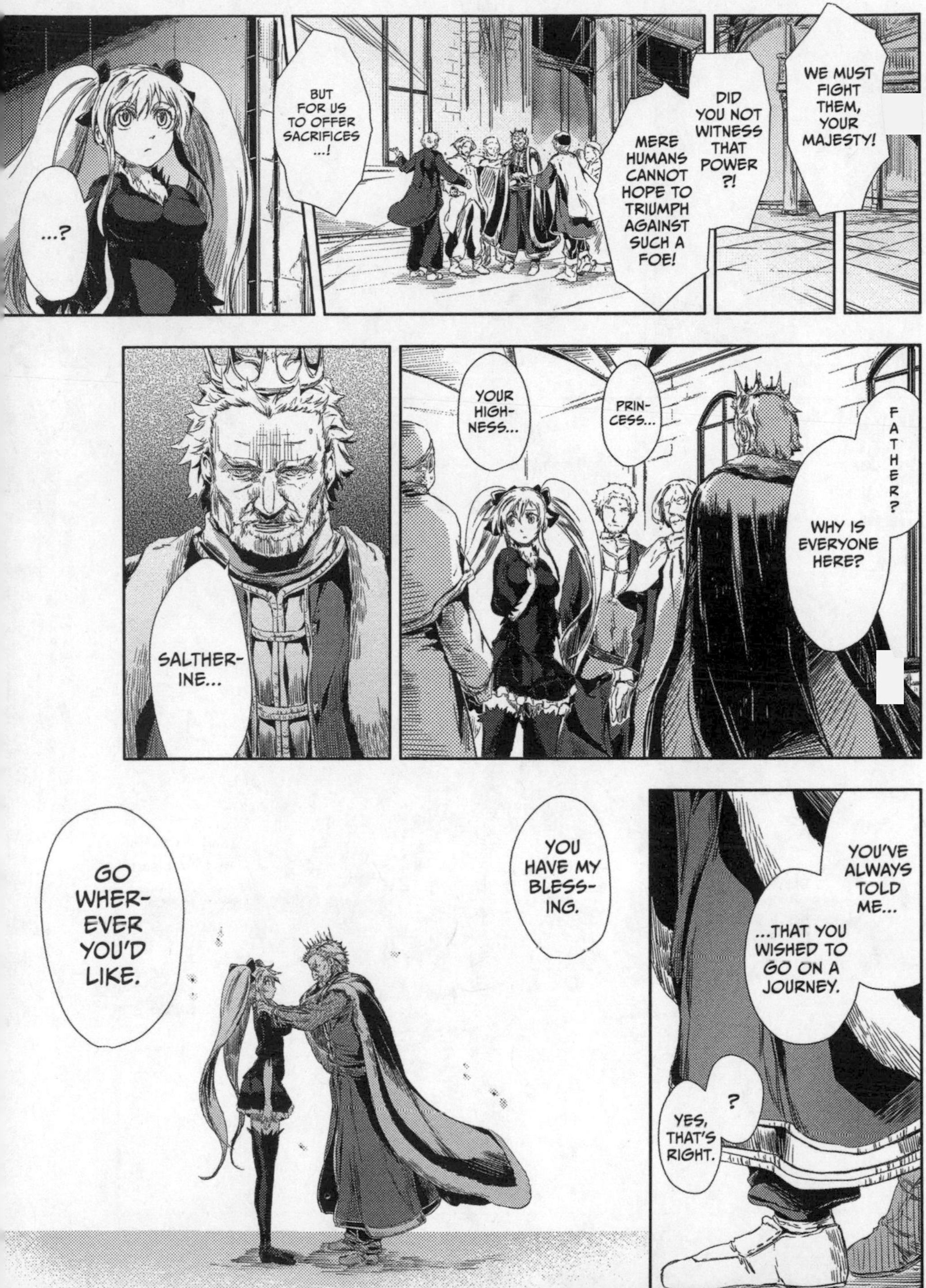
WE MUST FIGHT THEM, YOUR MAJESTY!
DID YOU NOT WITNESS THAT POWER?!
MERE HUMANS CANNOT HOPE TO TRIUMPH AGAINST SUCH A FOE!
BUT FOR US TO OFFER SACRIFICES...!
...?
FATHER?
WHY IS EVERYONE HERE?
PRINCESS...
YOUR HIGHNESS...
SALTHERINE...
YOU'VE ALWAYS TOLD ME...
...THAT YOU WISHED TO GO ON A JOURNEY.
?
YES, THAT'S RIGHT.
YOU HAVE MY BLESSING.
GO WHEREVER YOU'D LIKE.

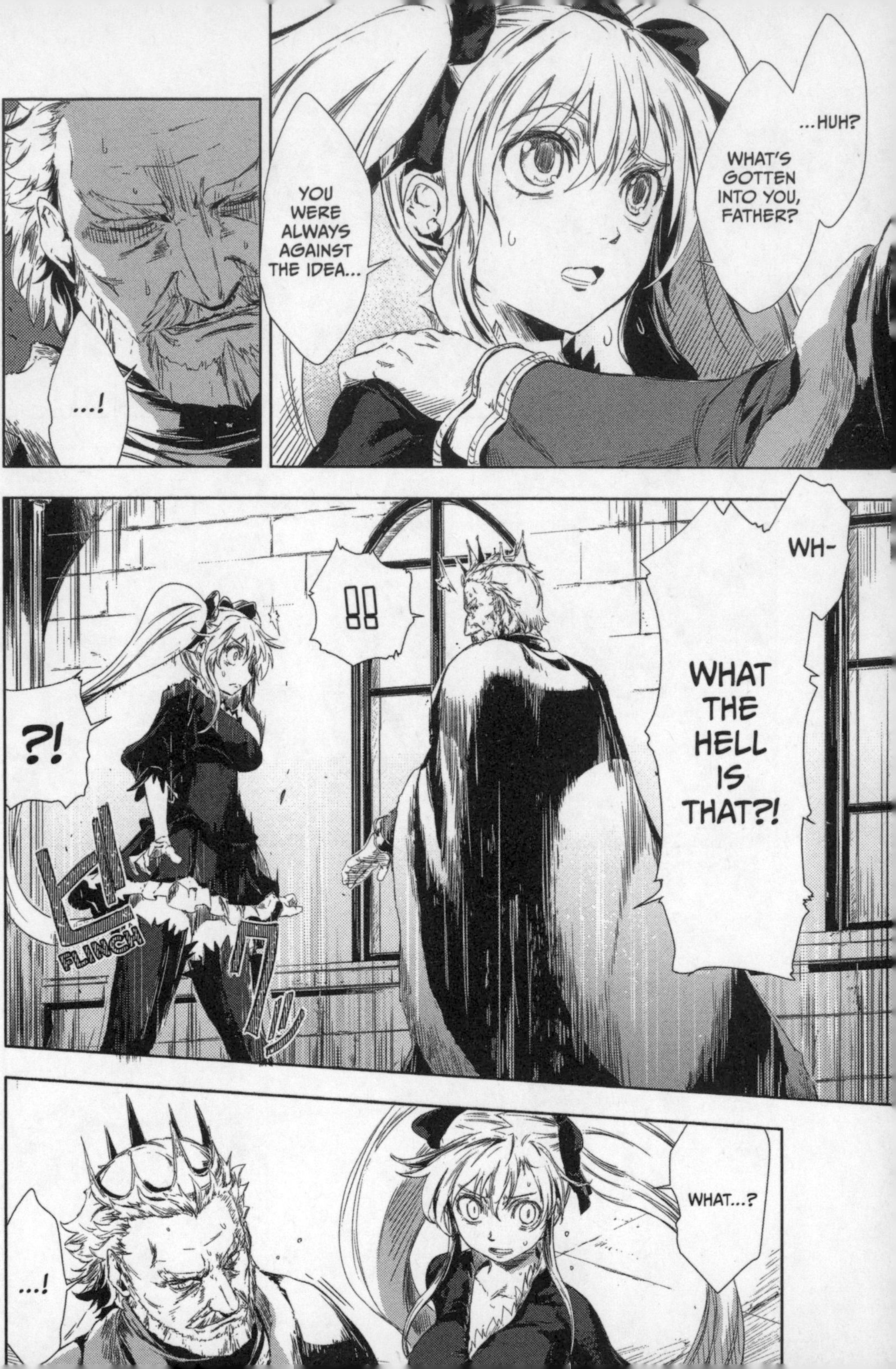
...HUH?
WHAT'S GOTTEN INTO YOU, FATHER?
YOU WERE ALWAYS AGAINST THE IDEA...
...!
WH-
WHAT THE HELL IS THAT?!
!!
?!
FLINCH
WHAT...?
...!

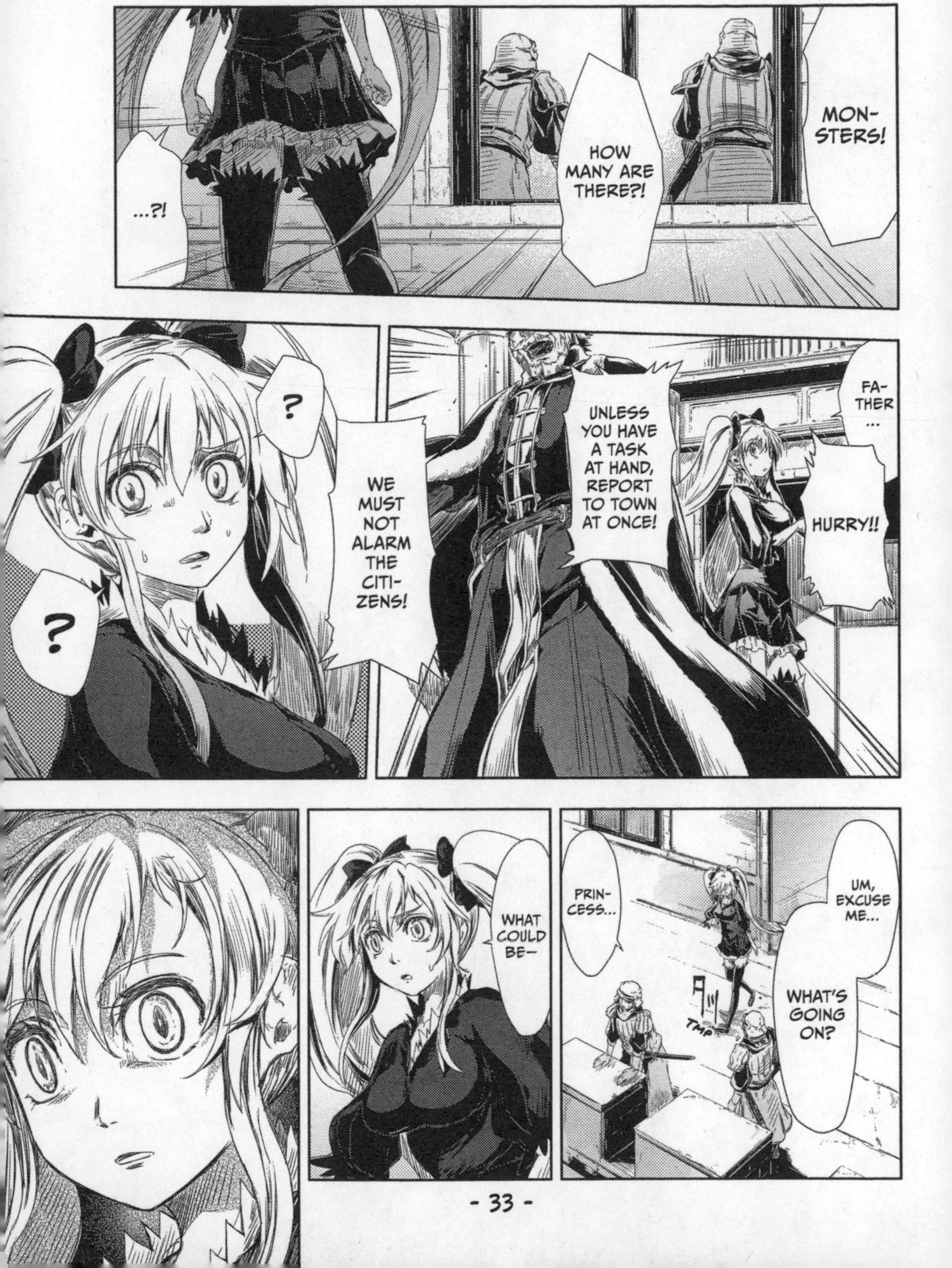
MON-STERS!
HOW MANY ARE THERE?!
...?!
FA-THER ...
UNLESS YOU HAVE A TASK AT HAND, REPORT TO TOWN AT ONCE!
HURRY!!
WE MUST NOT ALARM THE CITI-ZENS!
?
?
UM, EXCUSE ME...
WHAT'S GOING ON?
PRIN-CESS...
TMP
WHAT COULD BE-

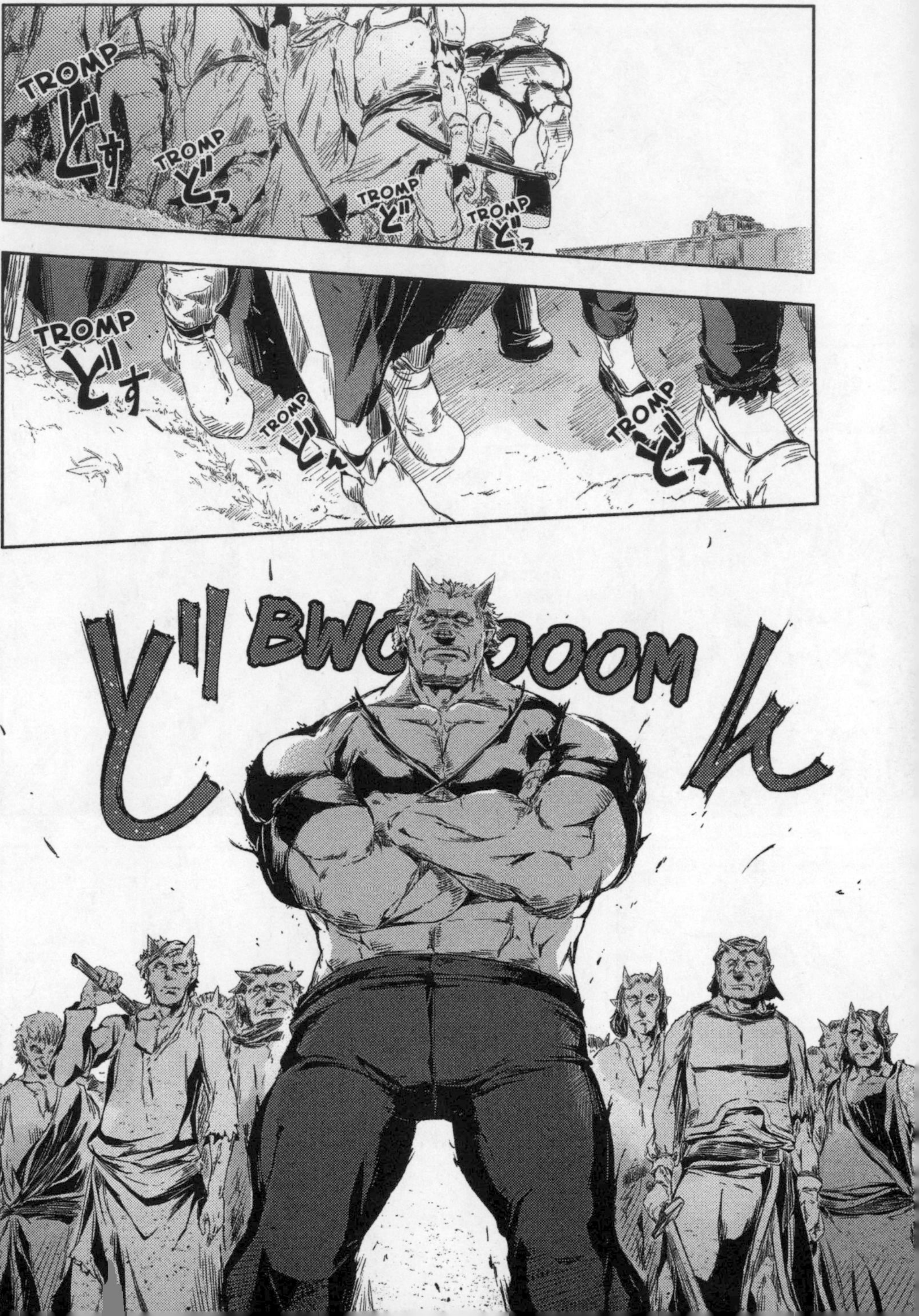
TROMP どっ
TROMP ど
TROMP どっ
TROMP どす
TROMP どっ
TROMP どん
TROMP どす
BWO OOOM
どん

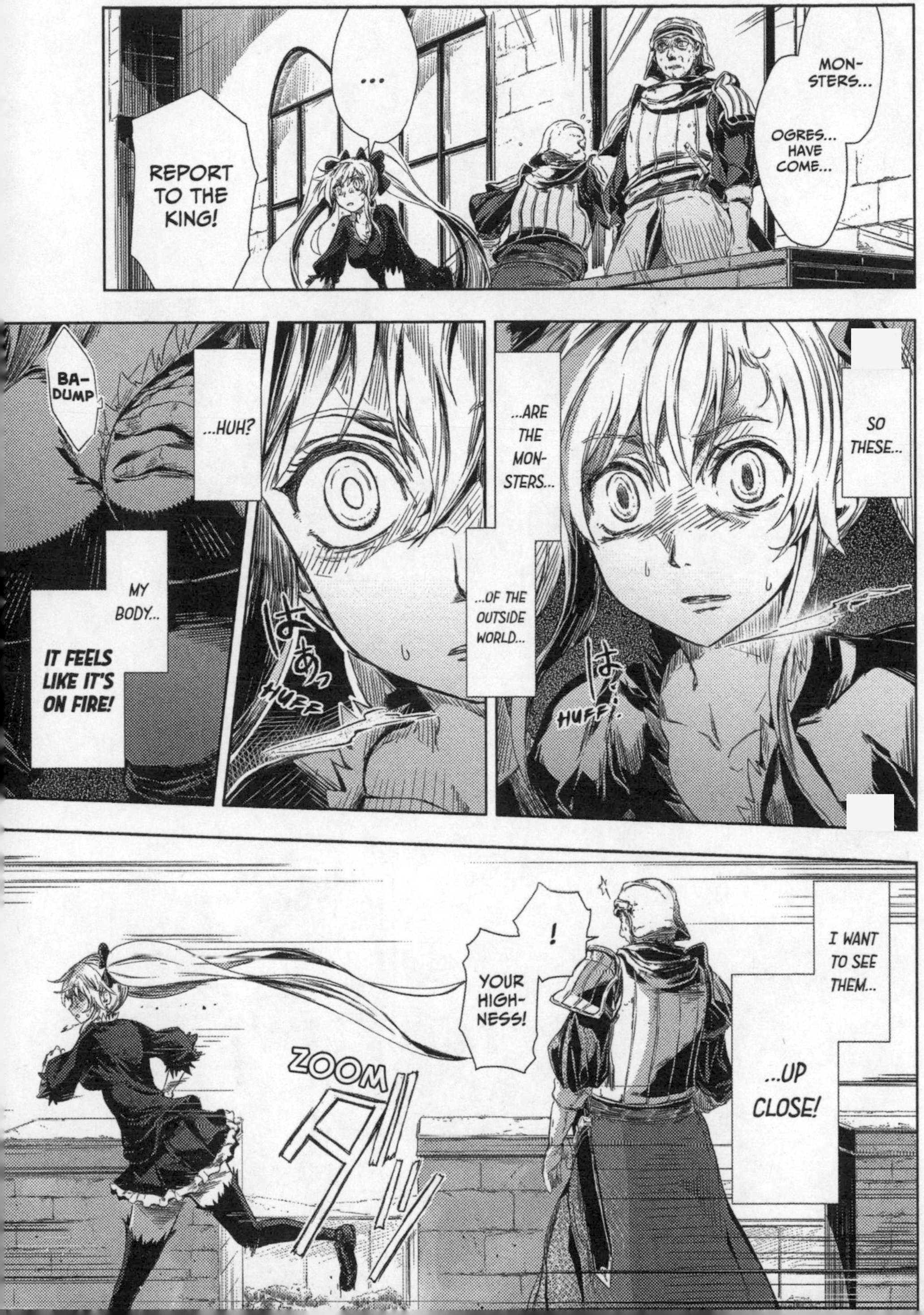
MON-STERS...
OGRES... HAVE COME...
...
REPORT TO THE KING!
SO THESE...
...ARE THE MON-STERS...
...OF THE OUTSIDE WORLD...
HUFF
...HUH?
HUFF
BA-DUMP
MY BODY...
IT FEELS LIKE IT'S ON FIRE!
I WANT TO SEE THEM...
...UP CLOSE!
!
YOUR HIGH-NESS!
ZOOM

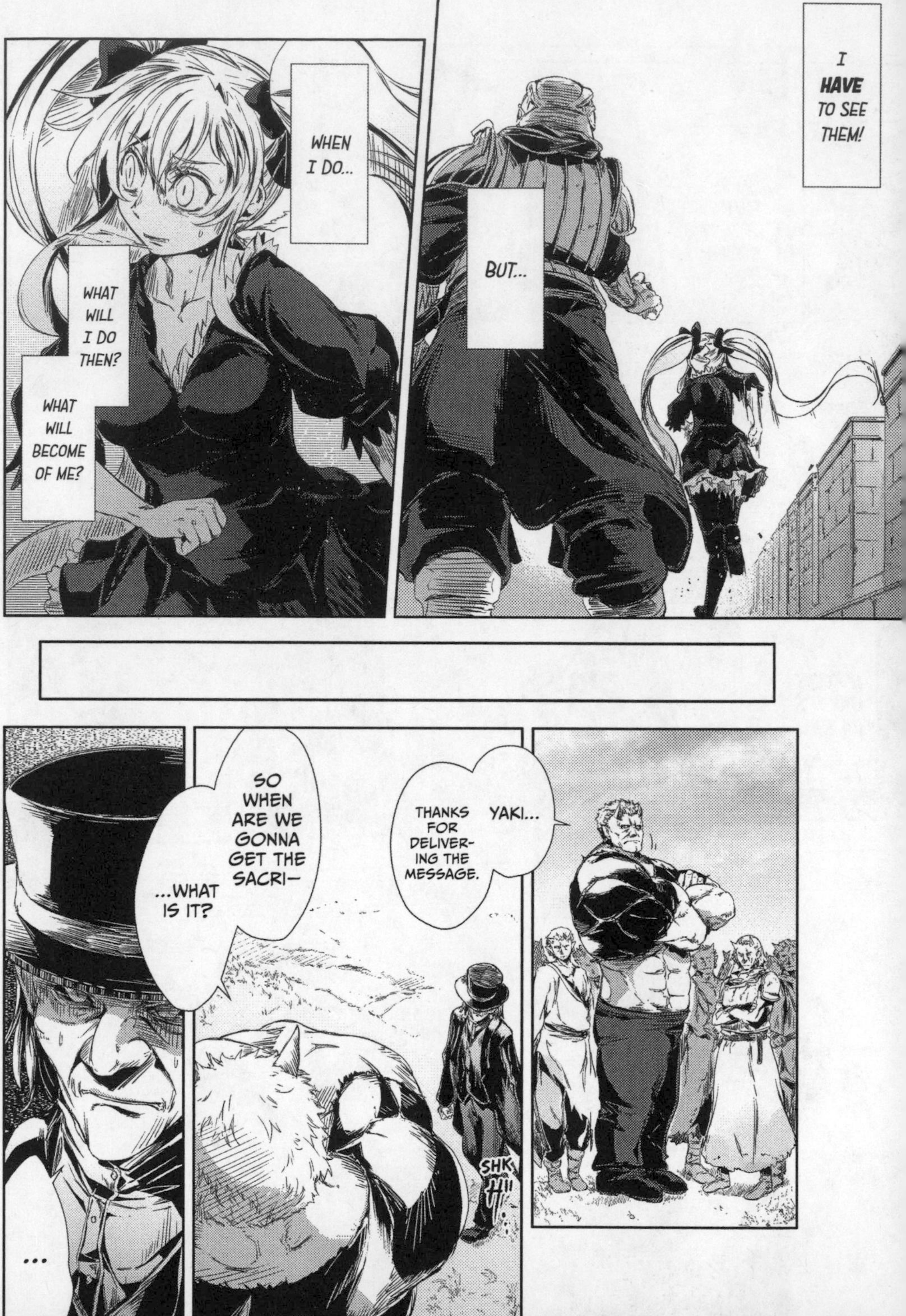
I HAVE TO SEE THEM!
BUT...
WHEN I DO...
WHAT WILL I DO THEN?
WHAT WILL BECOME OF ME?
YAKI...
THANKS FOR DELIVER-ING THE MESSAGE.
SO WHEN ARE WE GONNA GET THE SACRI—
...WHAT IS IT?
SHK
HI!
...

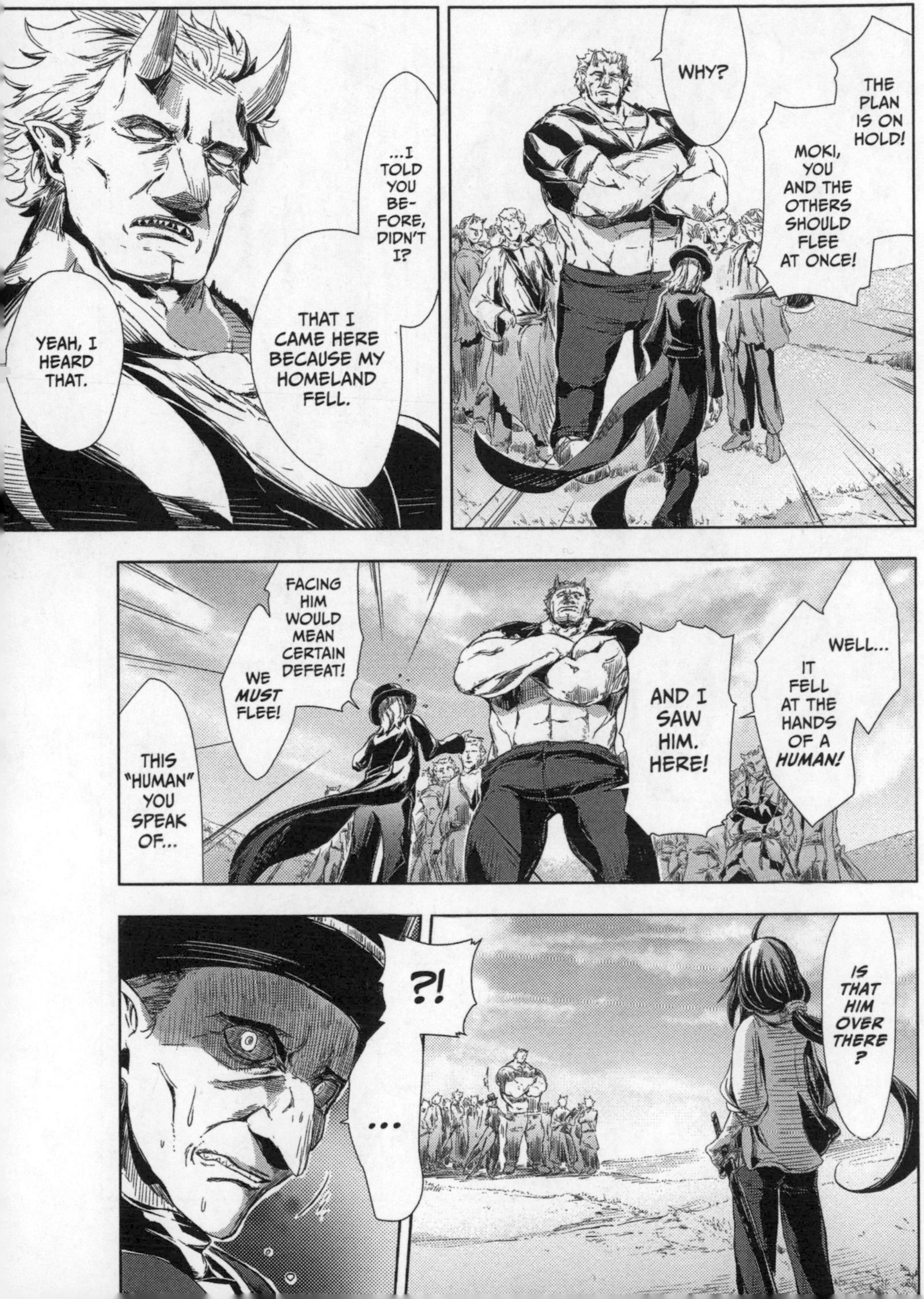
THE PLAN IS ON HOLD!
MOKI, YOU AND THE OTHERS SHOULD FLEE AT ONCE!
WHY?
...I TOLD YOU BEFORE, DIDN'T I?
THAT I CAME HERE BECAUSE MY HOMELAND FELL.
YEAH, I HEARD THAT.
WELL...
IT FELL AT THE HANDS OF A *HUMAN!*
AND I SAW HIM. HERE!
FACING HIM WOULD MEAN CERTAIN DEFEAT!
WE *MUST* FLEE!
THIS "HUMAN" YOU SPEAK OF...
IS THAT HIM OVER THERE?
?!
...

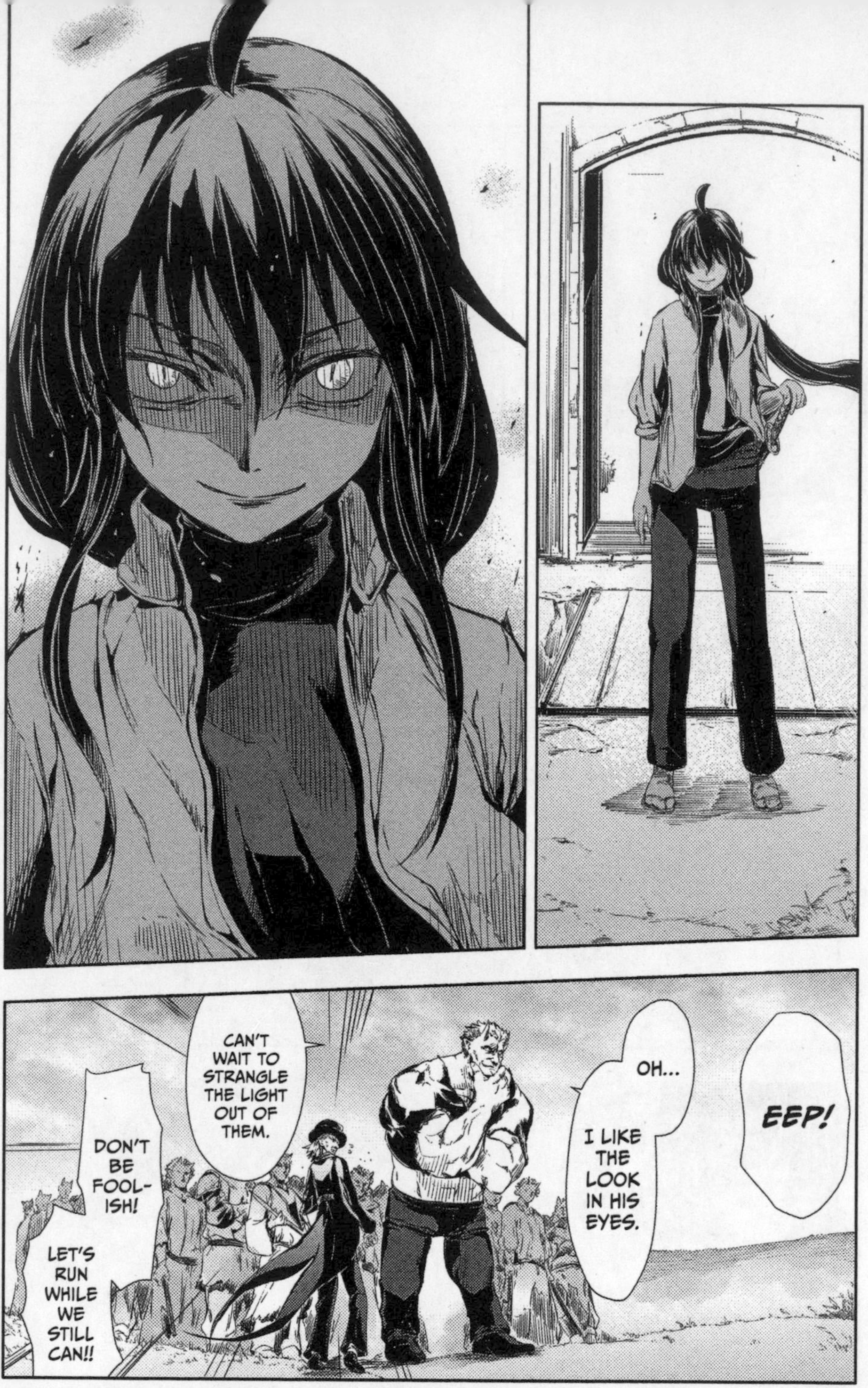
EEP!
OH...
I LIKE THE LOOK IN HIS EYES.
CAN'T WAIT TO STRANGLE THE LIGHT OUT OF THEM.
DON'T BE FOOL-ISH!
LET'S RUN WHILE WE STILL CAN!!

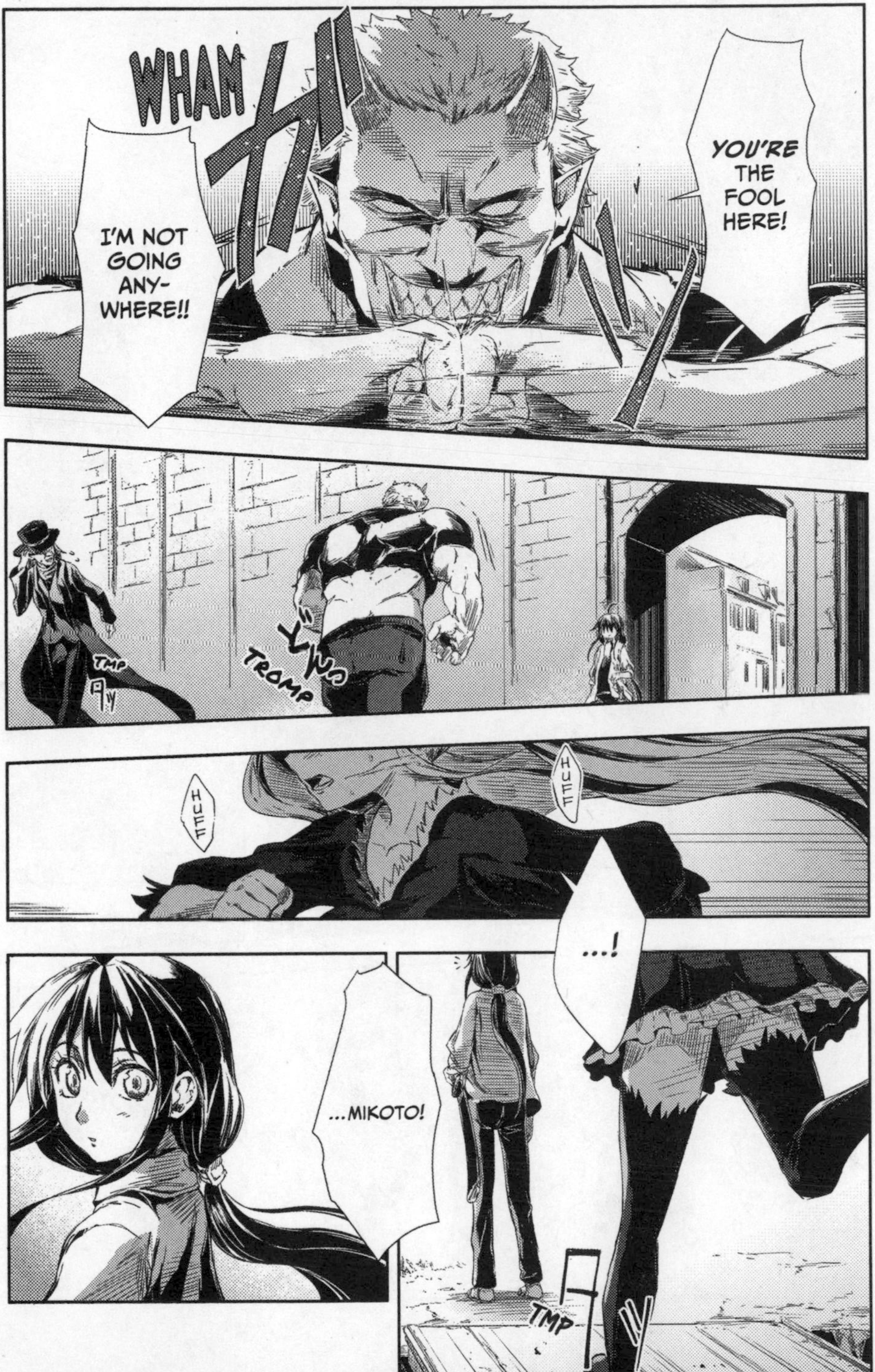
YOU'RE THE FOOL HERE!
WHAM
I'M NOT GOING ANY-WHERE!!
TROMP
TMP
HUFF
HUFF
...!
TMP
...MIKOTO!

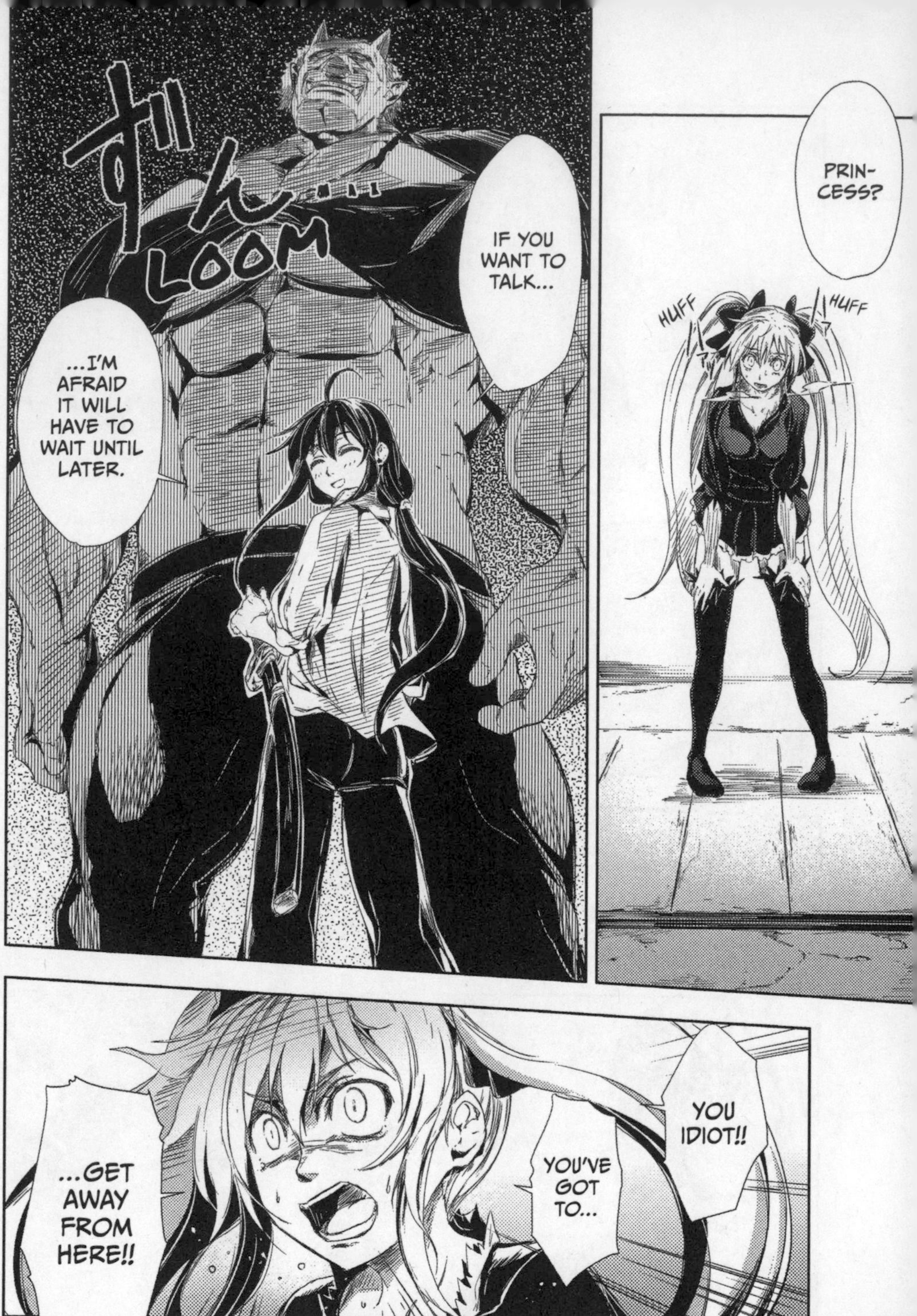
PRIN-CESS?
HUFF
HUFF
ずん
LOOM
IF YOU WANT TO TALK...
...I'M AFRAID IT WILL HAVE TO WAIT UNTIL LATER.
YOU IDIOT!!
YOU'VE GOT TO...
...GET AWAY FROM HERE!!

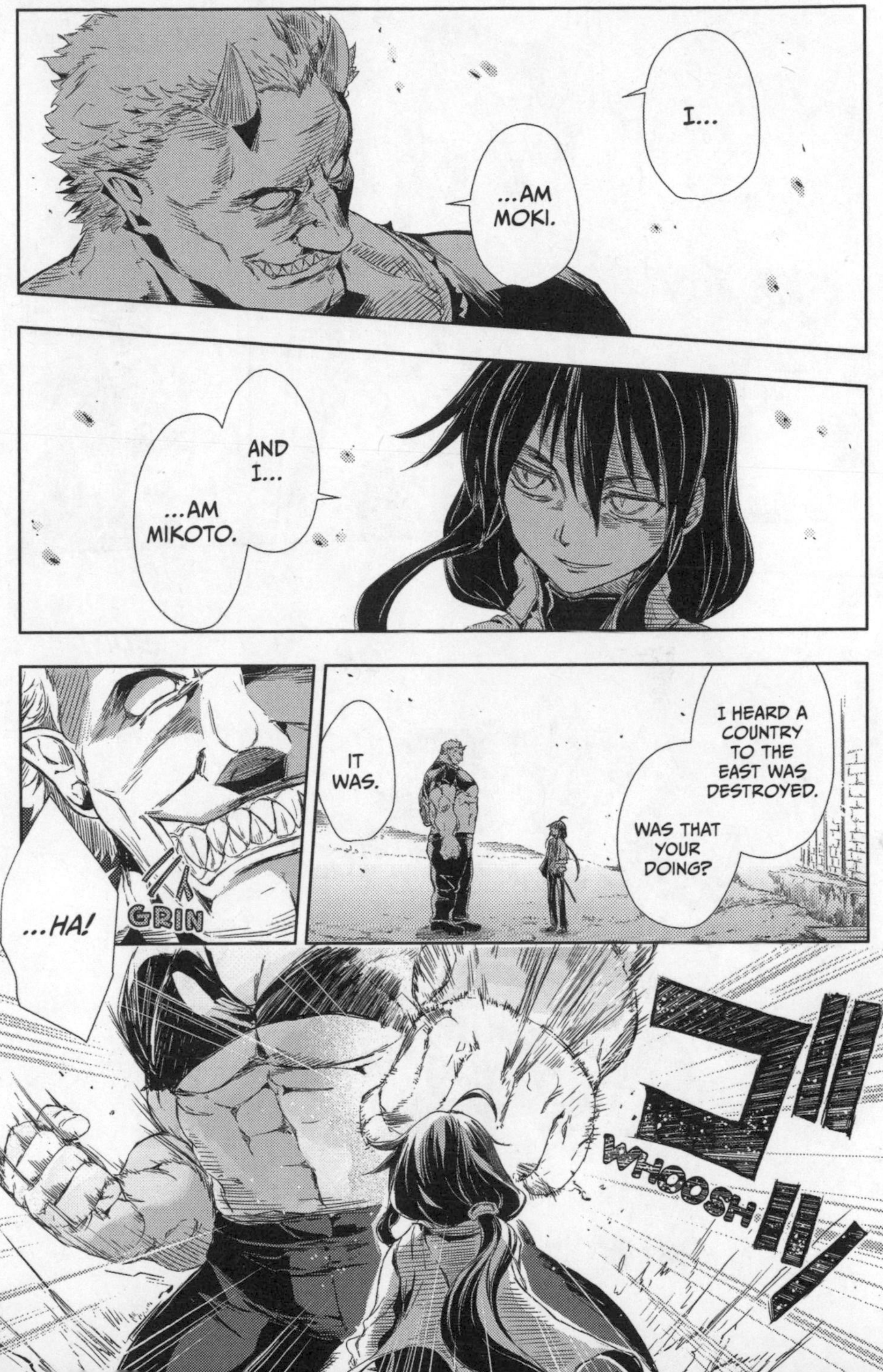
I...
...AM MOKI.
AND I...
...AM MIKOTO.
I HEARD A COUNTRY TO THE EAST WAS DESTROYED.
WAS THAT YOUR DOING?
IT WAS.
GRIN
...HA!
ゴ
WHOOSH

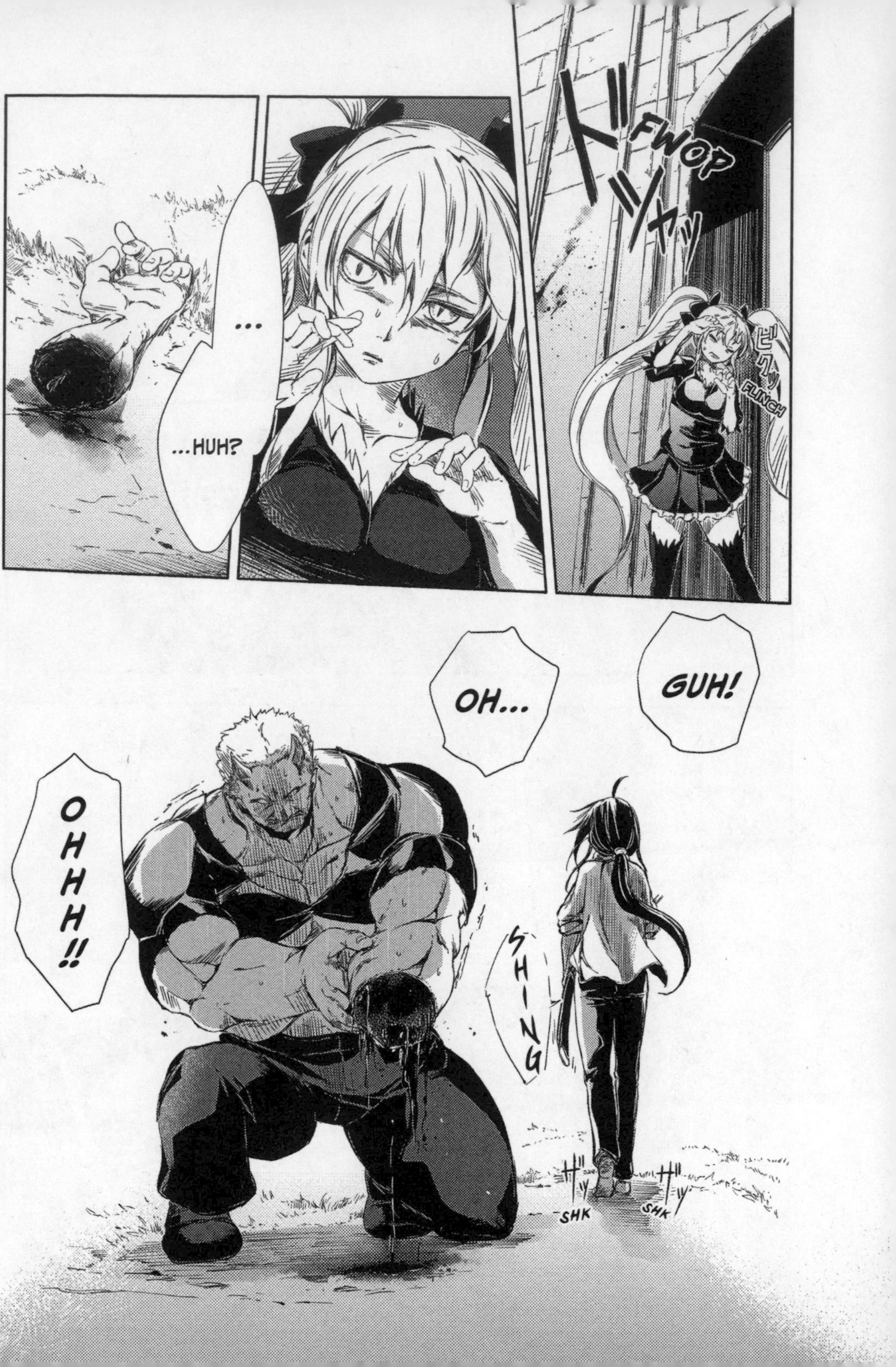
ドシャッ
FWOP
ビクッ
FLINCH
...
...HUH?
GUH!
OH...
OHHHH!!
SHING
ザッ
SHK
ザッ
SHK

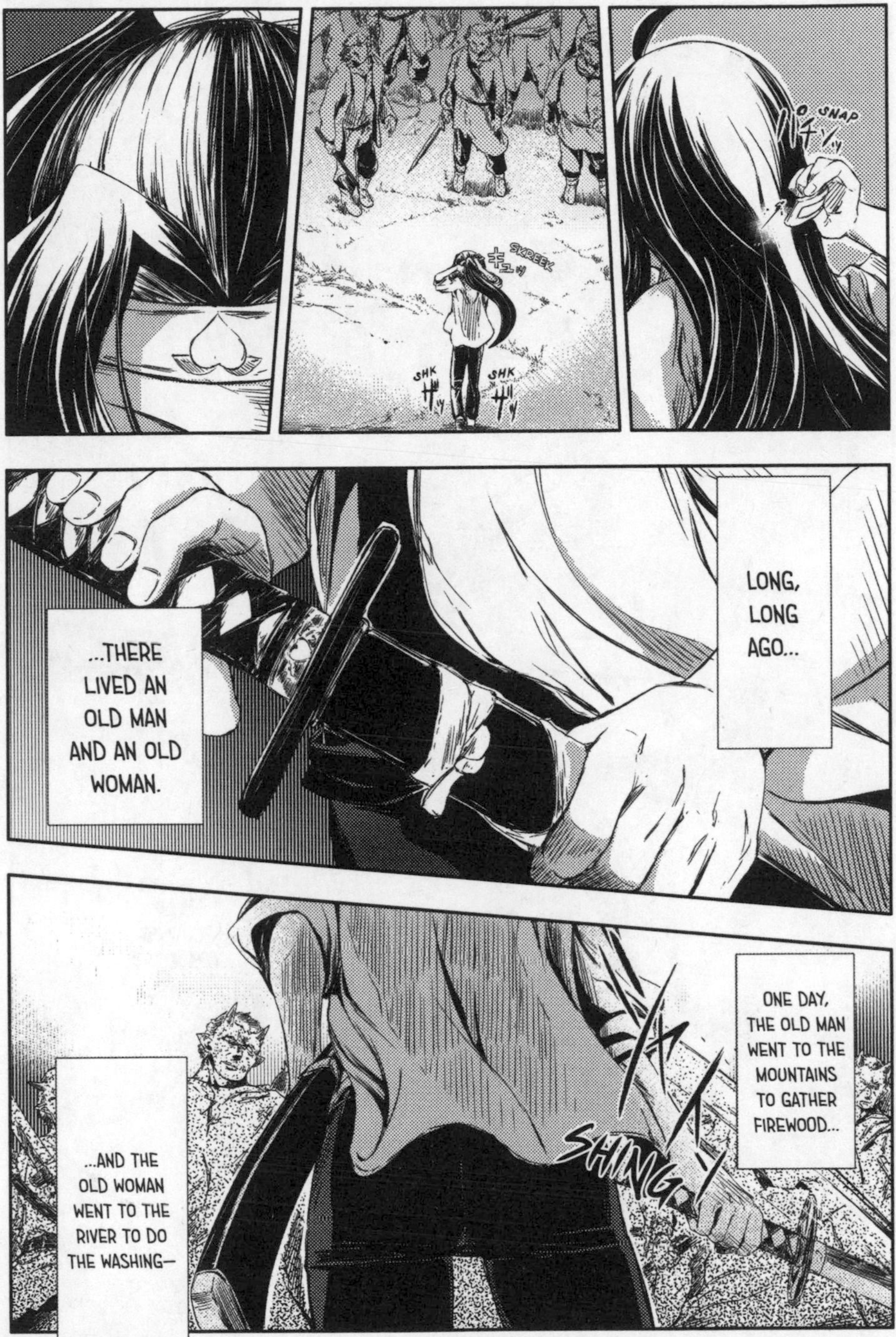
SNAP
SKREEK
SHK
SHK
LONG, LONG AGO...
...THERE LIVED AN OLD MAN AND AN OLD WOMAN.
ONE DAY, THE OLD MAN WENT TO THE MOUNTAINS TO GATHER FIREWOOD...
SHING
...AND THE OLD WOMAN WENT TO THE RIVER TO DO THE WASHING—

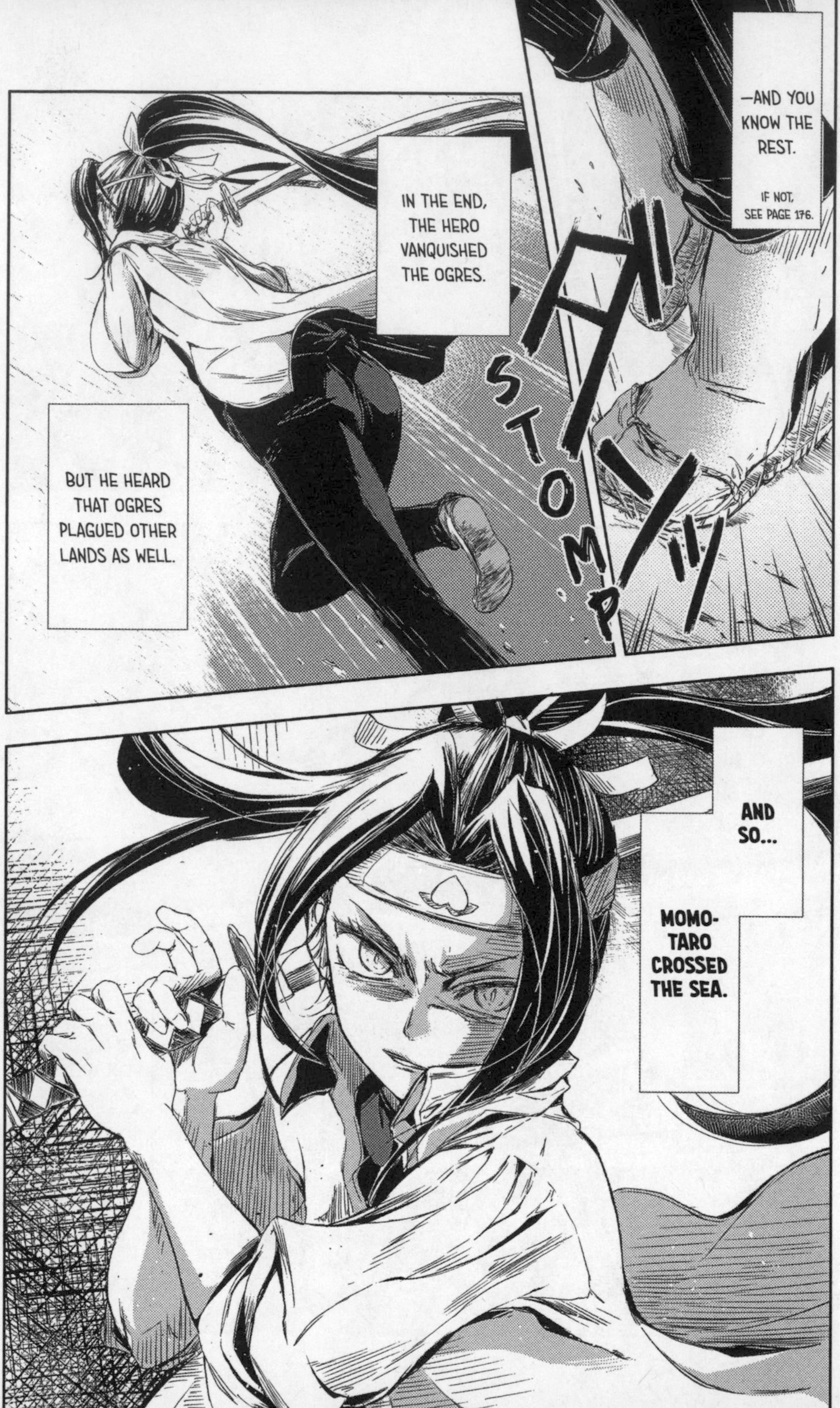
—AND YOU KNOW THE REST.
IF NOT, SEE PAGE 176.
STOMP
IN THE END, THE HERO VANQUISHED THE OGRES.
BUT HE HEARD THAT OGRES PLAGUED OTHER LANDS AS WELL.
AND SO...
MOMOTARO CROSSED THE SEA.

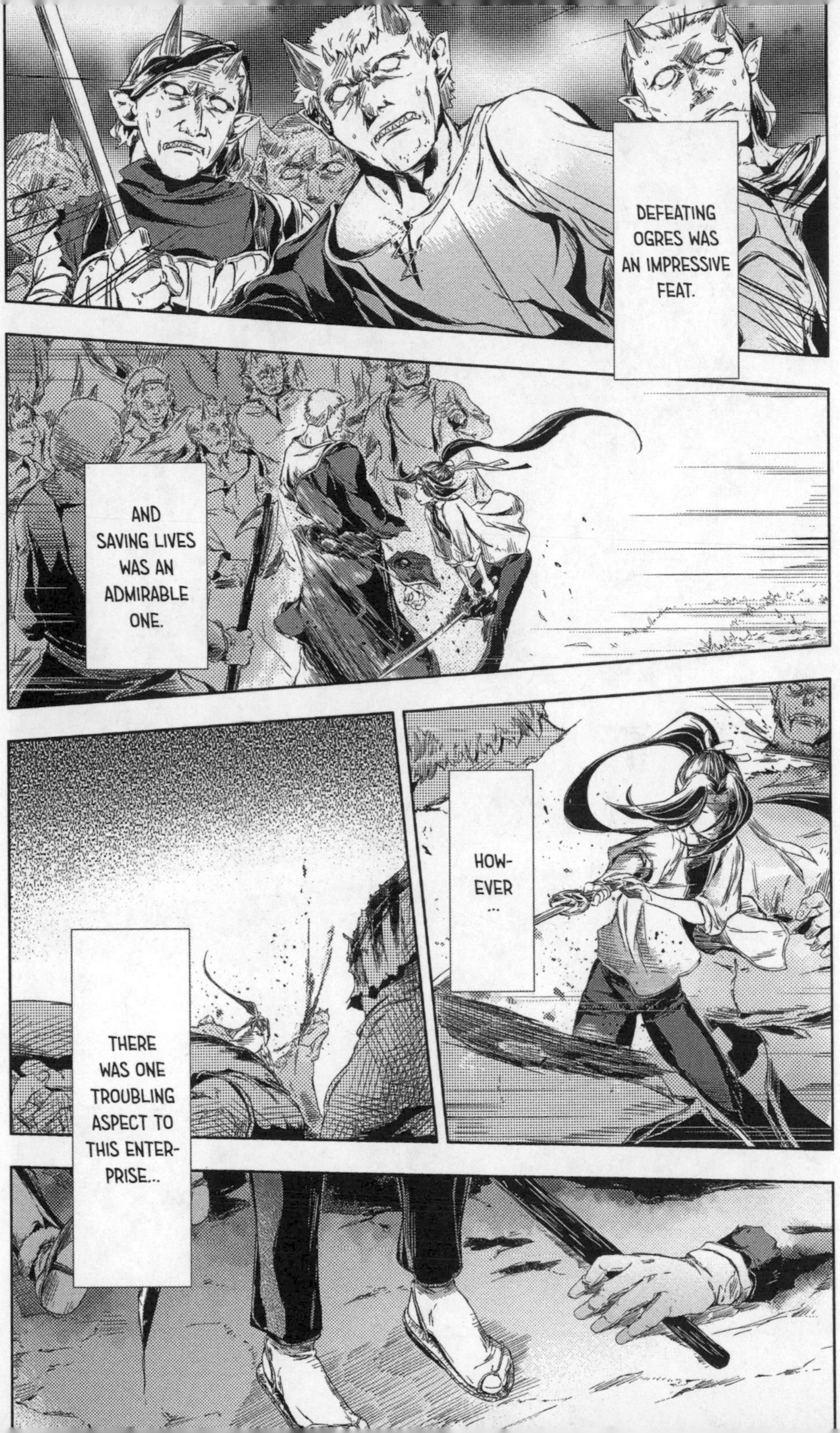
DEFEATING OGRES WAS AN IMPRESSIVE FEAT.
AND SAVING LIVES WAS AN ADMIRABLE ONE.
HOW-EVER...
THERE WAS ONE TROUBLING ASPECT TO THIS ENTER-PRISE...

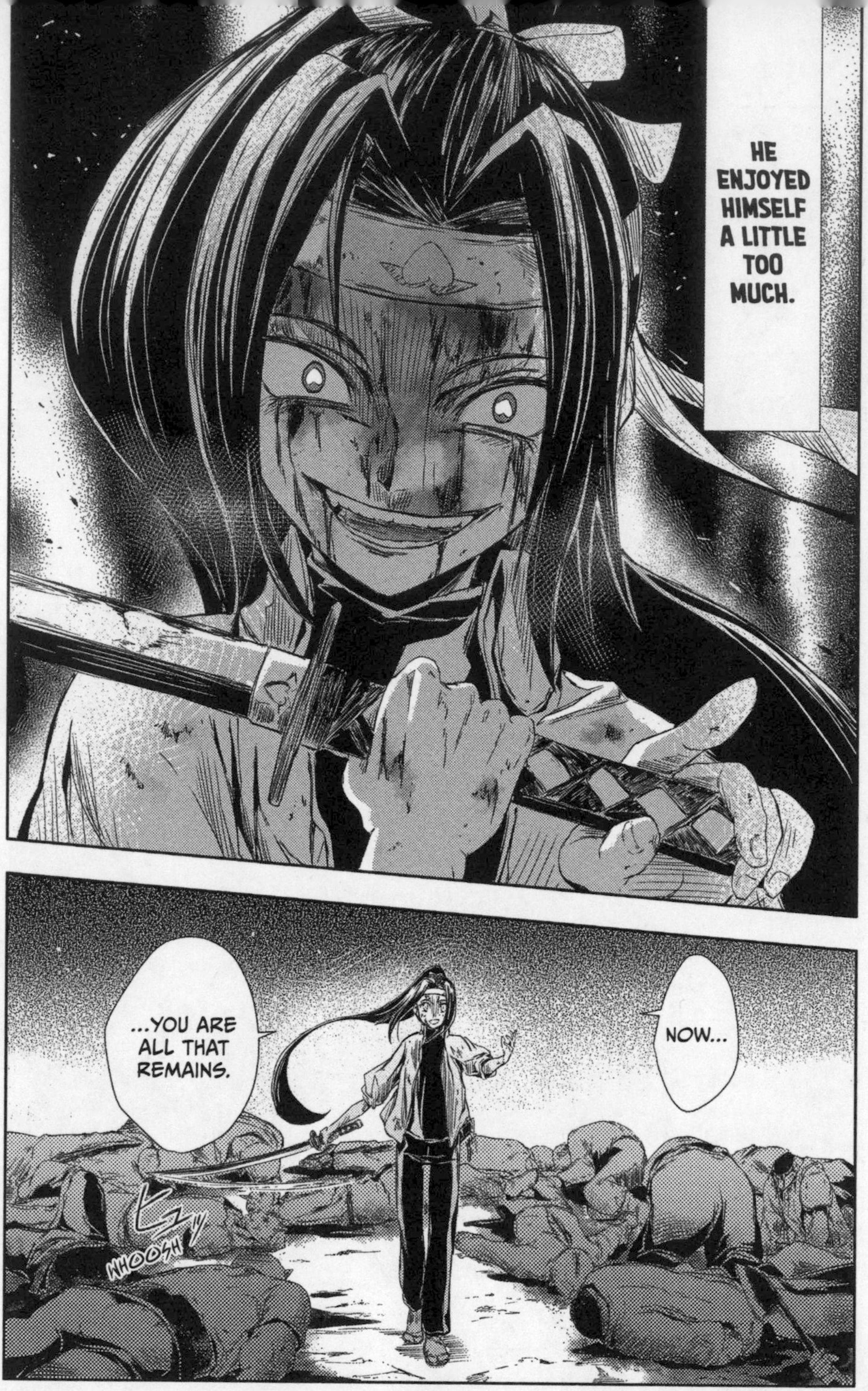
HE ENJOYED HIMSELF A LITTLE TOO MUCH.
NOW...
...YOU ARE ALL THAT REMAINS.
WHOOSH

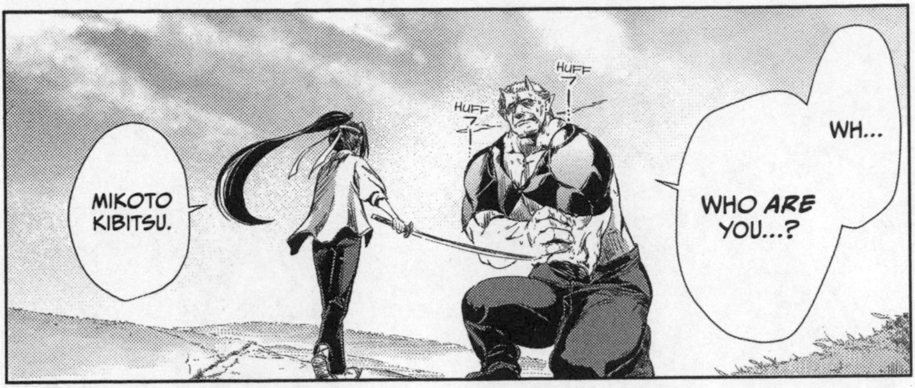
WH...
WHO ARE YOU...?
HUFF
HUFF
MIKOTO KIBITSU.

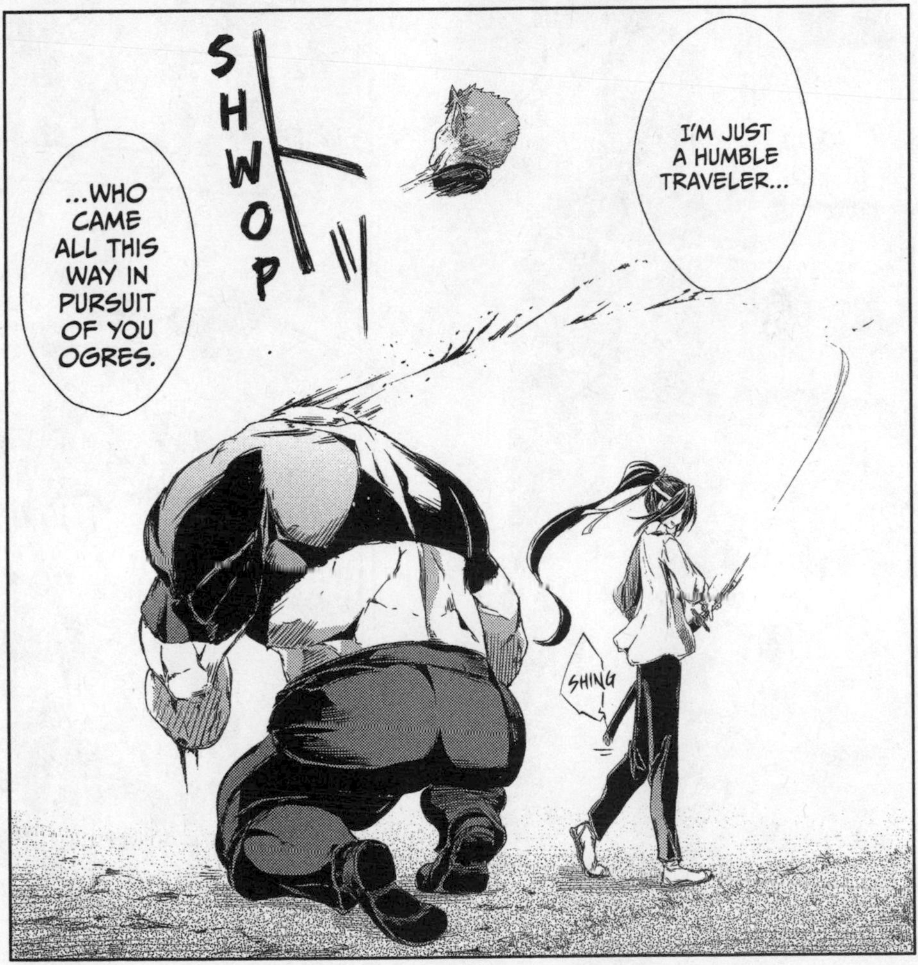
I'M JUST A HUMBLE TRAVELER...
SHWOP
...WHO CAME ALL THIS WAY IN PURSUIT OF YOU OGRES.
SHING

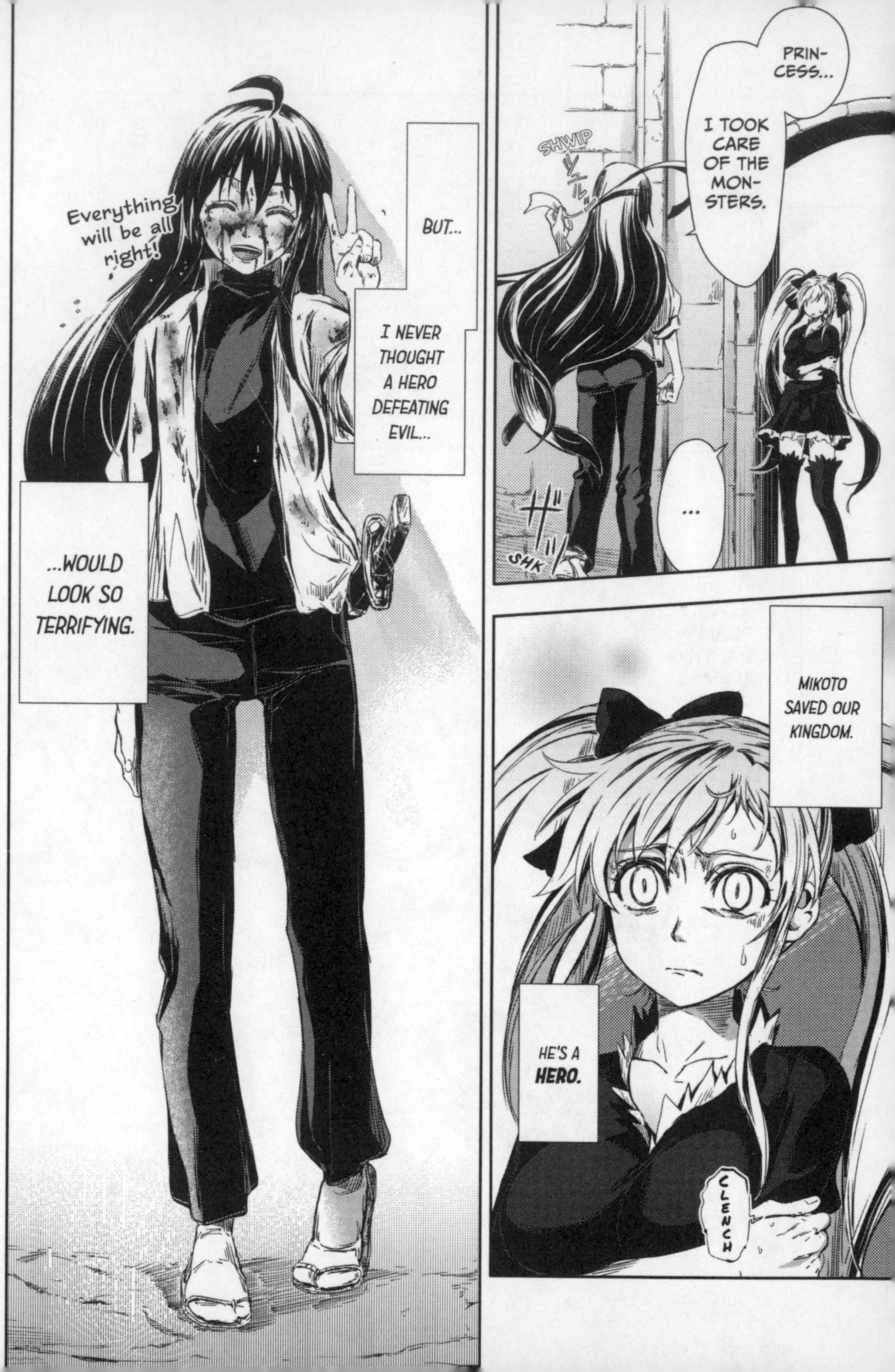
PRIN-
CESS...
I TOOK CARE OF THE MON-STERS.
SHWIP
...
SHK
MIKOTO SAVED OUR KINGDOM.
HE'S A **HERO.**
CLENCH
BUT...
I NEVER THOUGHT A HERO DEFEATING EVIL...
Everything will be all right!
...WOULD LOOK SO TERRIFYING.

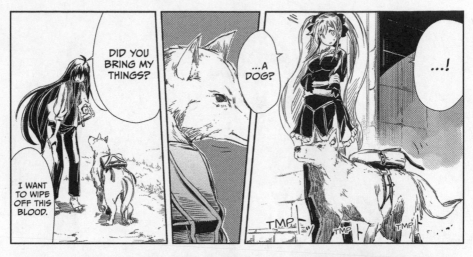

DID YOU BRING MY THINGS?

I WANT TO WIPE OFF THIS BLOOD.

...A DOG?

...!

TMP

TMP

TMP

WHY DON'T WE GET GOING?

ALL RIGHT.

...HUH?

...

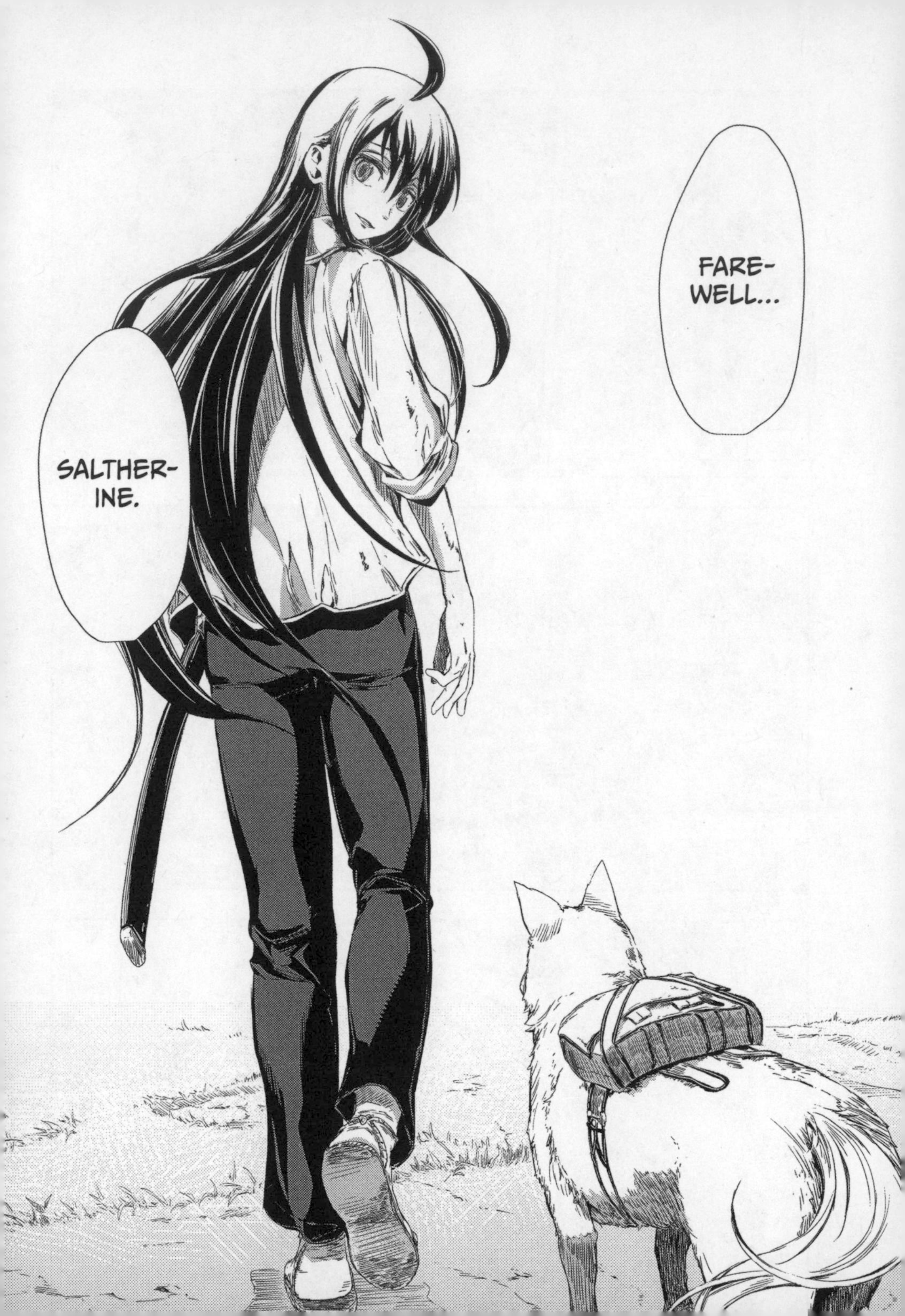
FARE-WELL...
SALTHER-INE.

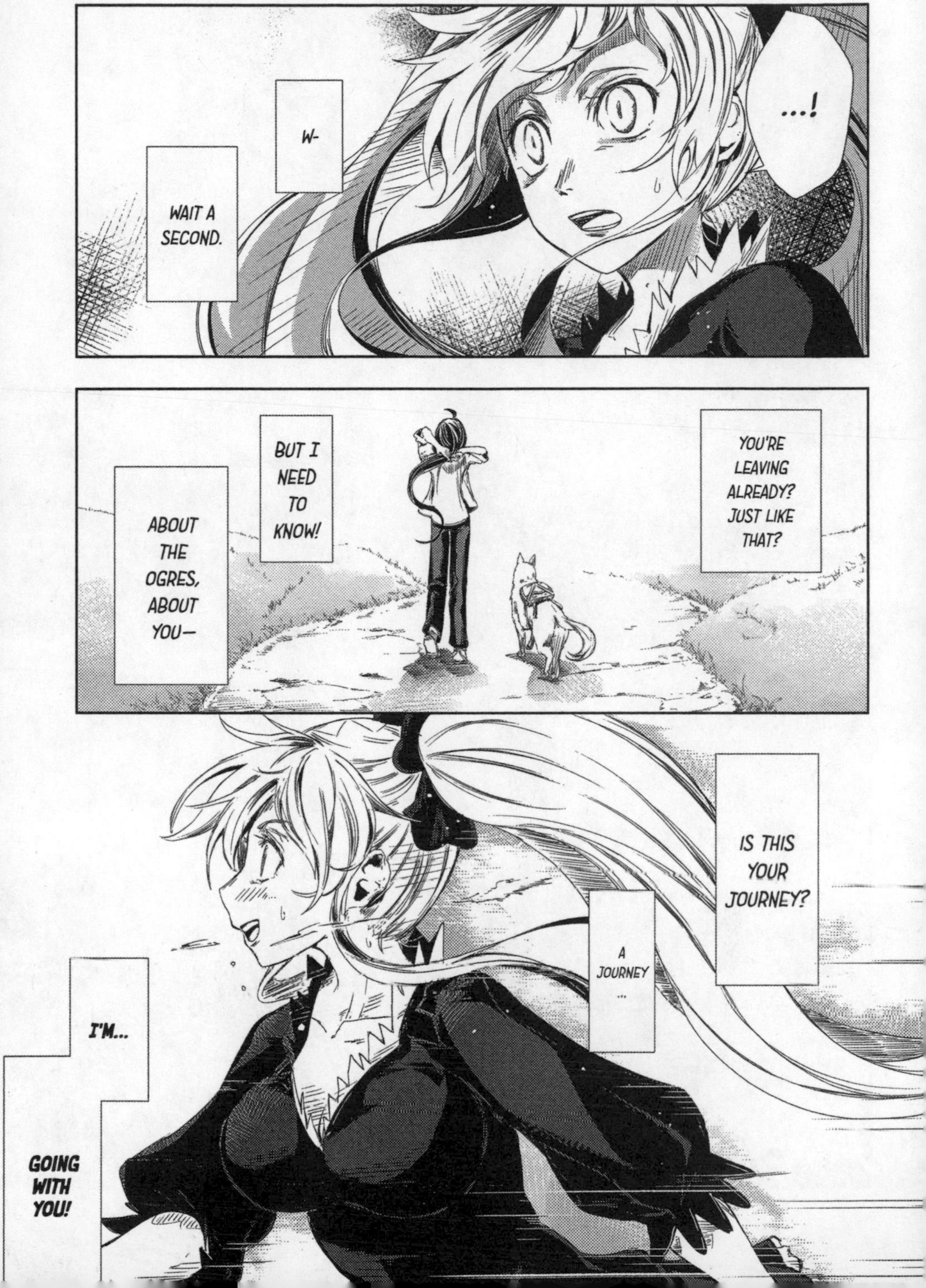
...!
W-
WAIT A SECOND.
YOU'RE LEAVING ALREADY? JUST LIKE THAT?
BUT I NEED TO KNOW!
ABOUT THE OGRES, ABOUT YOU—
IS THIS YOUR JOURNEY?
A JOURNEY...
I'M...
GOING WITH YOU!

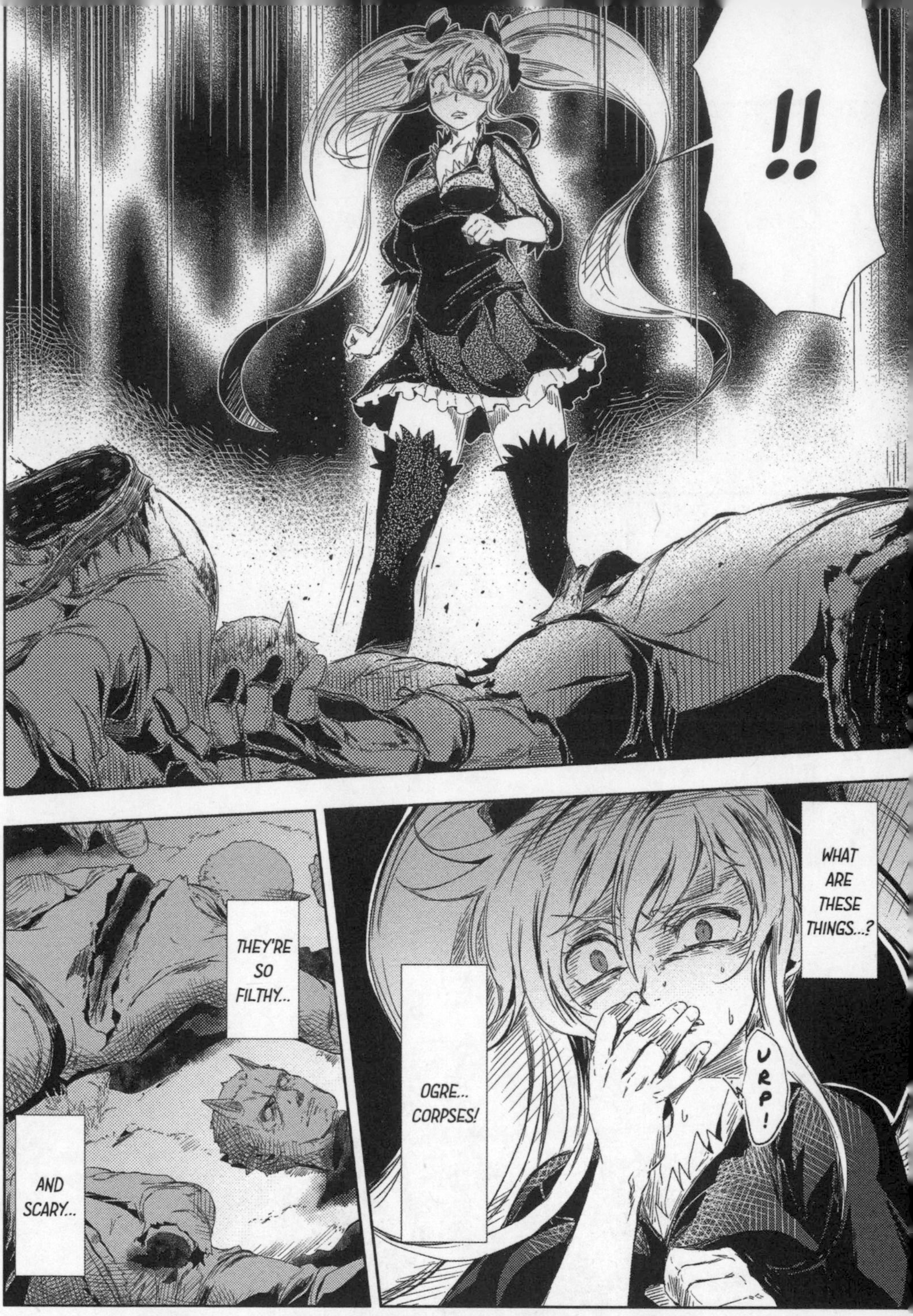
!!
WHAT ARE THESE THINGS...?
URP!
OGRE... CORPSES!
THEY'RE SO FILTHY...
AND SCARY...

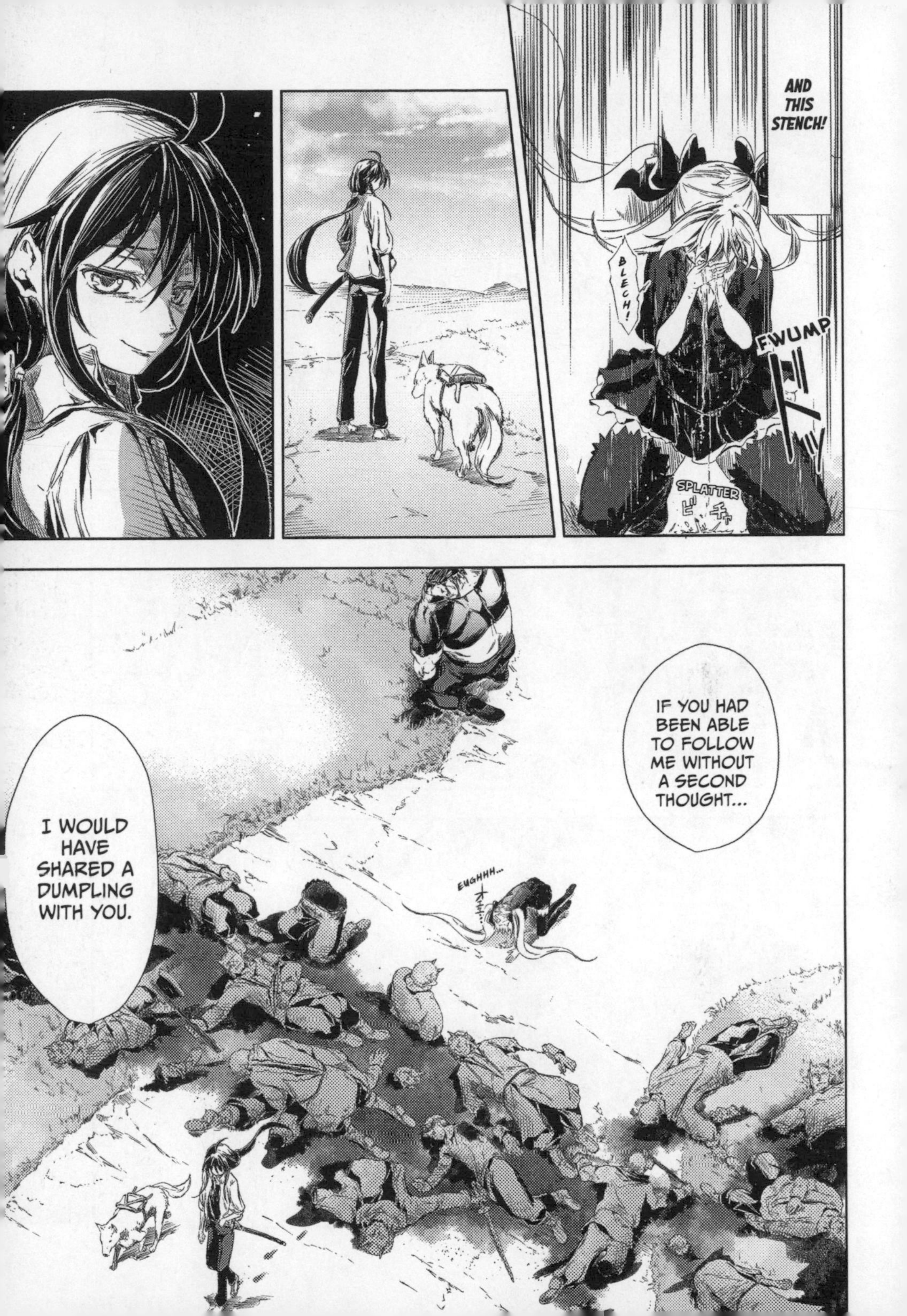
AND THIS STENCH!
BLECH!
FWUMP
SPLATTER
IF YOU HAD BEEN ABLE TO FOLLOW ME WITHOUT A SECOND THOUGHT...
I WOULD HAVE SHARED A DUMPLING WITH YOU.
EUGHHH...

WAIT FOR....!!

MIKOTO!

WAIT!

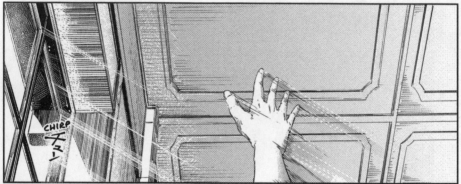

CHIRP

...

CHIRP

CHIRP

JUST A DREAM...

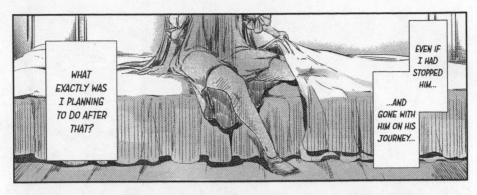

EVEN IF I HAD STOPPED HIM...
...AND GONE WITH HIM ON HIS JOURNEY...
WHAT EXACTLY WAS I PLANNING TO DO AFTER THAT?
IT'S BEEN ONE MONTH SINCE THEN.
LIFE HAS CONTINUED ON, UN-EVENTFULLY.
EVERY-THING HAS BEEN THE SAME AS IT ALWAYS IS.
BUT, AS THE DAYS GO BY, THERE ARE TWO THINGS I JUST CAN'T GET OFF MY MIND.
MIKOTO...
...AND...
FATHER...

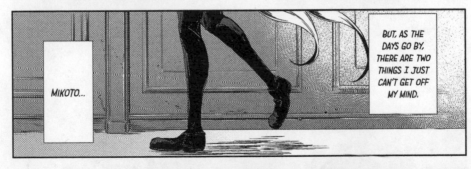

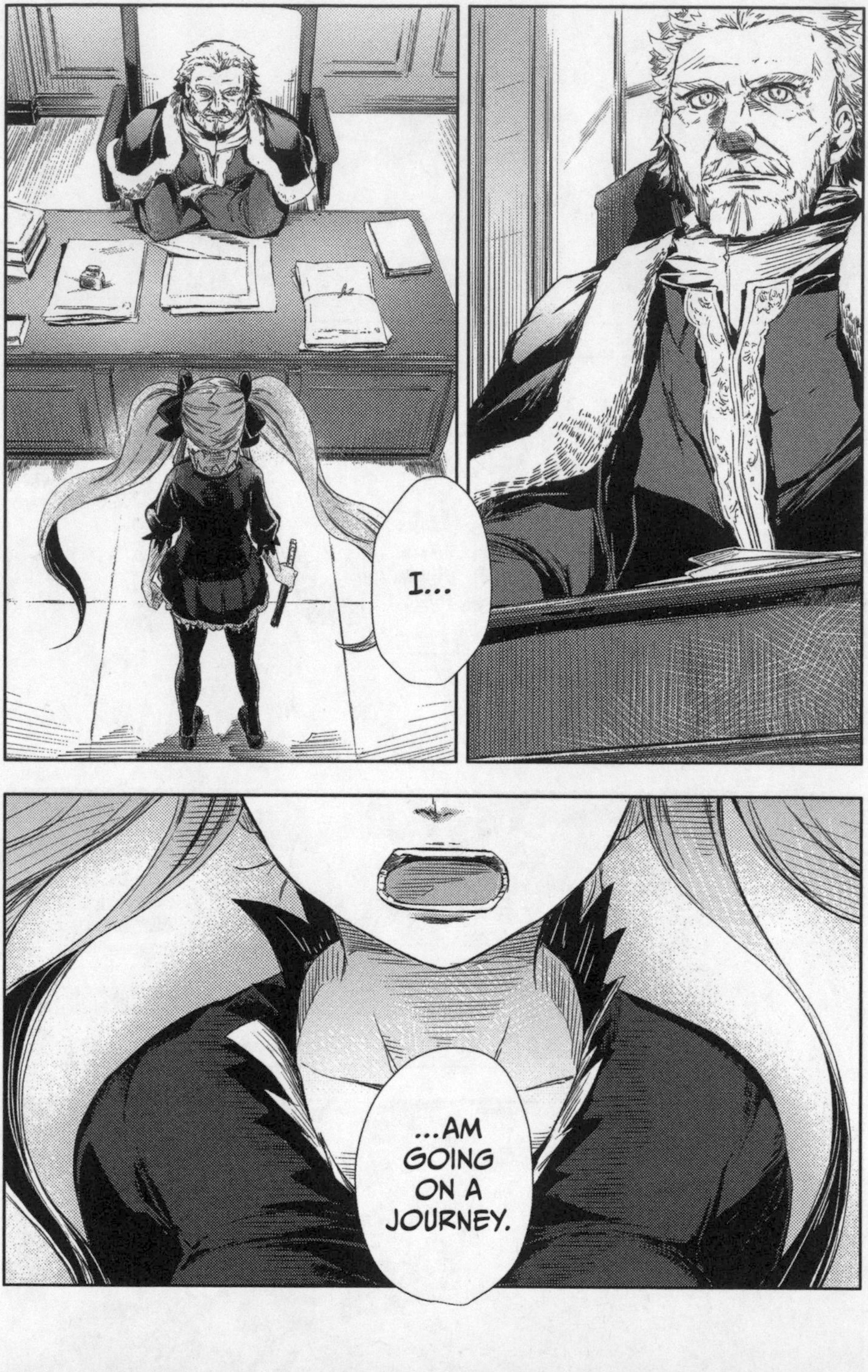
I...
...AM GOING ON A JOURNEY.

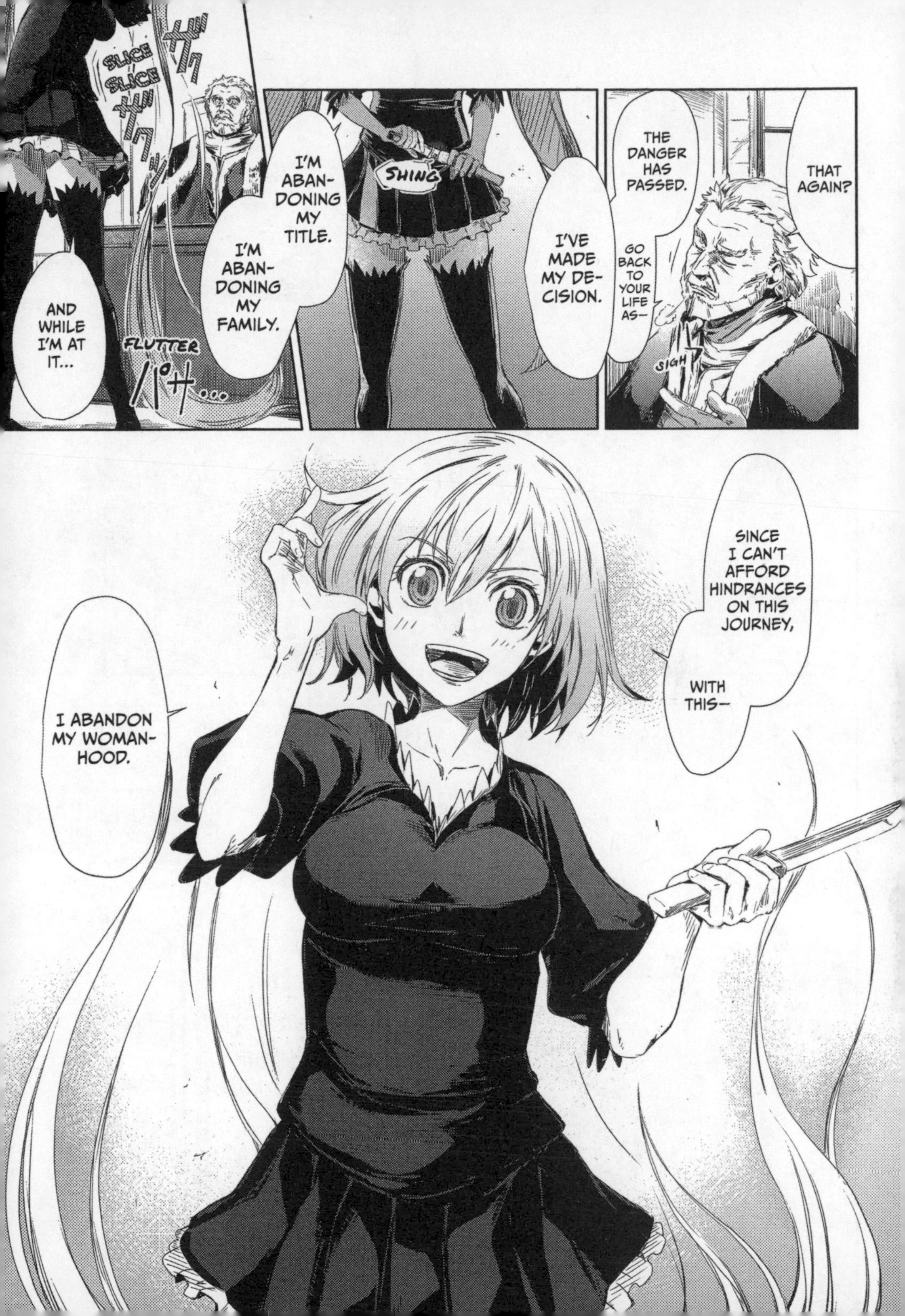
THAT AGAIN?
THE DANGER HAS PASSED.
GO BACK TO YOUR LIFE AS—
SIGH
I'VE MADE MY DECISION.
SHING
I'M ABANDONING MY TITLE.
I'M ABANDONING MY FAMILY.
SLICE SLICE
FLUTTER
パサ…
AND WHILE I'M AT IT...
SINCE I CAN'T AFFORD HINDRANCES ON THIS JOURNEY,
WITH THIS—
I ABANDON MY WOMANHOOD.

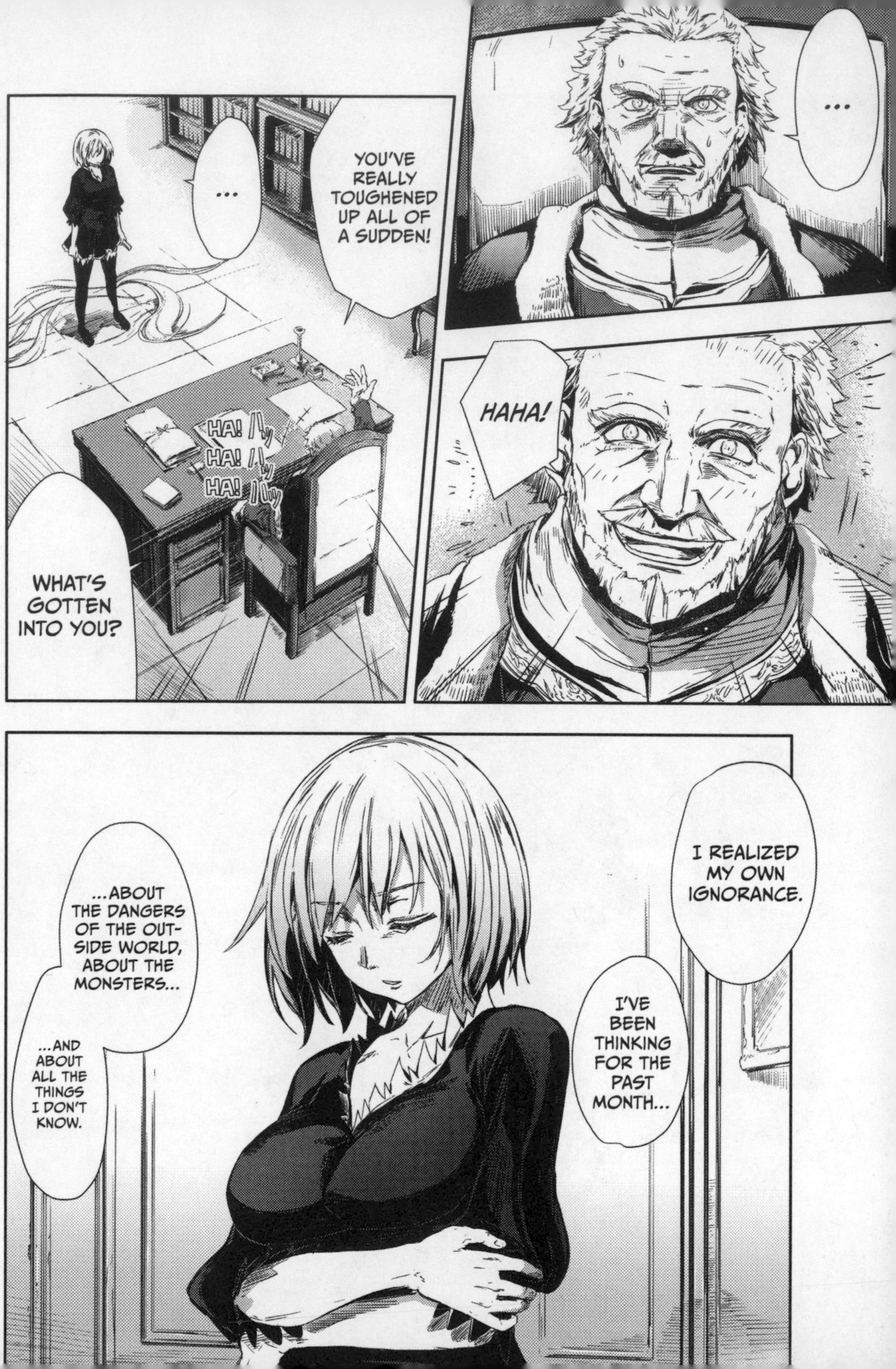
...
HAHA!
YOU'VE REALLY TOUGHENED UP ALL OF A SUDDEN!
...
HA! ハッ HA! ハッ HA! ハッ
WHAT'S GOTTEN INTO YOU?
I REALIZED MY OWN IGNORANCE.
I'VE BEEN THINKING FOR THE PAST MONTH...
...ABOUT THE DANGERS OF THE OUT-SIDE WORLD, ABOUT THE MONSTERS...
...AND ABOUT ALL THE THINGS I DON'T KNOW.

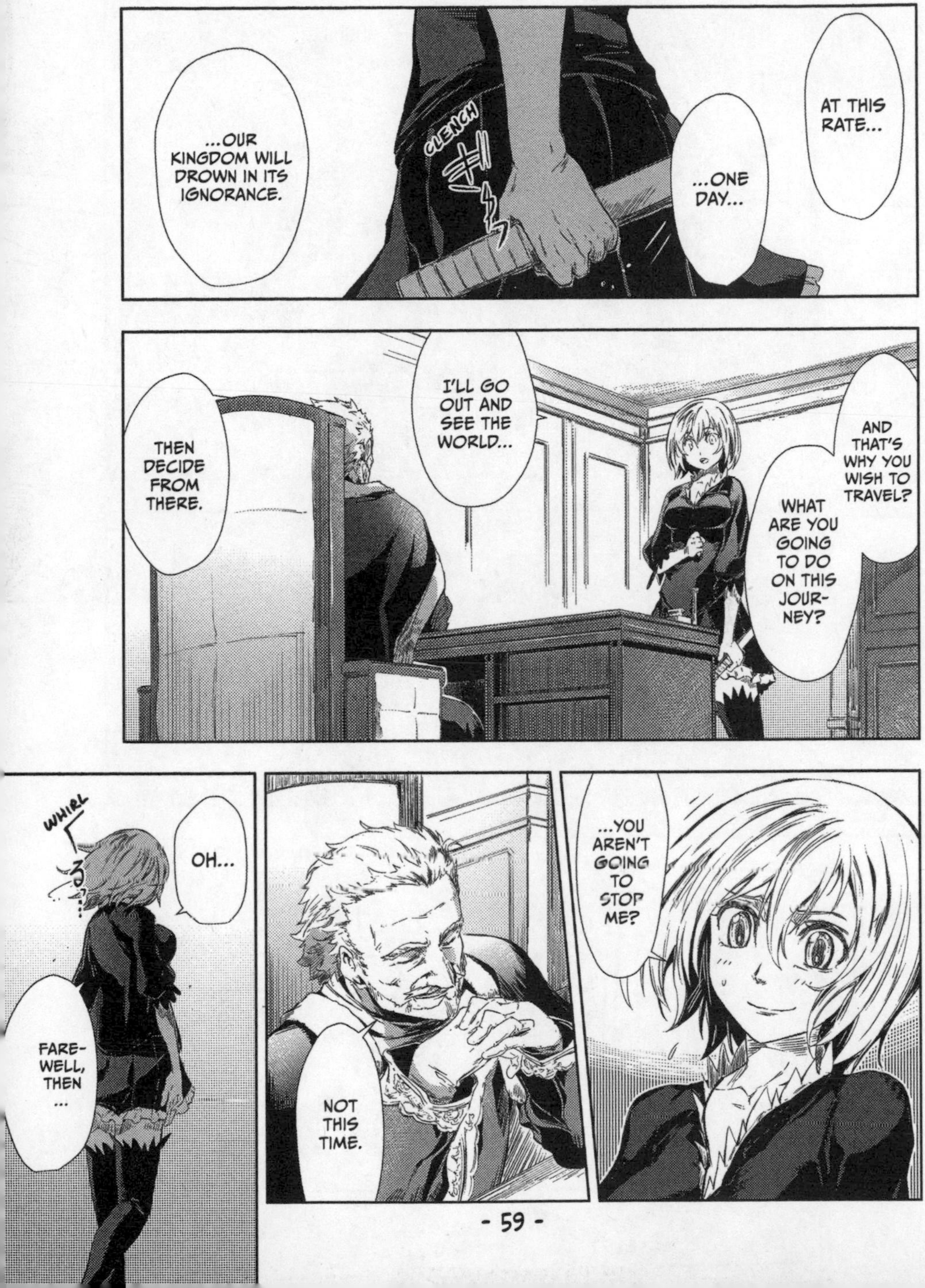
AT THIS RATE...
...ONE DAY...
CLENCH
...OUR KINGDOM WILL DROWN IN ITS IGNORANCE.
AND THAT'S WHY YOU WISH TO TRAVEL?
WHAT ARE YOU GOING TO DO ON THIS JOURNEY?
I'LL GO OUT AND SEE THE WORLD...
THEN DECIDE FROM THERE.
...YOU AREN'T GOING TO STOP ME?
NOT THIS TIME.
OH...
WHIRL
FARE-WELL, THEN ...

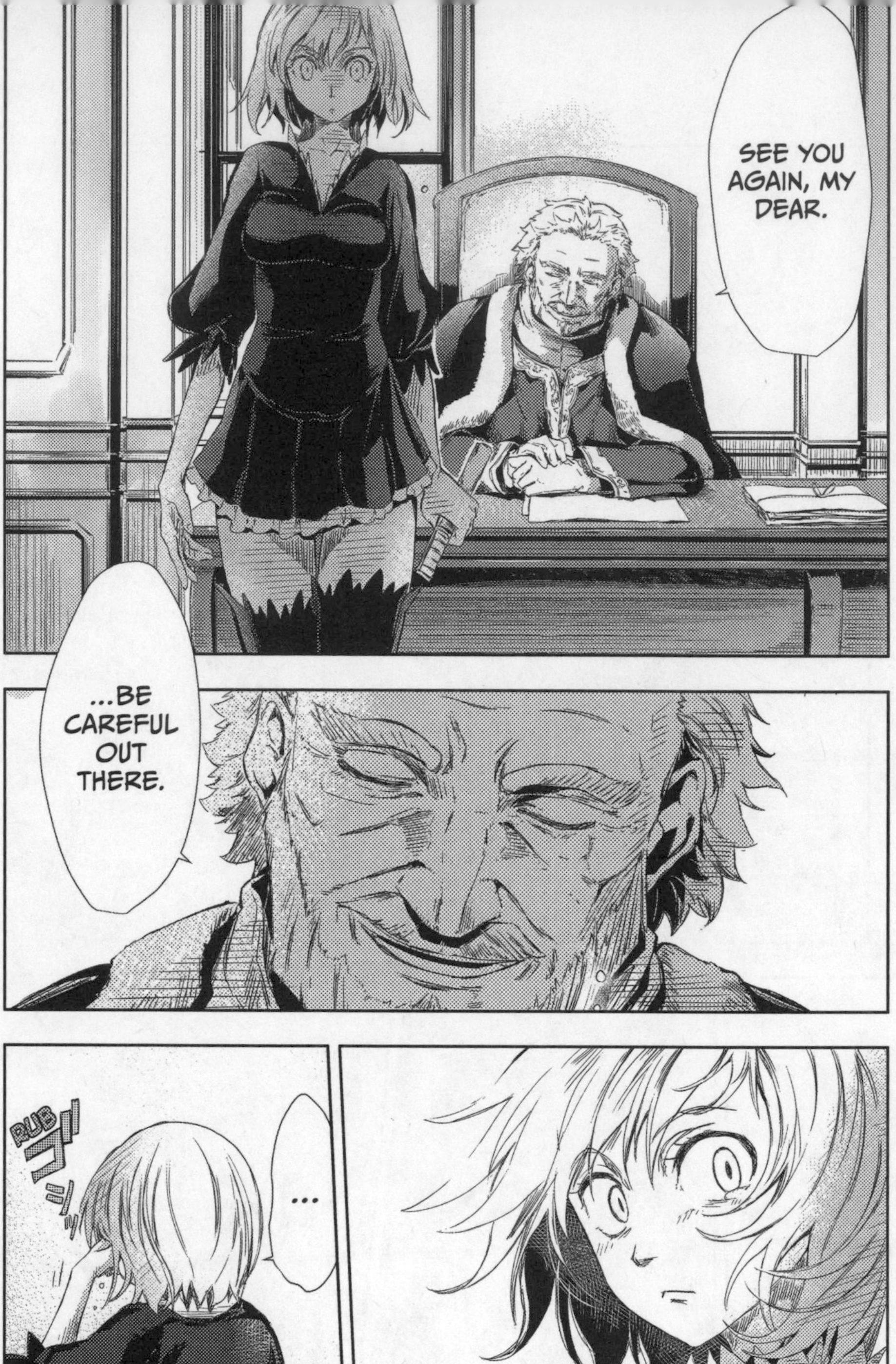
SEE YOU AGAIN, MY DEAR.
...BE CAREFUL OUT THERE.
RUB
...

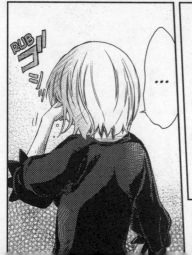

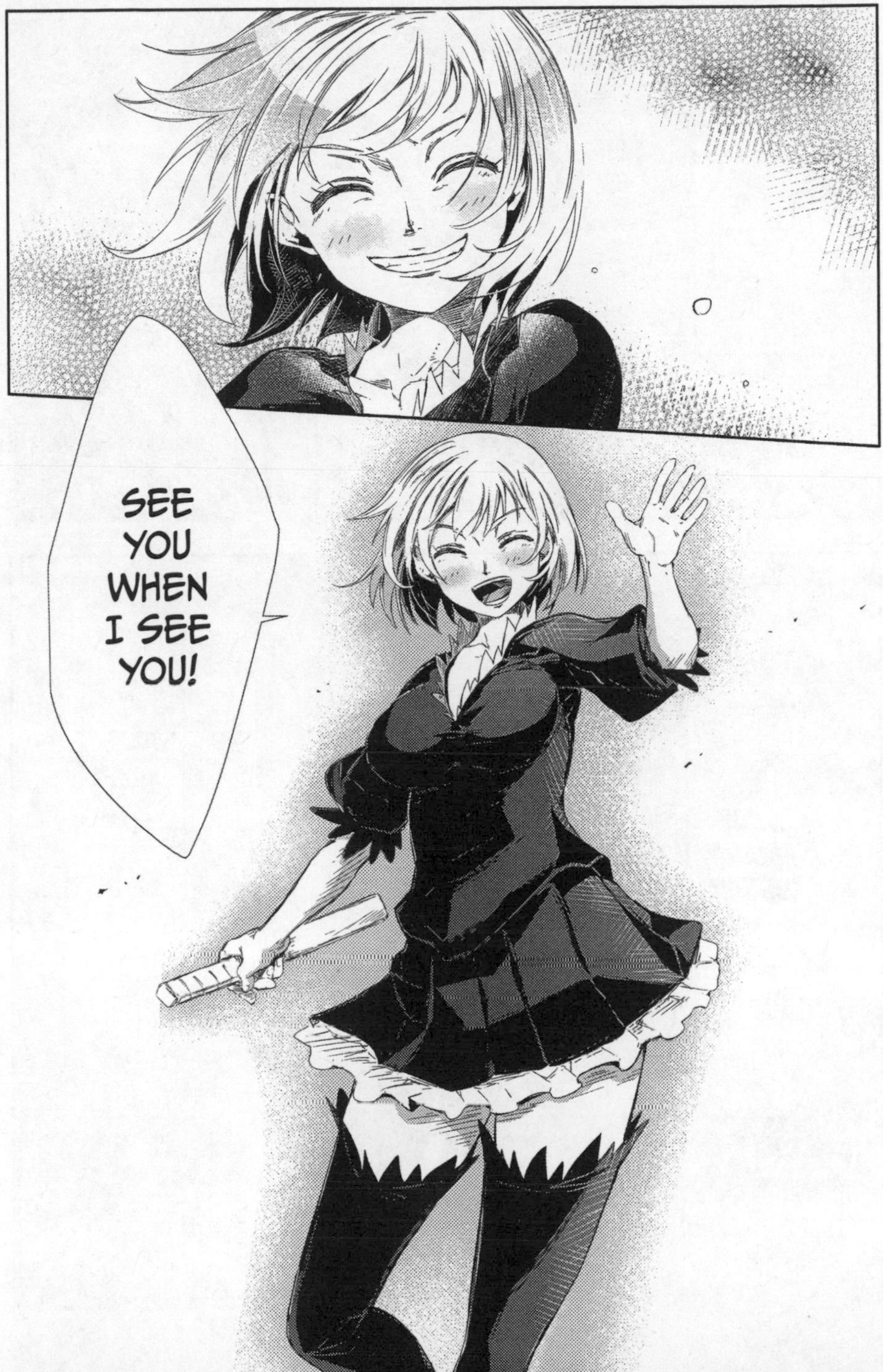
SEE YOU WHEN I SEE YOU!

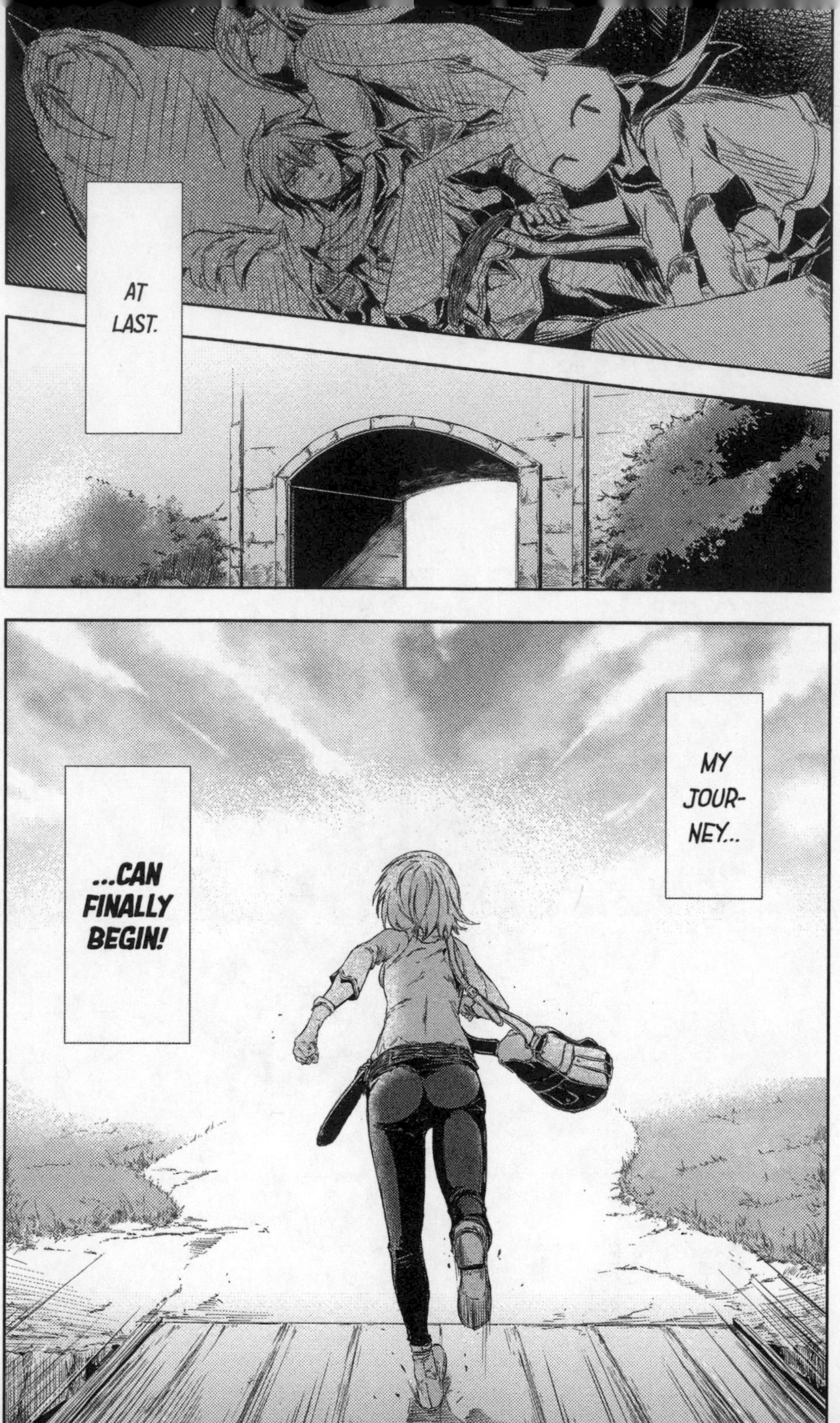
AT LAST.
MY JOURNEY...
...CAN FINALLY BEGIN!

PEACH BOY RIVERSIDE

CHAPTER 2:
THE FORMER PRINCESS AND THE RABBIT GIRL

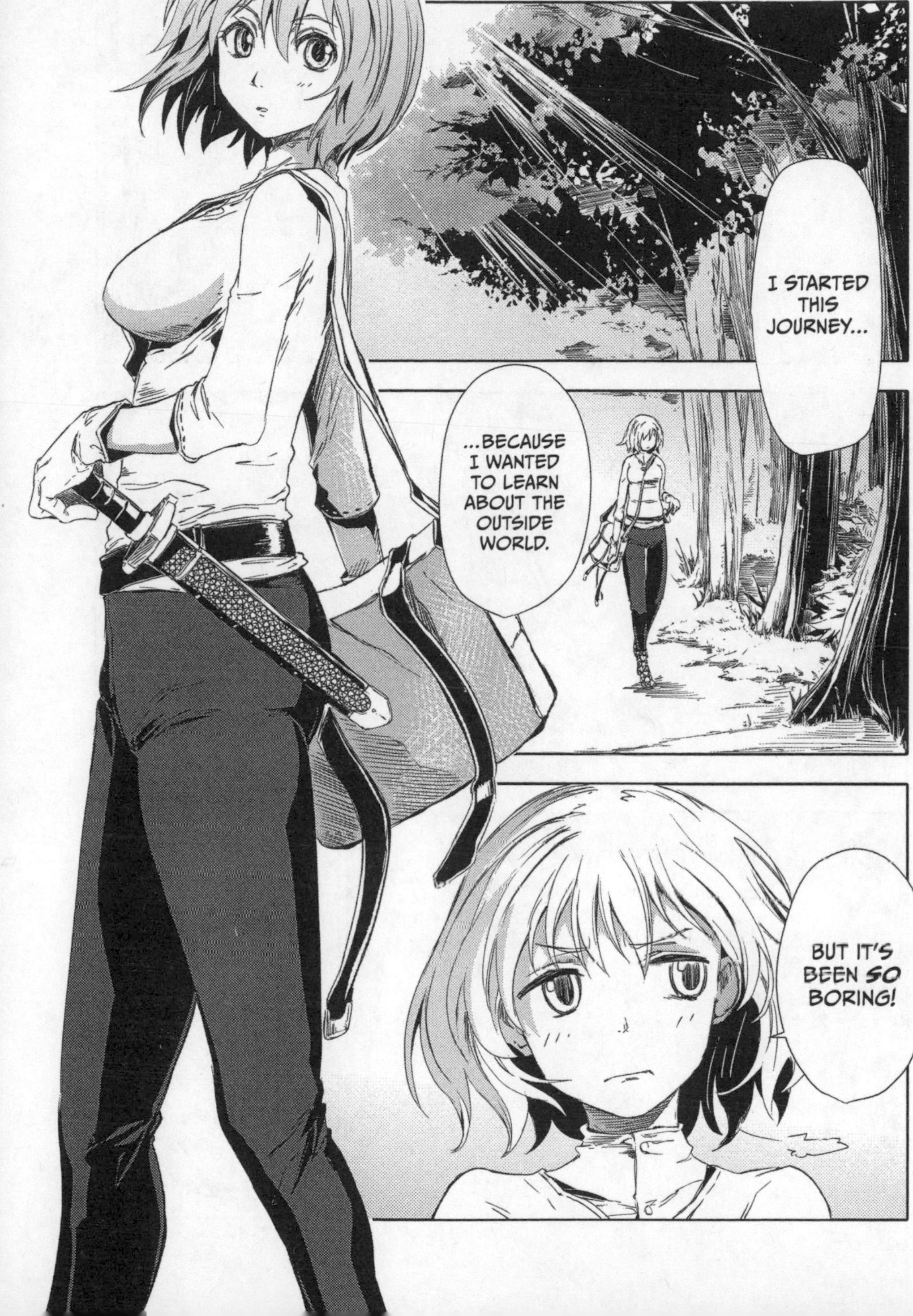
I STARTED THIS JOURNEY...
...BECAUSE I WANTED TO LEARN ABOUT THE OUTSIDE WORLD.
BUT IT'S BEEN *SO* BORING!

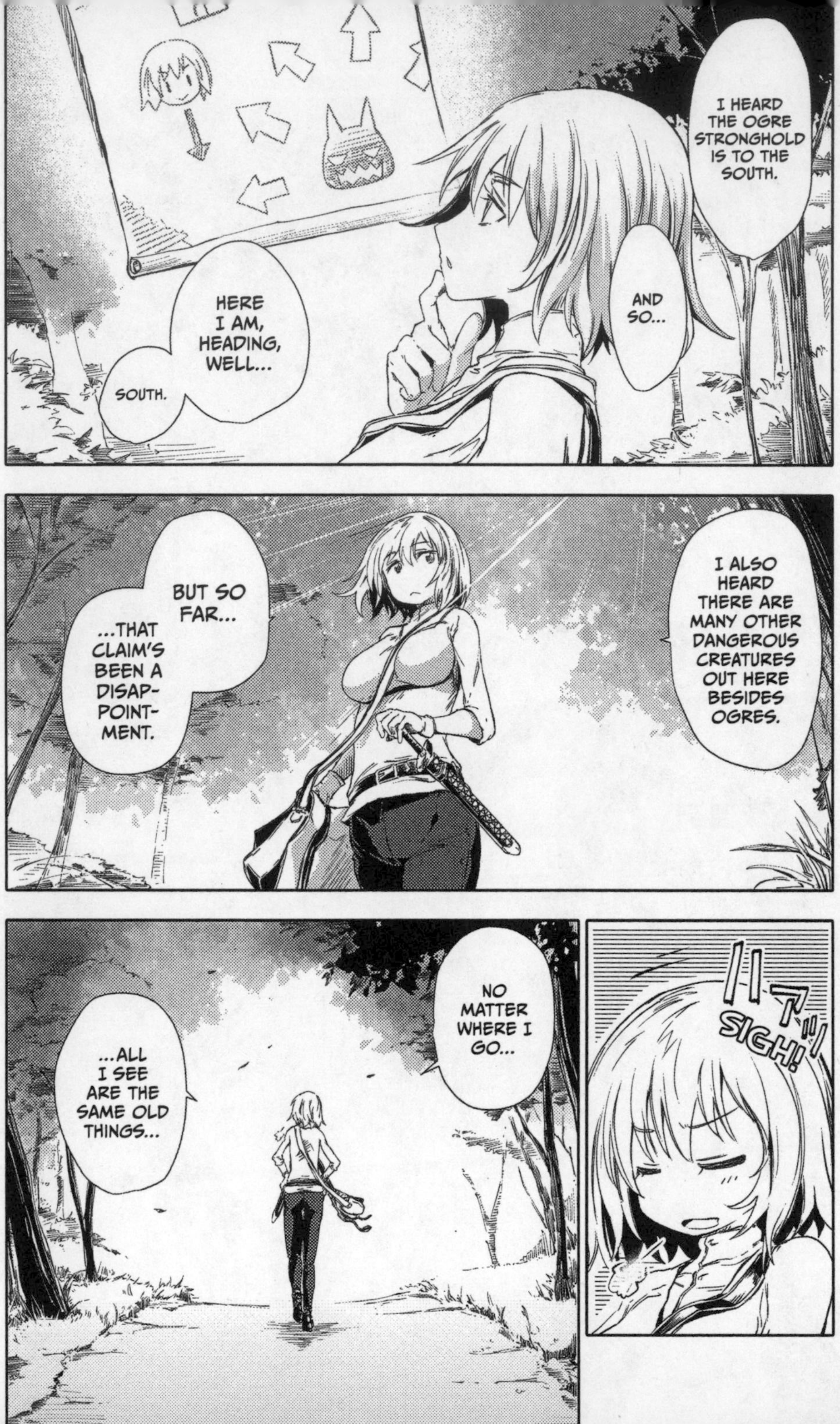
I HEARD THE OGRE STRONGHOLD IS TO THE SOUTH.
AND SO...
HERE I AM, HEADING, WELL...
SOUTH.
I ALSO HEARD THERE ARE MANY OTHER DANGEROUS CREATURES OUT HERE BESIDES OGRES.
BUT SO FAR...
...THAT CLAIM'S BEEN A DISAPPOINTMENT.
SIGH!
NO MATTER WHERE I GO...
...ALL I SEE ARE THE SAME OLD THINGS...

...OR MAYBE NOT.

...

WH-

WHAT...

...IS THAT?

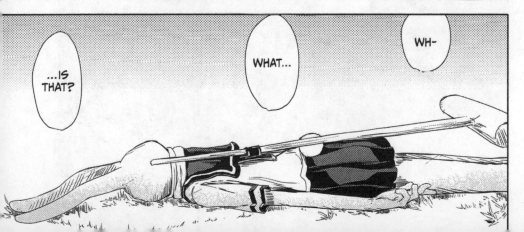

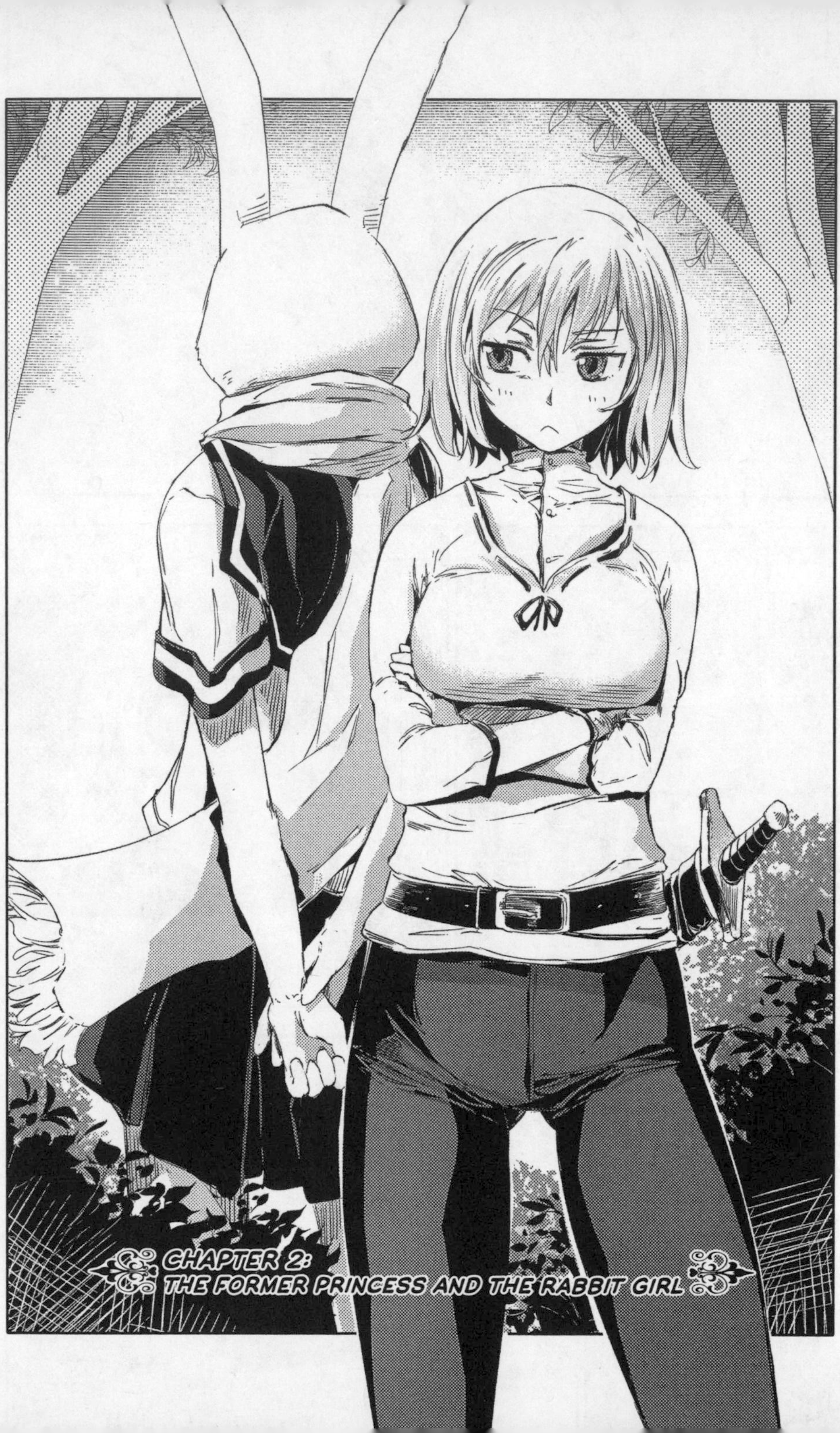
CHAPTER 2:
THE FORMER PRINCESS AND THE RABBIT GIRL

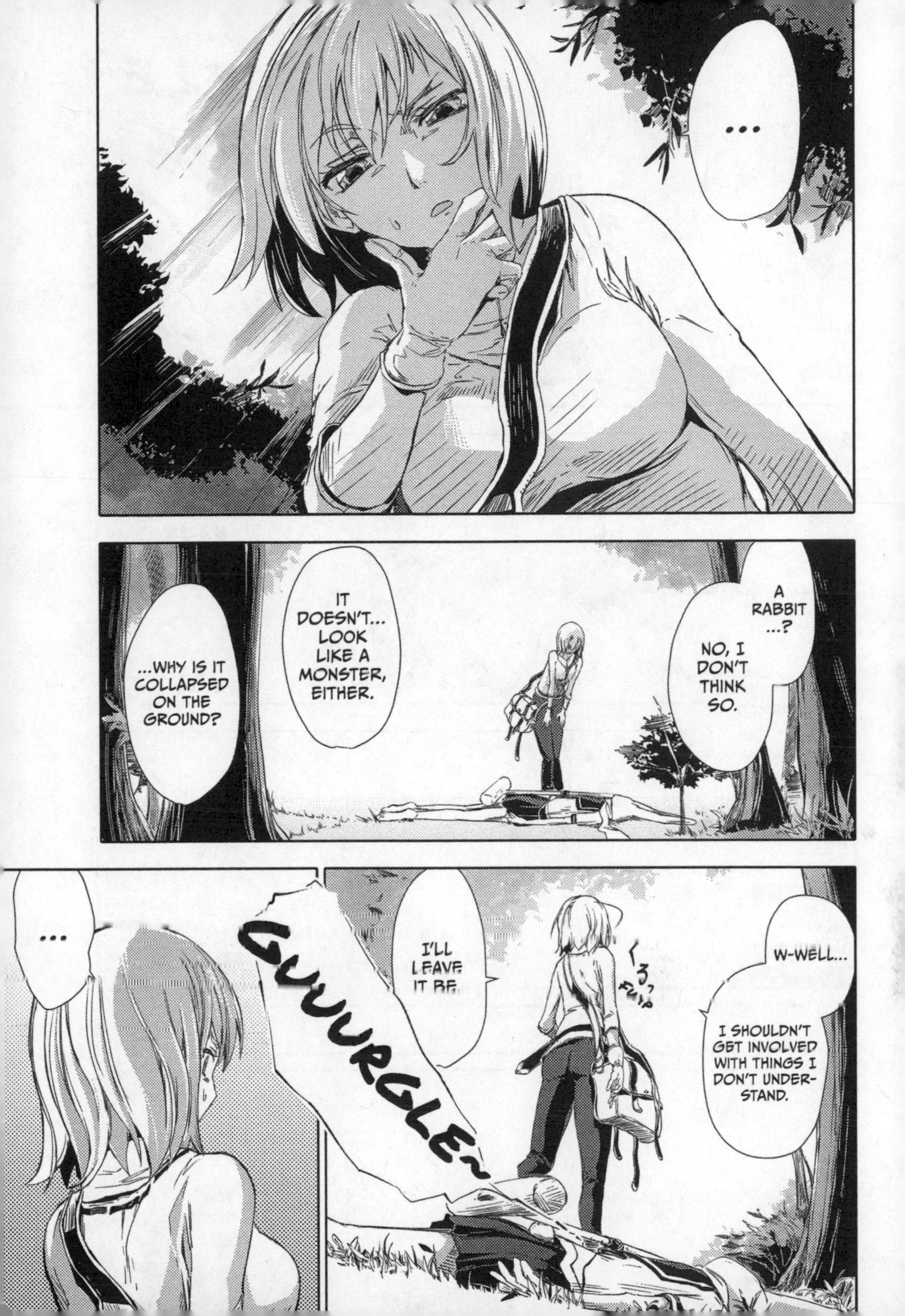
...
A RABBIT ...?
NO, I DON'T THINK SO.
IT DOESN'T... LOOK LIKE A MONSTER, EITHER.
...WHY IS IT COLLAPSED ON THE GROUND?
W-WELL...
I SHOULDN'T GET INVOLVED WITH THINGS I DON'T UNDERSTAND.
FLIP
I'LL LEAVE IT BE.
GUUURGLE~
...

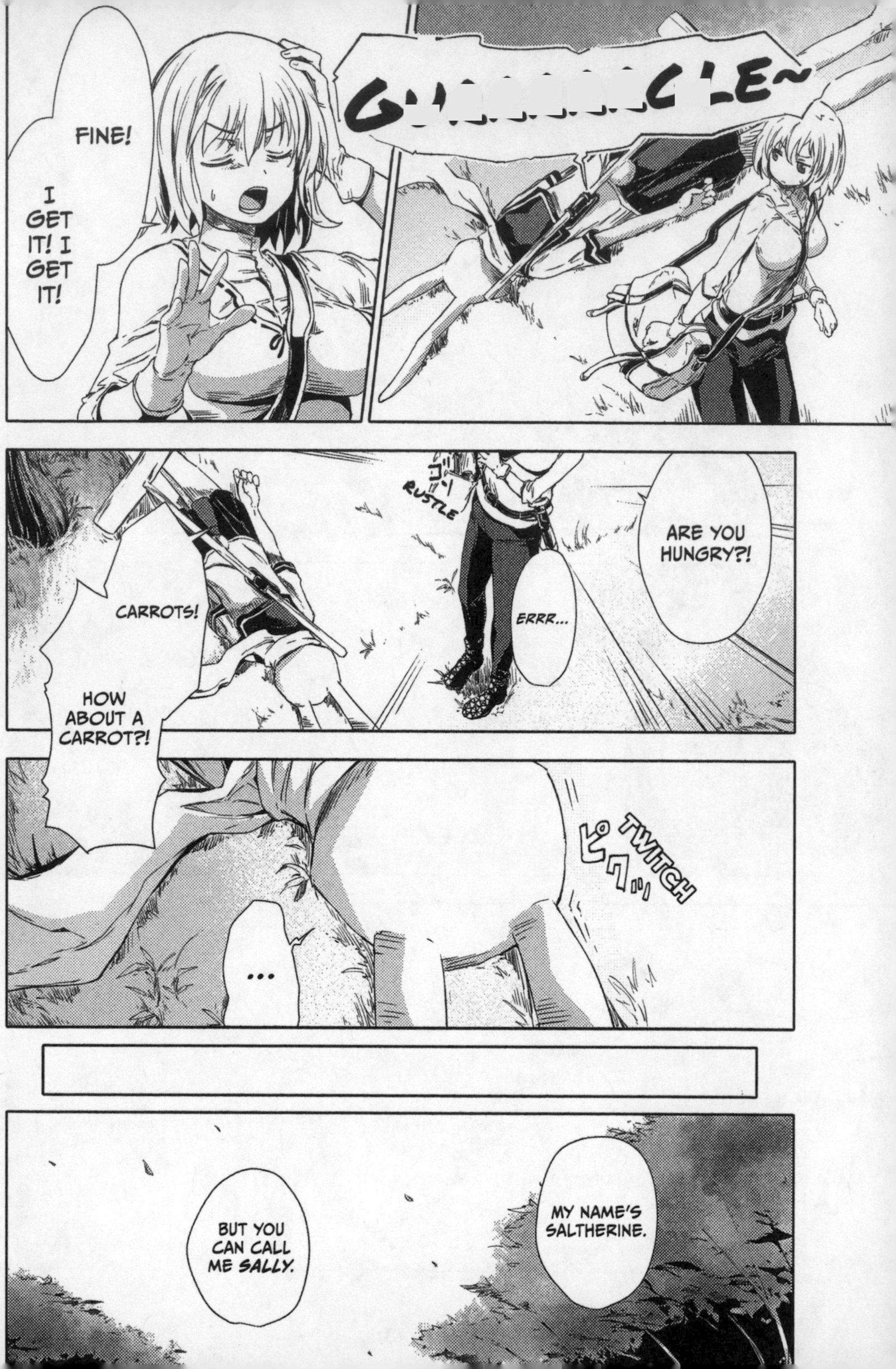
FINE!
I GET IT! I GET IT!
ARE YOU HUNGRY?!
ERRR...
RUSTLE
CARROTS!
HOW ABOUT A CARROT?!
TWITCH
...
MY NAME'S SALTHERINE.
BUT YOU CAN CALL ME SALLY.

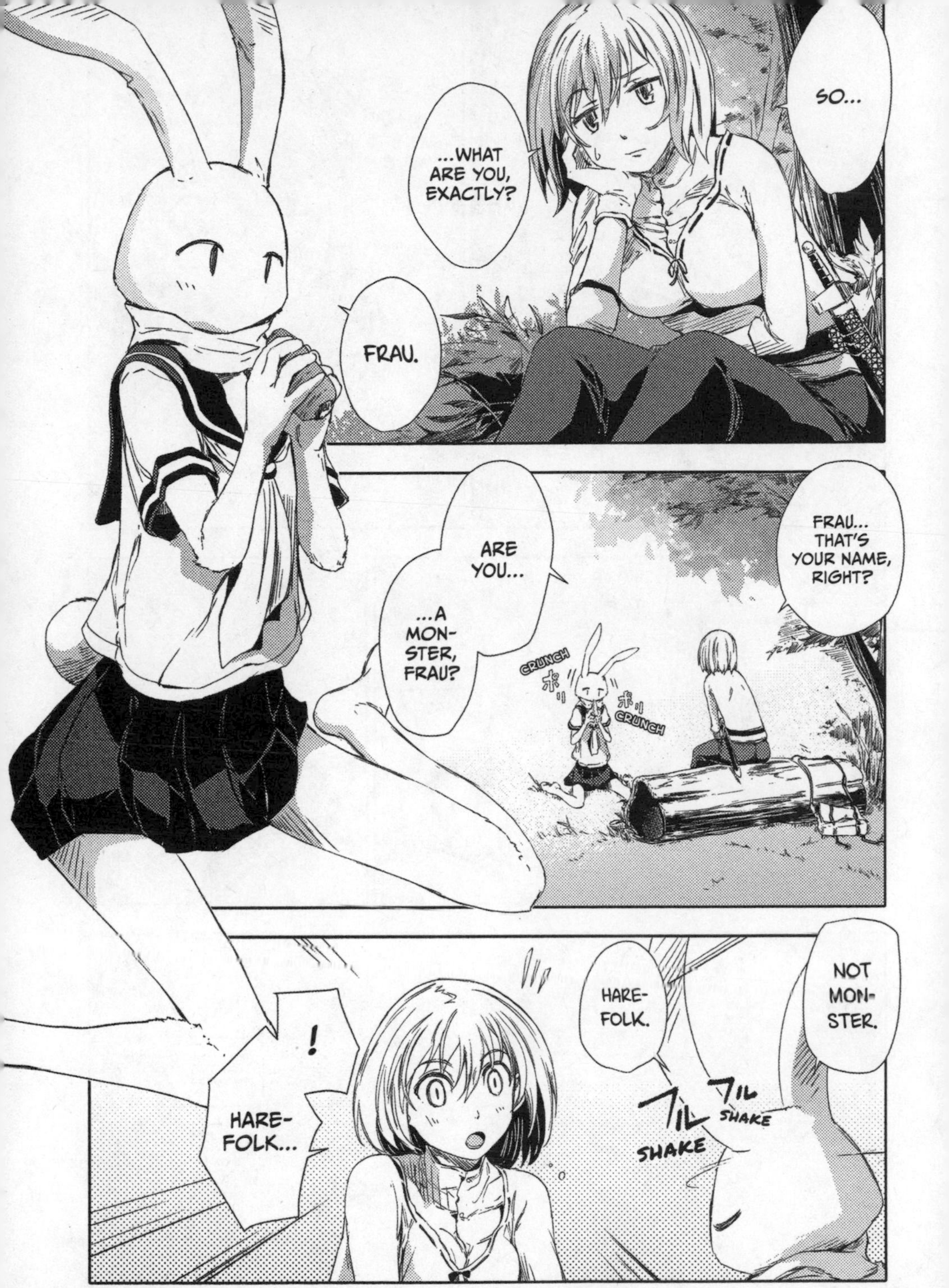
SO...
...WHAT ARE YOU, EXACTLY?
FRAU.
FRAU... THAT'S YOUR NAME, RIGHT?
ARE YOU...
...A MON-STER, FRAU?
ポリ CRUNCH
ポリ CRUNCH
NOT MON-STER.
HARE-FOLK.
フル SHAKE
フル SHAKE
!
HARE-FOLK...

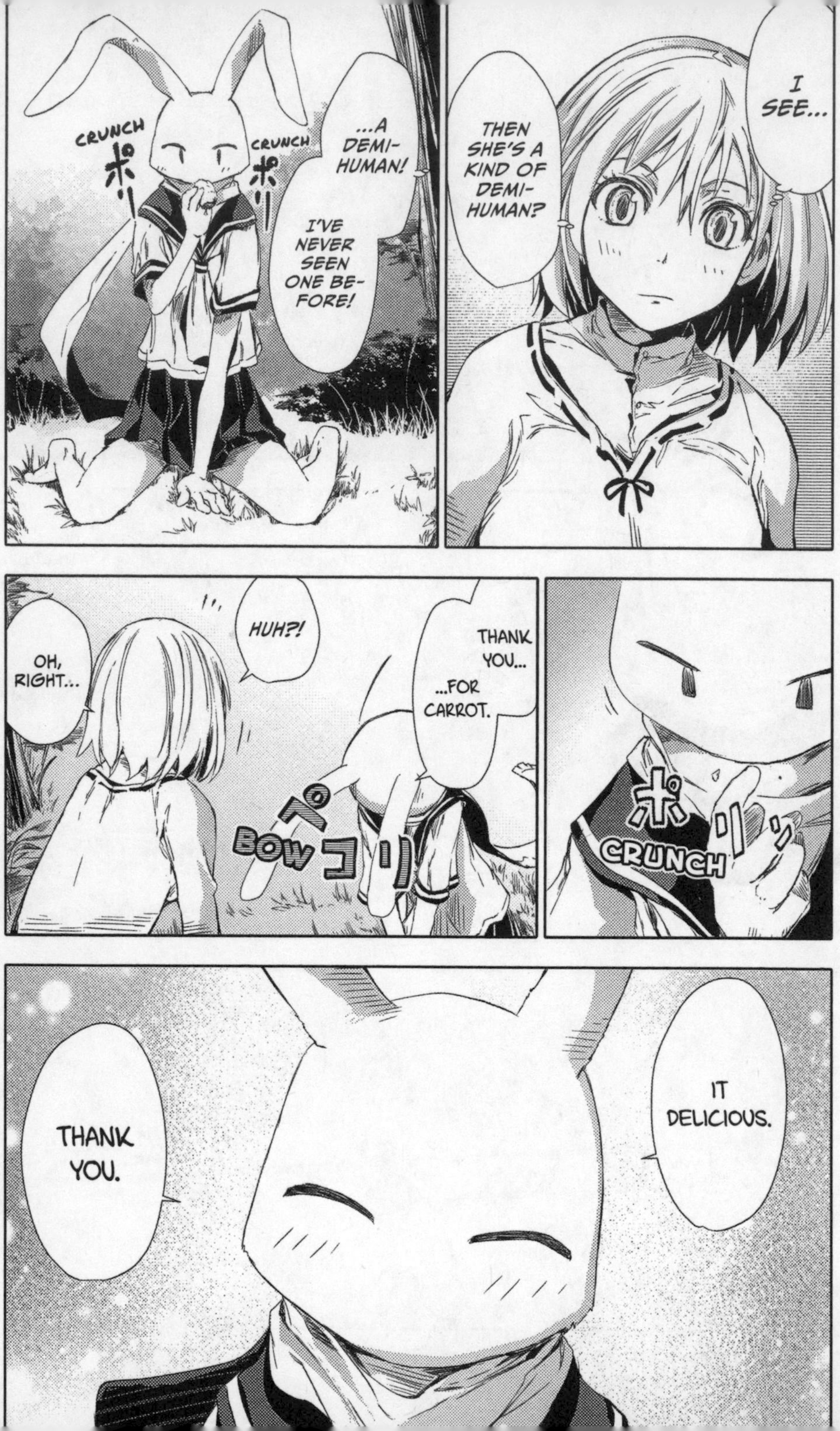
I SEE...
THEN SHE'S A KIND OF DEMI-HUMAN?
...A DEMI-HUMAN!
I'VE NEVER SEEN ONE BE-FORE!
CRUNCH
CRUNCH
CRUNCH
THANK YOU...
...FOR CARROT.
BOW
HUH?!
OH, RIGHT...
IT DELICIOUS.
THANK YOU.

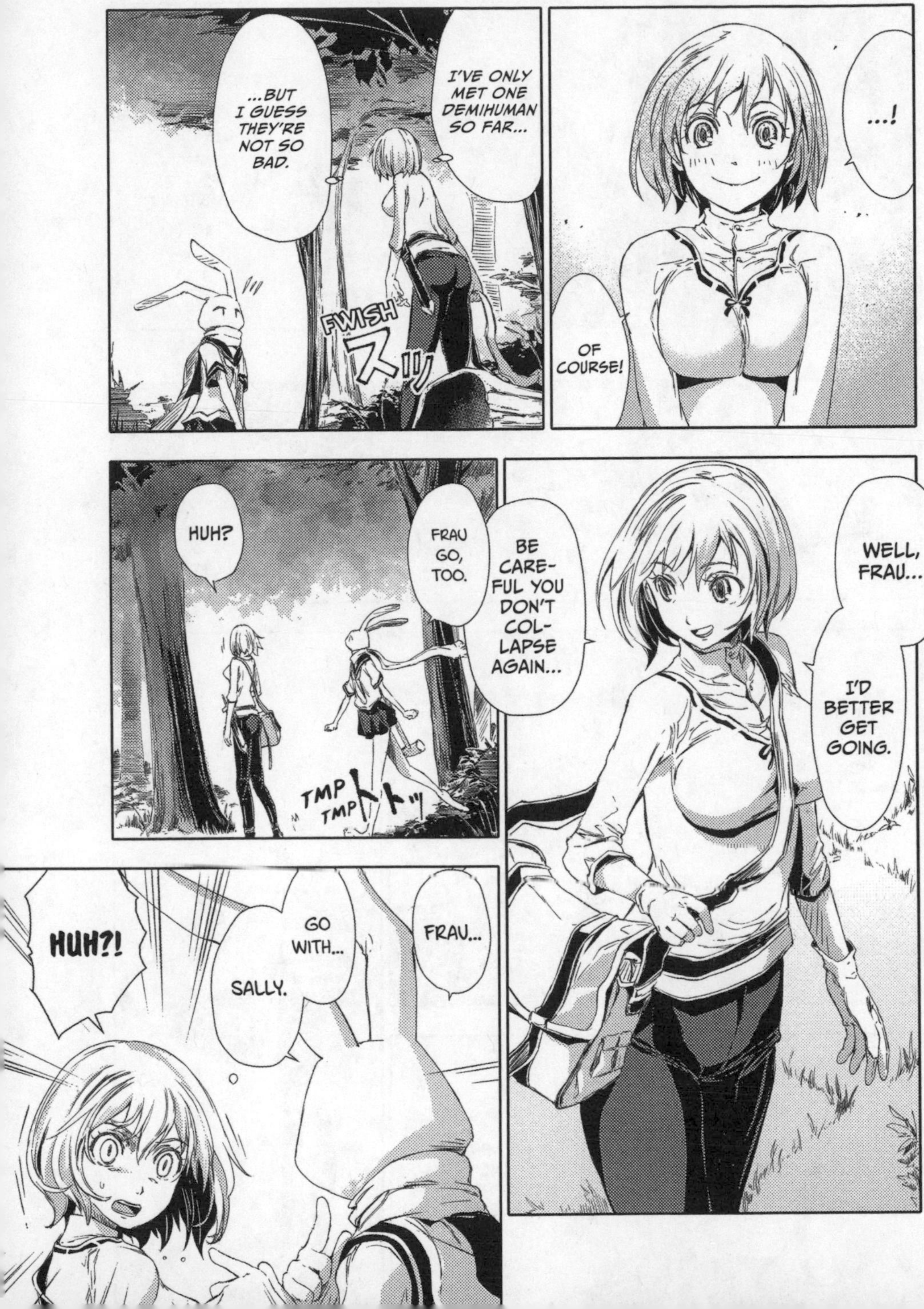
...!
OF COURSE!
I'VE ONLY MET ONE DEMIHUMAN SO FAR...
...BUT I GUESS THEY'RE NOT SO BAD.
FWISH
WELL, FRAU...
I'D BETTER GET GOING.
BE CARE-FUL YOU DON'T COL-LAPSE AGAIN...
FRAU GO, TOO.
HUH?
TMP TMP
FRAU...
GO WITH...
SALLY.
HUH?!

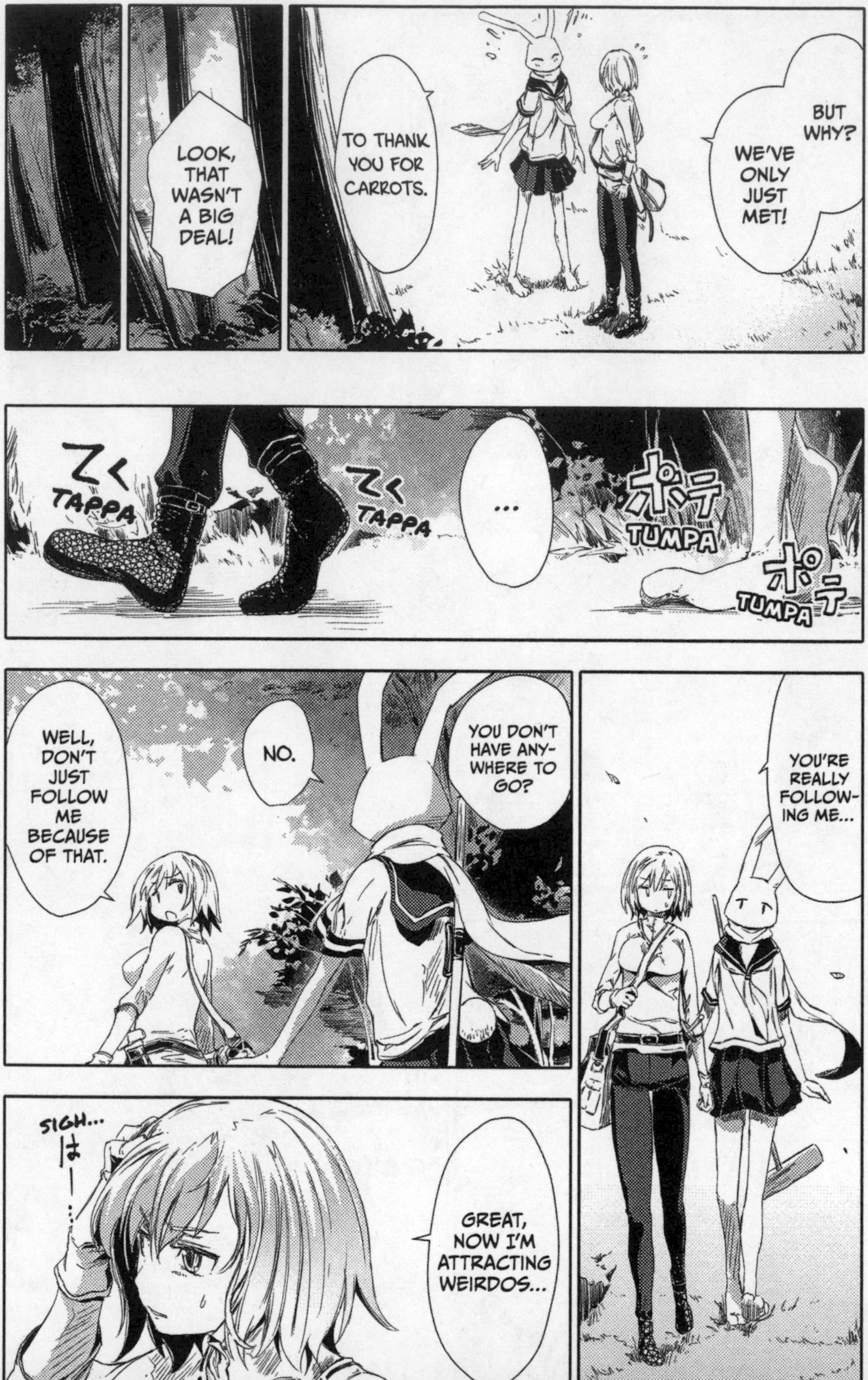
BUT WHY? WE'VE ONLY JUST MET!
TO THANK YOU FOR CARROTS.
LOOK, THAT WASN'T A BIG DEAL!
ポテ TUMPA
ポテ TUMPA
...
てく TAPPA
てく TAPPA
YOU'RE REALLY FOLLOWING ME...
YOU DON'T HAVE ANYWHERE TO GO?
NO.
WELL, DON'T JUST FOLLOW ME BECAUSE OF THAT.
GREAT, NOW I'M ATTRACTING WEIRDOS...
SIGH... はー…

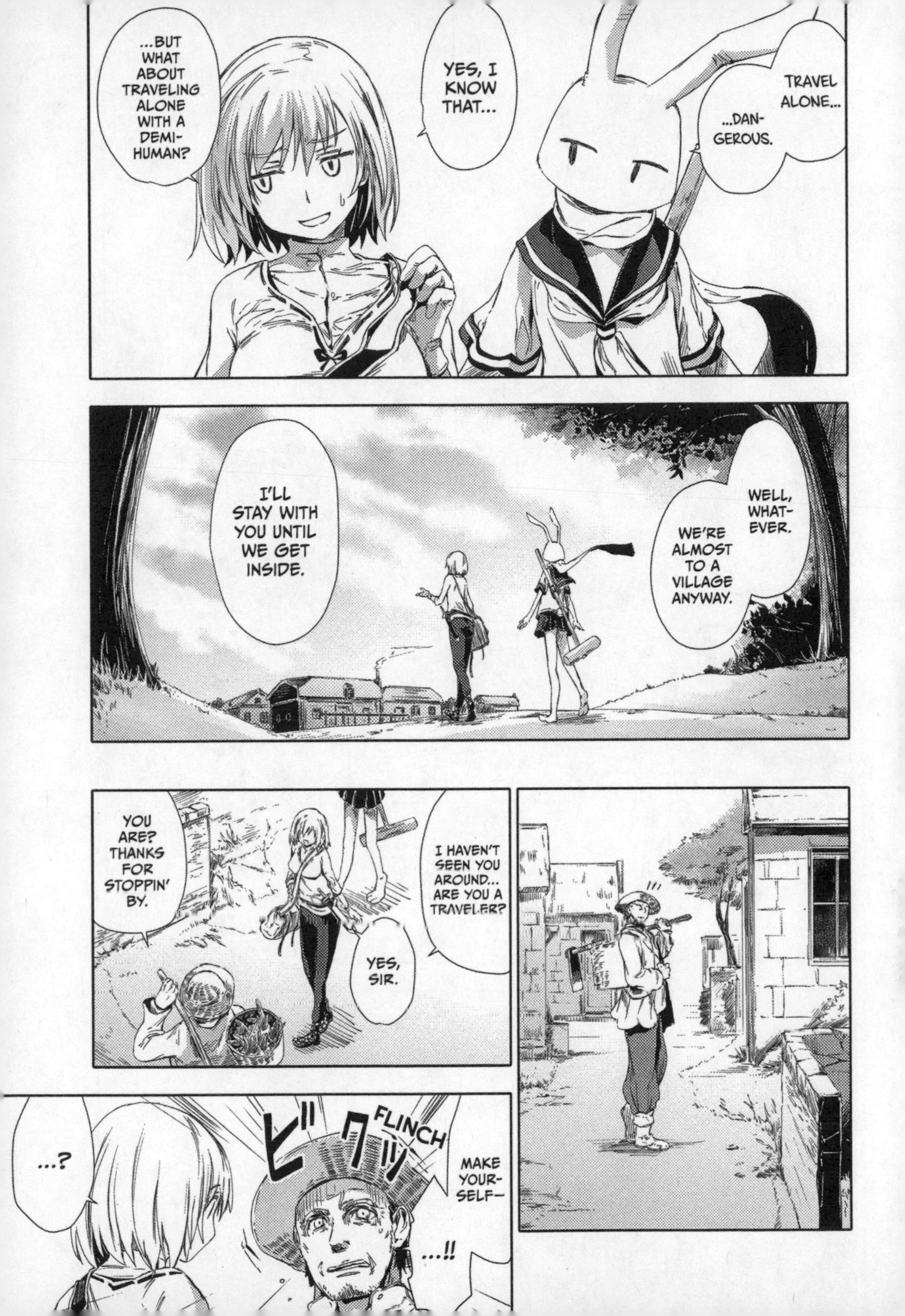
TRAVEL ALONE... ...DAN-GEROUS.
YES, I KNOW THAT...
...BUT WHAT ABOUT TRAVELING ALONE WITH A DEMI-HUMAN?
WELL, WHAT-EVER. WE'RE ALMOST TO A VILLAGE ANYWAY.
I'LL STAY WITH YOU UNTIL WE GET INSIDE.
I HAVEN'T SEEN YOU AROUND... ARE YOU A TRAVELER?
YES, SIR.
YOU ARE? THANKS FOR STOPPIN' BY.
MAKE YOUR-SELF-
FLINCH
...!!
...?

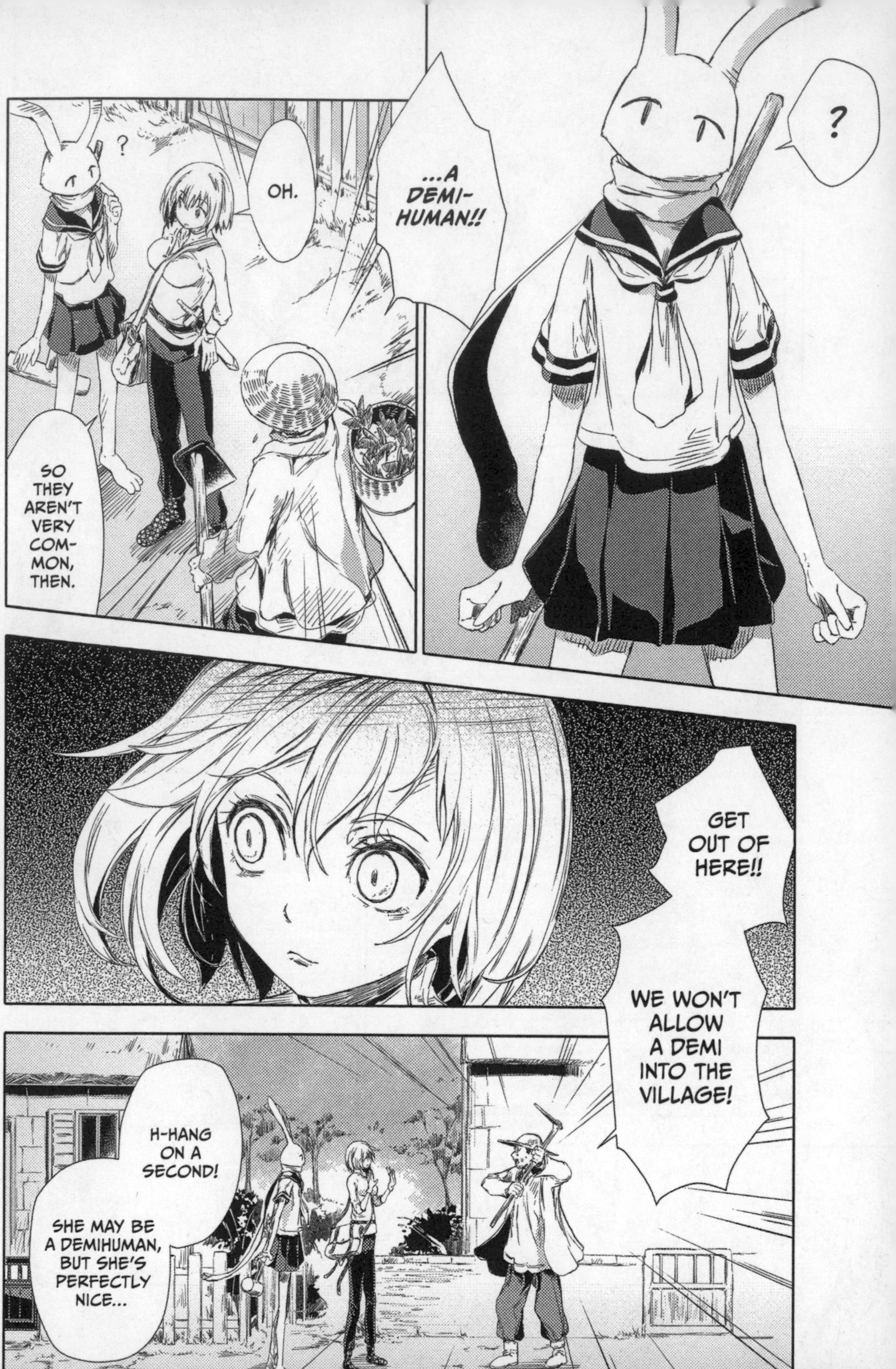
?
...A DEMI-HUMAN!!
OH.
?
SO THEY AREN'T VERY COM-MON, THEN.
GET OUT OF HERE!!
WE WON'T ALLOW A DEMI INTO THE VILLAGE!
H-HANG ON A SECOND!
SHE MAY BE A DEMIHUMAN, BUT SHE'S PERFECTLY NICE...

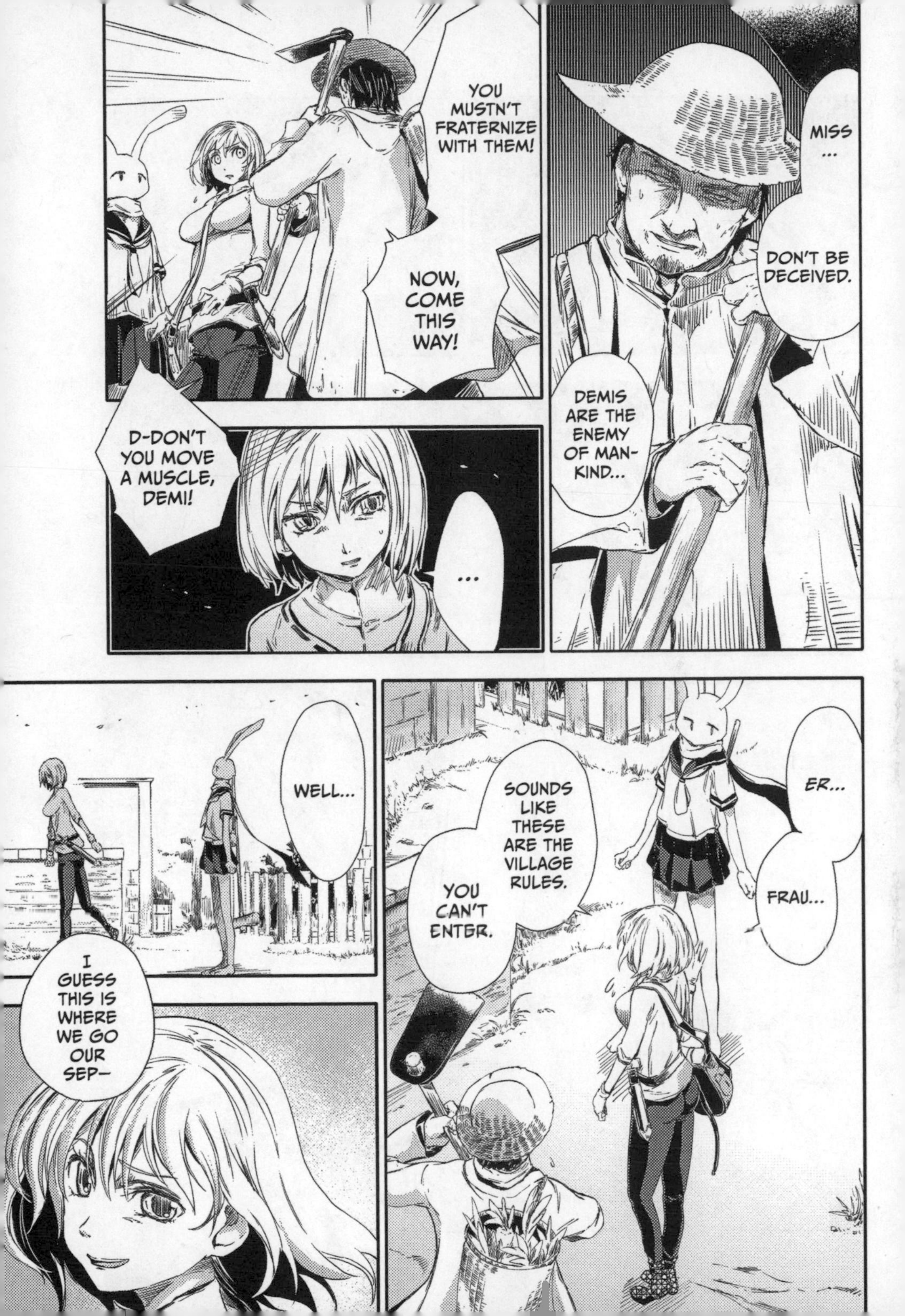
MISS ...
DON'T BE DECEIVED.
DEMIS ARE THE ENEMY OF MAN-KIND...
YOU MUSTN'T FRATERNIZE WITH THEM!
NOW, COME THIS WAY!
D-DON'T YOU MOVE A MUSCLE, DEMI!
...
ER...
FRAU...
SOUNDS LIKE THESE ARE THE VILLAGE RULES.
YOU CAN'T ENTER.
WELL...
I GUESS THIS IS WHERE WE GO OUR SEP–

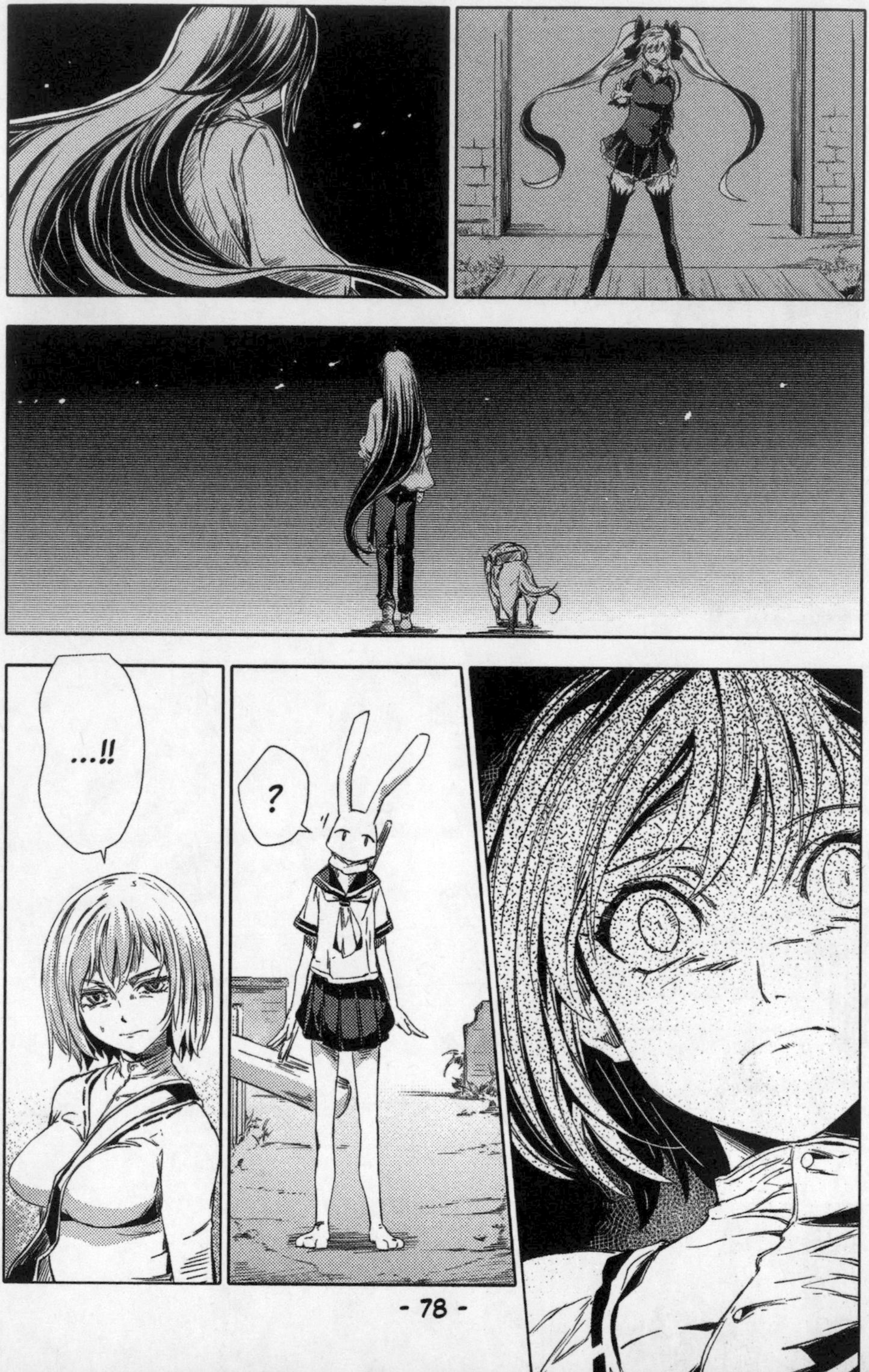
?
...!!

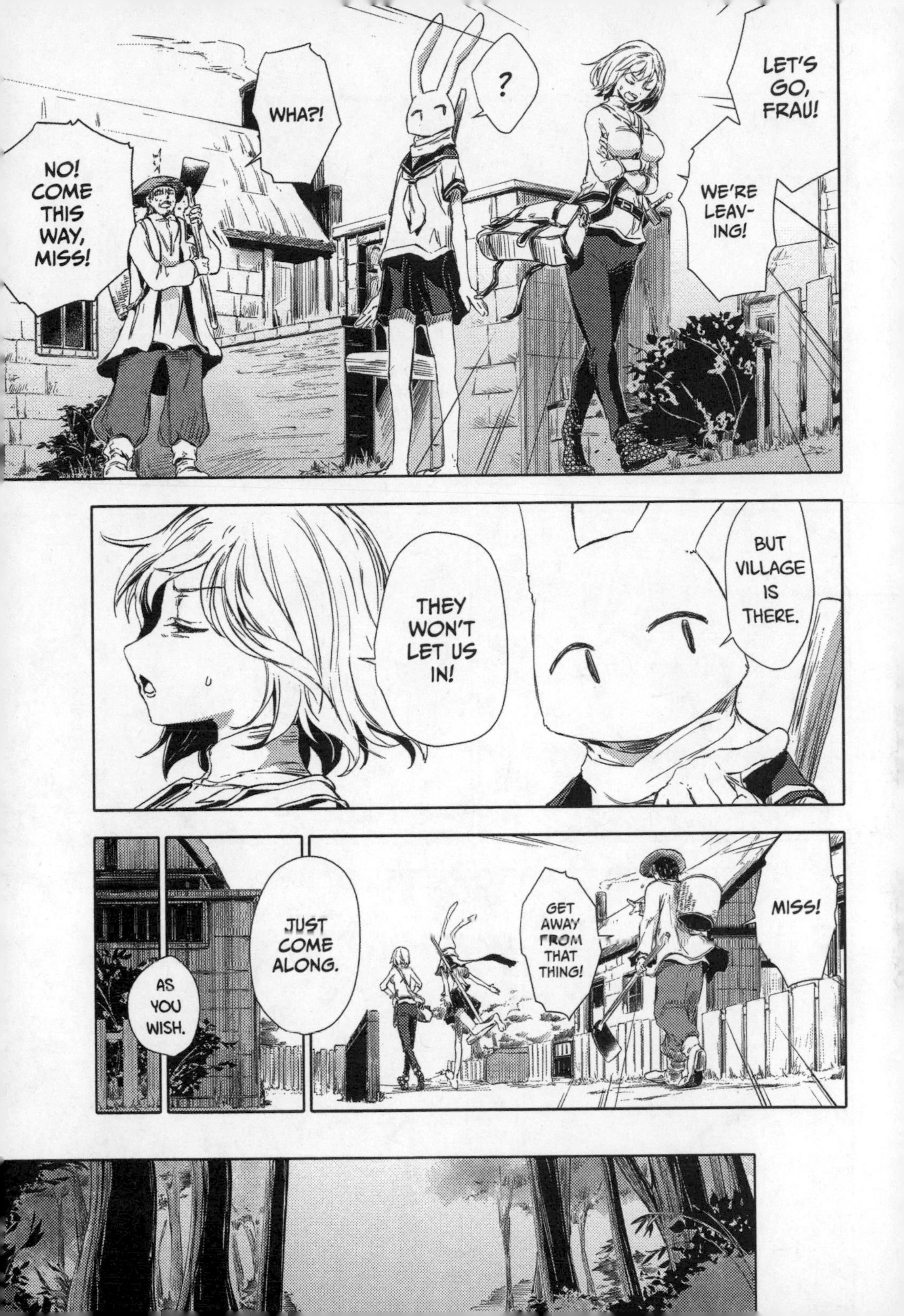
LET'S GO, FRAU!
WE'RE LEAVING!
?
WHA?!
NO! COME THIS WAY, MISS!
BUT VILLAGE IS THERE.
THEY WON'T LET US IN!
MISS!
GET AWAY FROM THAT THING!
JUST COME ALONG.
AS YOU WISH.

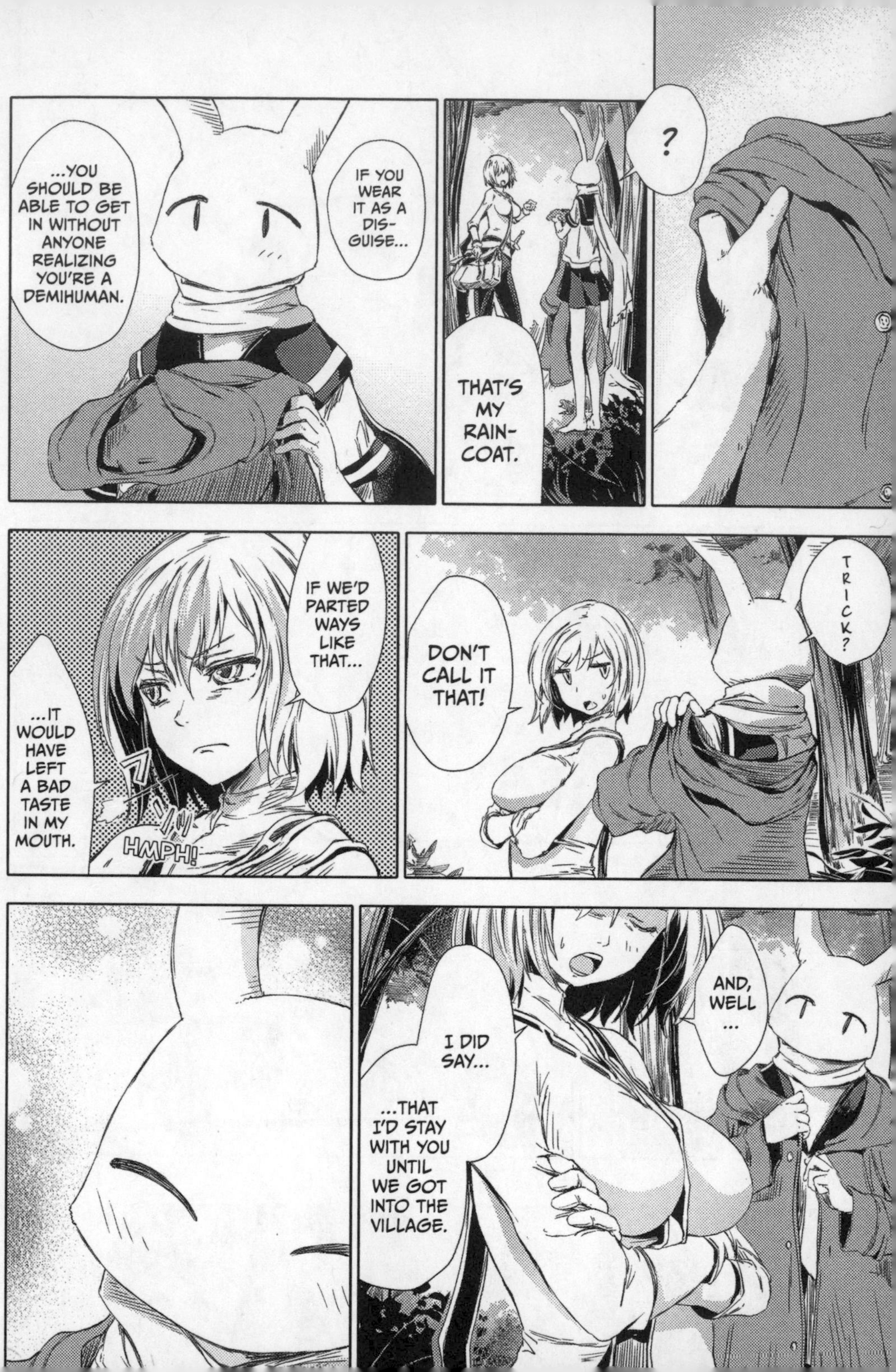
?
THAT'S MY RAINCOAT.
IF YOU WEAR IT AS A DISGUISE...
...YOU SHOULD BE ABLE TO GET IN WITHOUT ANYONE REALIZING YOU'RE A DEMIHUMAN.
TRICK?
DON'T CALL IT THAT!
IF WE'D PARTED WAYS LIKE THAT...
...IT WOULD HAVE LEFT A BAD TASTE IN MY MOUTH.
HMPH!
AND, WELL ...
I DID SAY...
...THAT I'D STAY WITH YOU UNTIL WE GOT INTO THE VILLAGE.

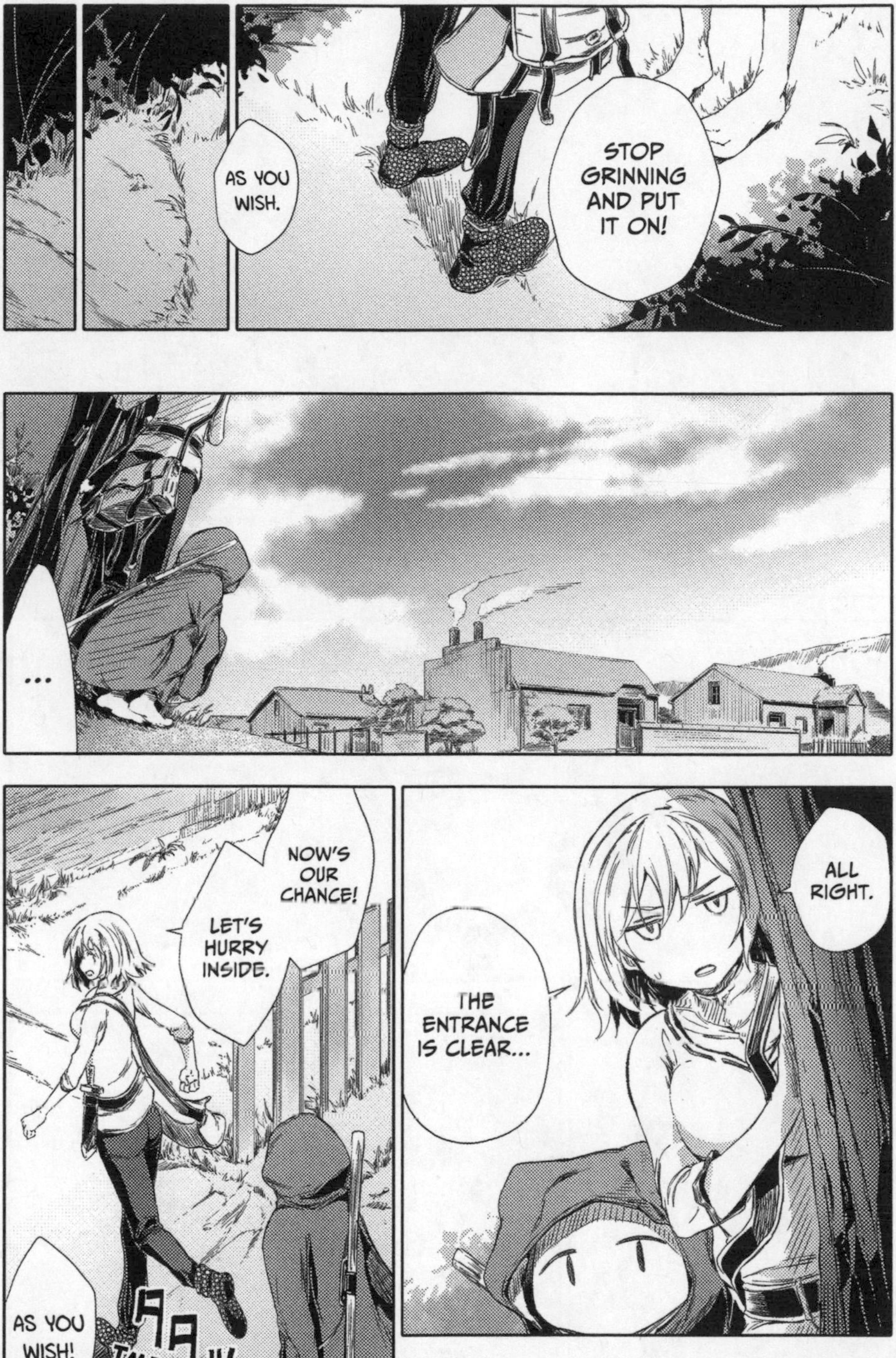
STOP GRINNING AND PUT IT ON!
AS YOU WISH.
...
ALL RIGHT.
THE ENTRANCE IS CLEAR...
NOW'S OUR CHANCE!
LET'S HURRY INSIDE.
AS YOU WISH!
TMP TMP

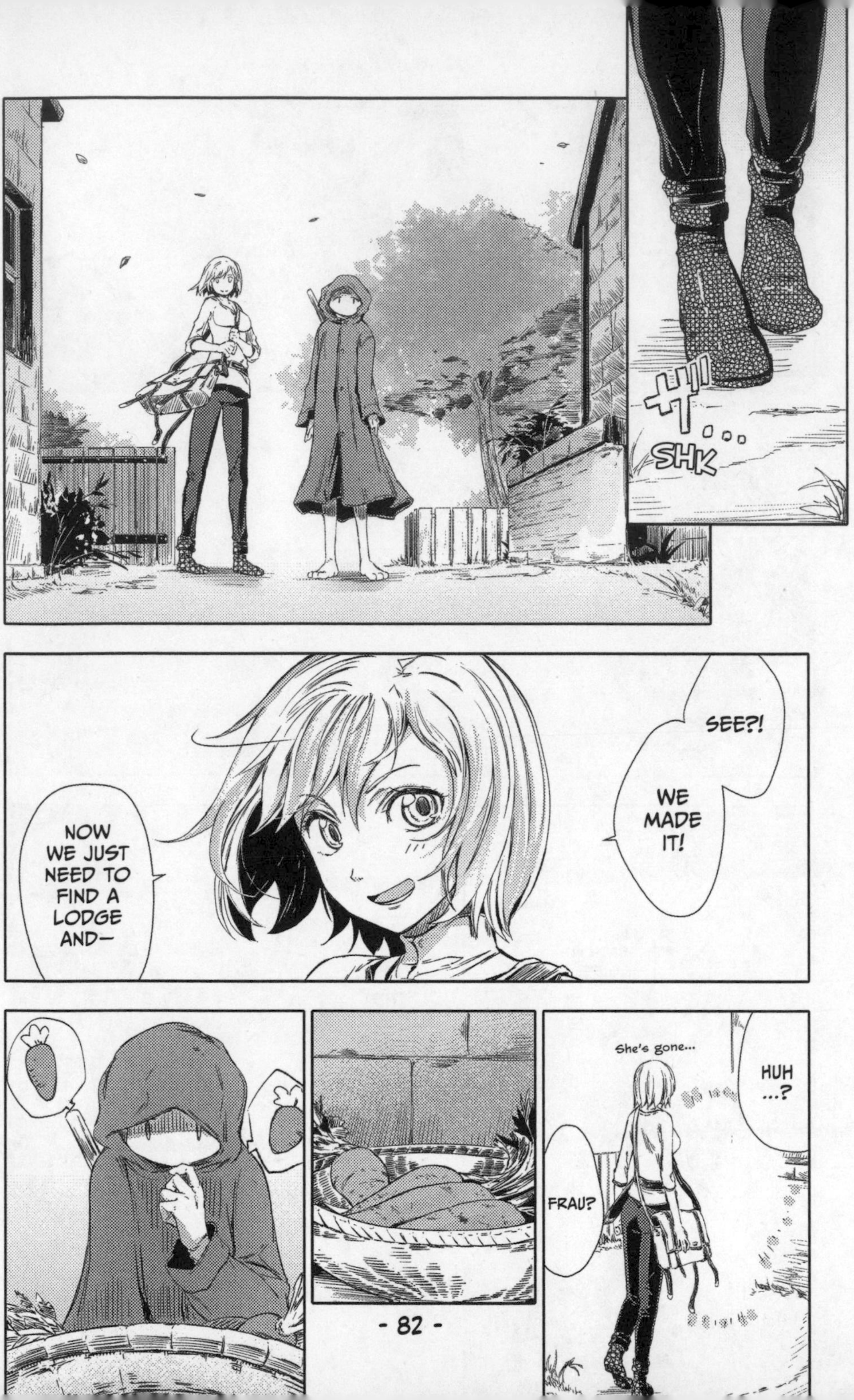

ザ...
SHK
SEE?!
WE MADE IT!
NOW WE JUST NEED TO FIND A LODGE AND—
HUH ...?
She's gone...
FRAU?

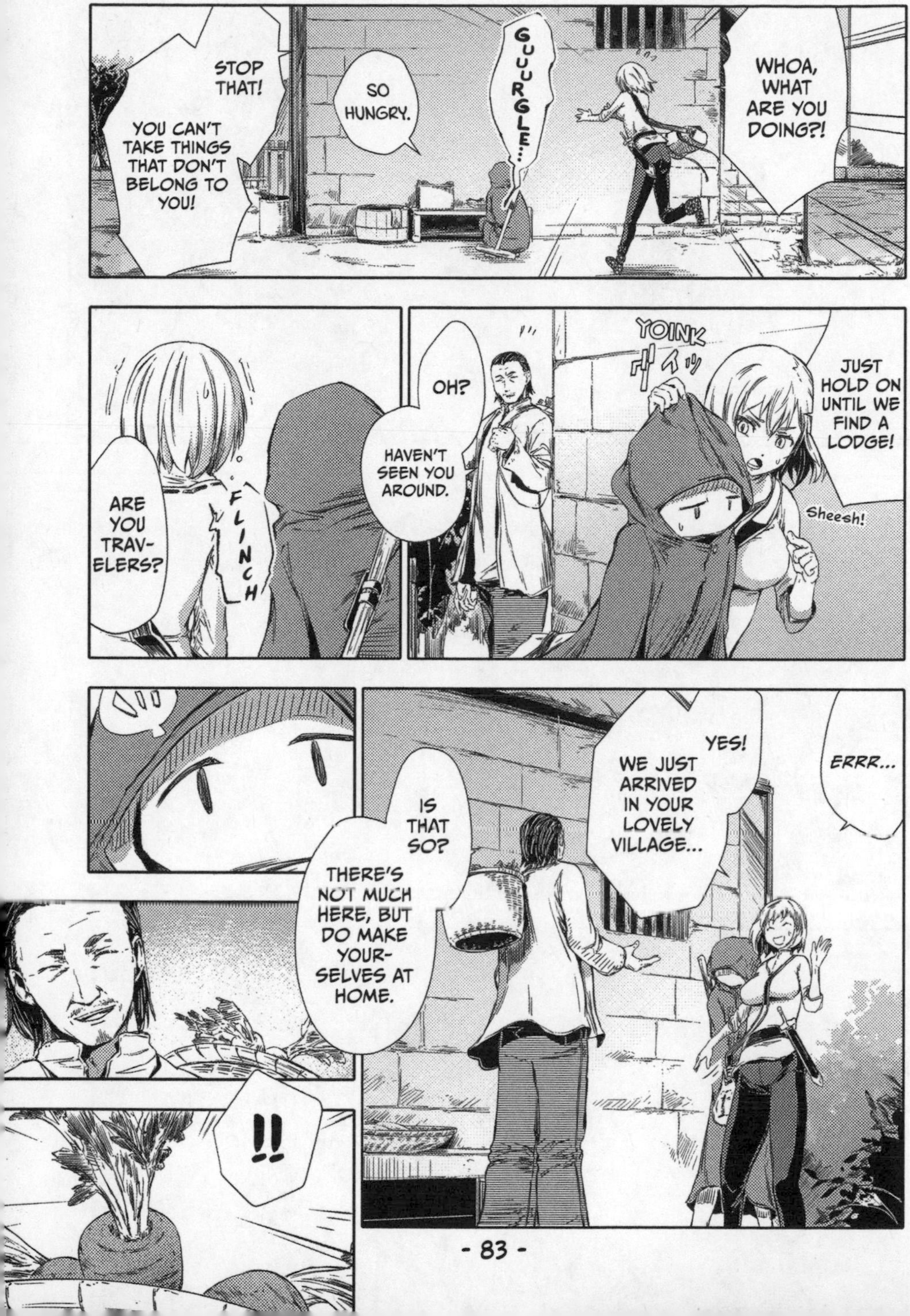
WHOA, WHAT ARE YOU DOING?!
GUUURGLE...
SO HUNGRY.
STOP THAT!
YOU CAN'T TAKE THINGS THAT DON'T BELONG TO YOU!
JUST HOLD ON UNTIL WE FIND A LODGE!
YOINK
Sheesh!
OH?
HAVEN'T SEEN YOU AROUND.
ARE YOU TRAV-ELERS?
FLINCH
ERRR...
YES!
WE JUST ARRIVED IN YOUR LOVELY VILLAGE...
IS THAT SO?
THERE'S NOT MUCH HERE, BUT DO MAKE YOUR-SELVES AT HOME.
!!

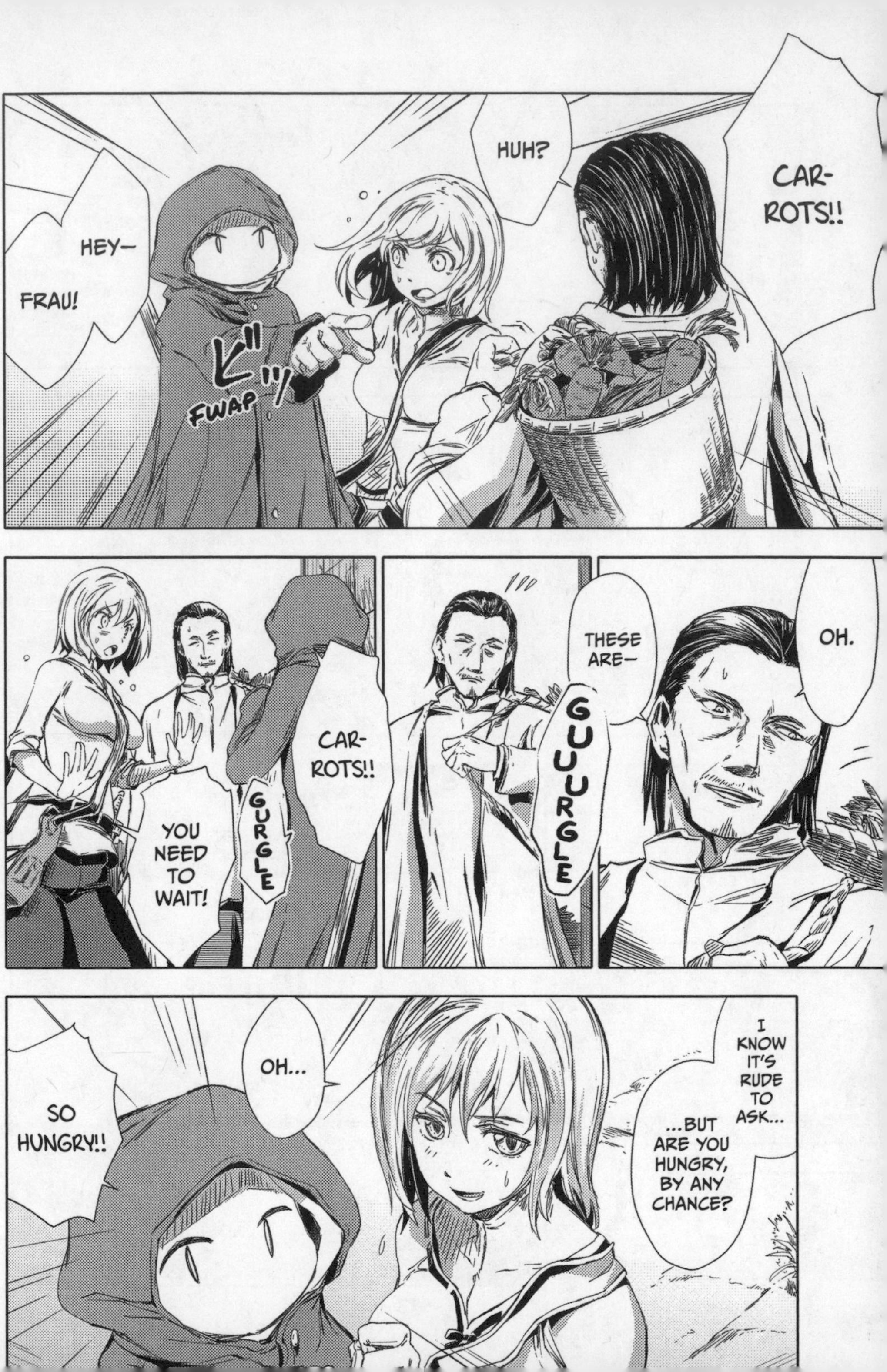
CAR-ROTS!!
HUH?
HEY—
FRAU!
FWAP
OH.
THESE ARE—
GUURGLE
CAR-ROTS!!
GURGLE
YOU NEED TO WAIT!
I KNOW IT'S RUDE TO ASK...
...BUT ARE YOU HUNGRY, BY ANY CHANCE?
OH...
SO HUNGRY!!

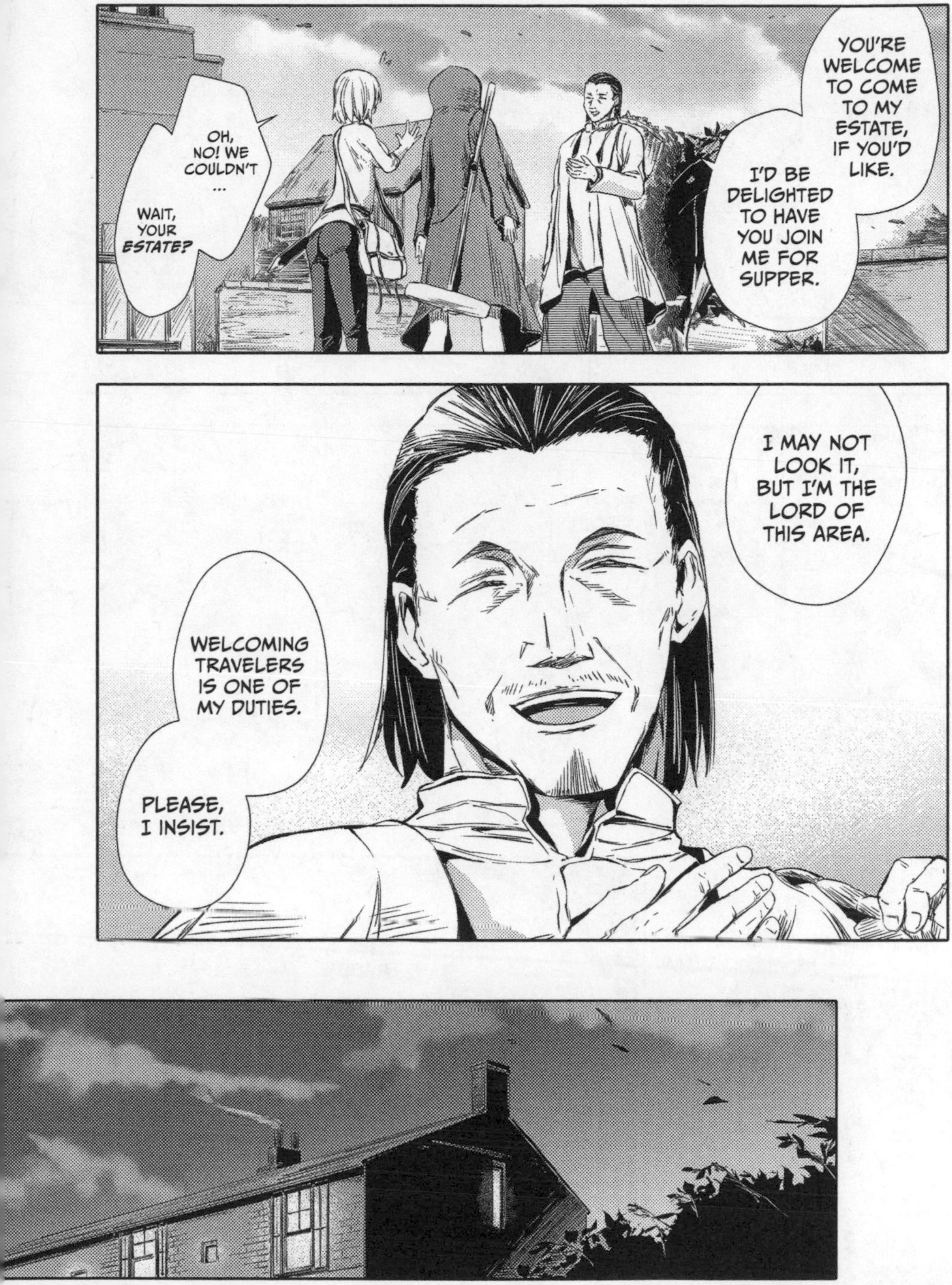
YOU'RE WELCOME TO COME TO MY ESTATE, IF YOU'D LIKE.
I'D BE DELIGHTED TO HAVE YOU JOIN ME FOR SUPPER.
OH, NO! WE COULDN'T ...
WAIT, YOUR *ESTATE?*
I MAY NOT LOOK IT, BUT I'M THE LORD OF THIS AREA.
WELCOMING TRAVELERS IS ONE OF MY DUTIES.
PLEASE, I INSIST.

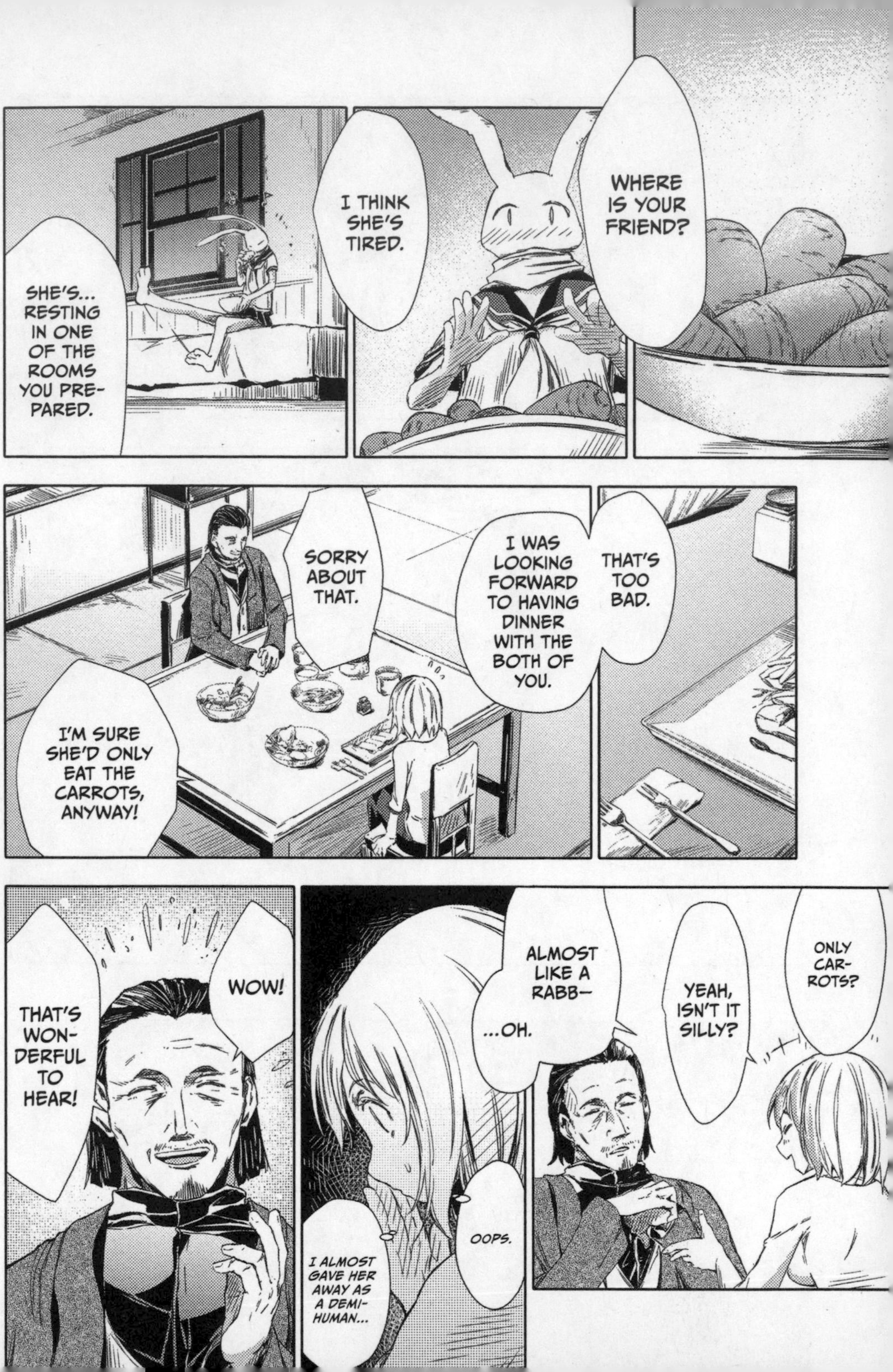
WHERE IS YOUR FRIEND?
I THINK SHE'S TIRED.
SHE'S... RESTING IN ONE OF THE ROOMS YOU PRE-PARED.
THAT'S TOO BAD.
I WAS LOOKING FORWARD TO HAVING DINNER WITH THE BOTH OF YOU.
SORRY ABOUT THAT.
I'M SURE SHE'D ONLY EAT THE CARROTS, ANYWAY!
ONLY CAR-ROTS?
YEAH, ISN'T IT SILLY?
ALMOST LIKE A RABB—
...OH.
OOPS.
I ALMOST GAVE HER AWAY AS A DEMI-HUMAN...
WOW!
THAT'S WON-DERFUL TO HEAR!

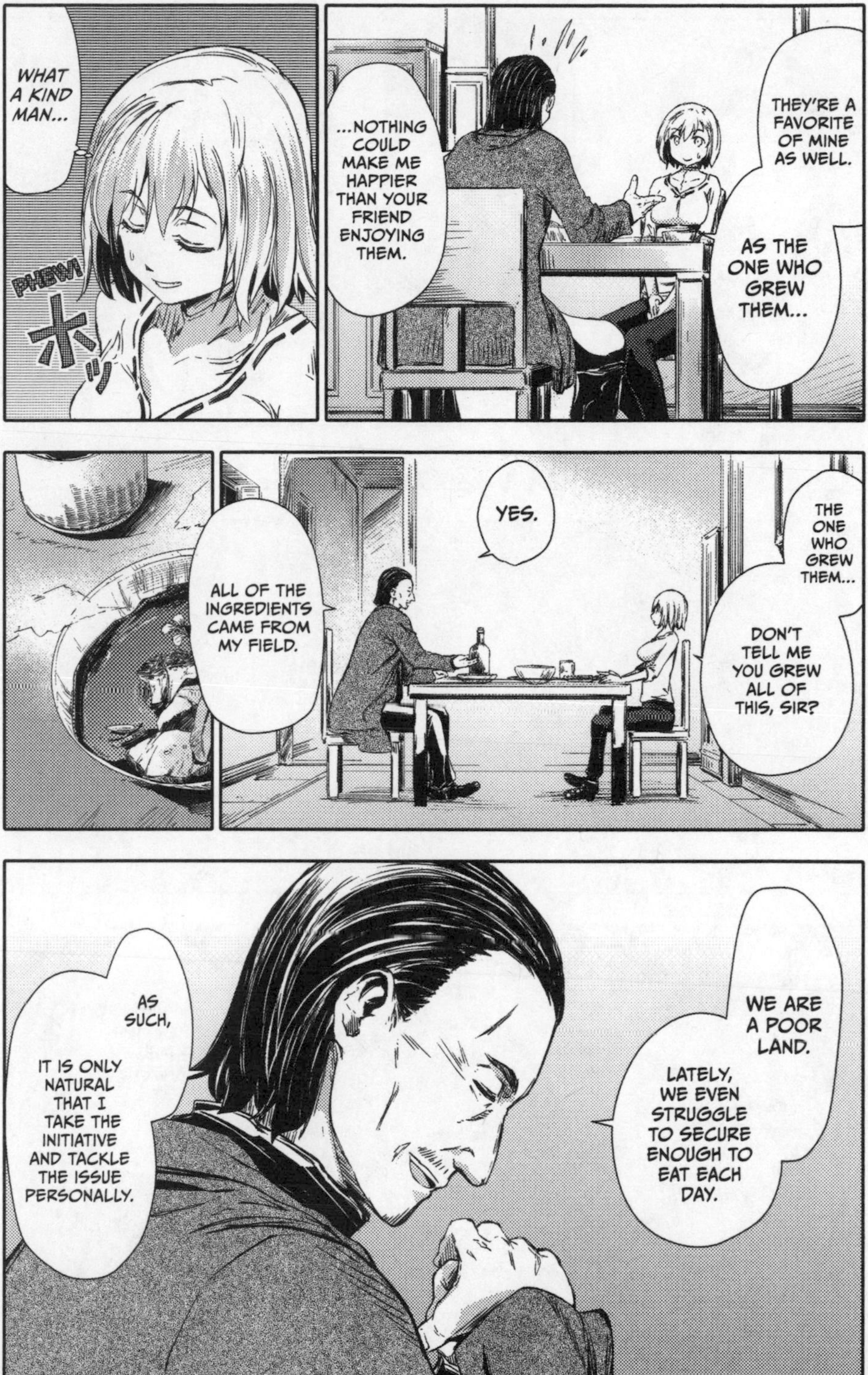
THEY'RE A FAVORITE OF MINE AS WELL.
AS THE ONE WHO GREW THEM...
...NOTHING COULD MAKE ME HAPPIER THAN YOUR FRIEND ENJOYING THEM.
WHAT A KIND MAN...
PHEW!
ホッ
THE ONE WHO GREW THEM...
DON'T TELL ME YOU GREW ALL OF THIS, SIR?
YES.
ALL OF THE INGREDIENTS CAME FROM MY FIELD.
WE ARE A POOR LAND.
LATELY, WE EVEN STRUGGLE TO SECURE ENOUGH TO EAT EACH DAY.
AS SUCH,
IT IS ONLY NATURAL THAT I TAKE THE INITIATIVE AND TACKLE THE ISSUE PERSONALLY.

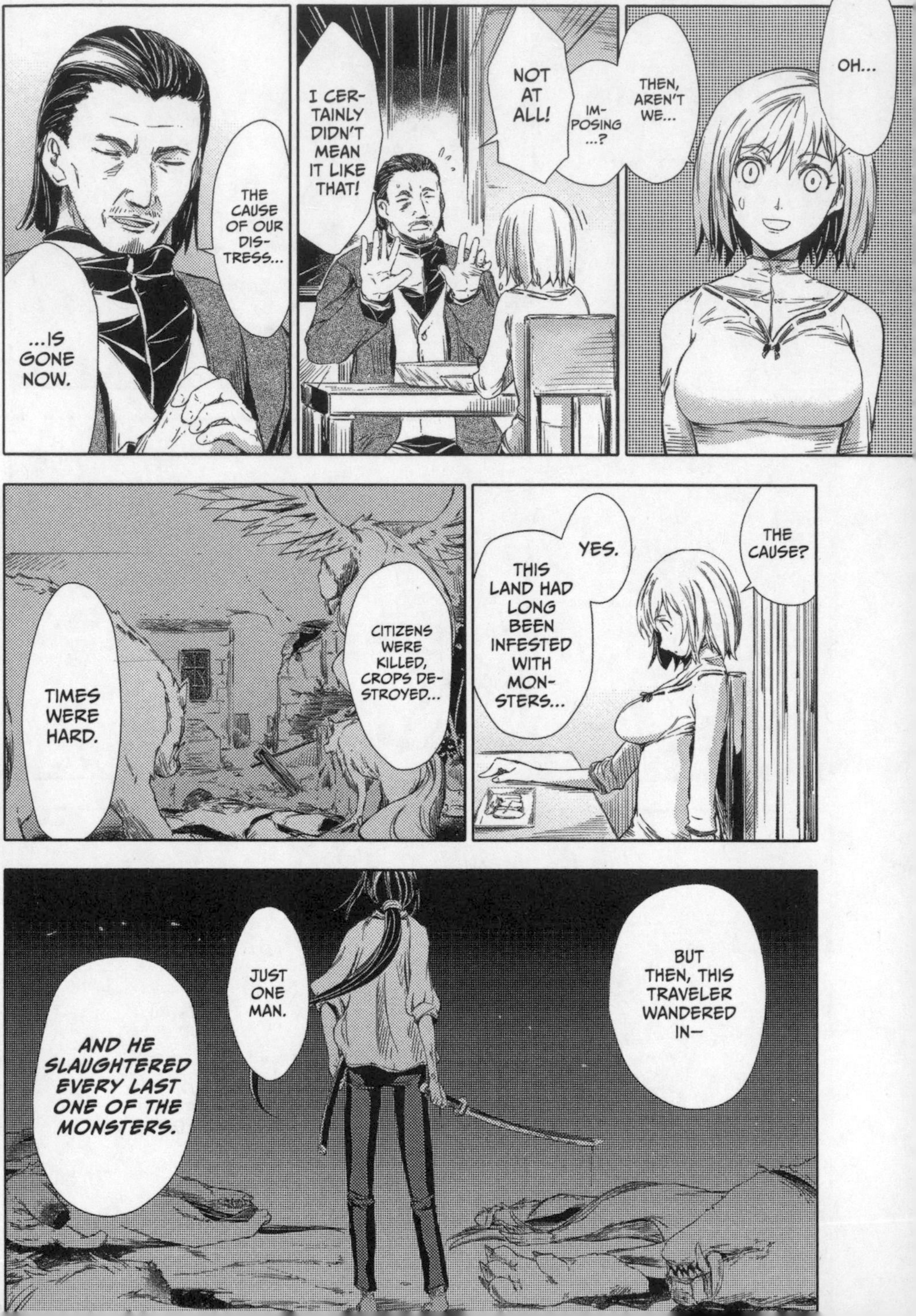
OH...
THEN, AREN'T WE...
IMPOSING ...?
NOT AT ALL!
I CERTAINLY DIDN'T MEAN IT LIKE THAT!
THE CAUSE OF OUR DISTRESS...
...IS GONE NOW.
THE CAUSE?
YES.
THIS LAND HAD LONG BEEN INFESTED WITH MONSTERS...
CITIZENS WERE KILLED, CROPS DESTROYED...
TIMES WERE HARD.
BUT THEN, THIS TRAVELER WANDERED IN—
JUST ONE MAN.
AND HE SLAUGHTERED EVERY LAST ONE OF THE MONSTERS.

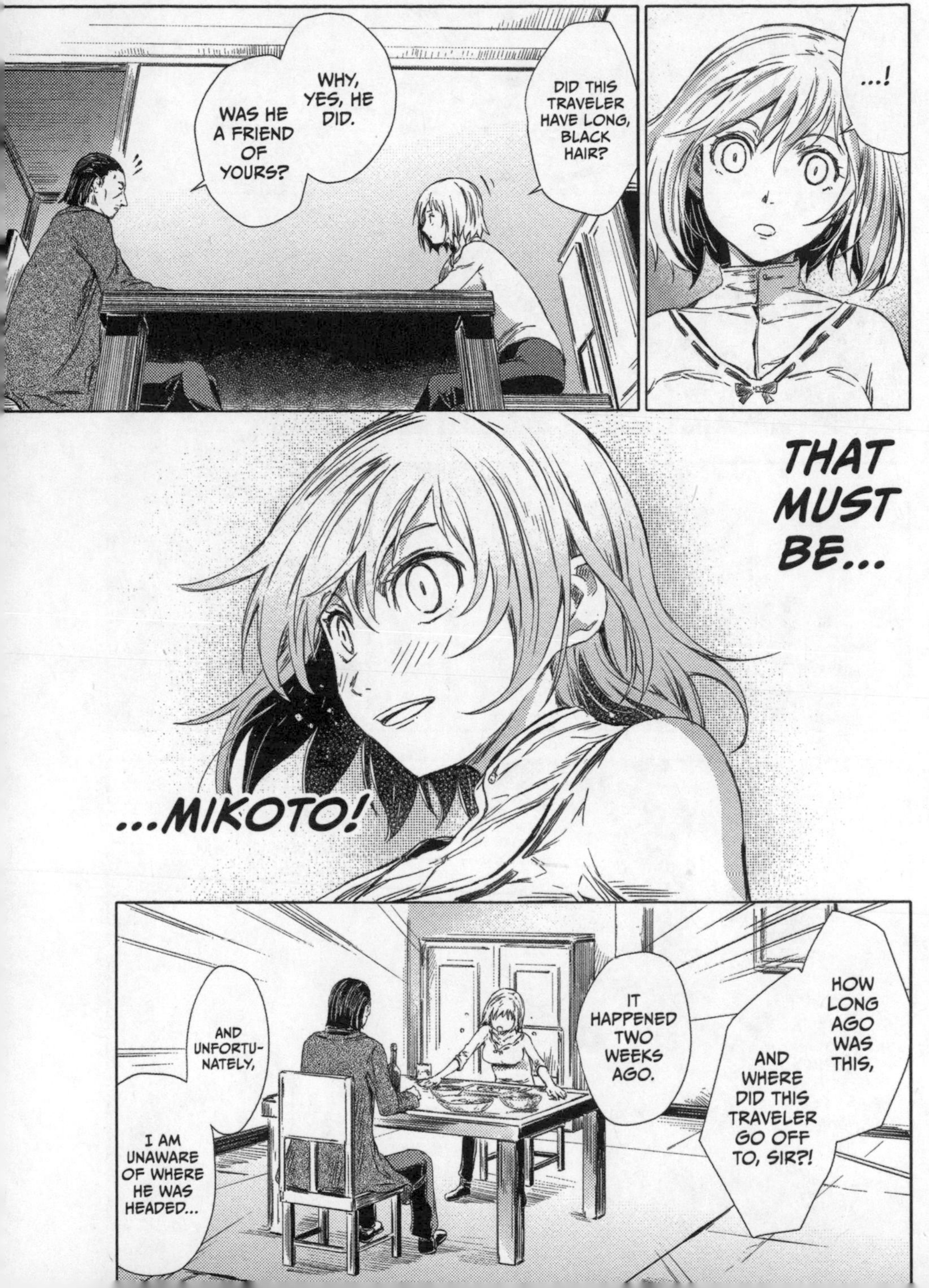
...!
DID THIS TRAVELER HAVE LONG, BLACK HAIR?
WHY, YES, HE DID.
WAS HE A FRIEND OF YOURS?
THAT MUST BE...
...MIKOTO!
HOW LONG AGO WAS THIS, AND WHERE DID THIS TRAVELER GO OFF TO, SIR?!
IT HAPPENED TWO WEEKS AGO.
AND UNFORTUNATELY, I AM UNAWARE OF WHERE HE WAS HEADED...

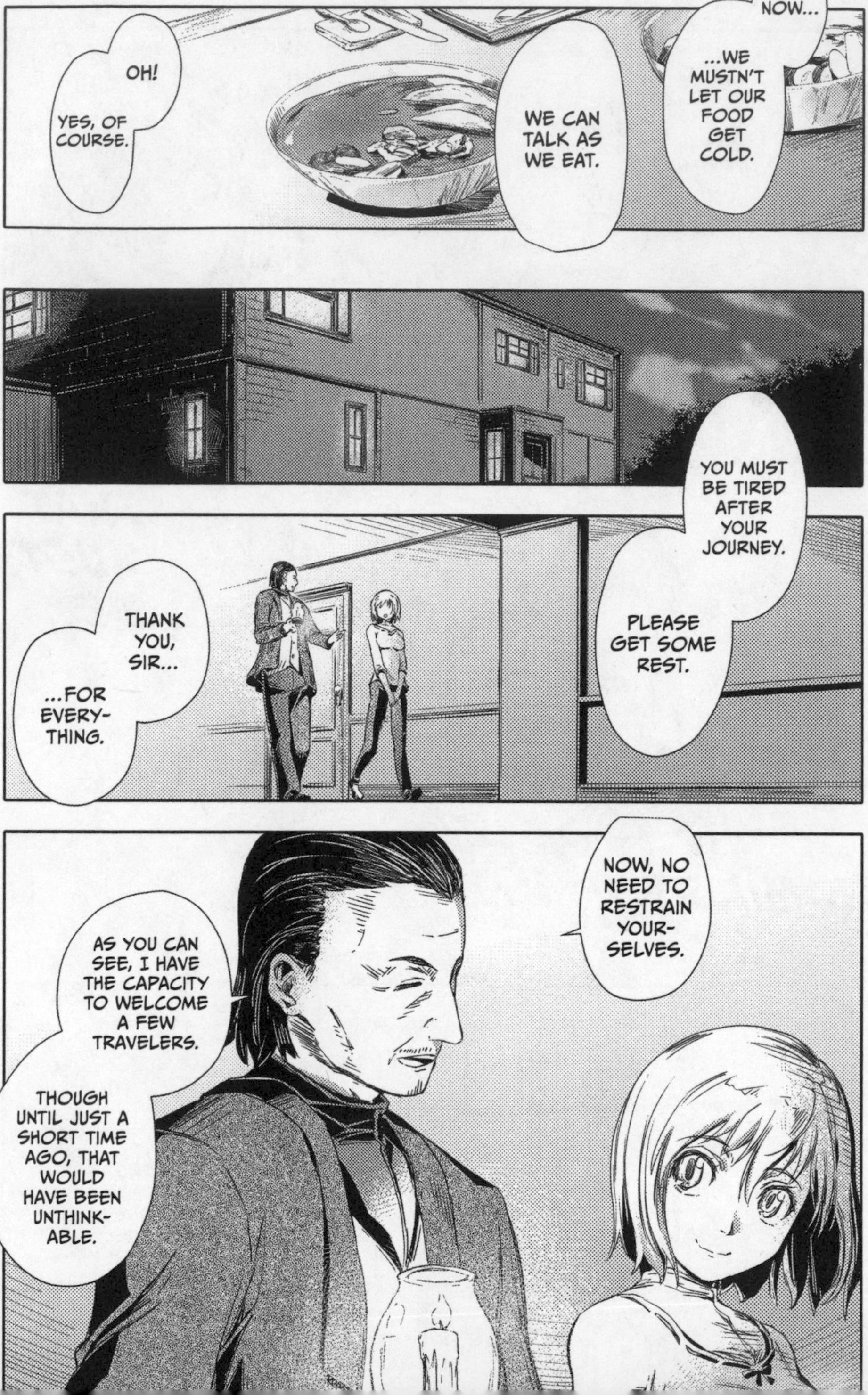
NOW...
...WE MUSTN'T LET OUR FOOD GET COLD.
WE CAN TALK AS WE EAT.
OH!
YES, OF COURSE.
YOU MUST BE TIRED AFTER YOUR JOURNEY.
PLEASE GET SOME REST.
THANK YOU, SIR...
...FOR EVERYTHING.
NOW, NO NEED TO RESTRAIN YOURSELVES.
AS YOU CAN SEE, I HAVE THE CAPACITY TO WELCOME A FEW TRAVELERS.
THOUGH UNTIL JUST A SHORT TIME AGO, THAT WOULD HAVE BEEN UNTHINKABLE.

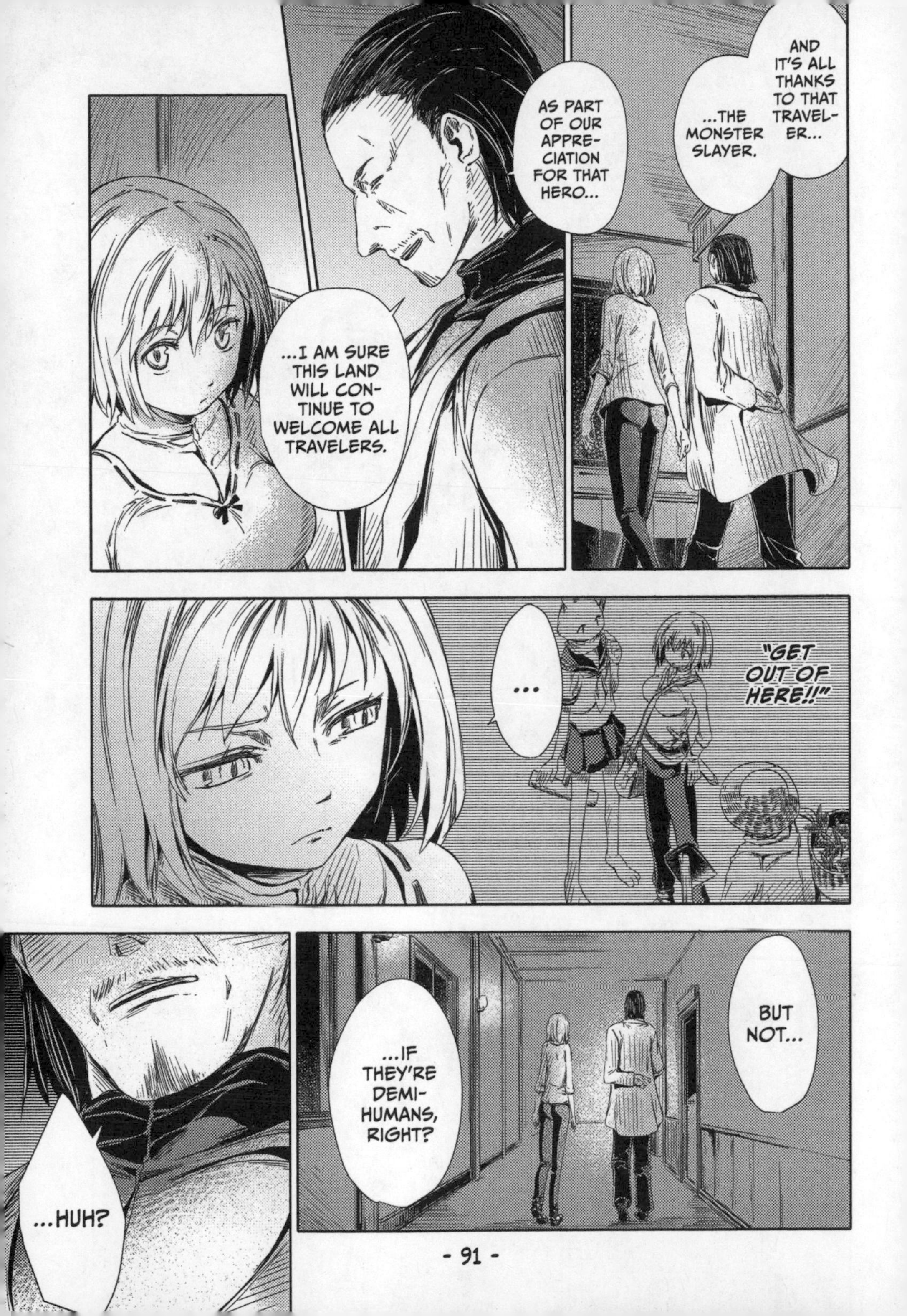
AND IT'S ALL THANKS TO THAT TRAVEL-ER...
...THE MONSTER SLAYER.
AS PART OF OUR APPRE-CIATION FOR THAT HERO...
...I AM SURE THIS LAND WILL CON-TINUE TO WELCOME ALL TRAVELERS.
"GET OUT OF HERE!!"
...
BUT NOT...
...IF THEY'RE DEMI-HUMANS, RIGHT?
...HUH?

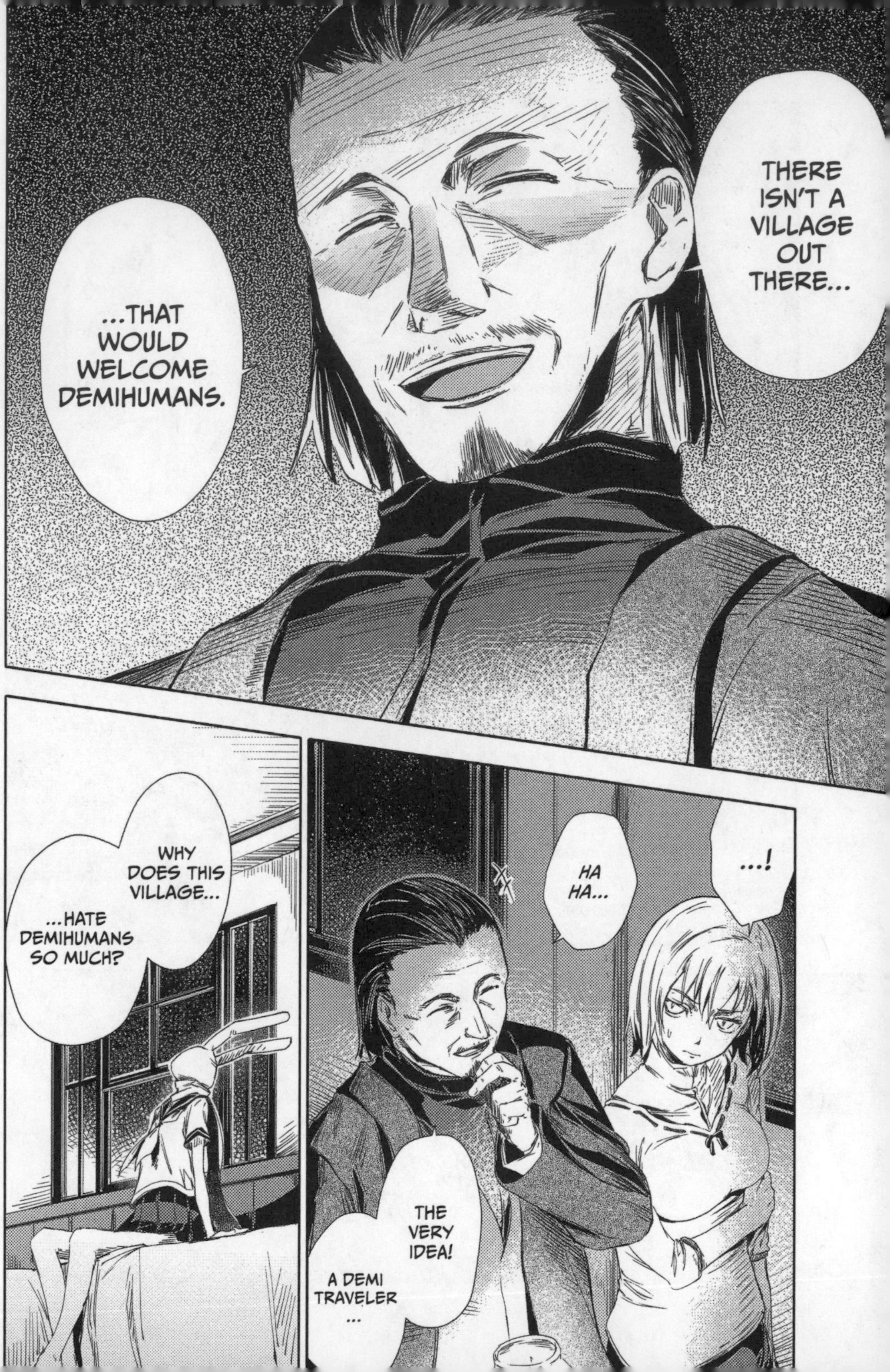
THERE ISN'T A VILLAGE OUT THERE...
...THAT WOULD WELCOME DEMIHUMANS.
...!
HA HA...
THE VERY IDEA!
A DEMI TRAVELER ...
WHY DOES THIS VILLAGE...
...HATE DEMIHUMANS SO MUCH?

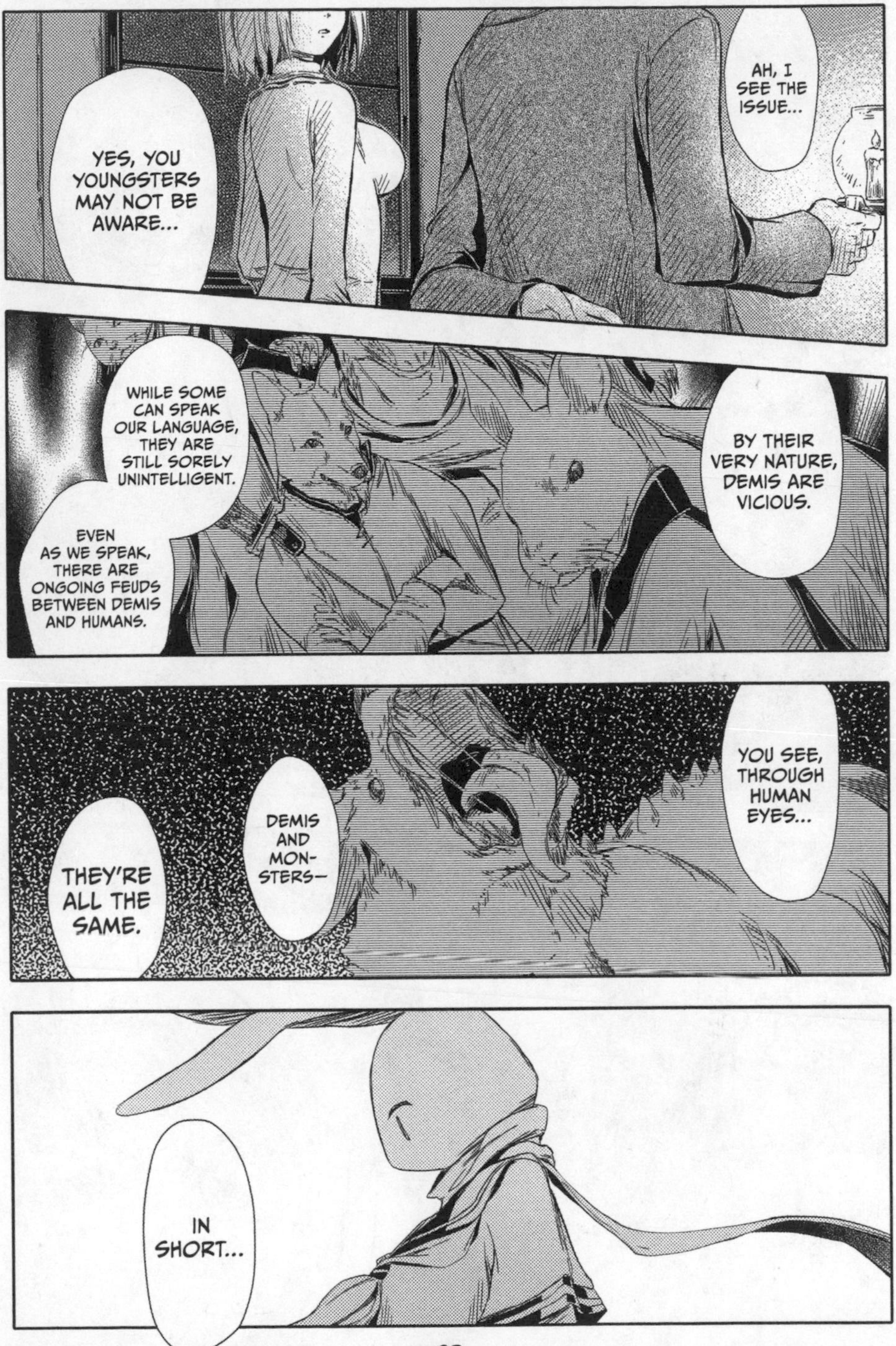
AH, I SEE THE ISSUE...
YES, YOU YOUNGSTERS MAY NOT BE AWARE...
BY THEIR VERY NATURE, DEMIS ARE VICIOUS.
WHILE SOME CAN SPEAK OUR LANGUAGE, THEY ARE STILL SORELY UNINTELLIGENT.
EVEN AS WE SPEAK, THERE ARE ONGOING FEUDS BETWEEN DEMIS AND HUMANS.
YOU SEE, THROUGH HUMAN EYES...
DEMIS AND MON-STERS—
THEY'RE ALL THE SAME.
IN SHORT...

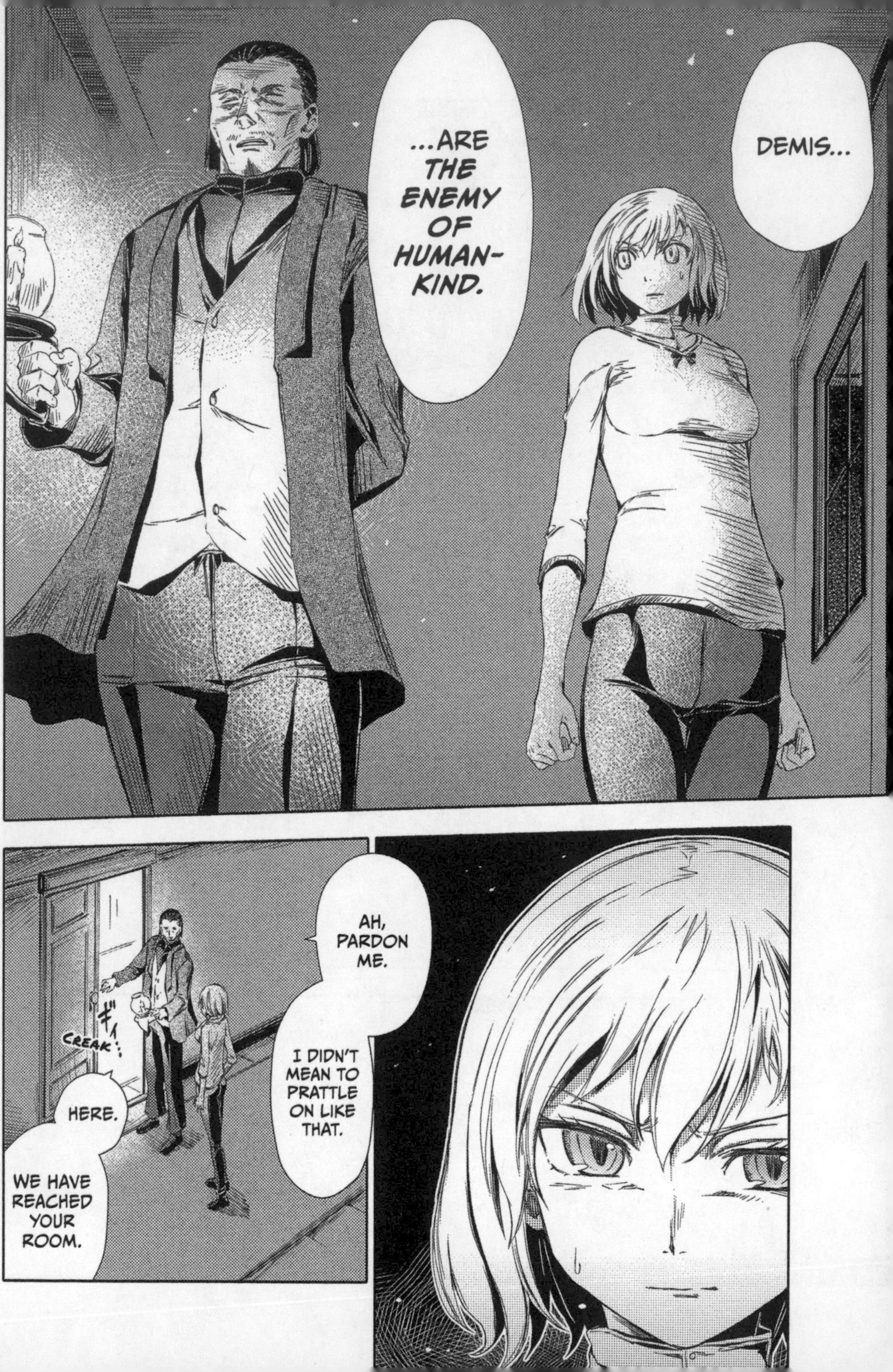
DEMIS...
...ARE THE ENEMY OF HUMAN-KIND.
AH, PARDON ME.
I DIDN'T MEAN TO PRATTLE ON LIKE THAT.
ギィ…
CREAK
HERE.
WE HAVE REACHED YOUR ROOM.

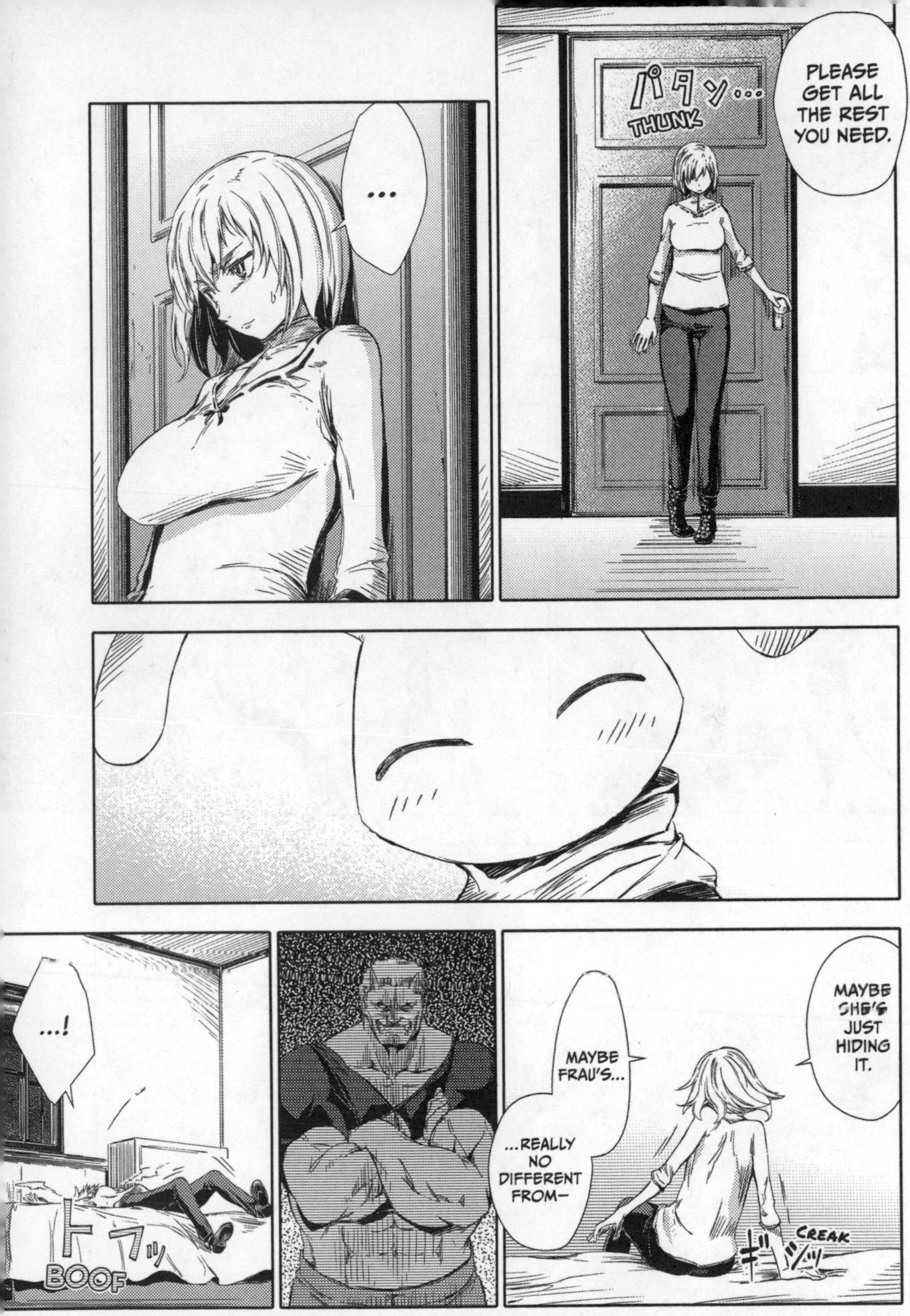
パタン…
THUNK
PLEASE GET ALL THE REST YOU NEED.
...
MAYBE SHE'S JUST HIDING IT.
MAYBE FRAU'S...
...REALLY NO DIFFERENT FROM—
ギシッ
CREAK
...!
トフッ
BOOF

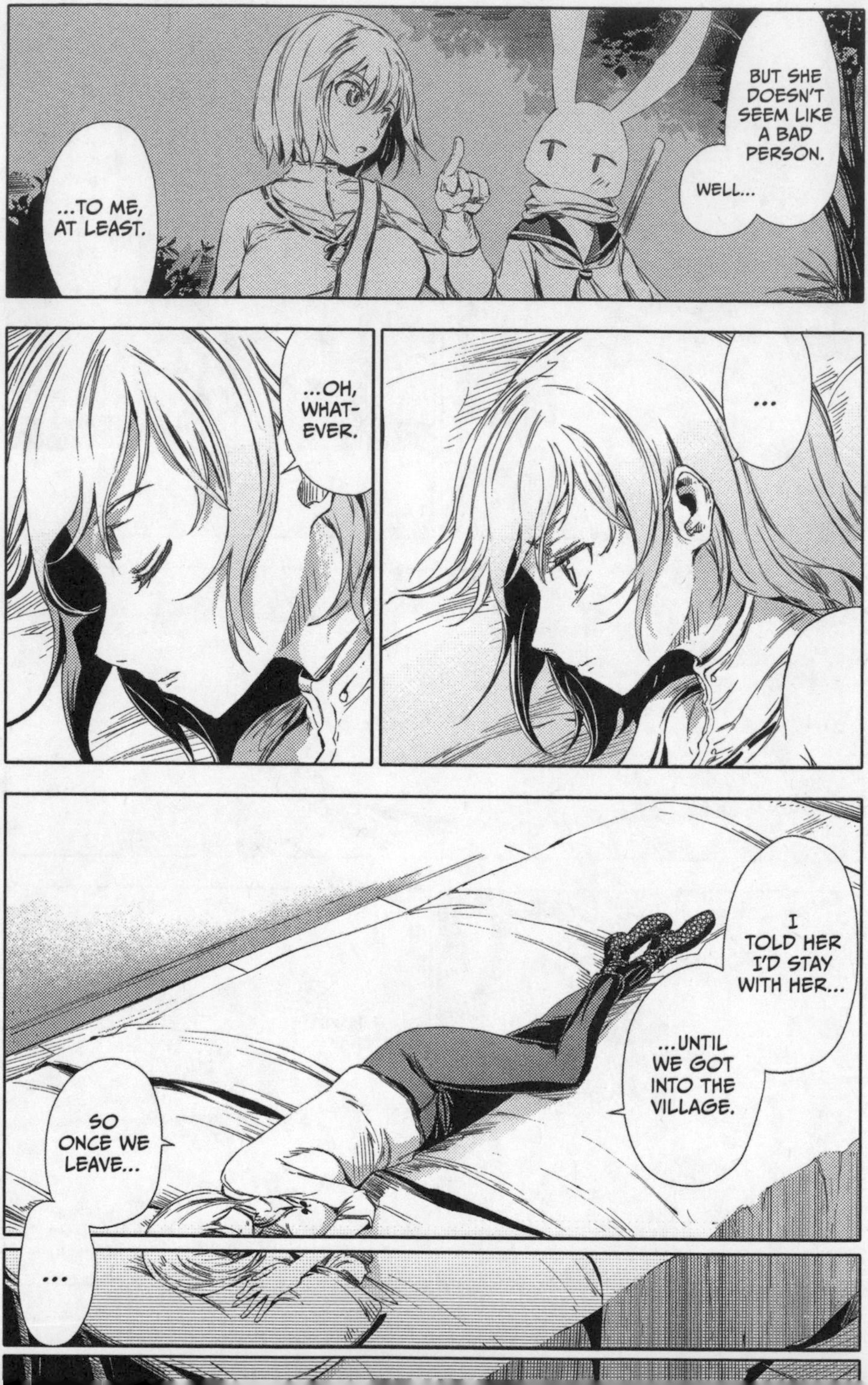
BUT SHE DOESN'T SEEM LIKE A BAD PERSON. WELL...
...TO ME, AT LEAST.
...
...OH, WHATEVER.
I TOLD HER I'D STAY WITH HER...
...UNTIL WE GOT INTO THE VILLAGE.
SO ONCE WE LEAVE...
...

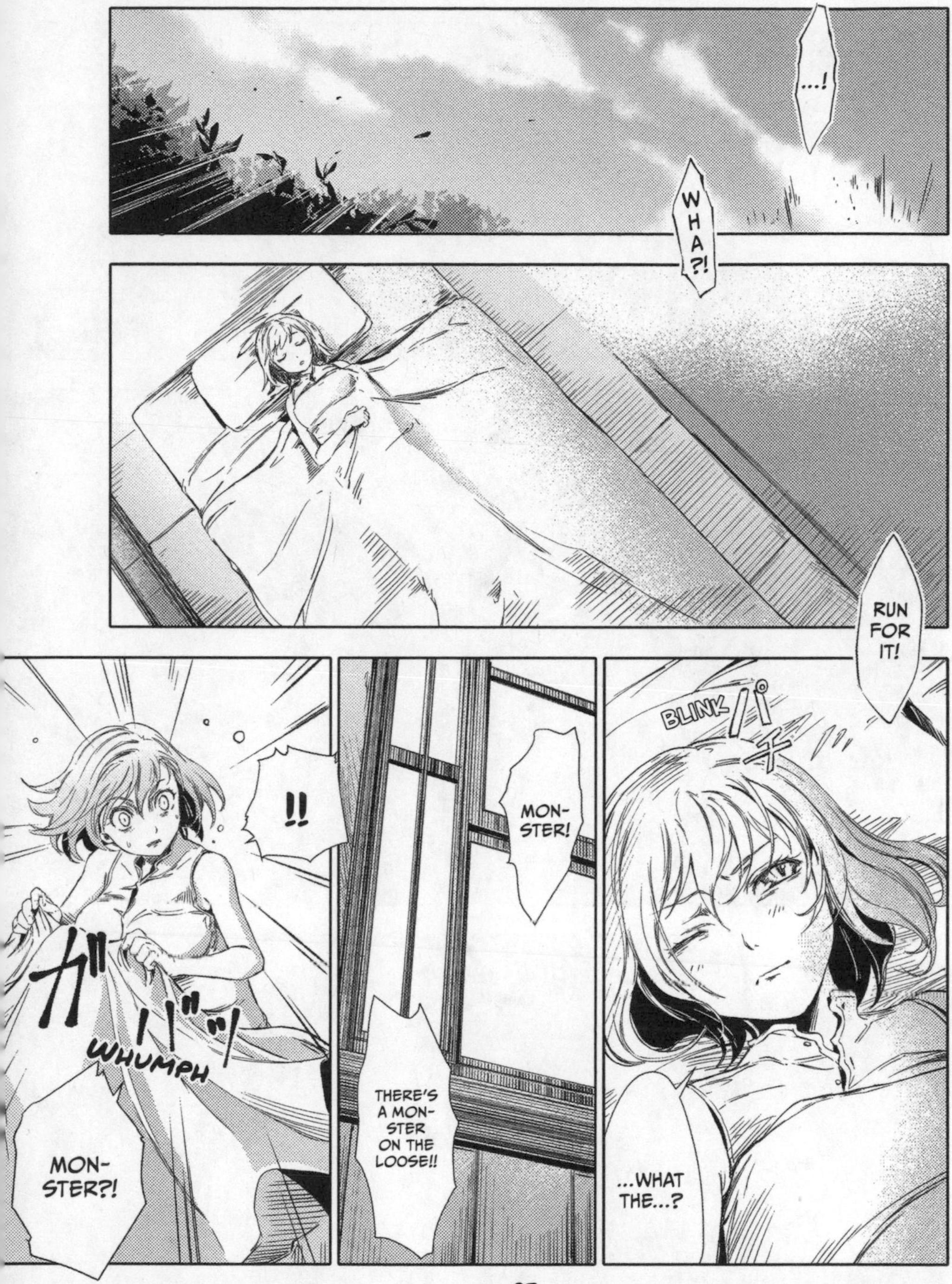
...!
WHA?!
RUN FOR IT!
BLINK パチ
...WHAT THE...?
MON-STER!
THERE'S A MON-STER ON THE LOOSE!!
!!
ガバッ WHUMPH
MON-STER?!

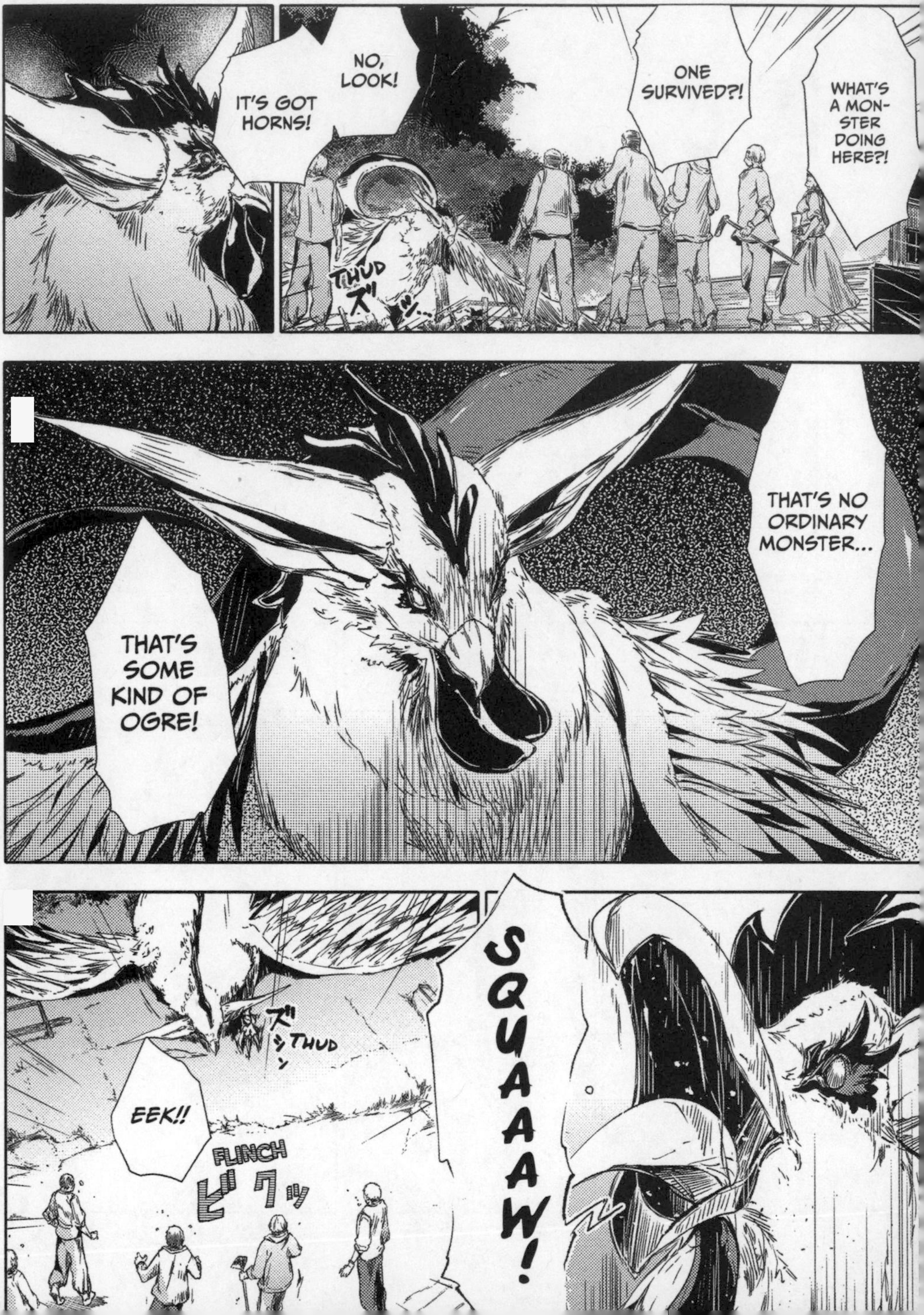
WHAT'S A MON-STER DOING HERE?!
ONE SURVIVED?!
NO, LOOK!
THUD ズシ...
IT'S GOT HORNS!
THAT'S NO ORDINARY MONSTER...
THAT'S SOME KIND OF OGRE!
SQUAAAAW!
ズシン THUD
EEK!!
FLINCH ビクッ

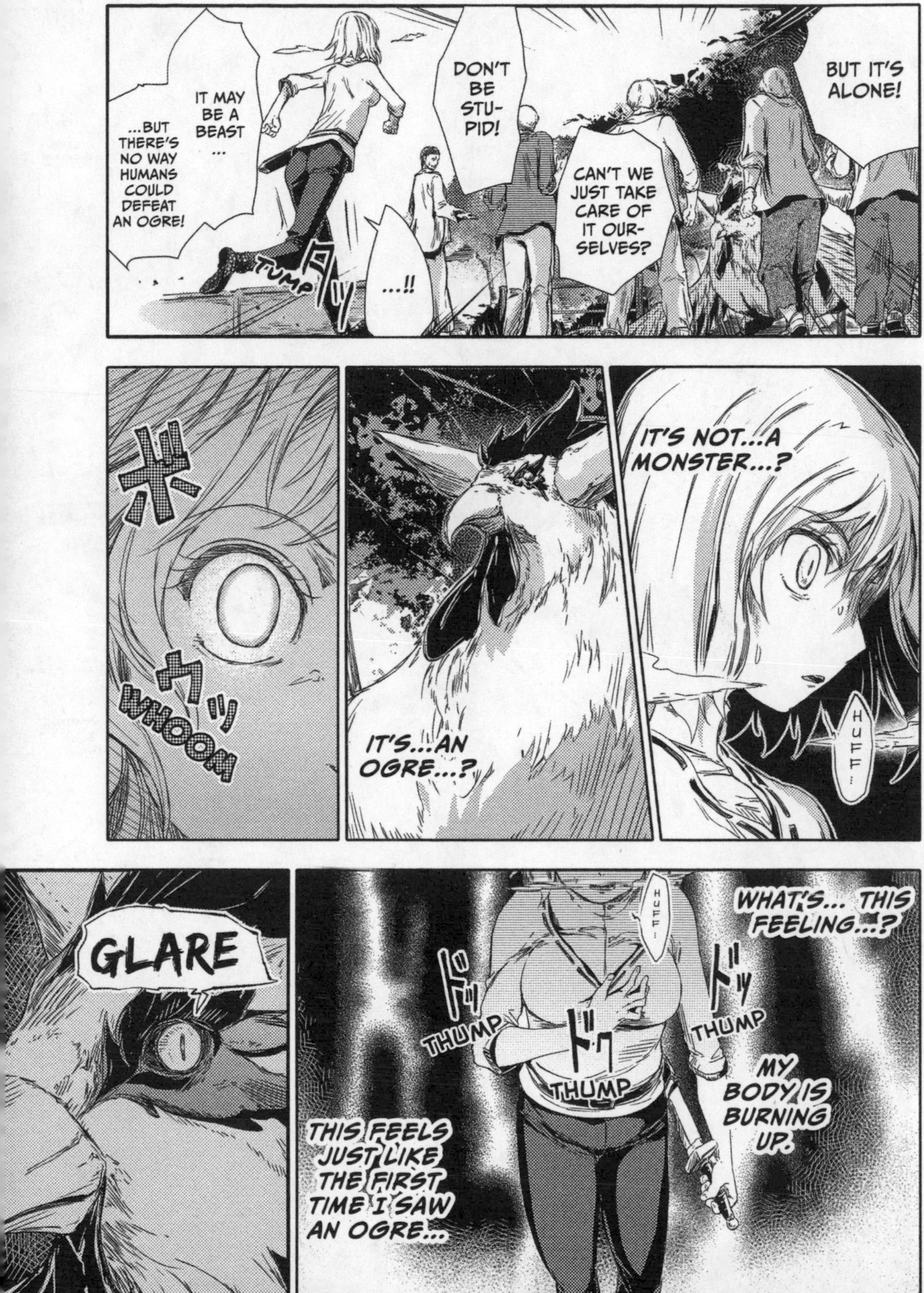
BUT IT'S ALONE!
CAN'T WE JUST TAKE CARE OF IT OUR-SELVES?
DON'T BE STU-PID!
IT MAY BE A BEAST ...
...BUT THERE'S NO WAY HUMANS COULD DEFEAT AN OGRE!
TUMP
...!!
IT'S NOT...A MONSTER...?
HUFF...
IT'S...AN OGRE...?
WHOOM
WHAT'S... THIS FEELING...?
HUFF!
THUMP
THUMP
THUMP
MY BODY IS BURNING UP.
THIS FEELS JUST LIKE THE FIRST TIME I SAW AN OGRE...
GLARE

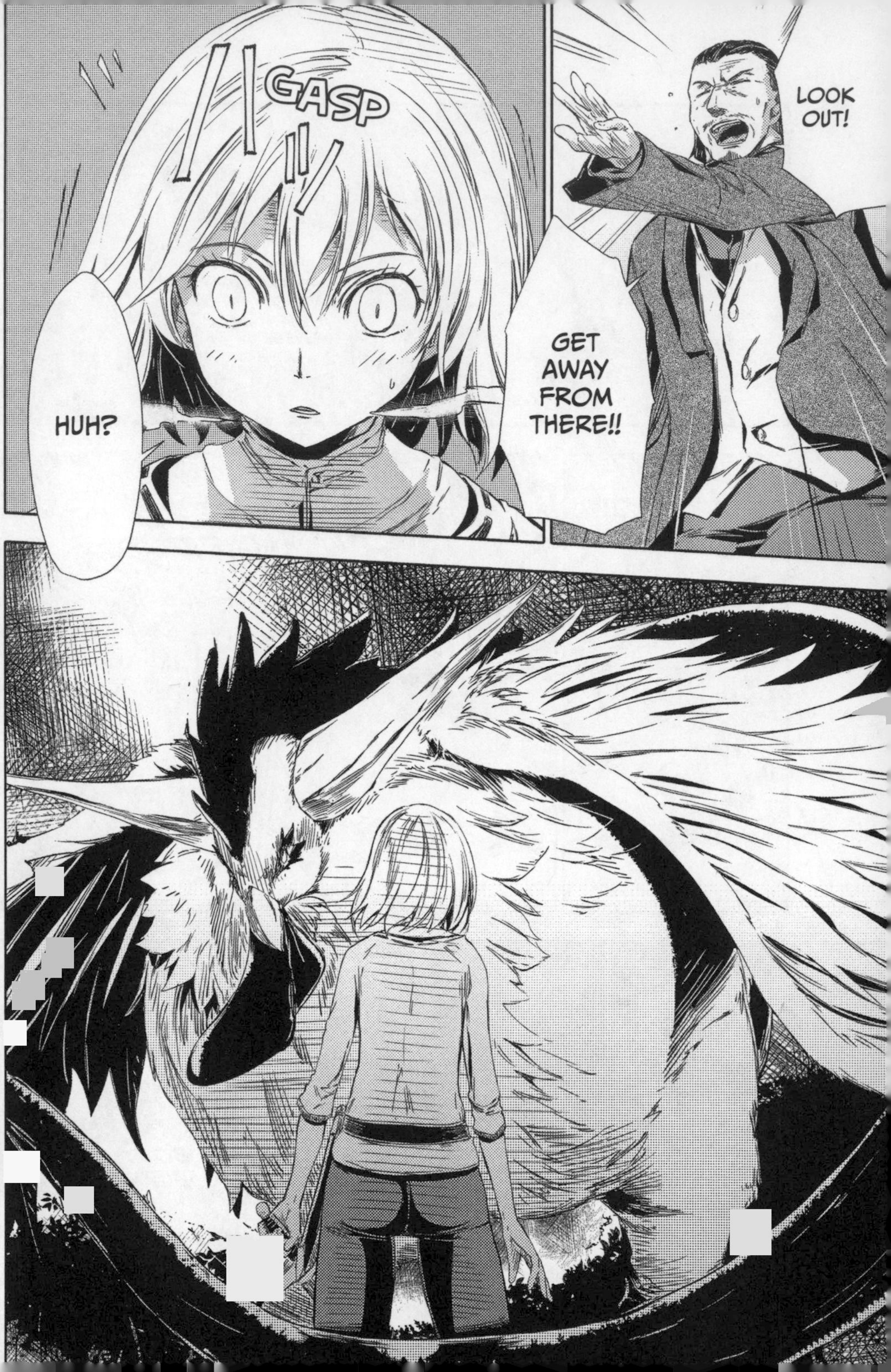
LOOK OUT!
GET AWAY FROM THERE!!
GASP
HUH?

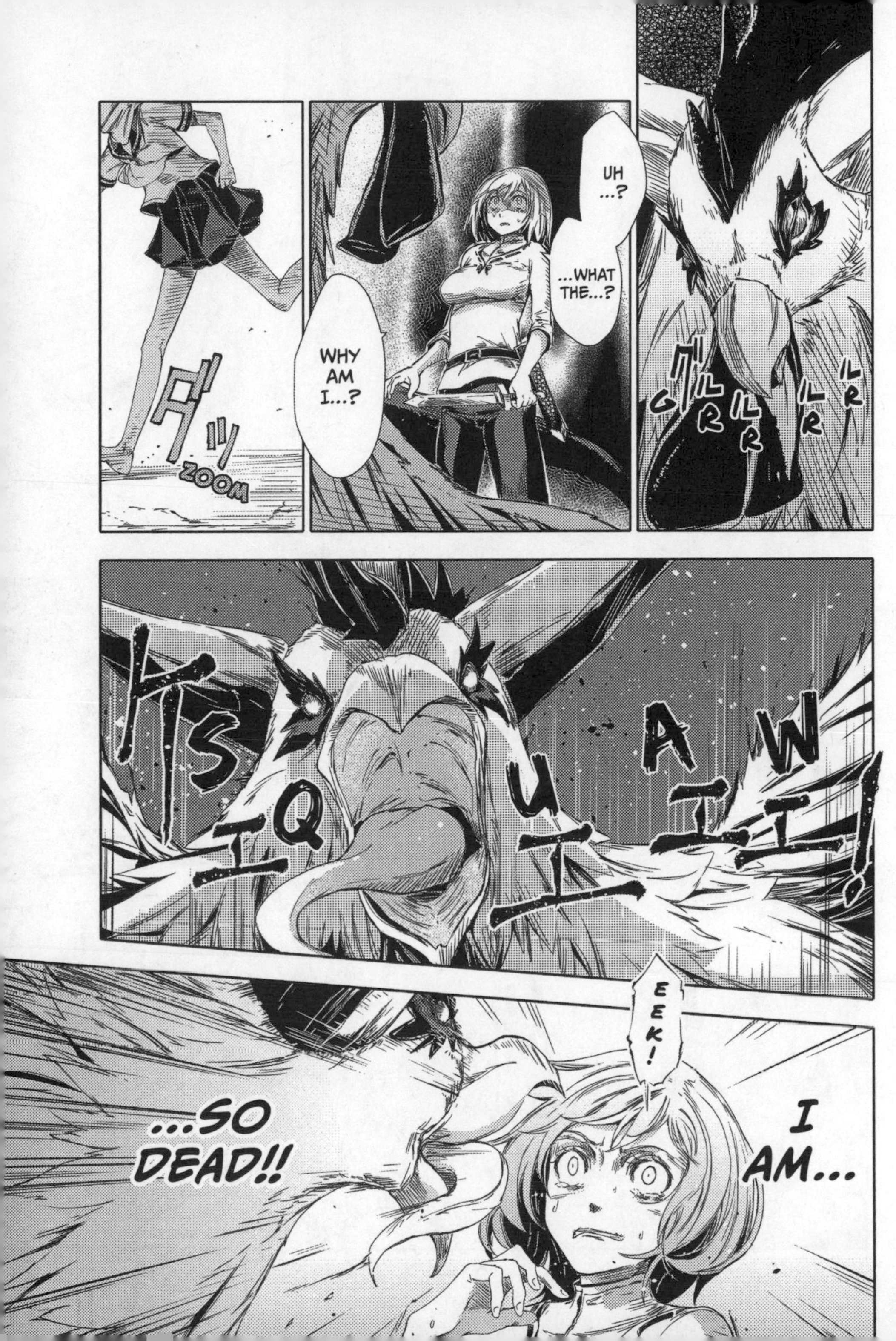
GRRRR
UH ...?
...WHAT THE...?
WHY AM I...?
ZOOM
SQUAWK!
EEK!
I AM...
...SO DEAD!!

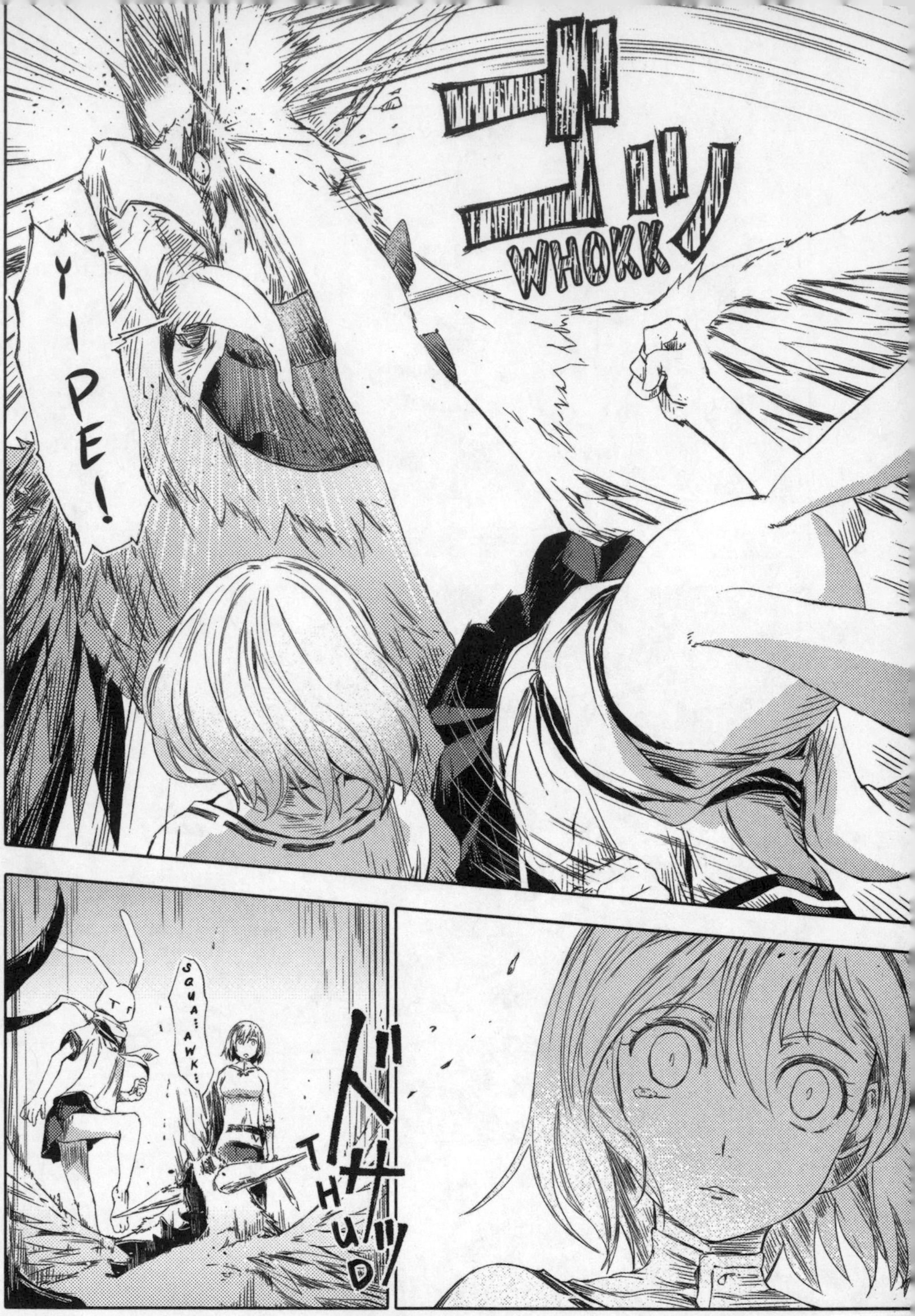
ゴッ
WHOKK
YIPE!
SQUA... AWK...
ドサッ
THUD

SQUAW...

SQUAW...

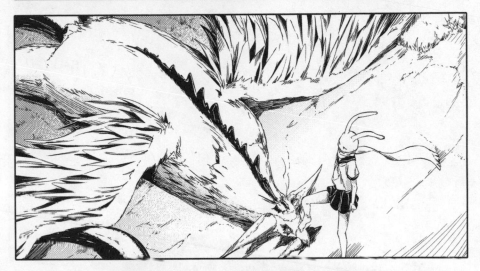

HUH?

...SALLY.

PRO-
TECT-
ED...

FLINCH

FWIA

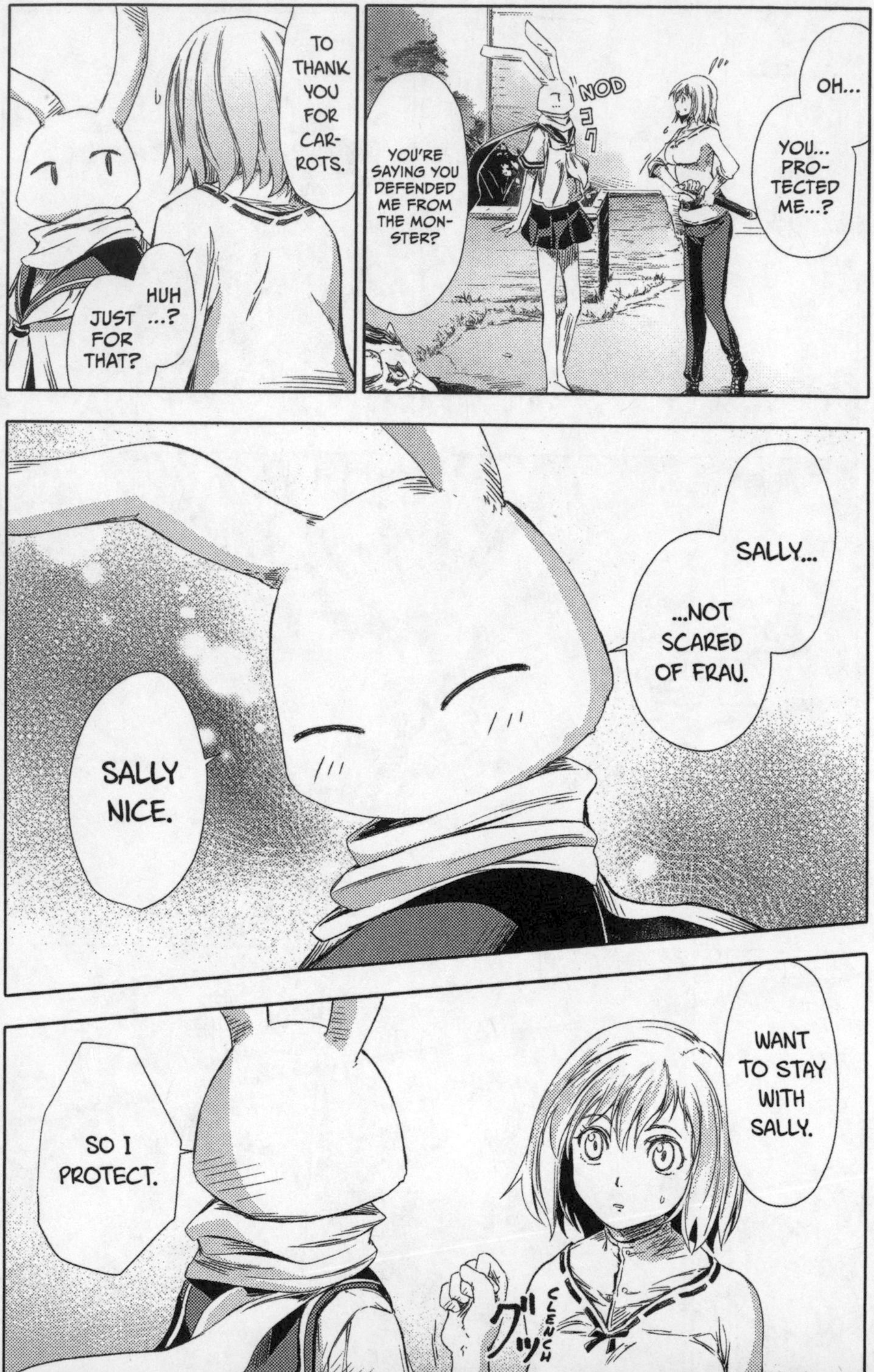
OH...
YOU... PRO-TECTED ME...?
NOD
YOU'RE SAYING YOU DEFENDED ME FROM THE MON-STER?
TO THANK YOU FOR CAR-ROTS.
HUH ...?
JUST FOR THAT?
SALLY...
...NOT SCARED OF FRAU.
SALLY NICE.
WANT TO STAY WITH SALLY.
SO I PROTECT.
CLENCH

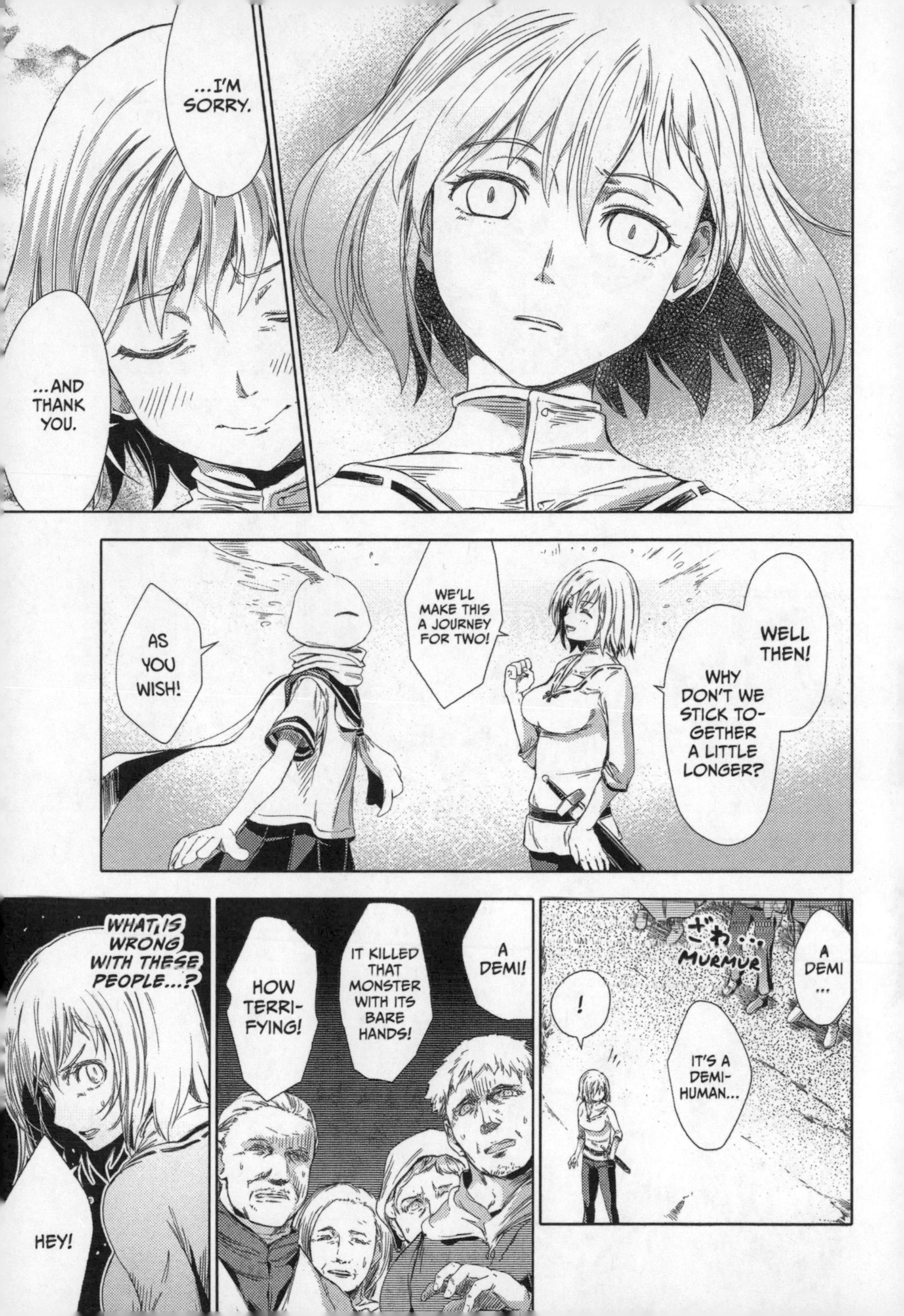
...I'M SORRY.
...AND THANK YOU.
WELL THEN! WHY DON'T WE STICK TO-GETHER A LITTLE LONGER?
WE'LL MAKE THIS A JOURNEY FOR TWO!
AS YOU WISH!
A DEMI ...
ざわ… MURMUR
IT'S A DEMI-HUMAN...
!
A DEMI!
IT KILLED THAT MONSTER WITH ITS BARE HANDS!
HOW TERRI-FYING!
WHAT IS WRONG WITH THESE PEOPLE...?
HEY!

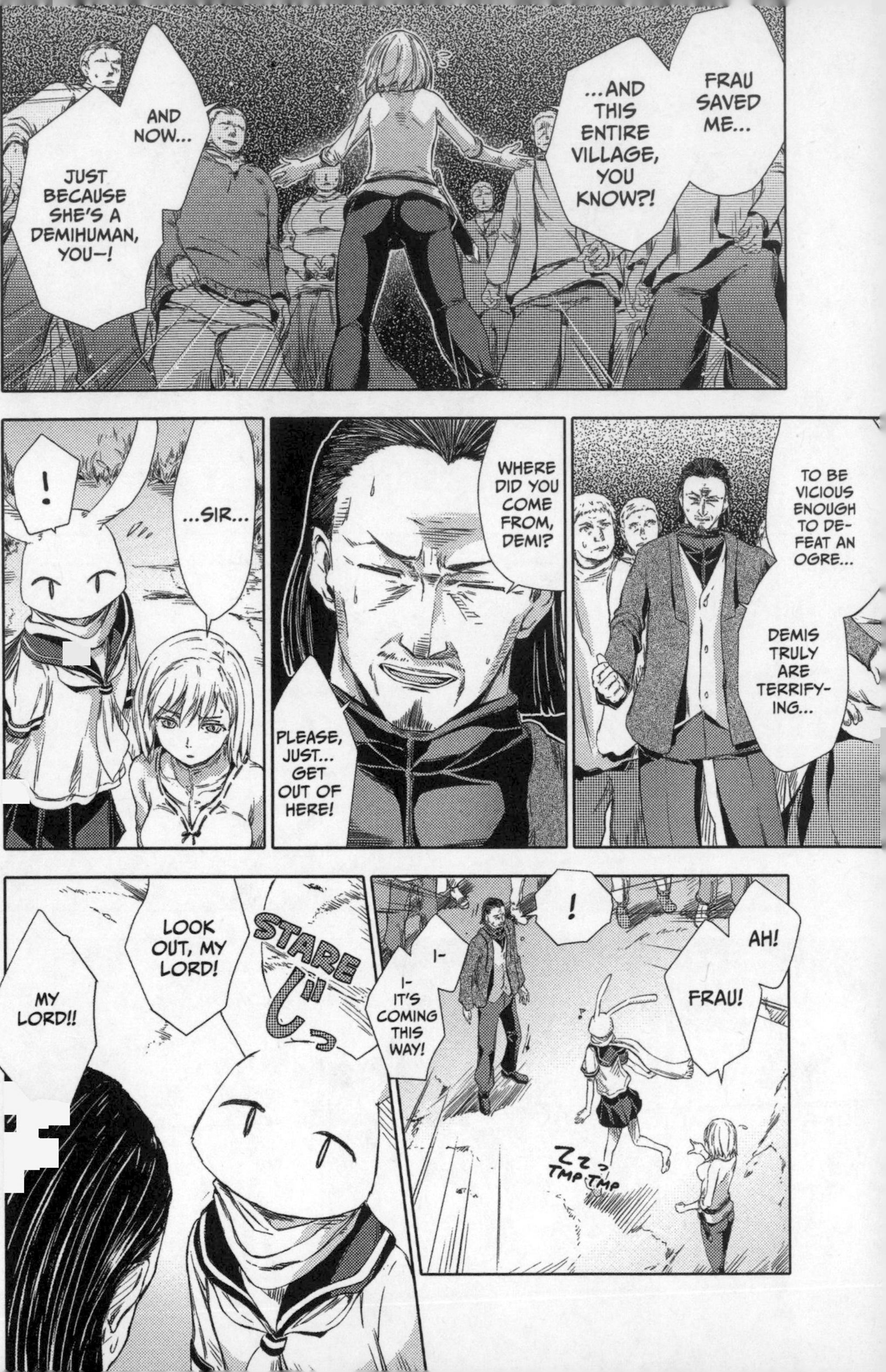
FRAU SAVED ME...
...AND THIS ENTIRE VILLAGE, YOU KNOW?!
AND NOW...
JUST BECAUSE SHE'S A DEMIHUMAN, YOU—!
TO BE VICIOUS ENOUGH TO DE-FEAT AN OGRE...
DEMIS TRULY ARE TERRIFY-ING...
WHERE DID YOU COME FROM, DEMI?
PLEASE, JUST... GET OUT OF HERE!
...SIR...
!
AH!
FRAU!
!
I-
I- IT'S COMING THIS WAY!
TMP TMP
STARE
LOOK OUT, MY LORD!
MY LORD!!

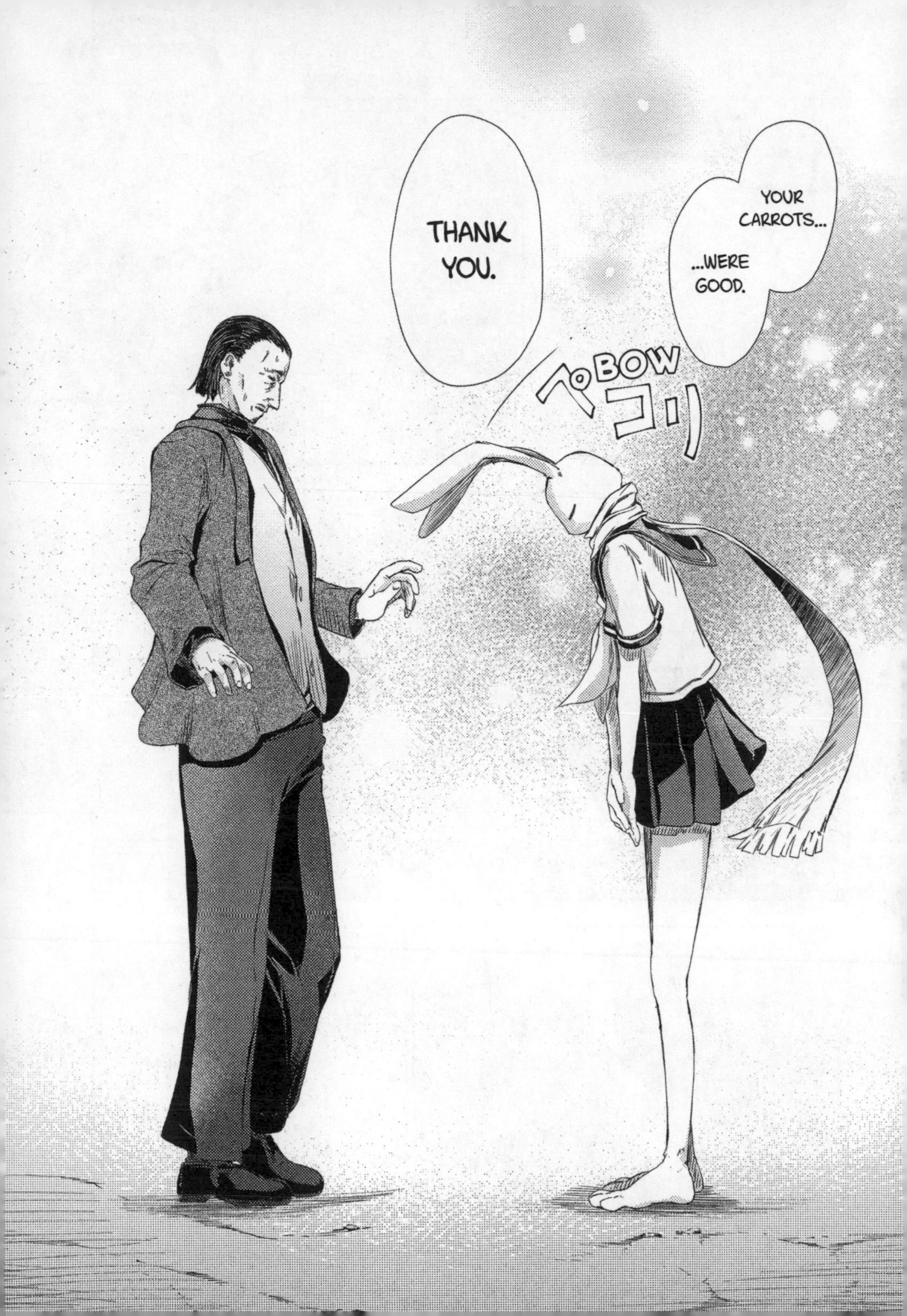
YOUR CARROTS...
...WERE GOOD.
THANK YOU.
ペ BOW コリ

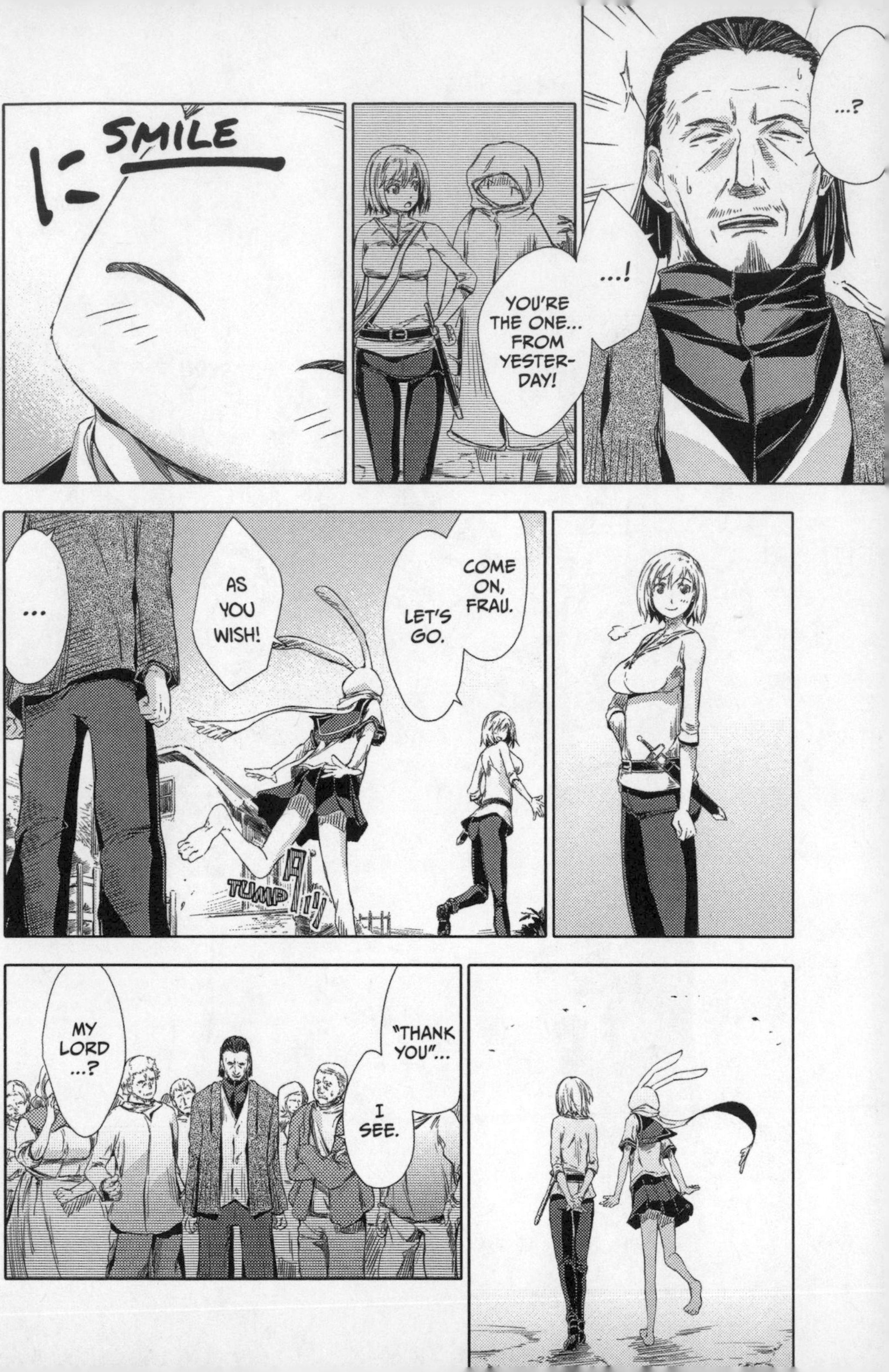
...?
...!
YOU'RE THE ONE... FROM YESTER-DAY!
SMILE
COME ON, FRAU.
LET'S GO.
AS YOU WISH!
...
TUMP
"THANK YOU"...
I SEE.
MY LORD ...?

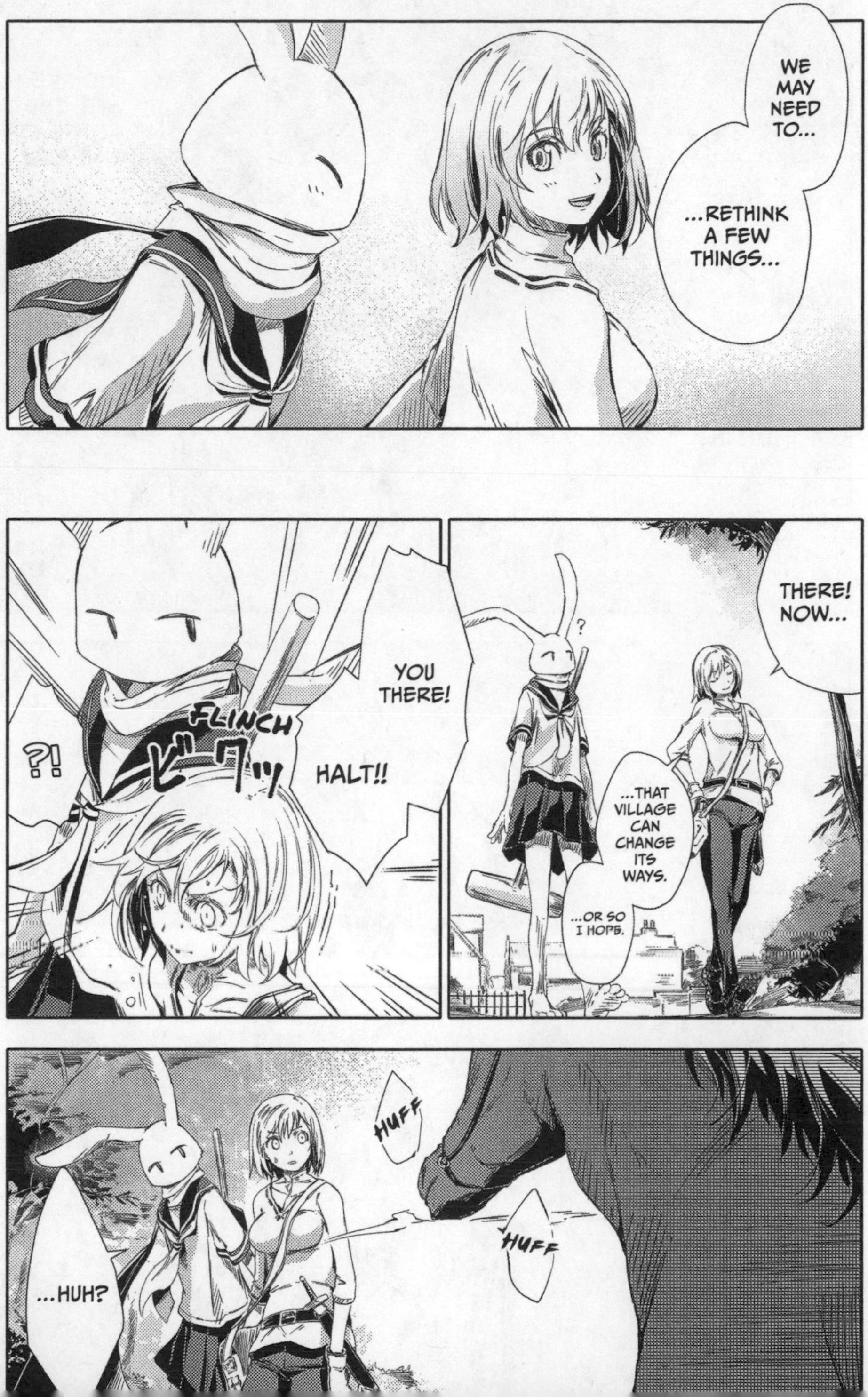
WE MAY NEED TO...
...RETHINK A FEW THINGS...
THERE! NOW...
...THAT VILLAGE CAN CHANGE ITS WAYS.
...OR SO I HOPE.
YOU THERE!
HALT!!
FLINCH
ビクッ
?!
HUFF
HUFF
...HUH?

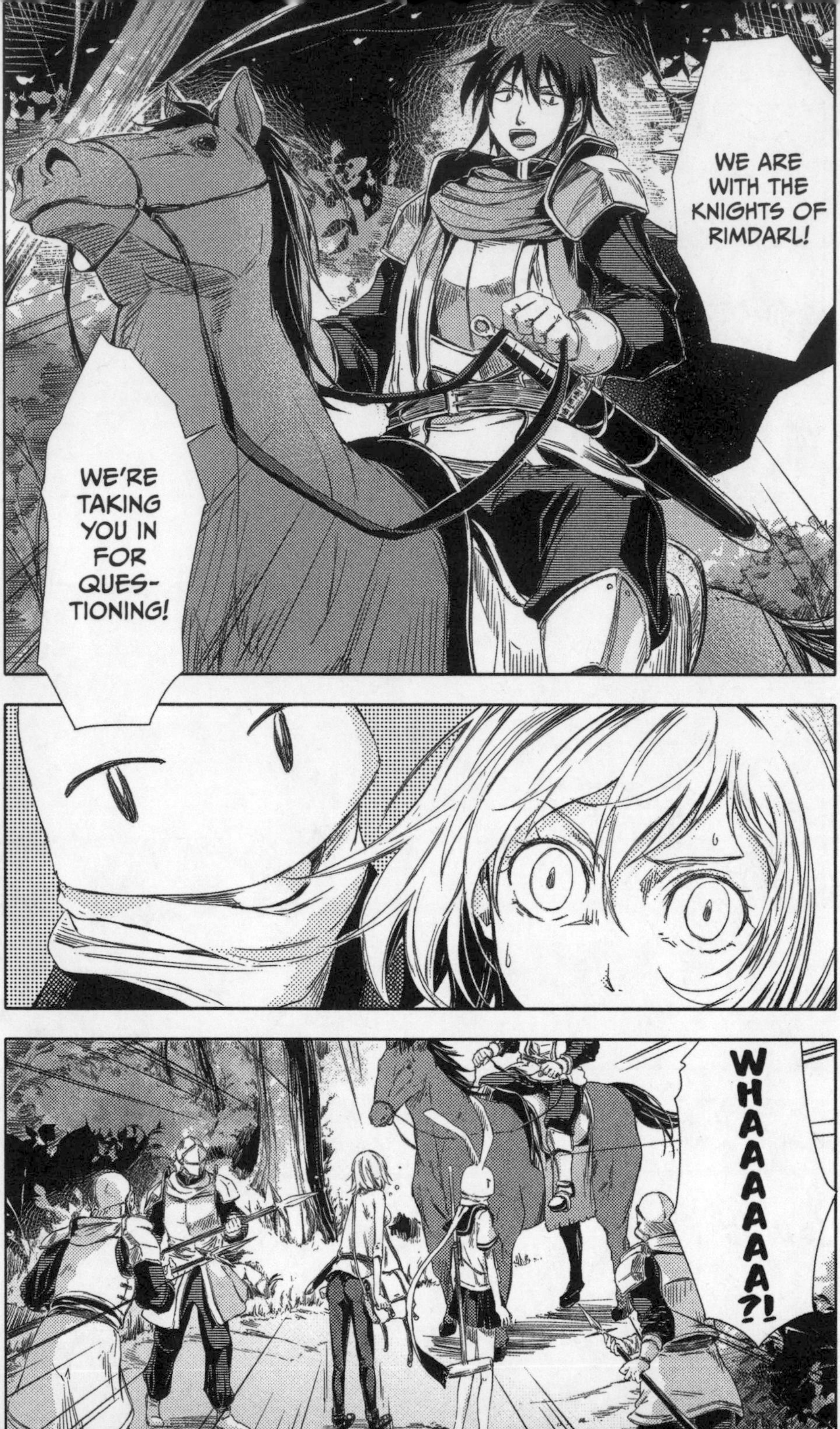
WE ARE WITH THE KNIGHTS OF RIMDARL!
WE'RE TAKING YOU IN FOR QUES-TIONING!
WHAAAAAAA?!

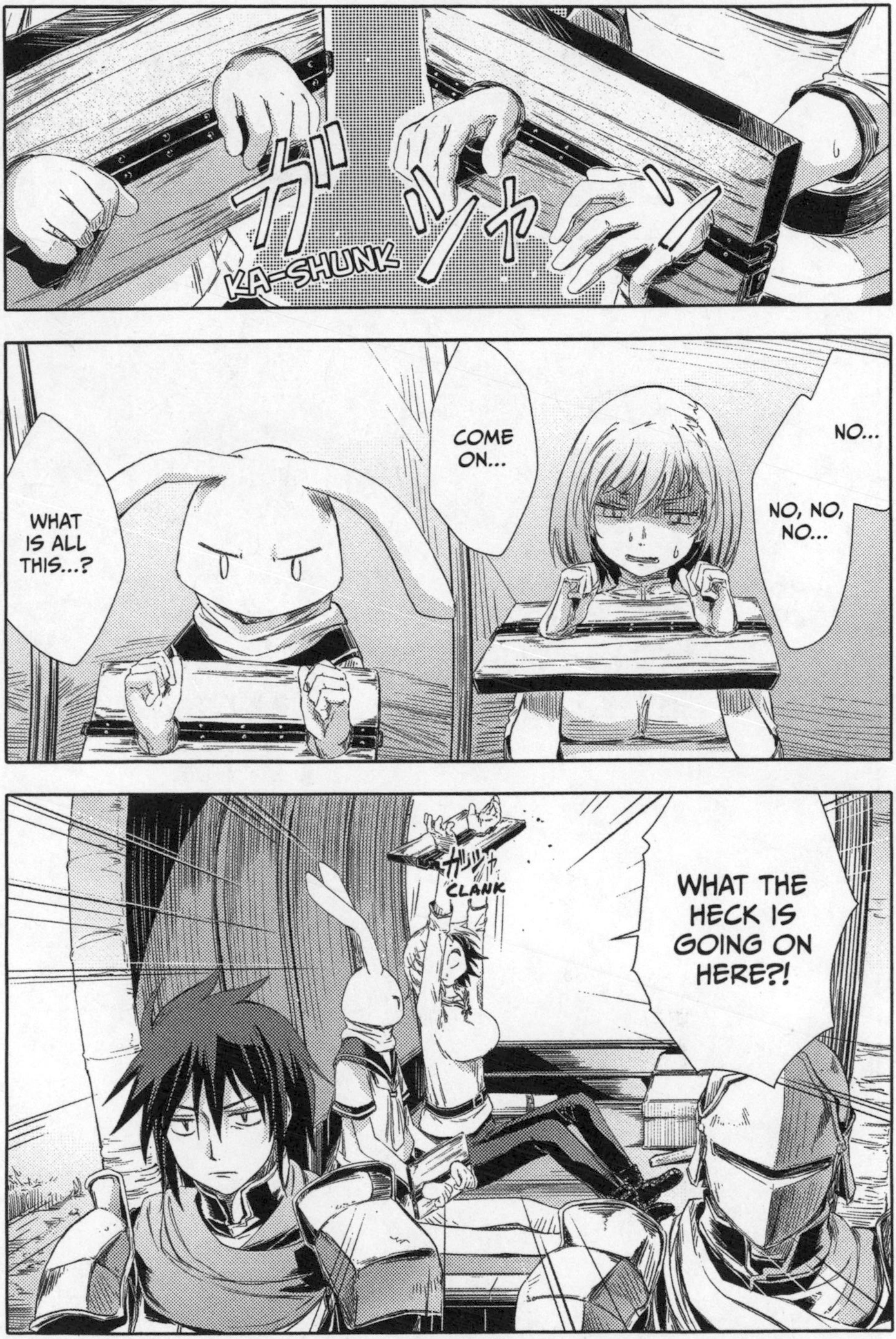
ガシャン
KA-SHUNK
NO...
NO, NO, NO...
COME ON...
WHAT IS ALL THIS...?
WHAT THE HECK IS GOING ON HERE?!
ガシャ
CLANK

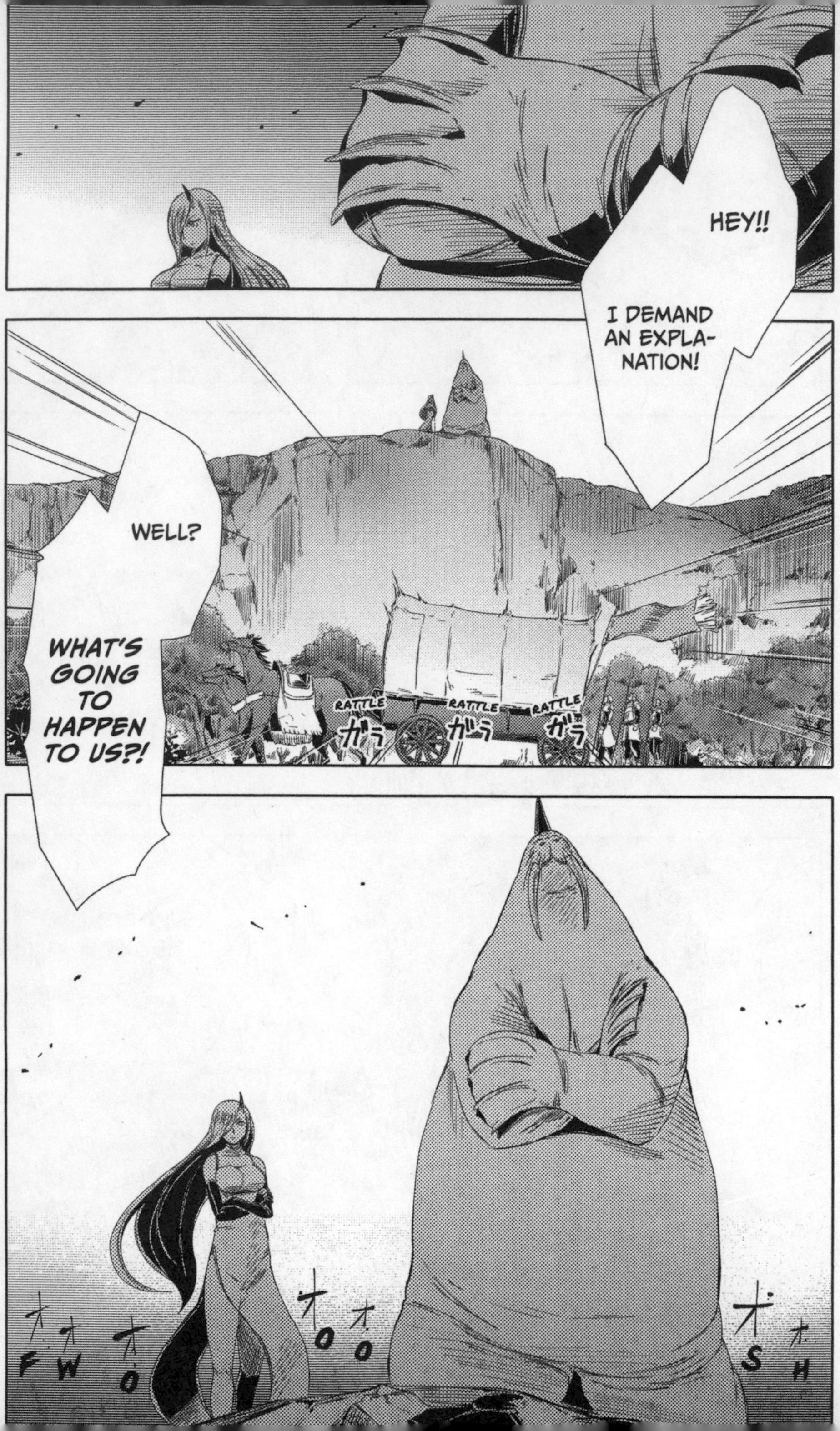
HEY!!
I DEMAND AN EXPLA-NATION!
WELL?
WHAT'S GOING TO HAPPEN TO US?!
RATTLE ガラ
RATTLE ガラ
RATTLE ガラ
FWOOOSH

MUNCH カリ

MUNCH カリ

PEACH BOY RIVERSIDE

CHAPTER 3:
THE PEACH AND I

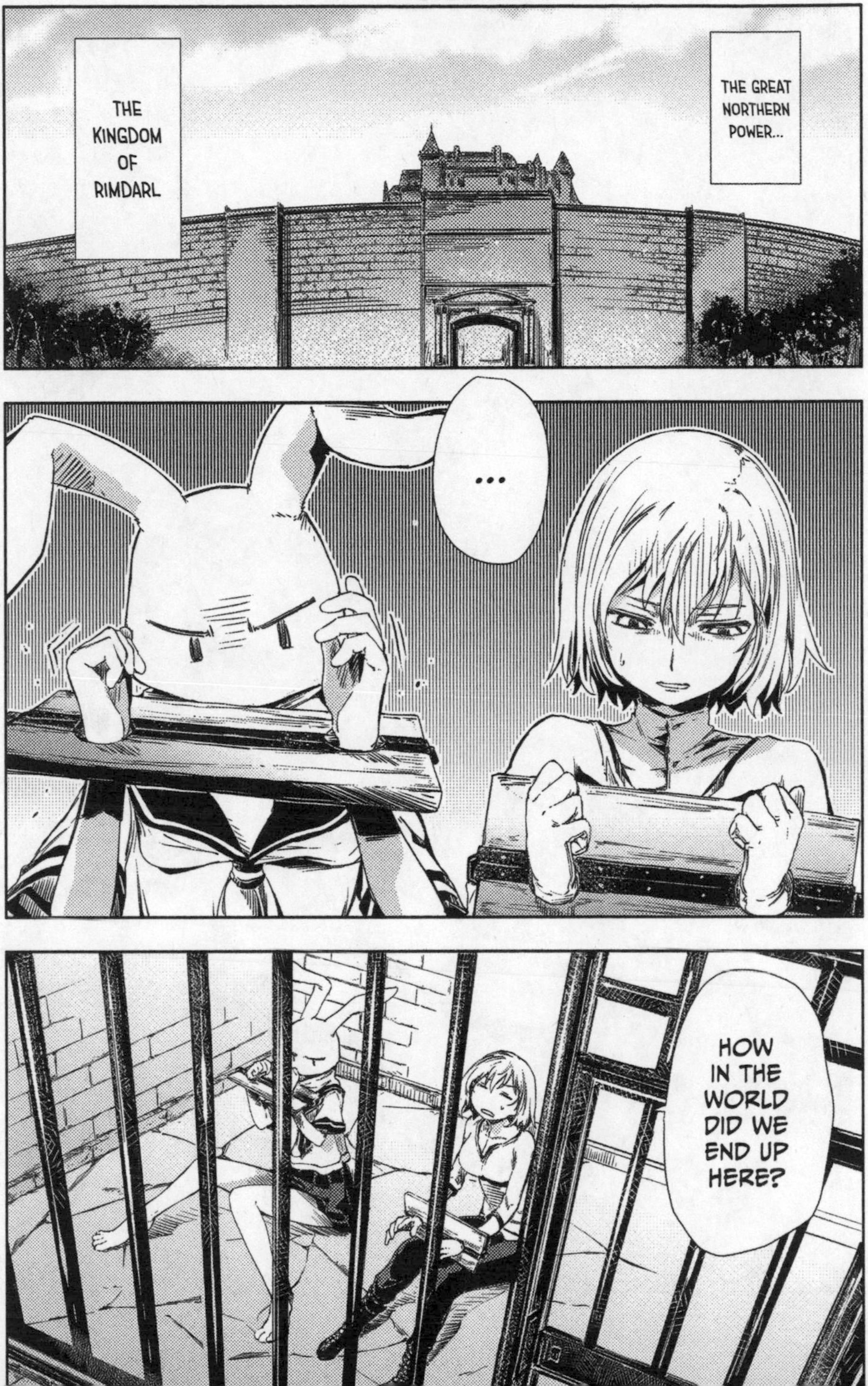
THE GREAT NORTHERN POWER...
THE KINGDOM OF RIMDARL
...
HOW IN THE WORLD DID WE END UP HERE?

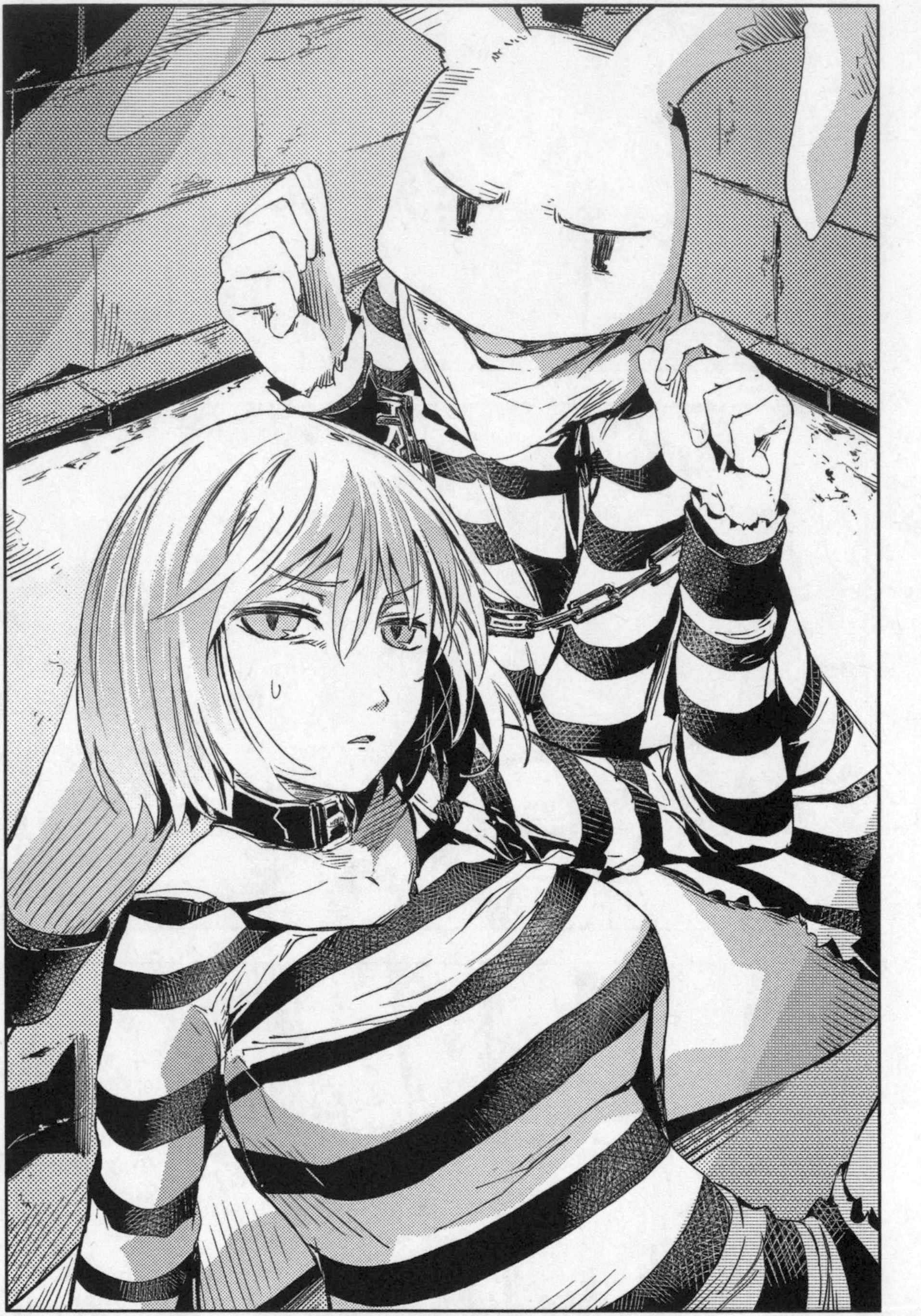

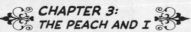

CHAPTER 3:
THE PEACH AND I

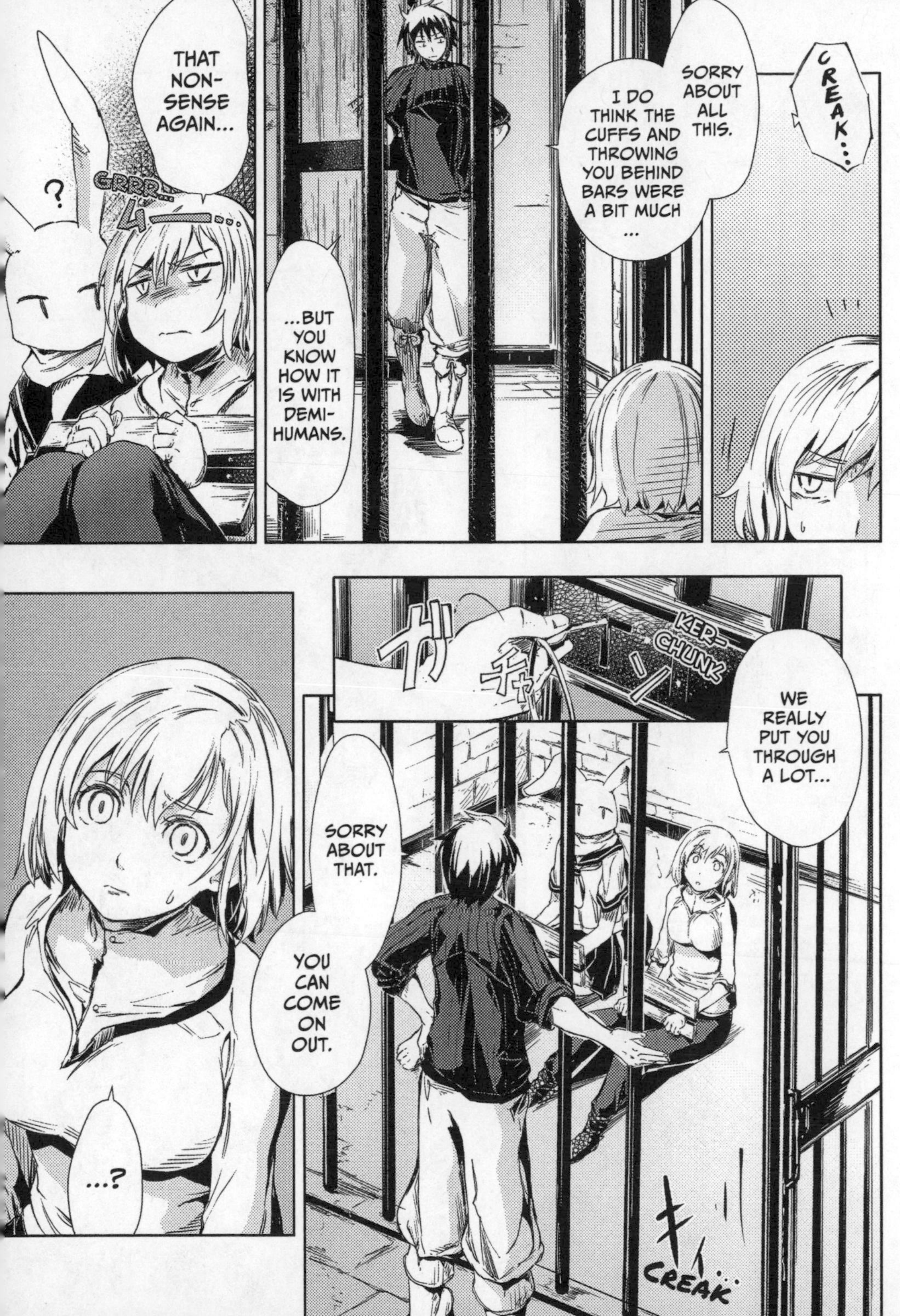
CREAK...
SORRY ABOUT ALL THIS.
I DO THINK THE CUFFS AND THROWING YOU BEHIND BARS WERE A BIT MUCH ...
...BUT YOU KNOW HOW IT IS WITH DEMI-HUMANS.
THAT NON-SENSE AGAIN...
GRRR...
?
KER-CHUNK
WE REALLY PUT YOU THROUGH A LOT...
SORRY ABOUT THAT.
YOU CAN COME ON OUT.
CREAK
...?

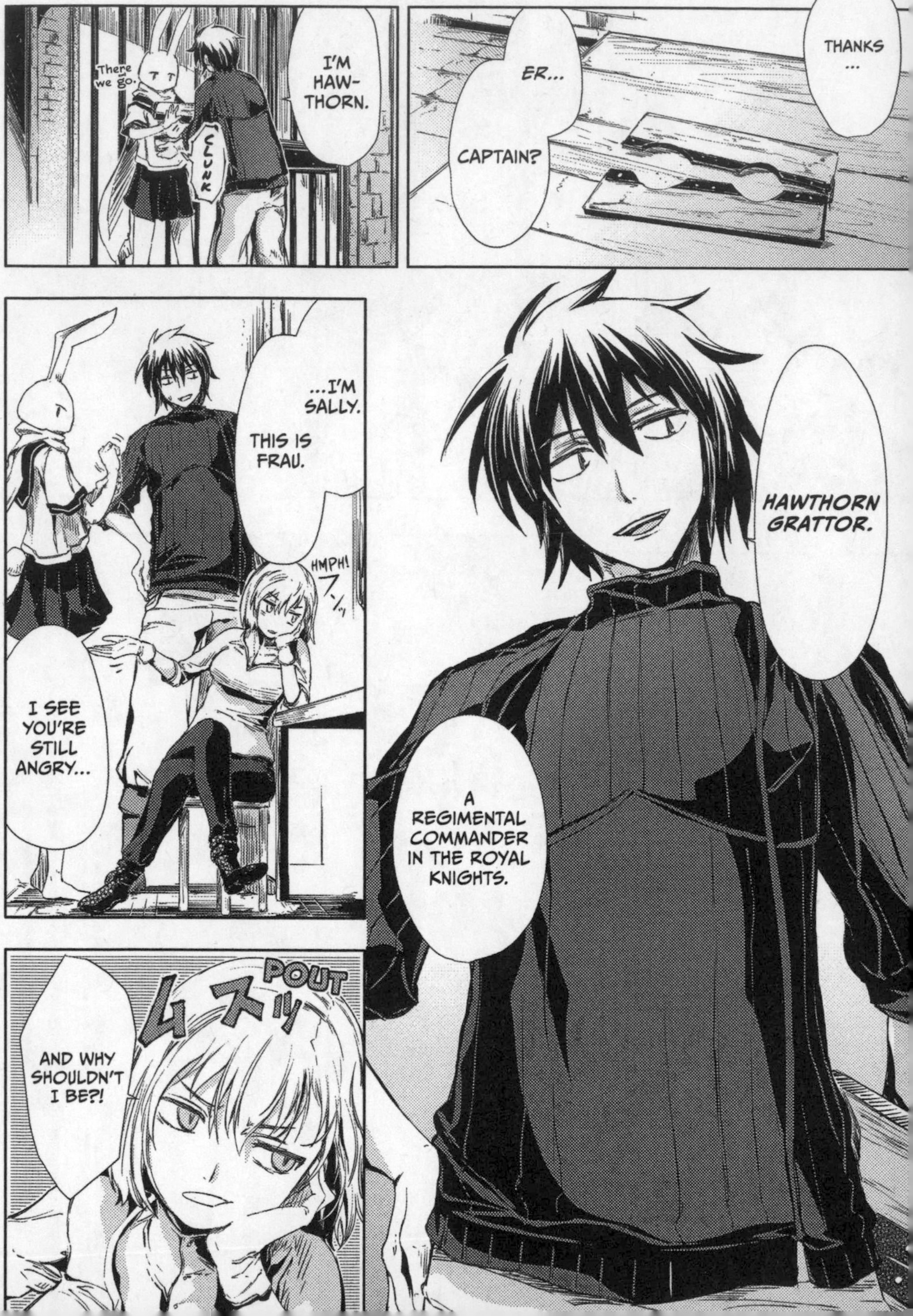
THANKS ...
ER...
CAPTAIN?
I'M HAW-THORN.
There we go.
CLUNK
HAWTHORN GRATTOR.
A REGIMENTAL COMMANDER IN THE ROYAL KNIGHTS.
...I'M SALLY.
THIS IS FRAU.
HMPH!
I SEE YOU'RE STILL ANGRY...
POUT
AND WHY SHOULDN'T I BE?!

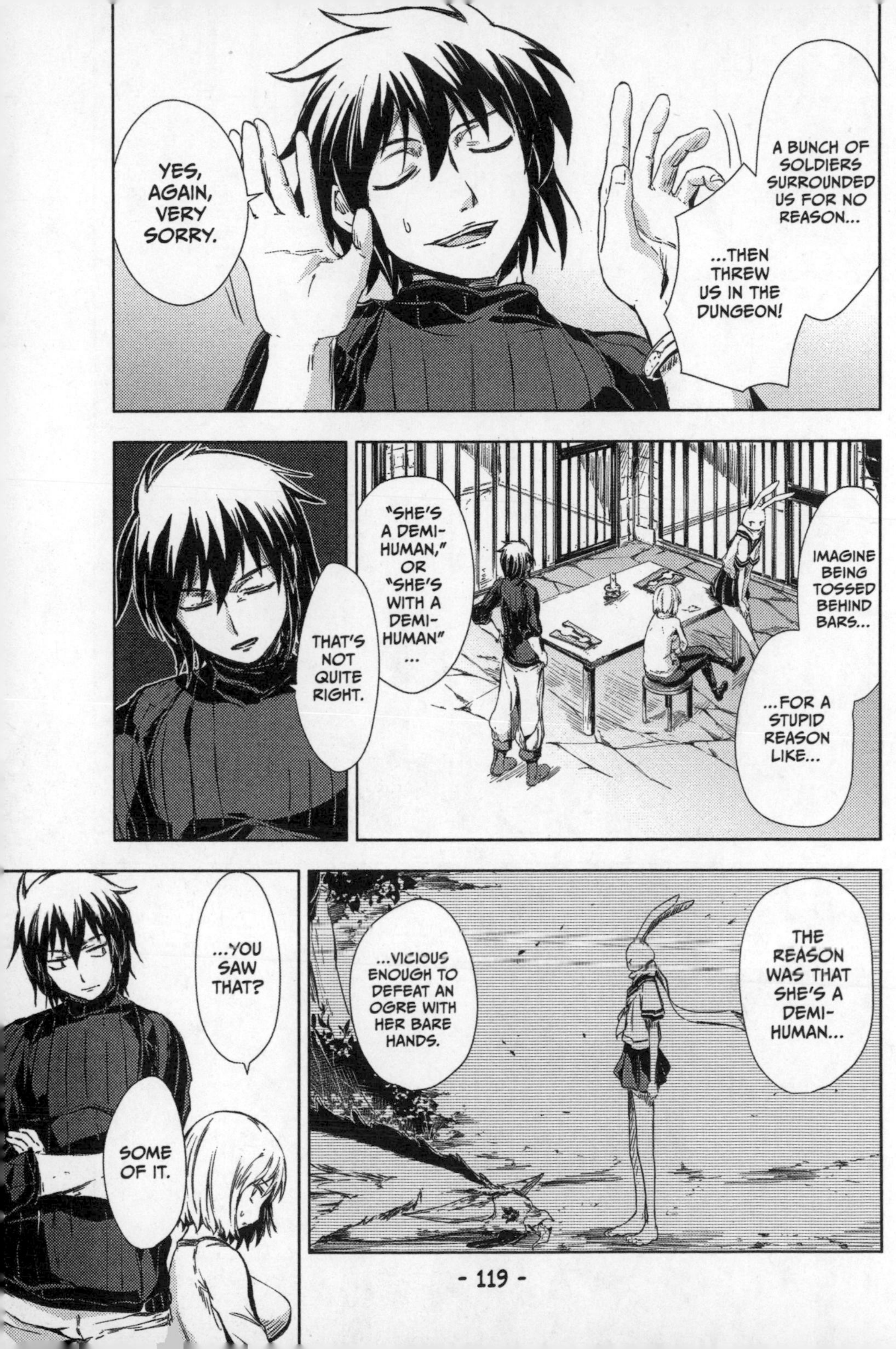
A BUNCH OF SOLDIERS SURROUNDED US FOR NO REASON...
...THEN THREW US IN THE DUNGEON!
YES, AGAIN, VERY SORRY.
IMAGINE BEING TOSSED BEHIND BARS...
...FOR A STUPID REASON LIKE...
"SHE'S A DEMI-HUMAN," OR "SHE'S WITH A DEMI-HUMAN"...
THAT'S NOT QUITE RIGHT.
THE REASON WAS THAT SHE'S A DEMI-HUMAN...
...VICIOUS ENOUGH TO DEFEAT AN OGRE WITH HER BARE HANDS.
...YOU SAW THAT?
SOME OF IT.

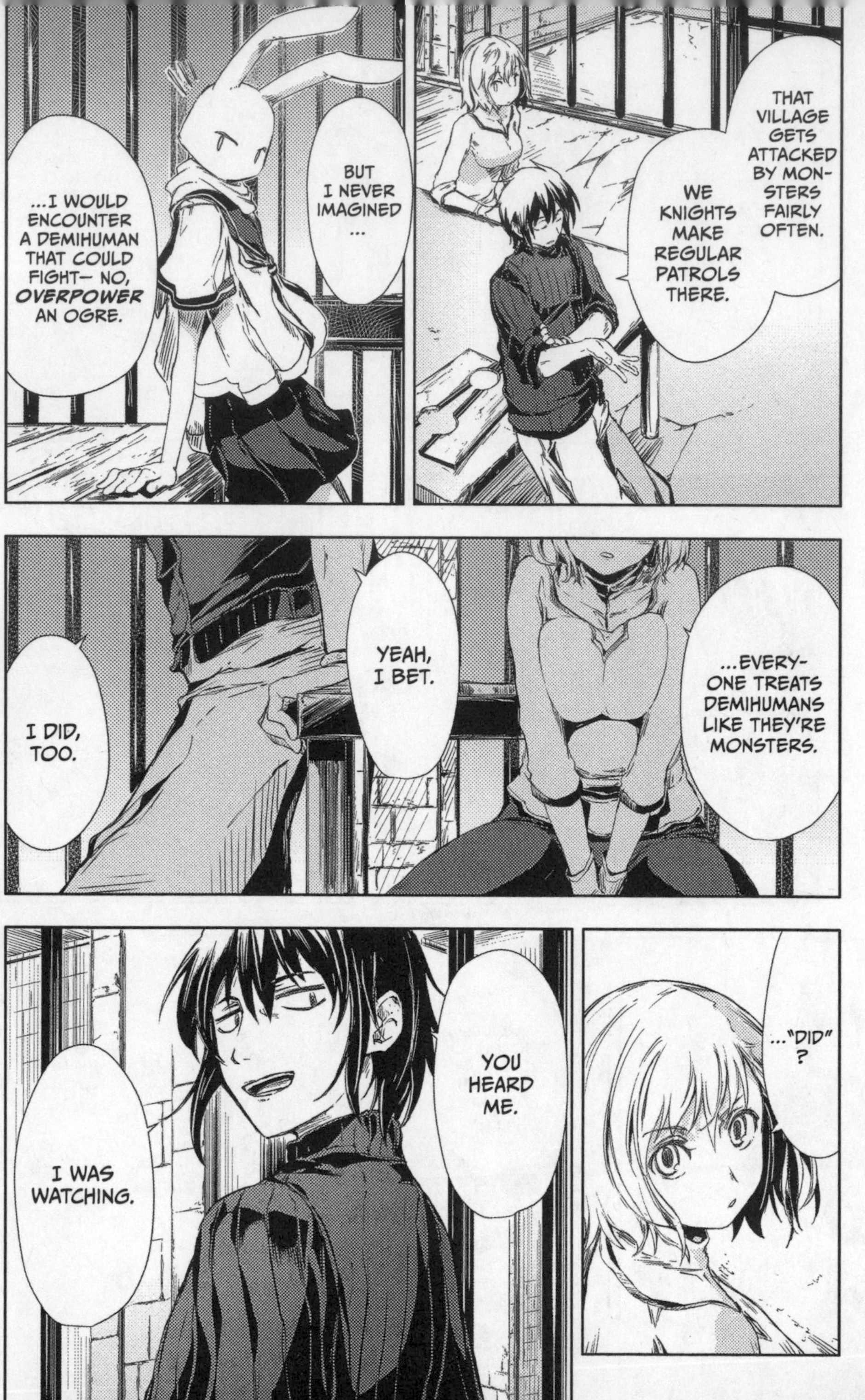
THAT VILLAGE GETS ATTACKED BY MON-STERS FAIRLY OFTEN.
WE KNIGHTS MAKE REGULAR PATROLS THERE.
BUT I NEVER IMAGINED ...
...I WOULD ENCOUNTER A DEMIHUMAN THAT COULD FIGHT— NO, OVERPOWER AN OGRE.
...EVERY-ONE TREATS DEMIHUMANS LIKE THEY'RE MONSTERS.
YEAH, I BET.
I DID, TOO.
..."DID"?
YOU HEARD ME.
I WAS WATCHING.

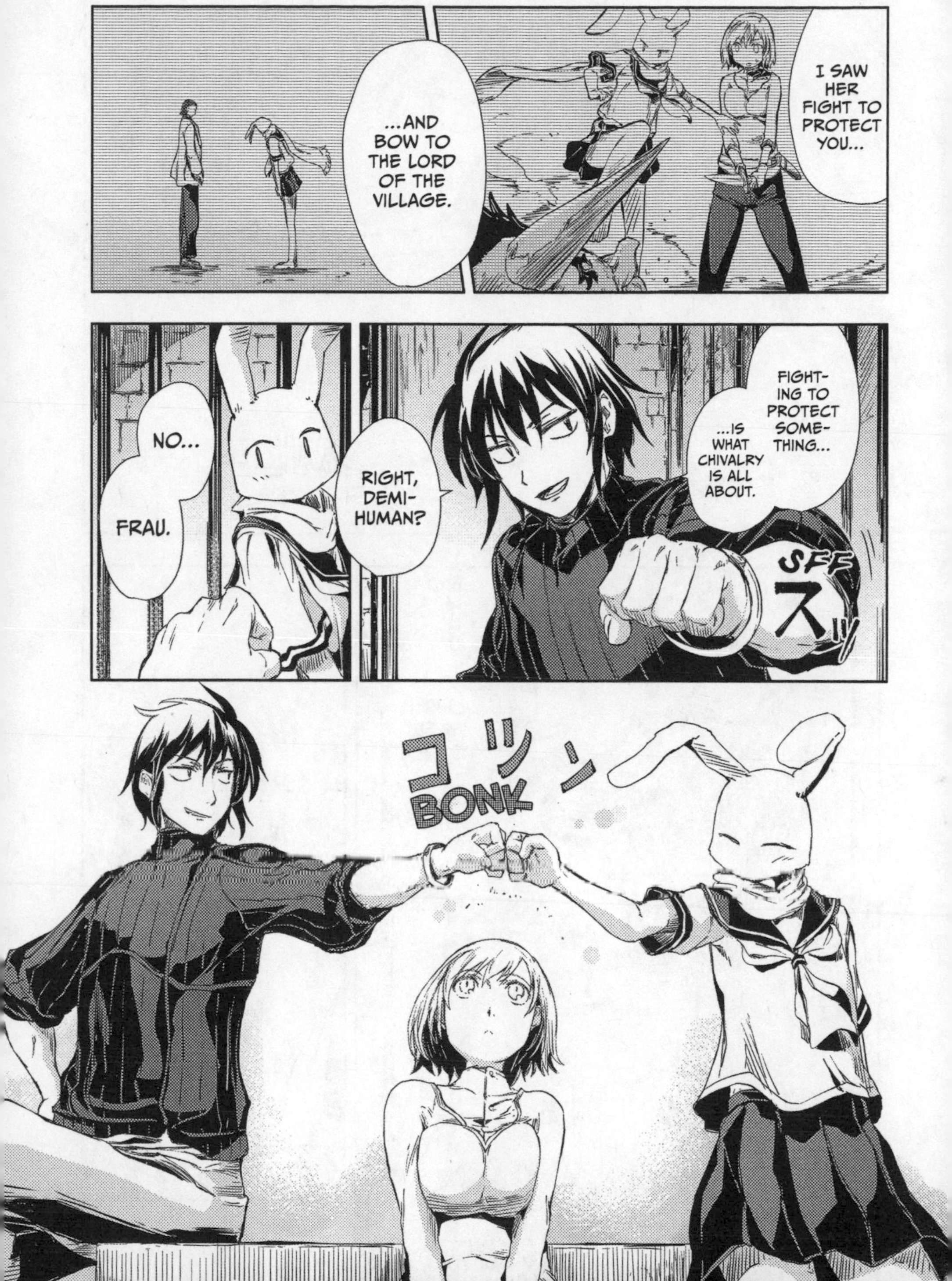
I SAW HER FIGHT TO PROTECT YOU...
...AND BOW TO THE LORD OF THE VILLAGE.
FIGHT-ING TO PROTECT SOME-THING...
...IS WHAT CHIVALRY IS ALL ABOUT.
SFF
スッ
RIGHT, DEMI-HUMAN?
NO...
FRAU.
コツン
BONK

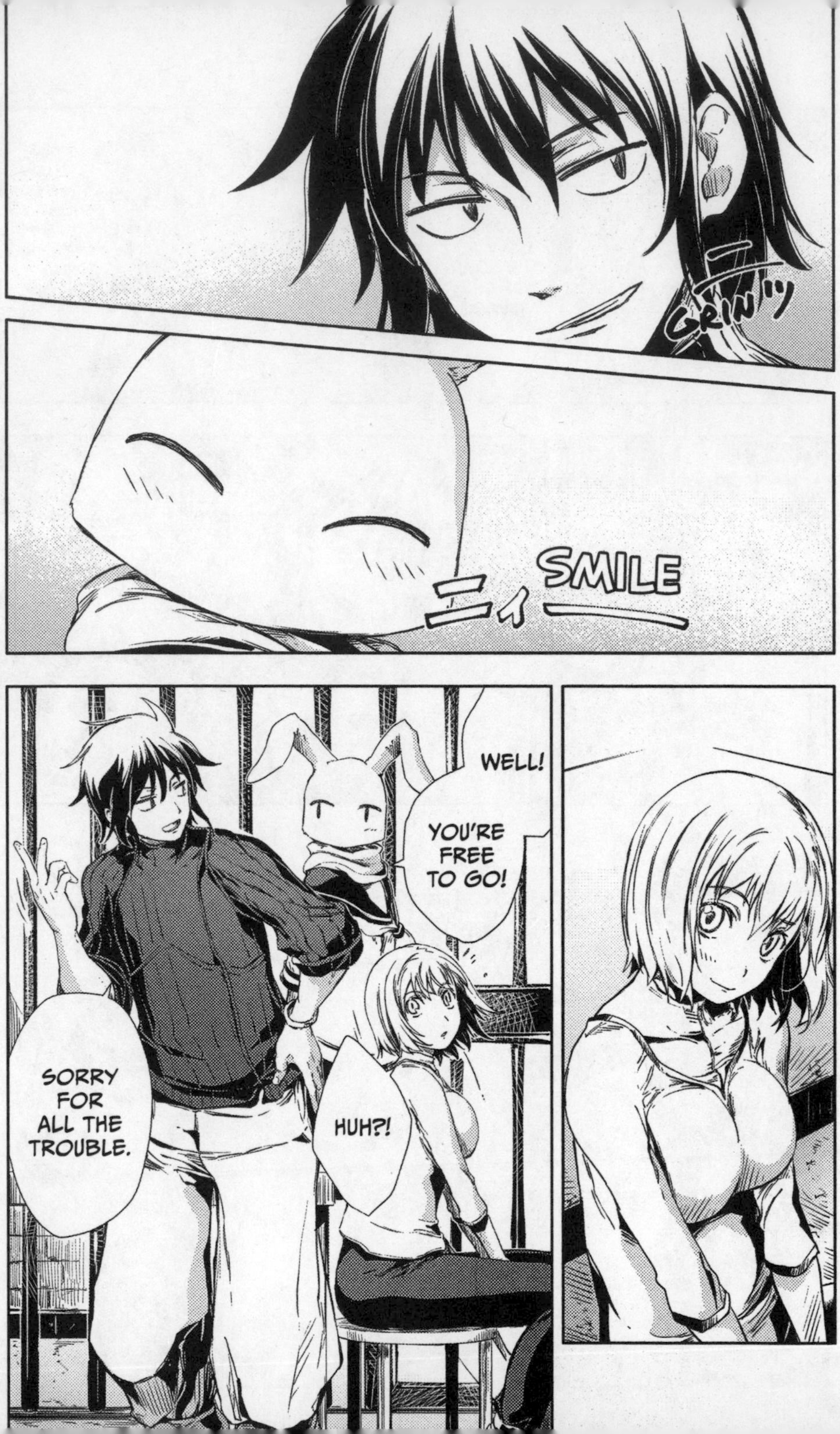
GRIN
SMILE
WELL!
YOU'RE FREE TO GO!
HUH?!
SORRY FOR ALL THE TROUBLE.

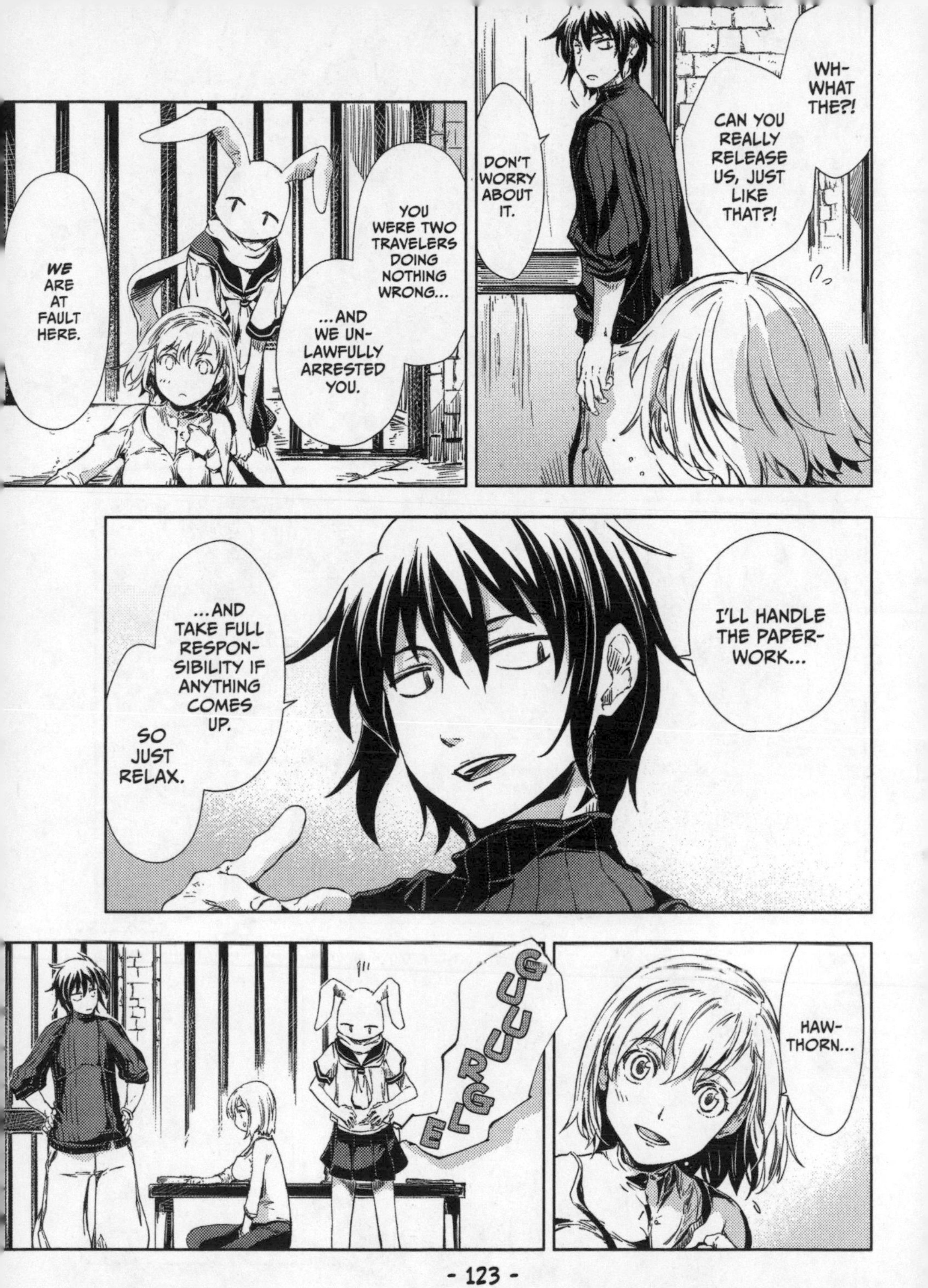
WH- WHAT THE?!
CAN YOU REALLY RELEASE US, JUST LIKE THAT?!
DON'T WORRY ABOUT IT.
YOU WERE TWO TRAVELERS DOING NOTHING WRONG...
...AND WE UNLAWFULLY ARRESTED YOU.
WE ARE AT FAULT HERE.
I'LL HANDLE THE PAPERWORK...
...AND TAKE FULL RESPONSIBILITY IF ANYTHING COMES UP.
SO JUST RELAX.
HAWTHORN...
GUUURGLE

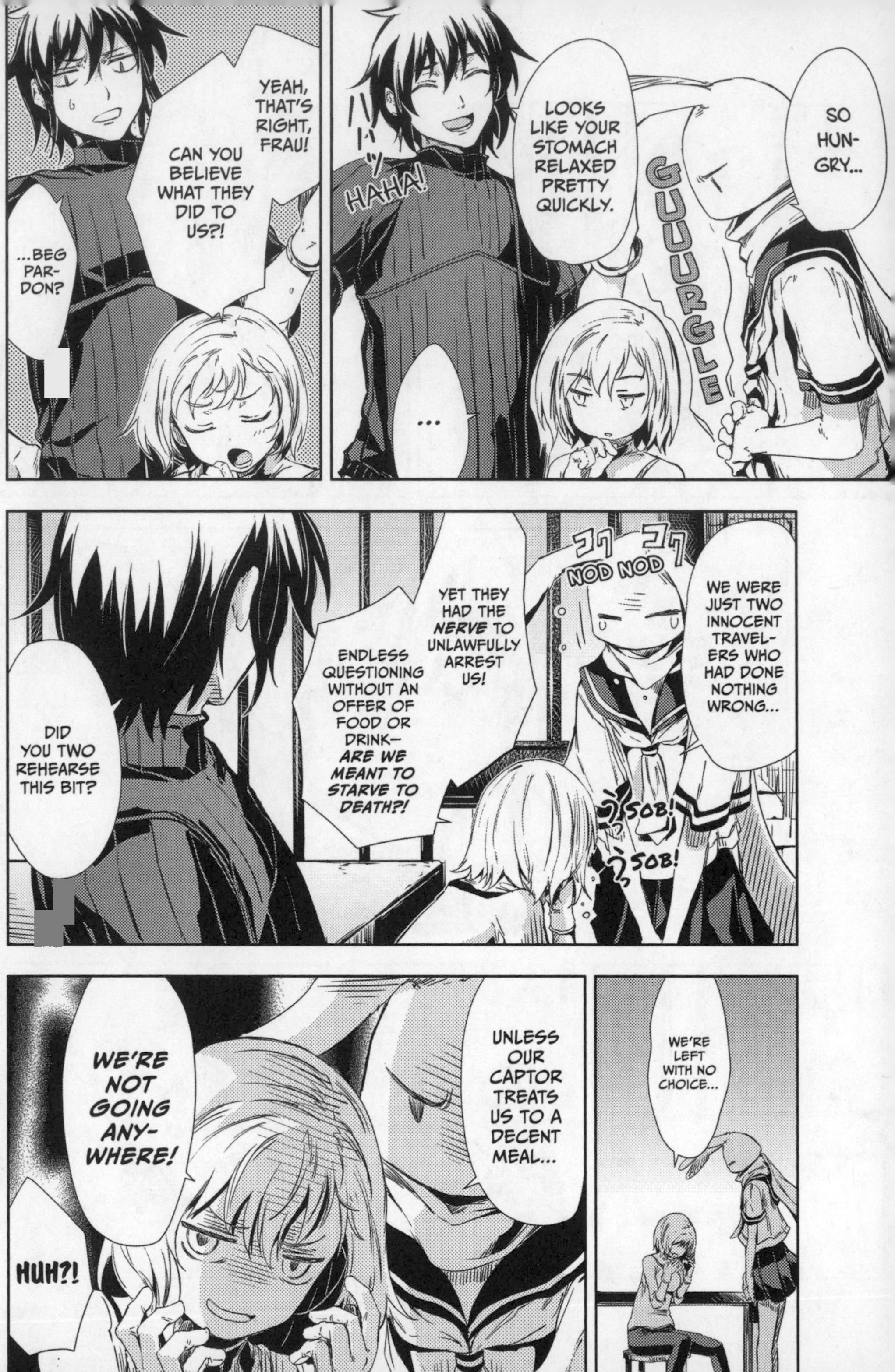
SO HUN-GRY...
GUUURGLE
LOOKS LIKE YOUR STOMACH RELAXED PRETTY QUICKLY.
HAHA!
...
YEAH, THAT'S RIGHT, FRAU!
CAN YOU BELIEVE WHAT THEY DID TO US?!
...BEG PAR-DON?
コク コク
NOD NOD
WE WERE JUST TWO INNOCENT TRAVEL-ERS WHO HAD DONE NOTHING WRONG...
YET THEY HAD THE *NERVE* TO UNLAWFULLY ARREST US!
ENDLESS QUESTIONING WITHOUT AN OFFER OF FOOD OR DRINK— *ARE WE MEANT TO STARVE TO DEATH?!*
SOB! SOB!
DID YOU TWO REHEARSE THIS BIT?
WE'RE LEFT WITH NO CHOICE...
UNLESS OUR CAPTOR TREATS US TO A DECENT MEAL...
WE'RE NOT GOING ANY-WHERE!
HUH?!

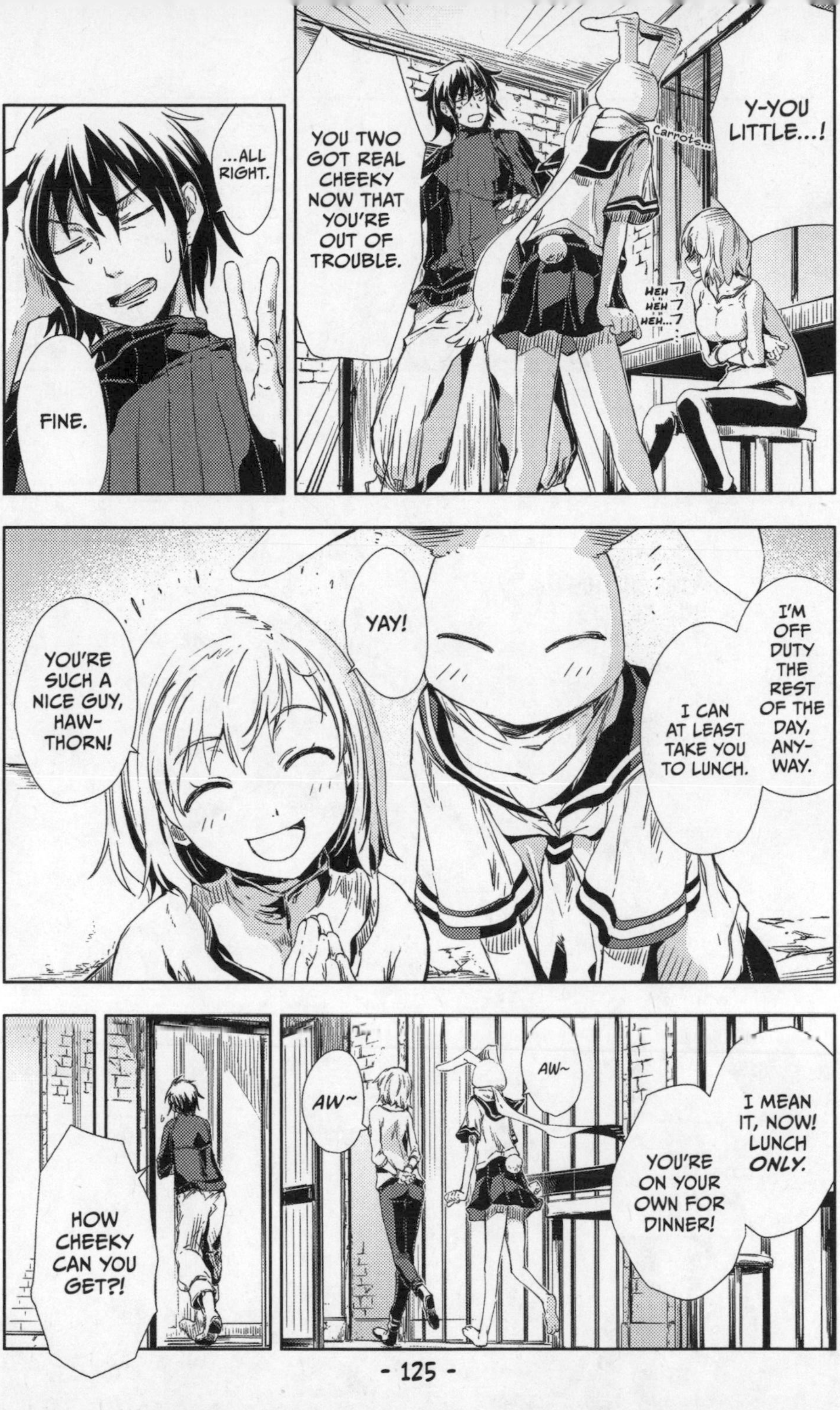
Y-YOU LITTLE...!
Carrots...
YOU TWO GOT REAL CHEEKY NOW THAT YOU'RE OUT OF TROUBLE.
HEH HEH HEH...
...ALL RIGHT.
FINE.
I'M OFF DUTY THE REST OF THE DAY, ANY-WAY.
I CAN AT LEAST TAKE YOU TO LUNCH.
YAY!
YOU'RE SUCH A NICE GUY, HAW-THORN!
I MEAN IT, NOW! LUNCH *ONLY.*
YOU'RE ON YOUR OWN FOR DINNER!
AW~
AW~
HOW CHEEKY CAN YOU GET?!

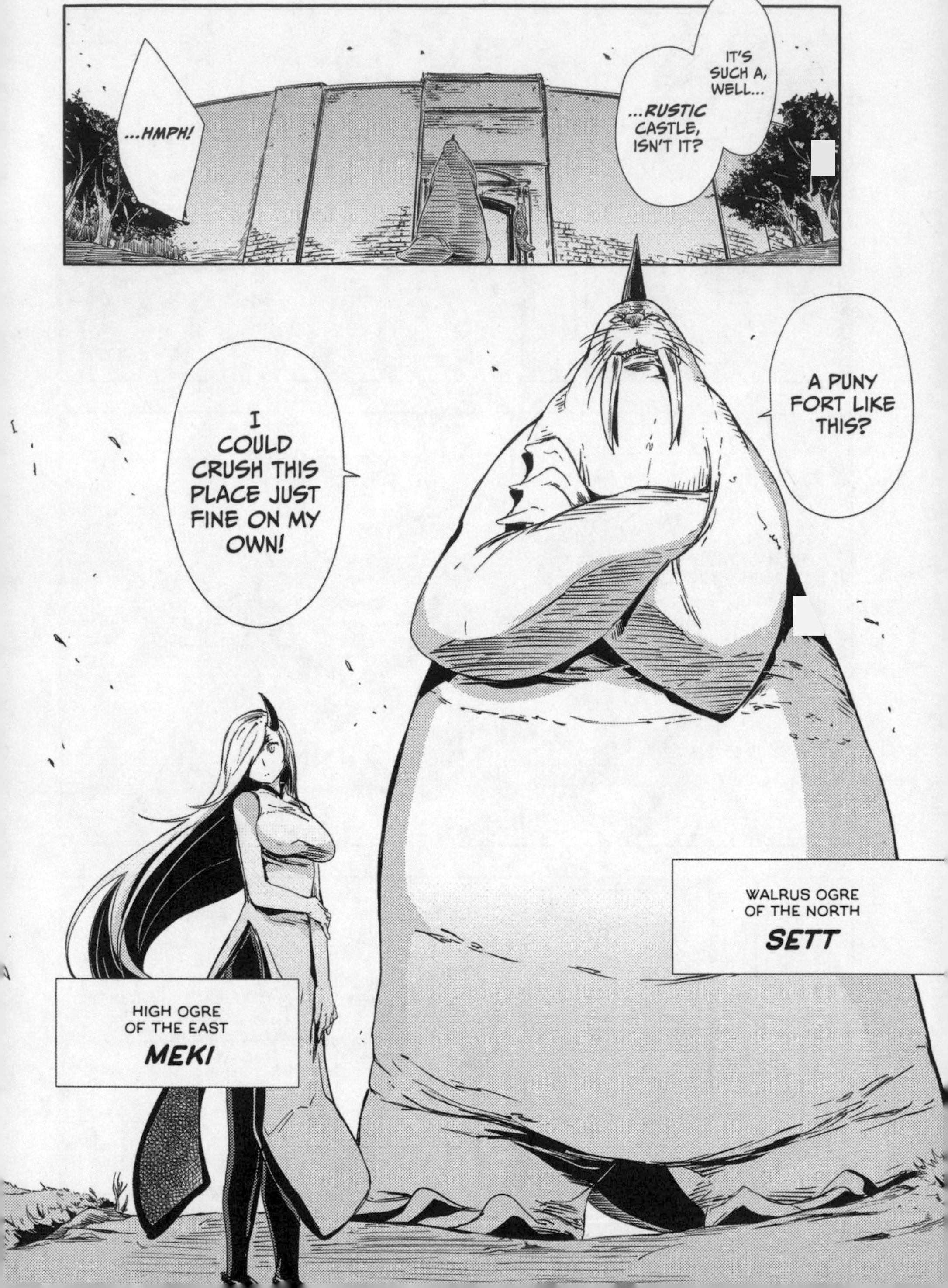
IT'S SUCH A, WELL... ...RUSTIC CASTLE, ISN'T IT?
...HMPH!
A PUNY FORT LIKE THIS?
I COULD CRUSH THIS PLACE JUST FINE ON MY OWN!
WALRUS OGRE OF THE NORTH SETT
HIGH OGRE OF THE EAST MEKI

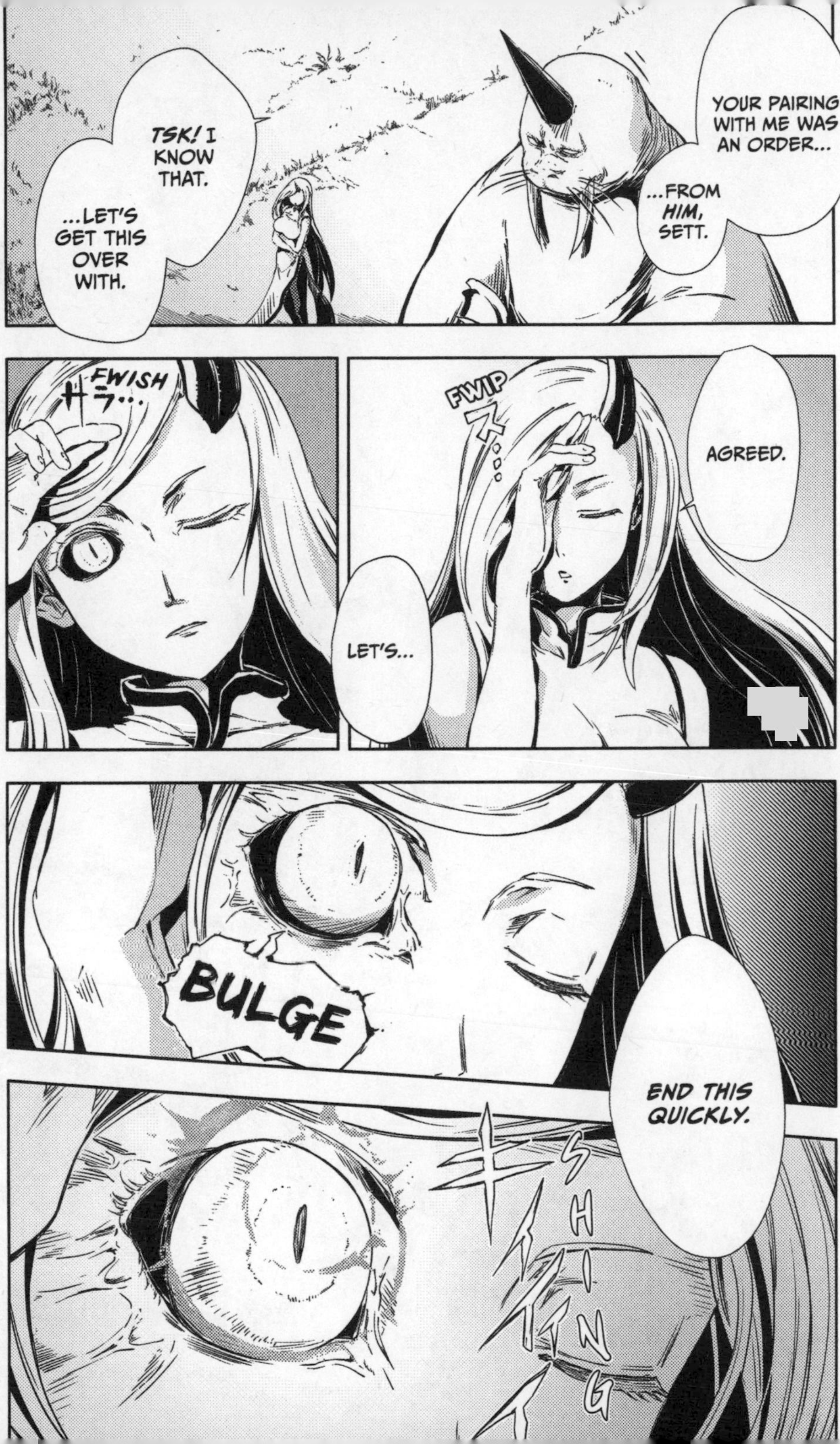
YOUR PAIRING WITH ME WAS AN ORDER...
...FROM HIM, SETT.
TSK! I KNOW THAT.
...LET'S GET THIS OVER WITH.
FWIP
AGREED.
LET'S...
FWISH
BULGE
END THIS QUICKLY.
SHING

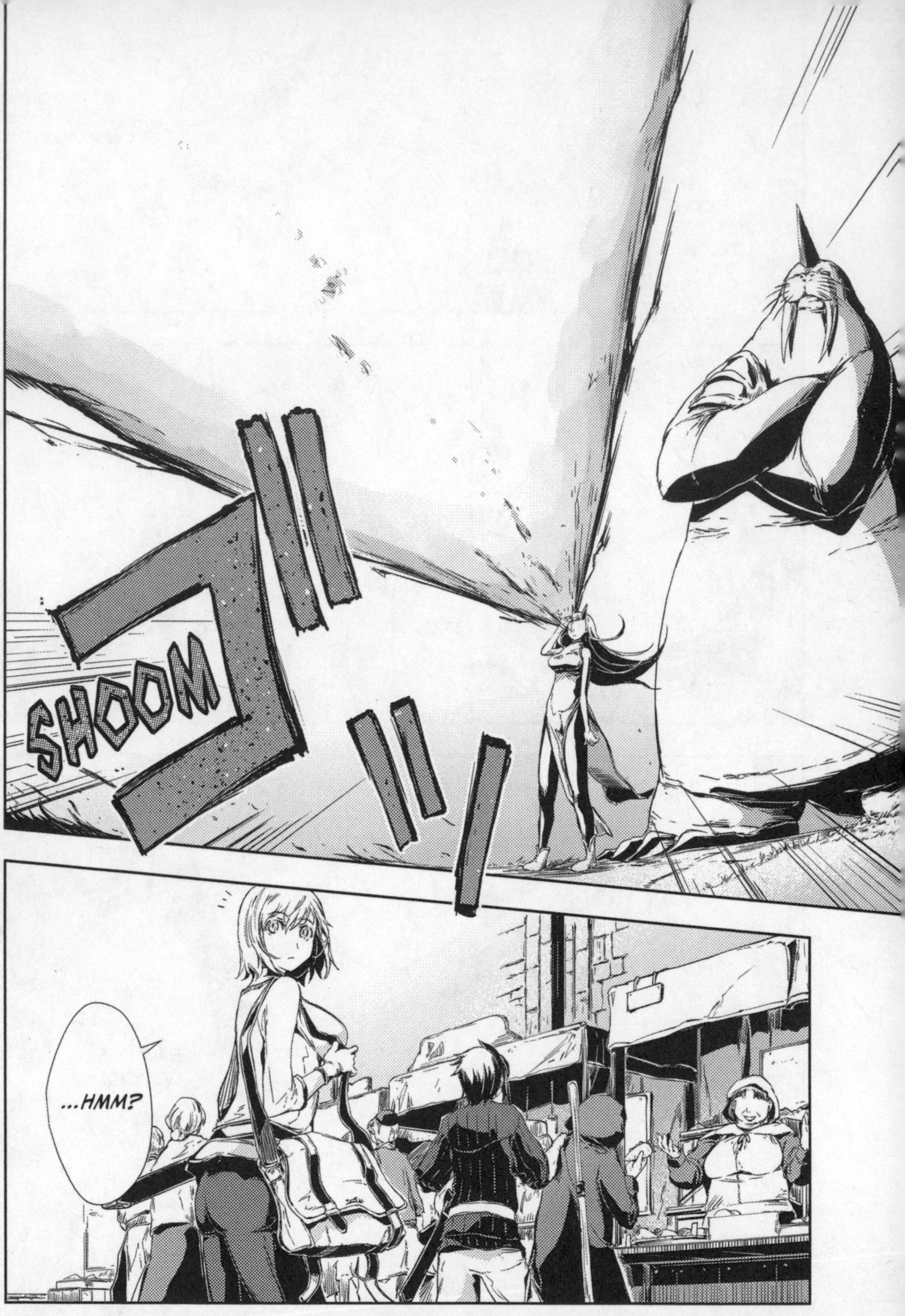
SHOOM
...HMM?

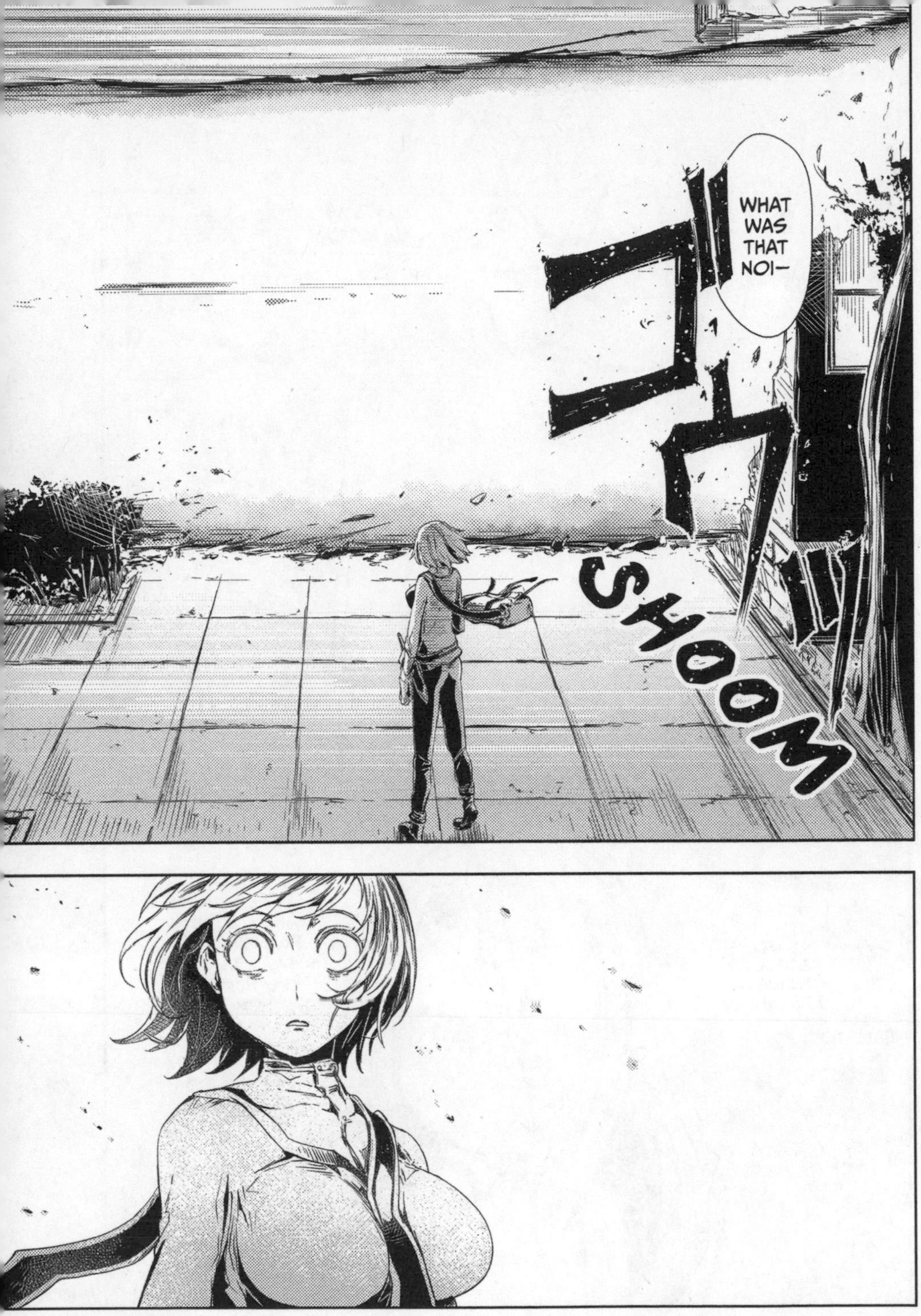
WHAT WAS THAT NOI—
ゴゴ
SHOOM

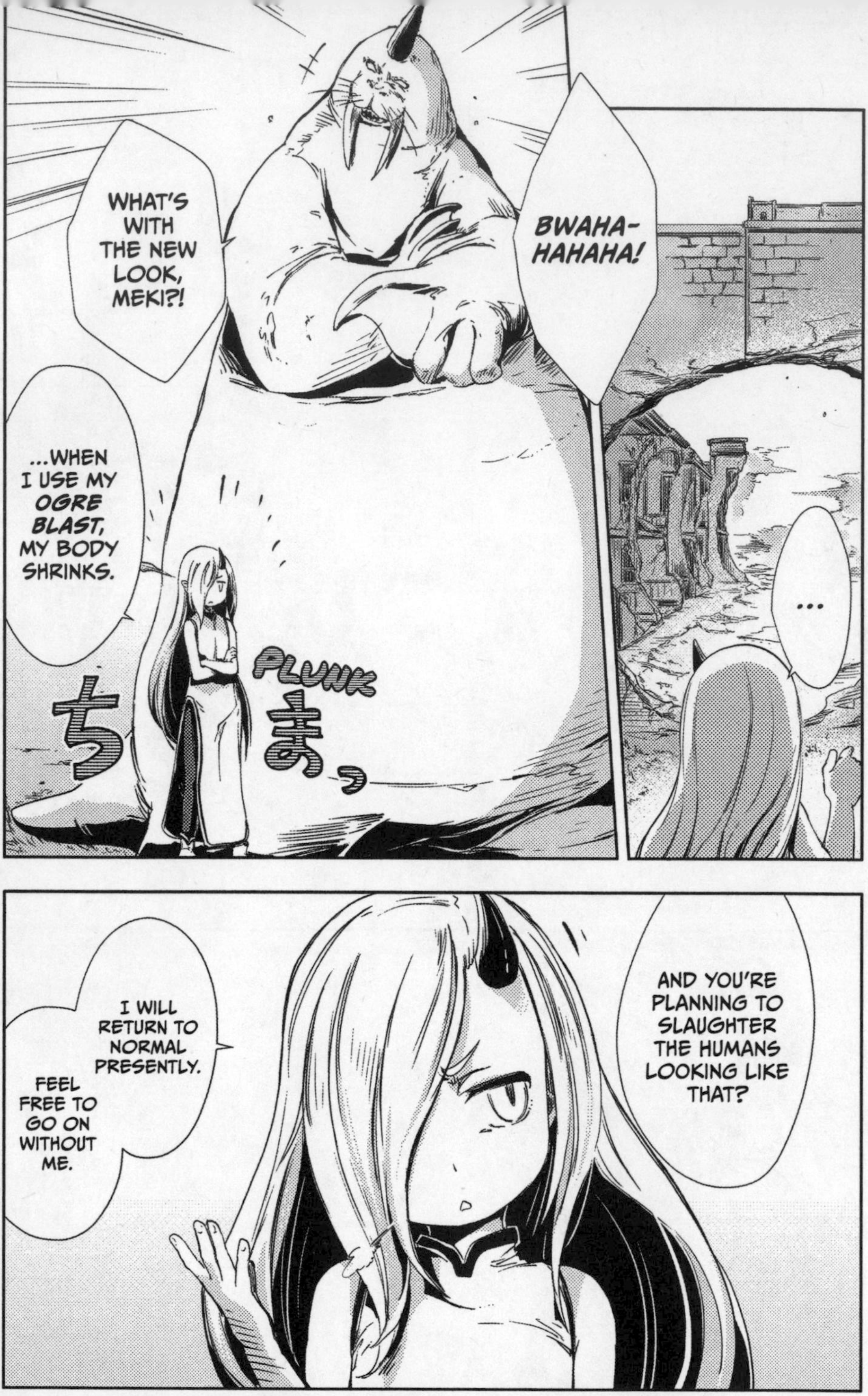
...
BWAHA-HAHAHA!
WHAT'S WITH THE NEW LOOK, MEKI?!
...WHEN I USE MY OGRE BLAST, MY BODY SHRINKS.
PLUNK
ちまっ
AND YOU'RE PLANNING TO SLAUGHTER THE HUMANS LOOKING LIKE THAT?
I WILL RETURN TO NORMAL PRESENTLY.
FEEL FREE TO GO ON WITHOUT ME.

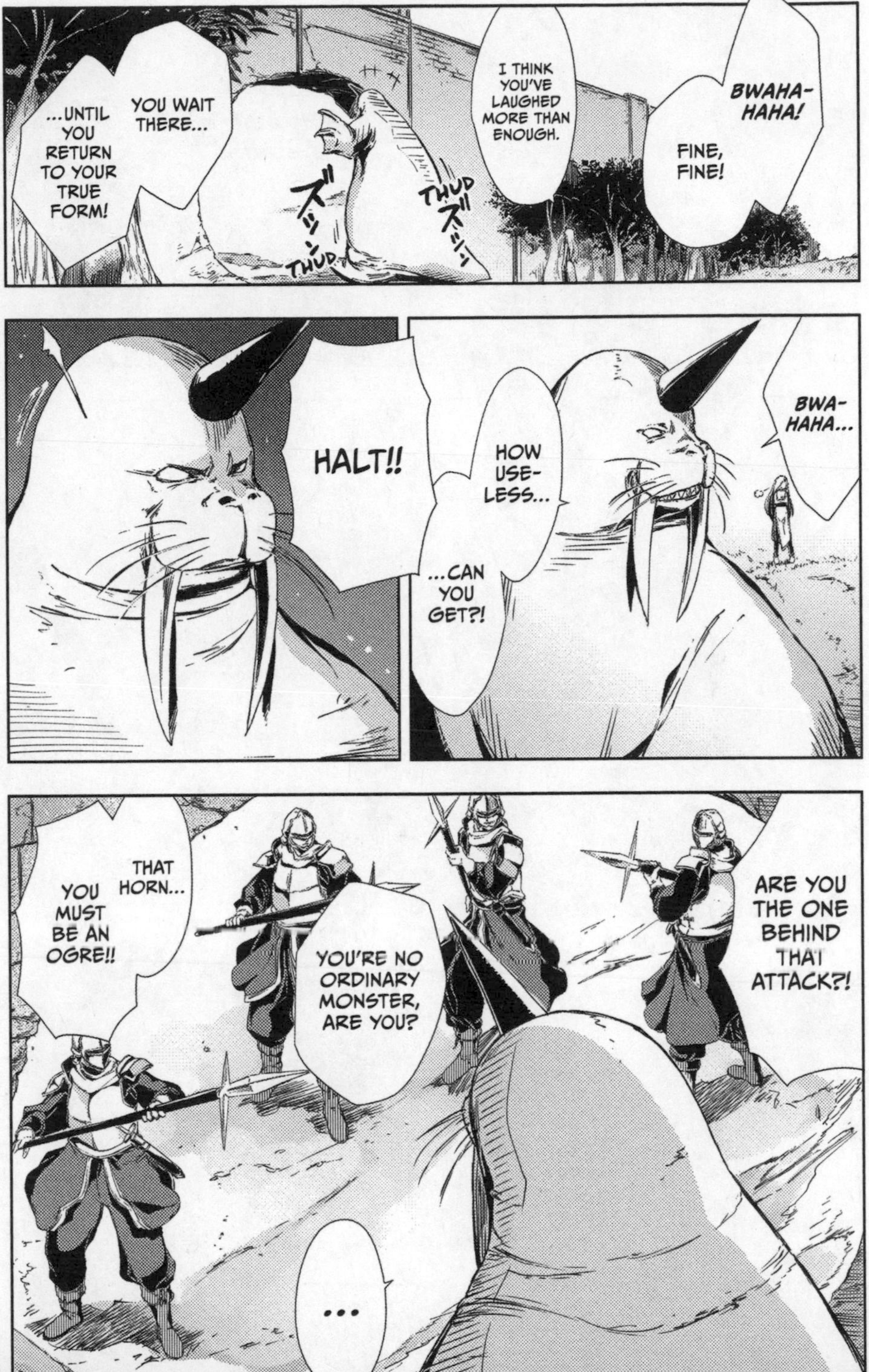
BWAHA-HAHA!
FINE, FINE!
I THINK YOU'VE LAUGHED MORE THAN ENOUGH.
THUD
THUD
YOU WAIT THERE...
...UNTIL YOU RETURN TO YOUR TRUE FORM!
BWAHA-HAHA...
HOW USELESS...
...CAN YOU GET?!
HALT!!
ARE YOU THE ONE BEHIND THAT ATTACK?!
YOU'RE NO ORDINARY MONSTER, ARE YOU?
THAT HORN...
YOU MUST BE AN OGRE!!
...

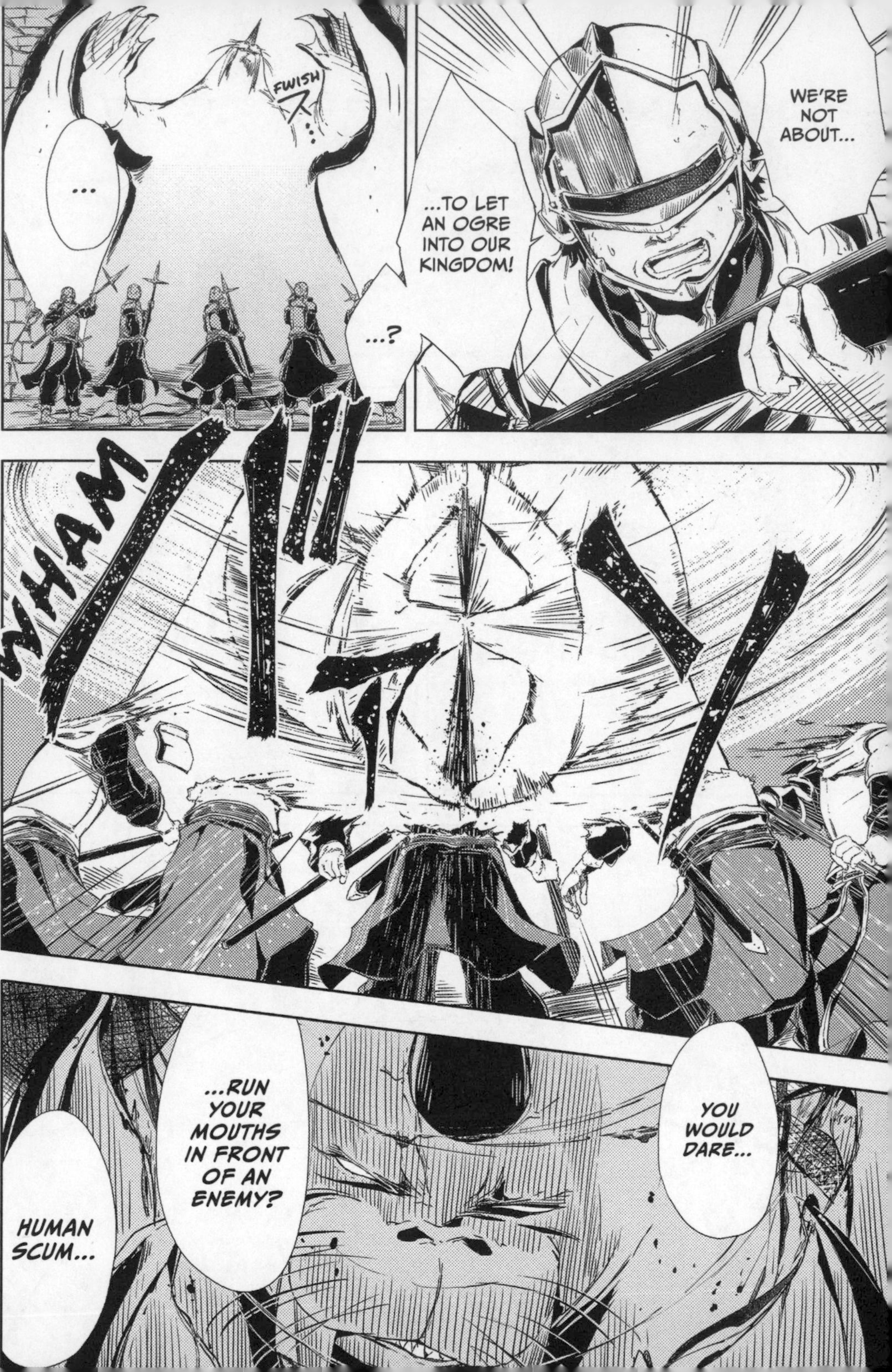
WE'RE NOT ABOUT...
...TO LET AN OGRE INTO OUR KINGDOM!
...?
FWISH
...
WHAM
YOU WOULD DARE...
...RUN YOUR MOUTHS IN FRONT OF AN ENEMY?
HUMAN SCUM...

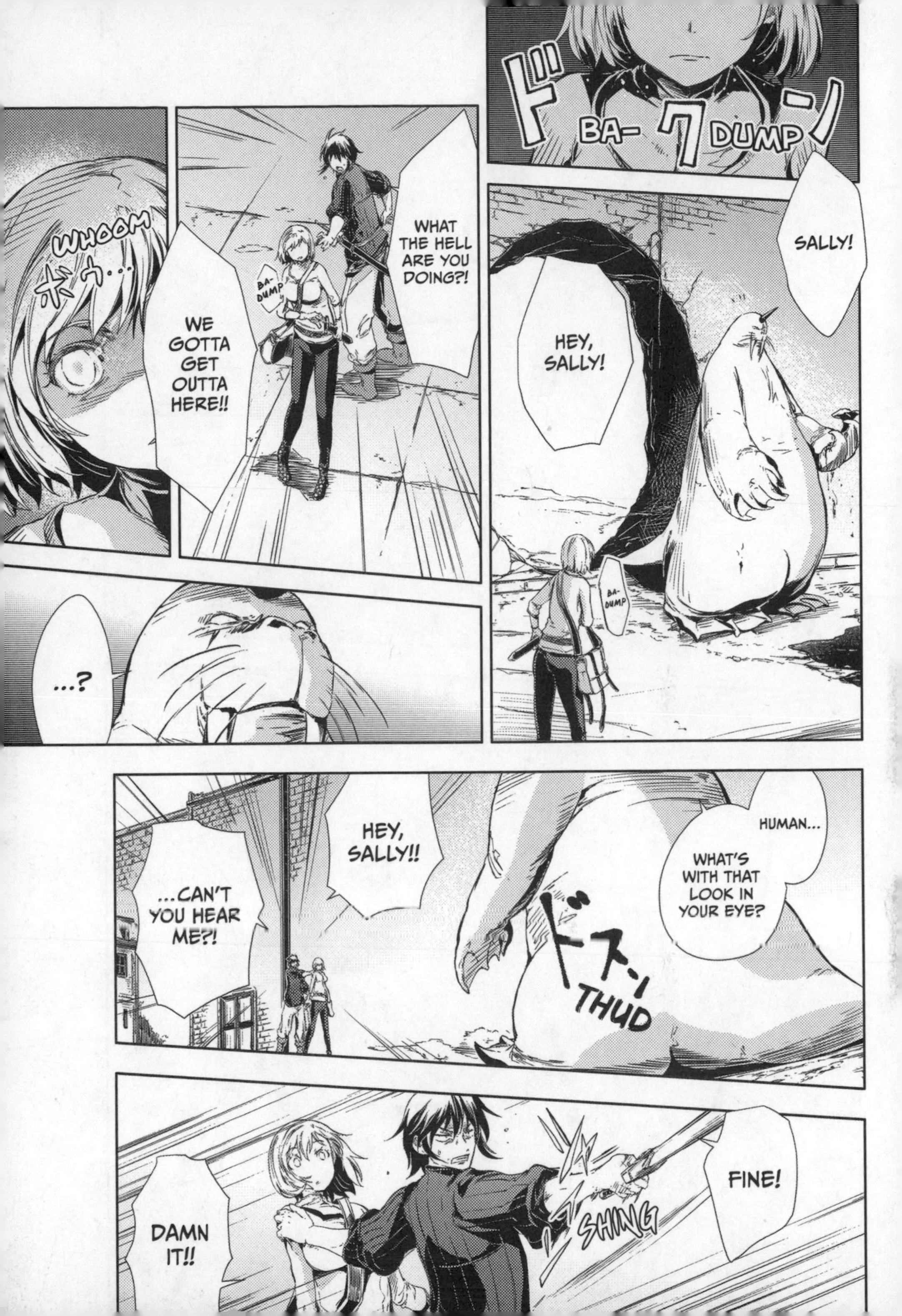
ド
BA-
ク
DUMP
ン
WHAT THE HELL ARE YOU DOING?!
BA-DUMP
WE GOTTA GET OUTTA HERE!!
WHOOM
ボウ…
SALLY!
HEY, SALLY!
BA-DUMP
...?
HUMAN...
WHAT'S WITH THAT LOOK IN YOUR EYE?
ドスーン
THUD
HEY, SALLY!!
...CAN'T YOU HEAR ME?!
FINE!
SHING
DAMN IT!!

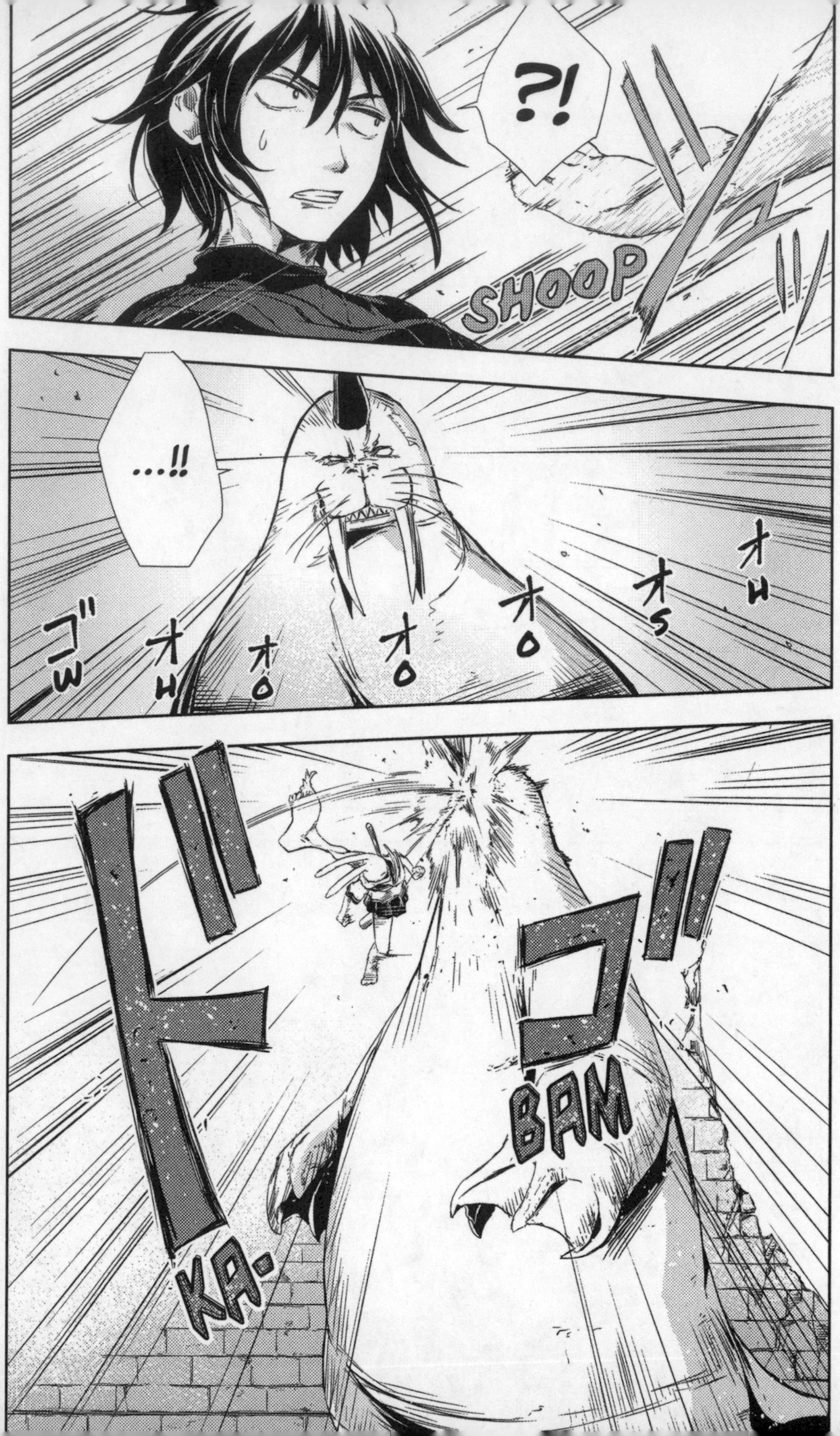
?!
SHOOP
...!!
WHOOOSH
ドゴ
KA-
BAM

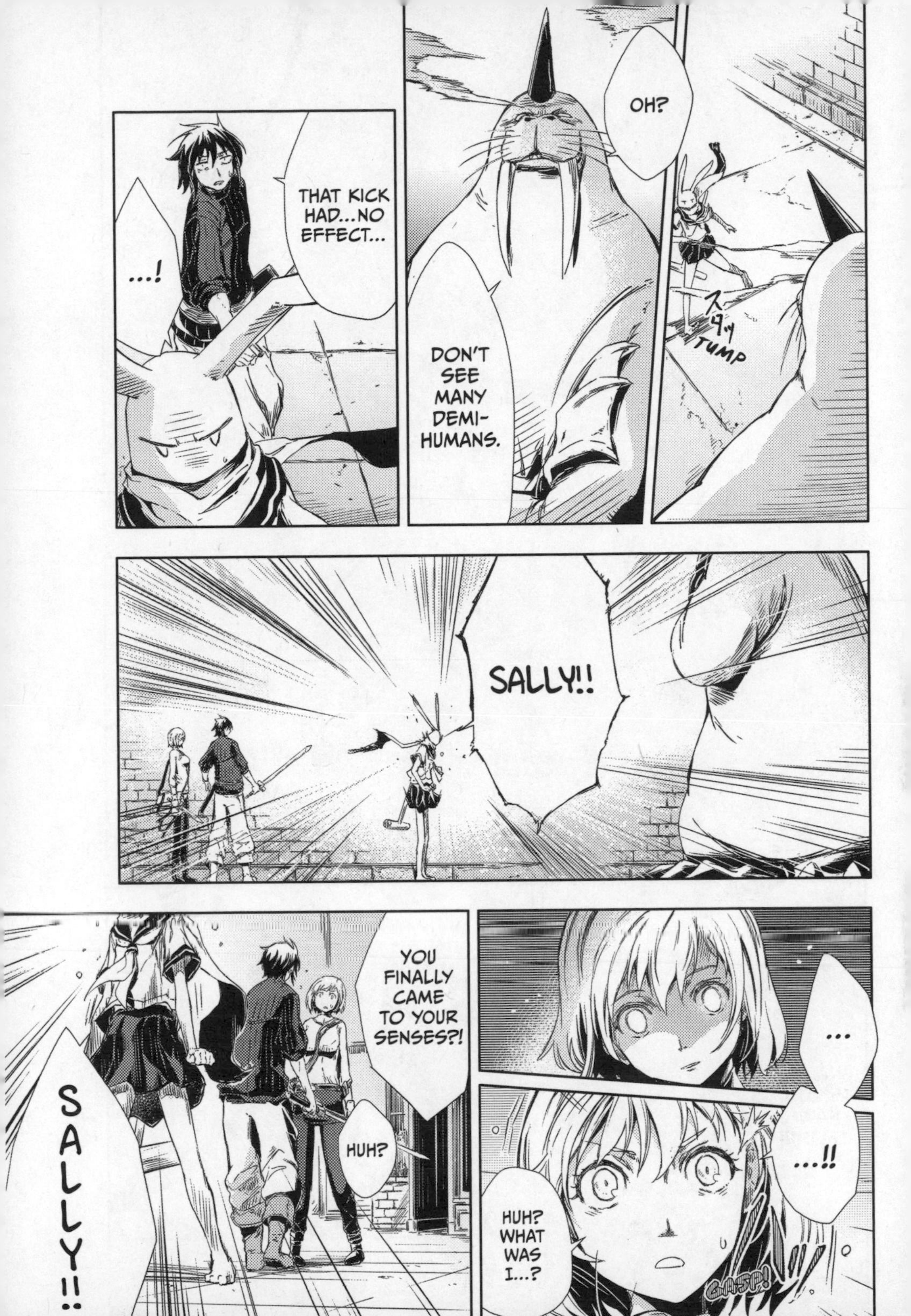

TUMP
OH?
DON'T SEE MANY DEMI-HUMANS.
THAT KICK HAD...NO EFFECT...
...!
SALLY!!
...
...!!
HUH? WHAT WAS I...?
YOU FINALLY CAME TO YOUR SENSES?!
HUH?
SALLY!!

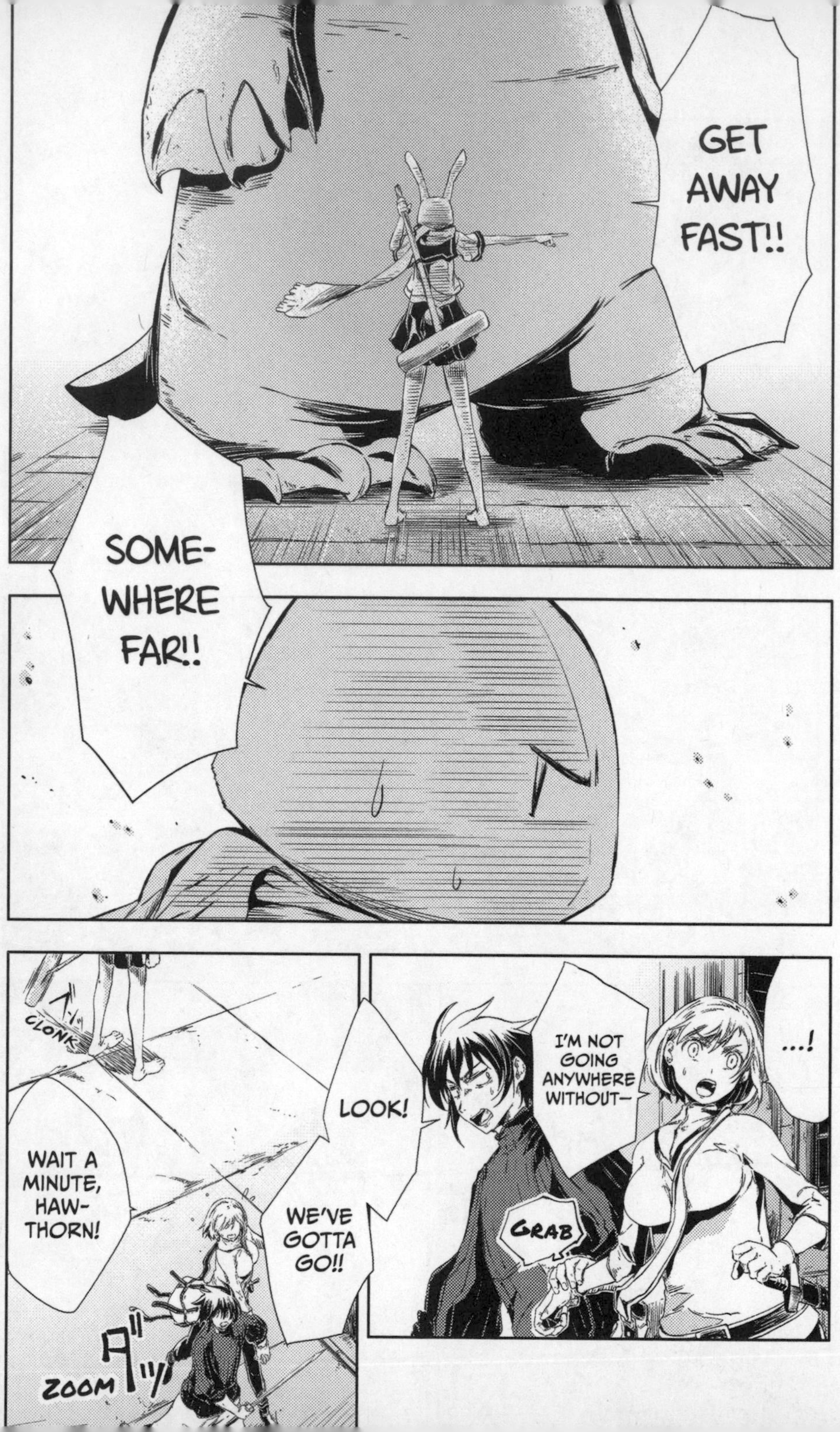
GET AWAY FAST!!
SOME-WHERE FAR!!
...!
I'M NOT GOING ANYWHERE WITHOUT—
LOOK!
WE'VE GOTTA GO!!
GRAB
CLONK
WAIT A MINUTE, HAW-THORN!
ZOOM

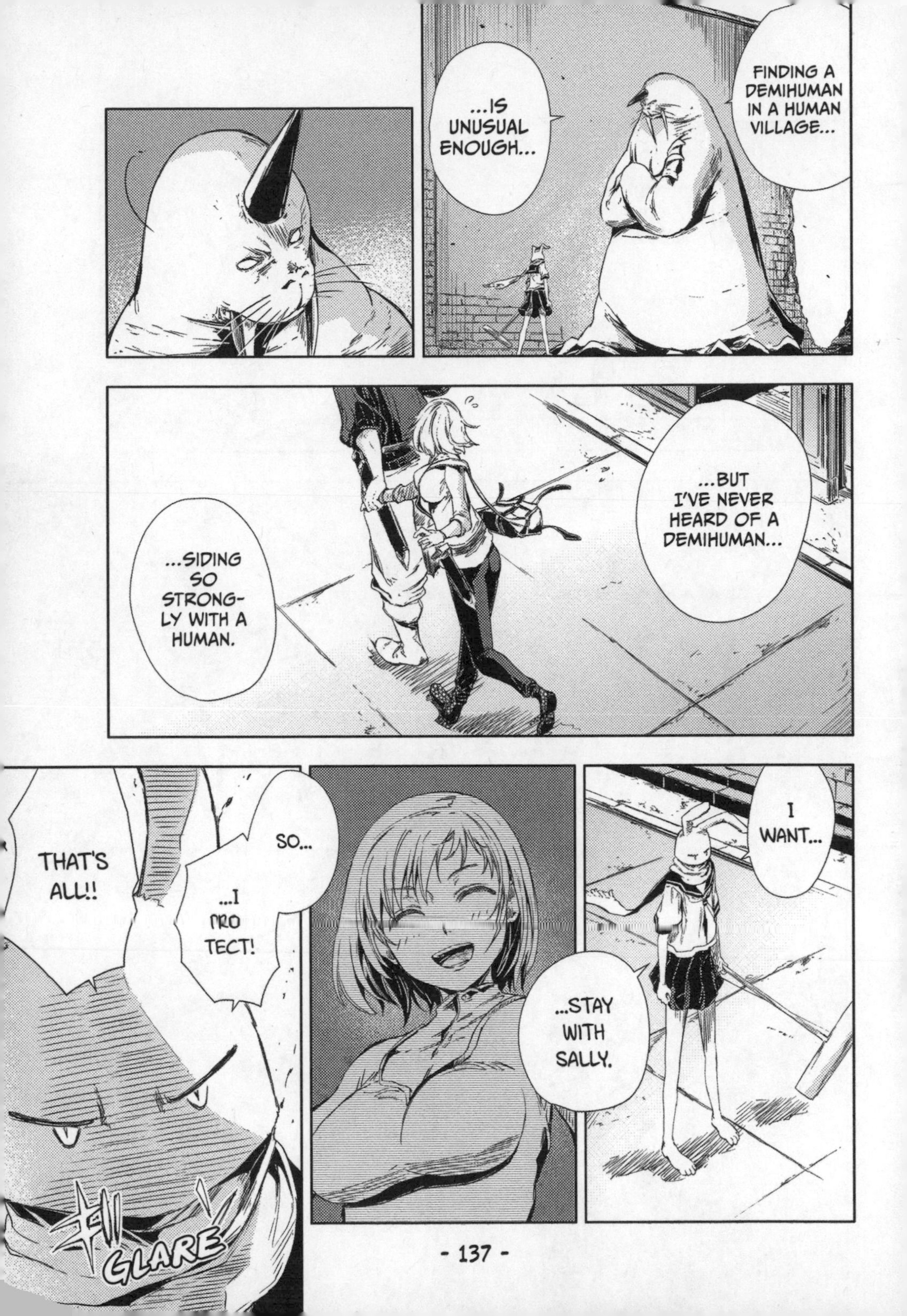
FINDING A DEMIHUMAN IN A HUMAN VILLAGE...
...IS UNUSUAL ENOUGH...
...BUT I'VE NEVER HEARD OF A DEMIHUMAN...
...SIDING SO STRONG-LY WITH A HUMAN.
I WANT...
...STAY WITH SALLY.
SO...
...I PRO TECT!
THAT'S ALL!!
GLARE

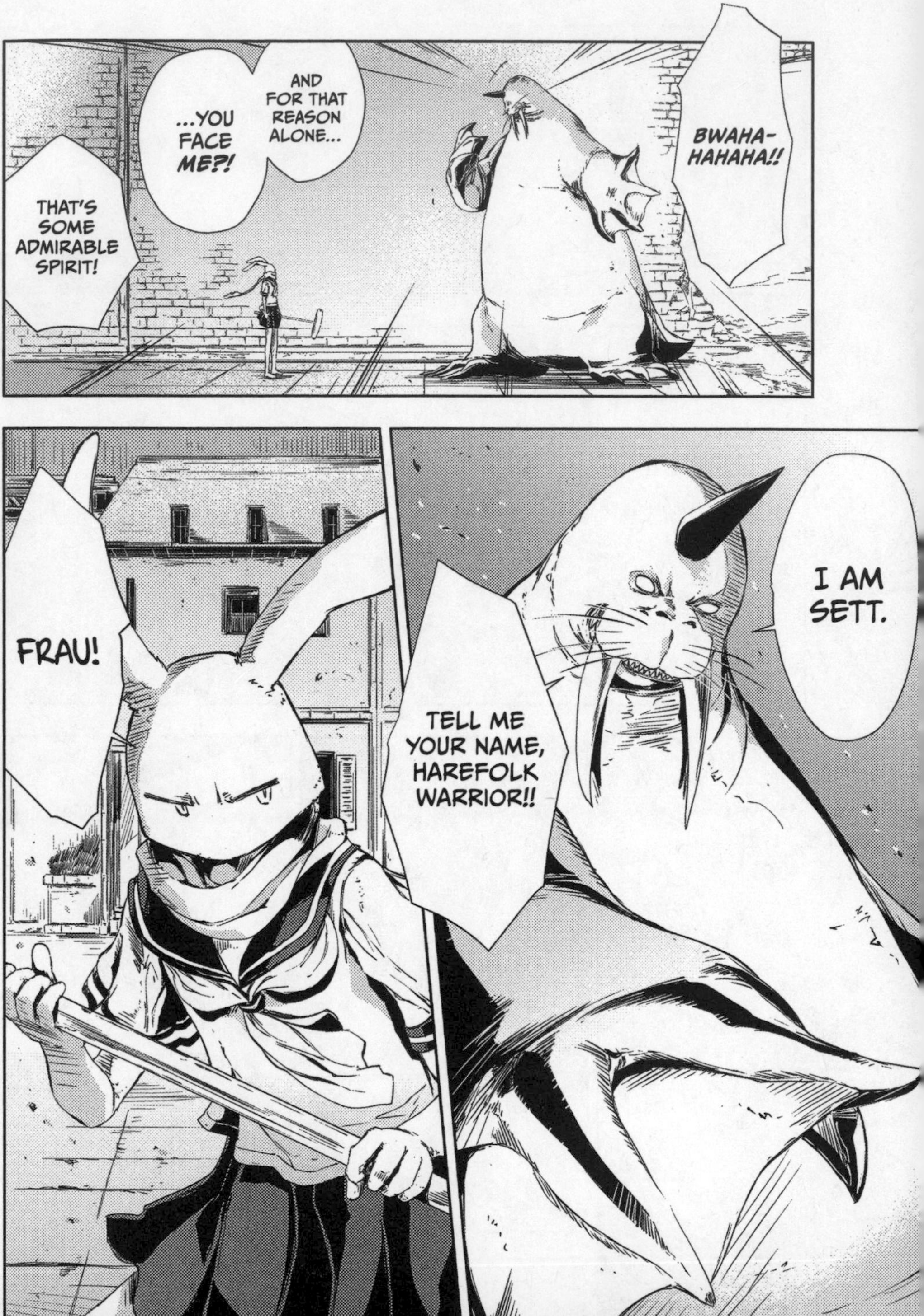
BWAHA-HAHAHA!!
AND FOR THAT REASON ALONE...
...YOU FACE ME?!
THAT'S SOME ADMIRABLE SPIRIT!
I AM SETT.
TELL ME YOUR NAME, HAREFOLK WARRIOR!!
FRAU!

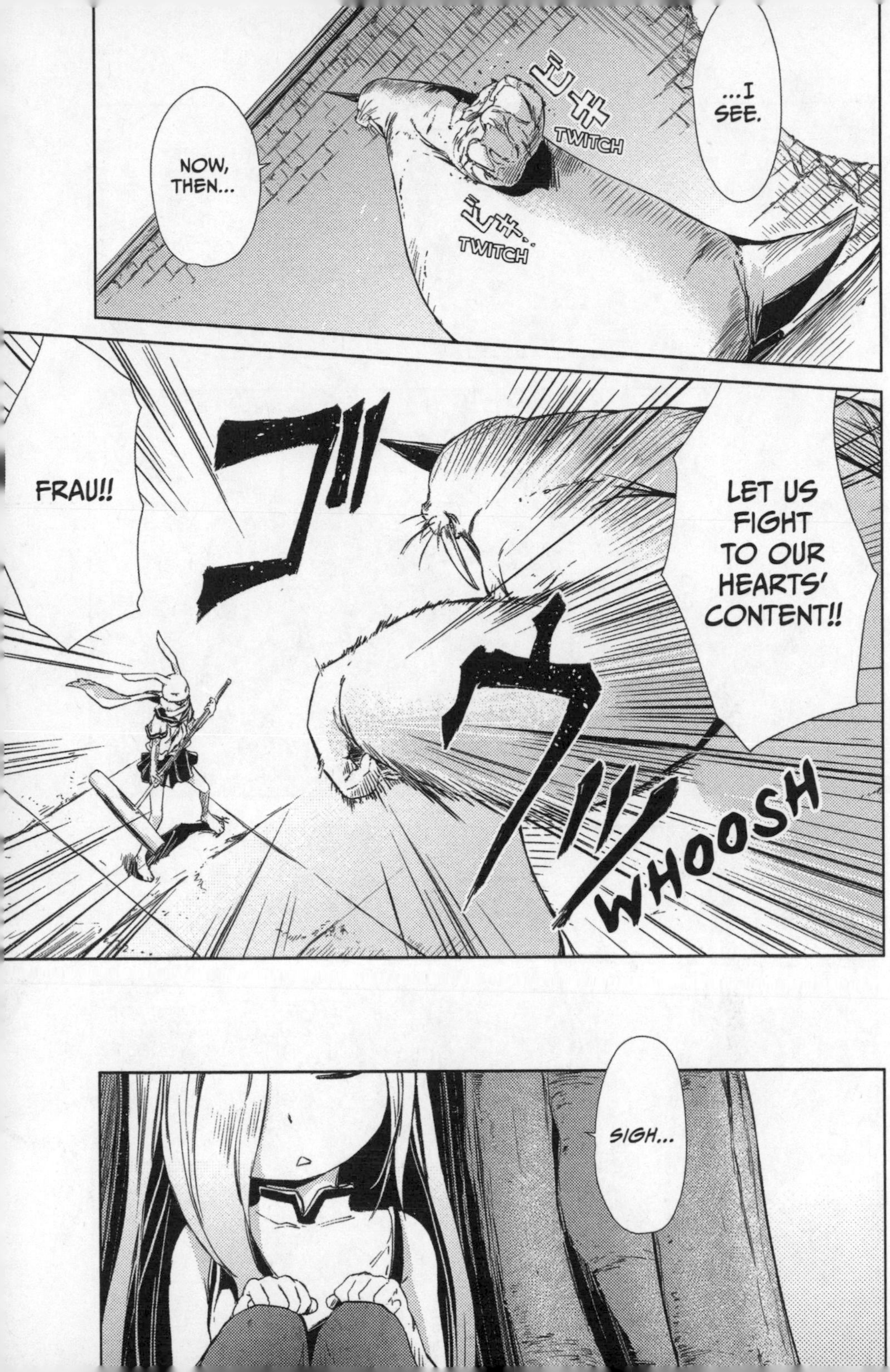
...I SEE.
TWITCH
TWITCH
NOW, THEN...
LET US FIGHT TO OUR HEARTS' CONTENT!!
WHOOSH
FRAU!!
SIGH...

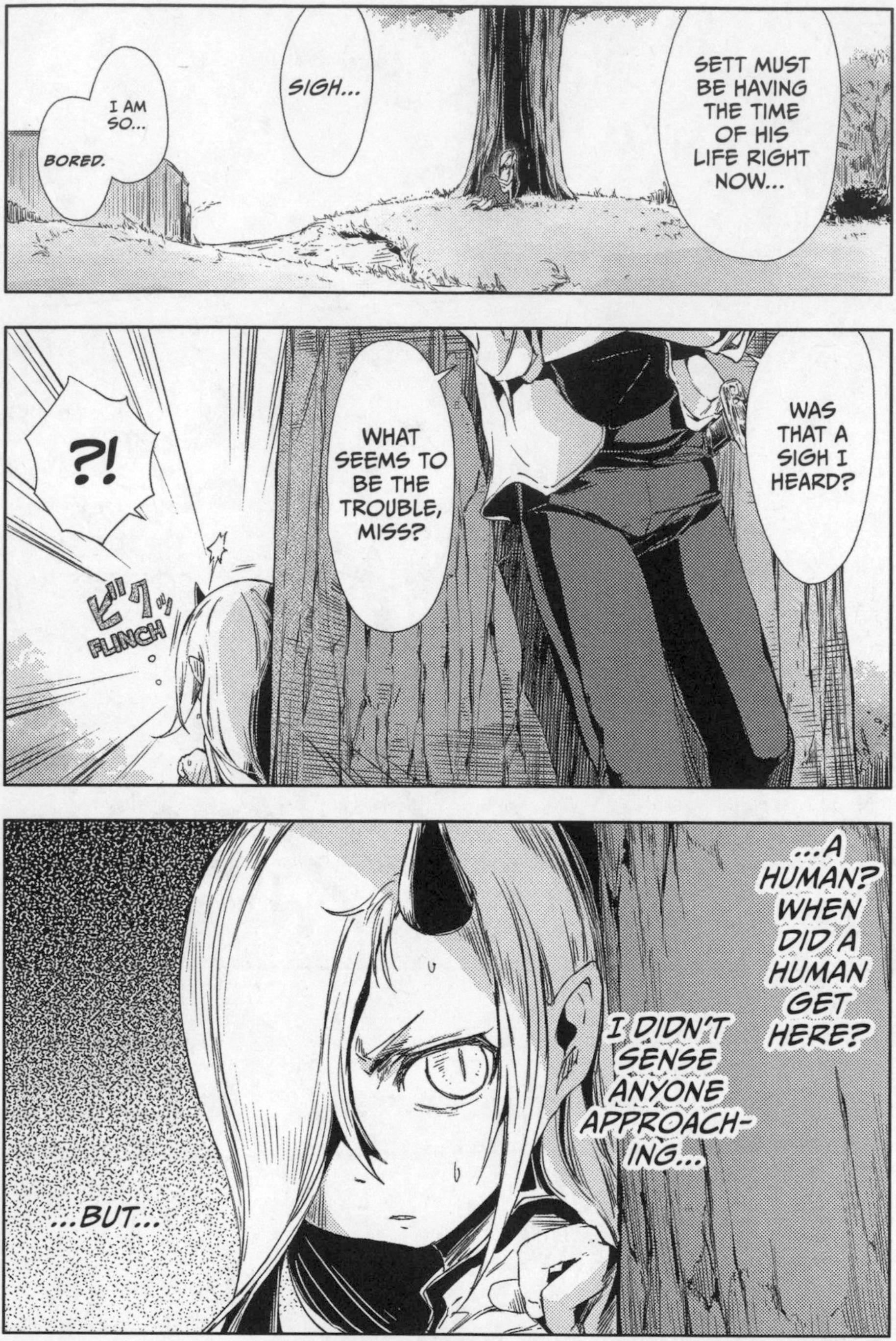
SETT MUST BE HAVING THE TIME OF HIS LIFE RIGHT NOW...
SIGH...
I AM SO...
BORED.
WAS THAT A SIGH I HEARD?
WHAT SEEMS TO BE THE TROUBLE, MISS?
?!
ビクッ
FLINCH
...A HUMAN? WHEN DID A HUMAN GET HERE?
I DIDN'T SENSE ANYONE APPROACH-ING...
...BUT...

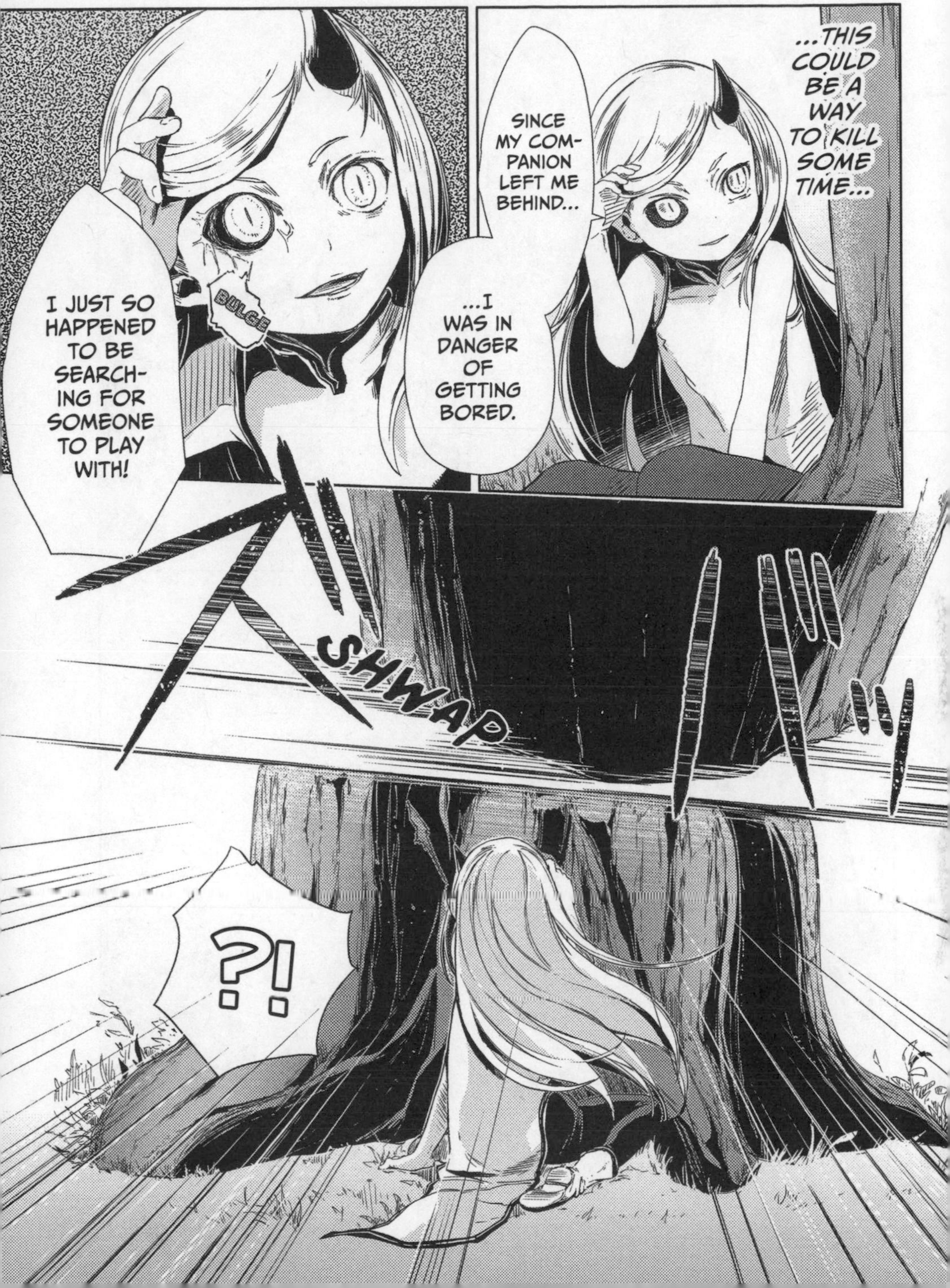
...THIS COULD BE A WAY TO KILL SOME TIME...
SINCE MY COM-PANION LEFT ME BEHIND...
...I WAS IN DANGER OF GETTING BORED.
I JUST SO HAPPENED TO BE SEARCH-ING FOR SOMEONE TO PLAY WITH!
BULGE
SHWAP
?!

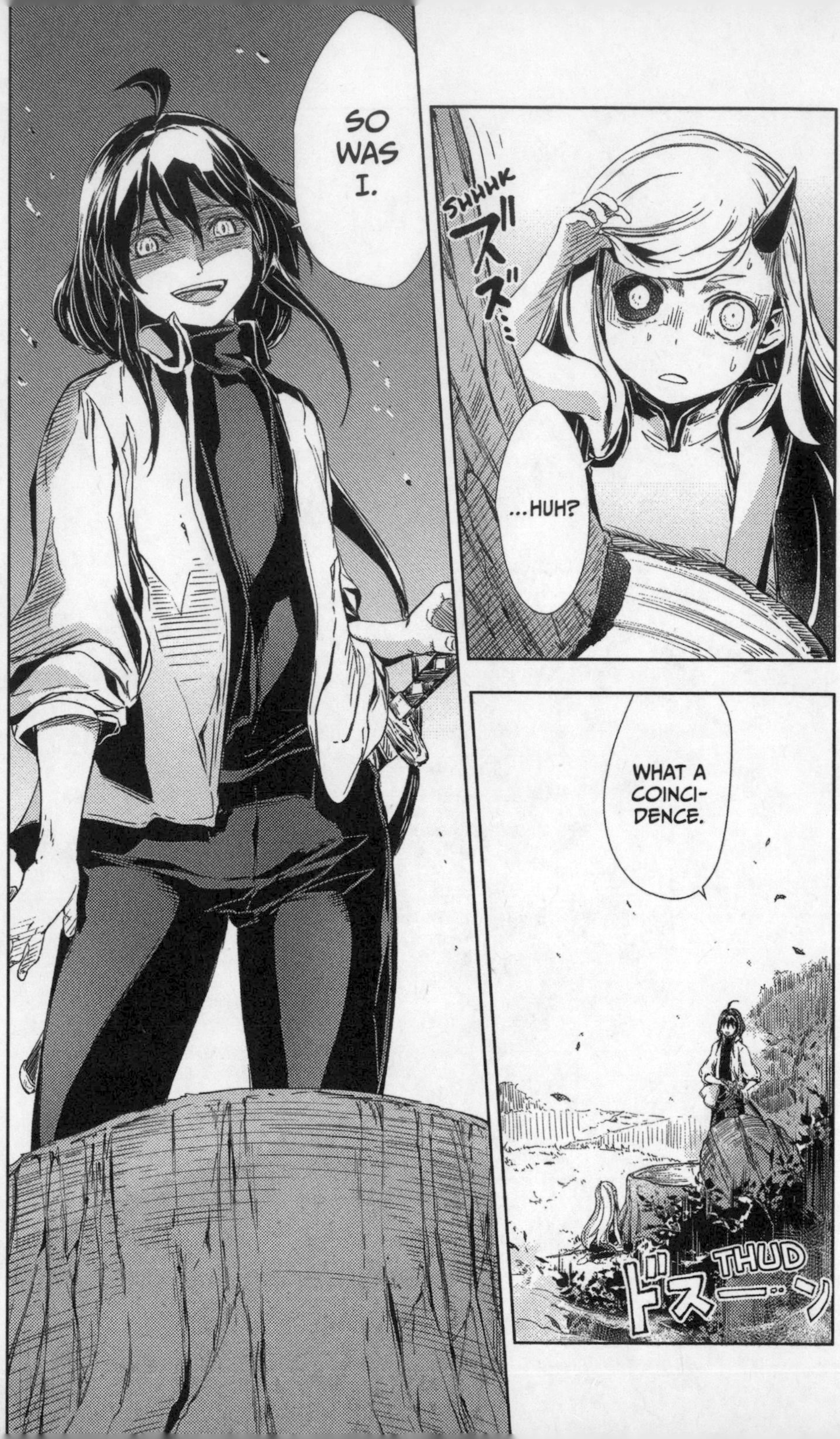
SHHUK
ズズ…
...HUH?
WHAT A COINCI-DENCE.
THUD
ドスーン
SO WAS I.

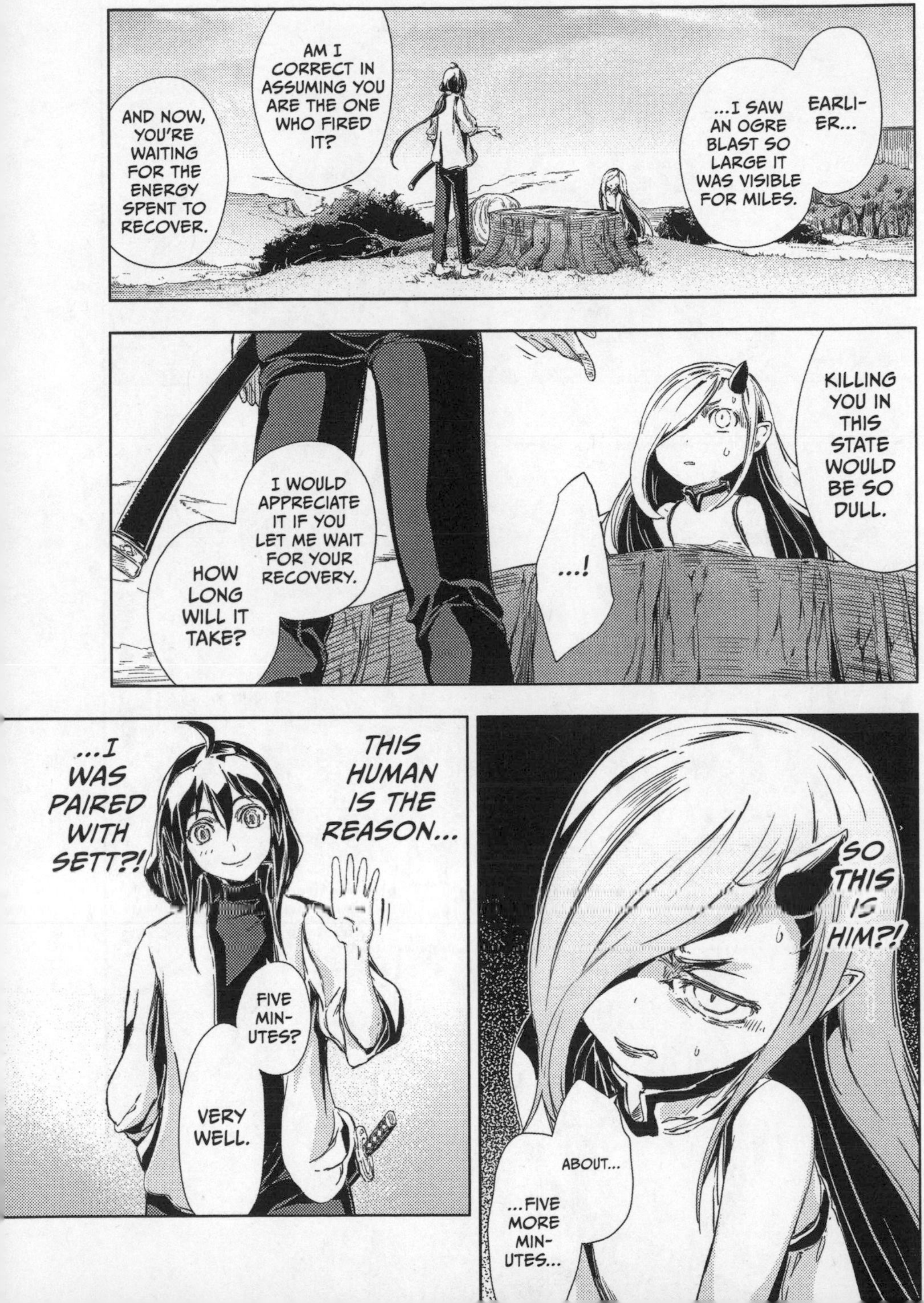
EARLIER...
...I SAW AN OGRE BLAST SO LARGE IT WAS VISIBLE FOR MILES.
AM I CORRECT IN ASSUMING YOU ARE THE ONE WHO FIRED IT?
AND NOW, YOU'RE WAITING FOR THE ENERGY SPENT TO RECOVER.
KILLING YOU IN THIS STATE WOULD BE SO DULL.
...!
I WOULD APPRECIATE IT IF YOU LET ME WAIT FOR YOUR RECOVERY.
HOW LONG WILL IT TAKE?
SO THIS IS HIM?!
ABOUT...
...FIVE MORE MIN-UTES...
THIS HUMAN IS THE REASON...
...I WAS PAIRED WITH SETT?!
FIVE MIN-UTES?
VERY WELL.

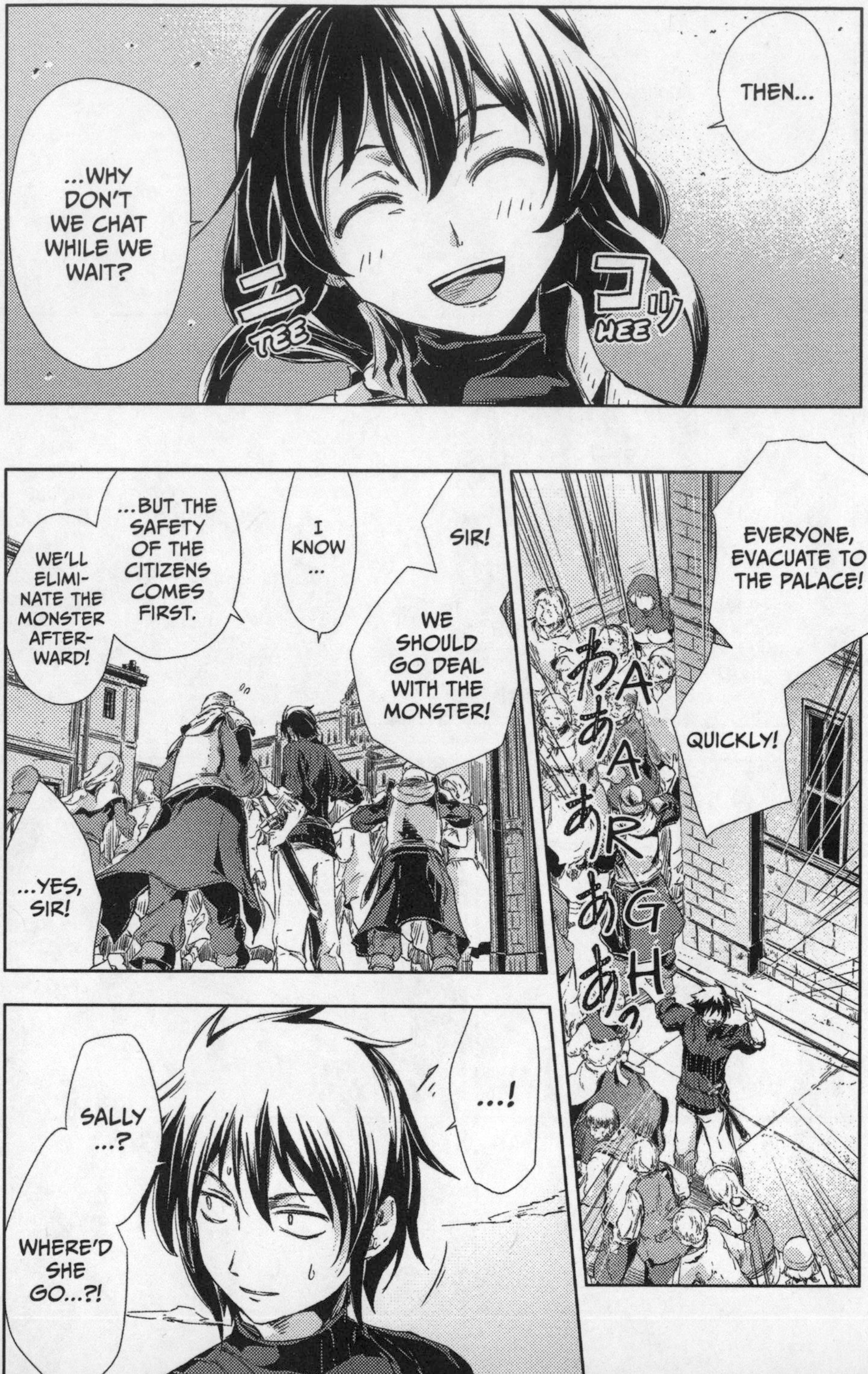
THEN...
...WHY DON'T WE CHAT WHILE WE WAIT?
ニ TEE
コッ HEE
EVERYONE, EVACUATE TO THE PALACE!
QUICKLY!
わあああああっ AARGH
SIR!
WE SHOULD GO DEAL WITH THE MONSTER!
I KNOW...
...BUT THE SAFETY OF THE CITIZENS COMES FIRST.
WE'LL ELIMINATE THE MONSTER AFTERWARD!
...YES, SIR!
...!
SALLY...?
WHERE'D SHE GO...?!

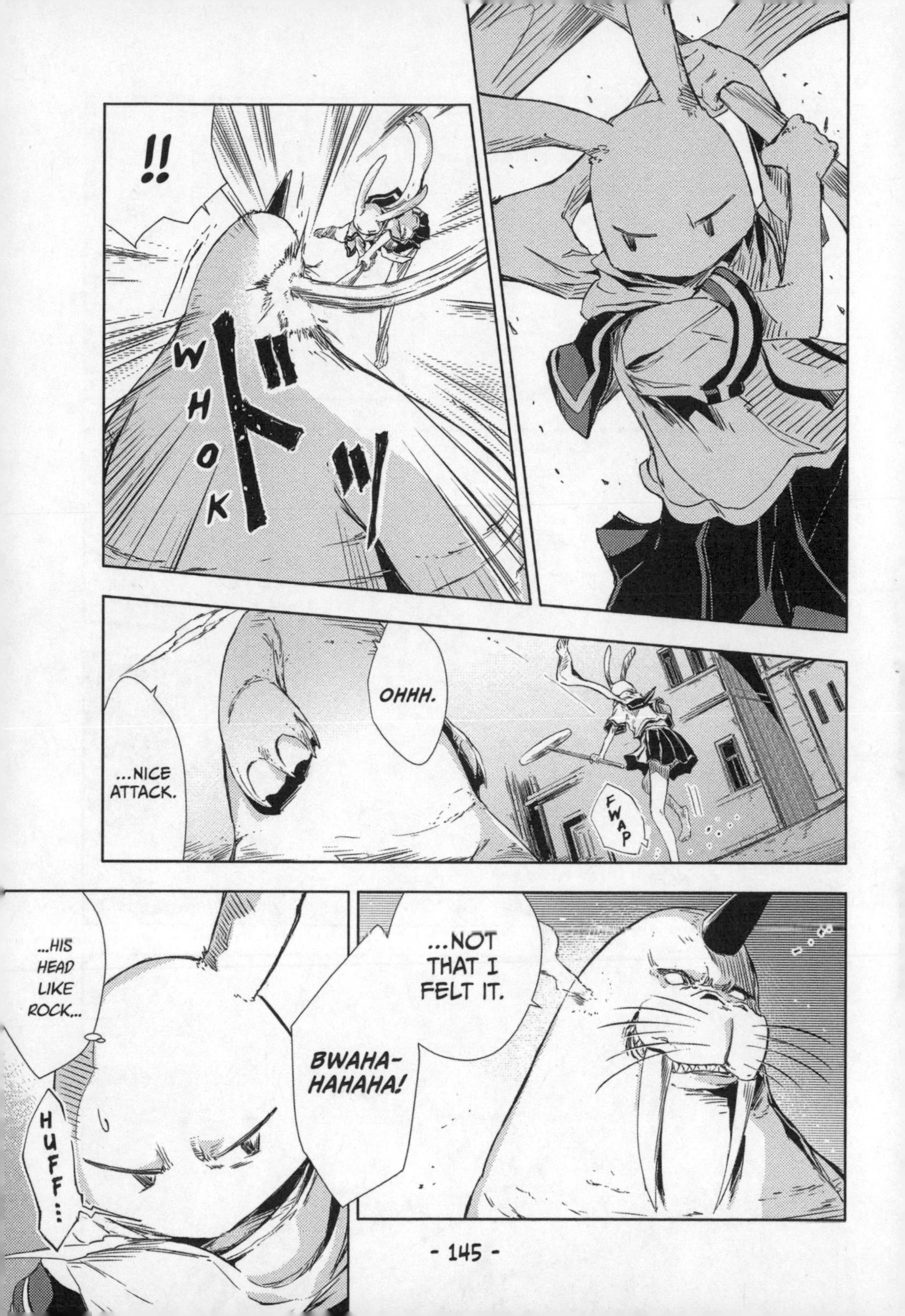
!!
WHOK
FWAP
OHHH.
...NICE ATTACK.
...NOT THAT I FELT IT.
BWAHA-HAHAHA!
...HIS HEAD LIKE ROCK...
HUFF...

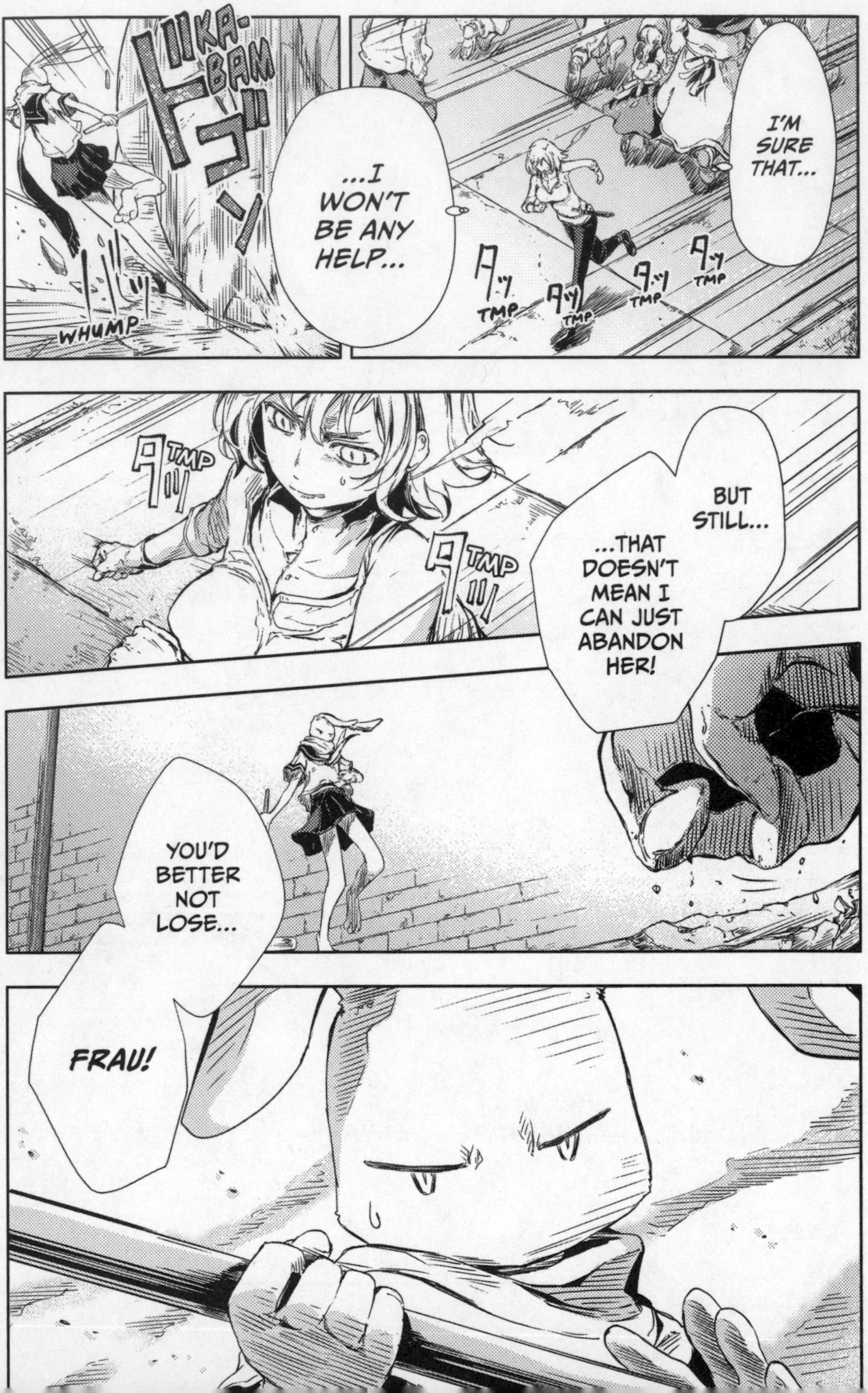
I'M SURE THAT...
...I WON'T BE ANY HELP...
TMP
TMP
TMP
TMP
KA-BAM
WHUMP
BUT STILL...
...THAT DOESN'T MEAN I CAN JUST ABANDON HER!
TMP
TMP
YOU'D BETTER NOT LOSE...
FRAU!

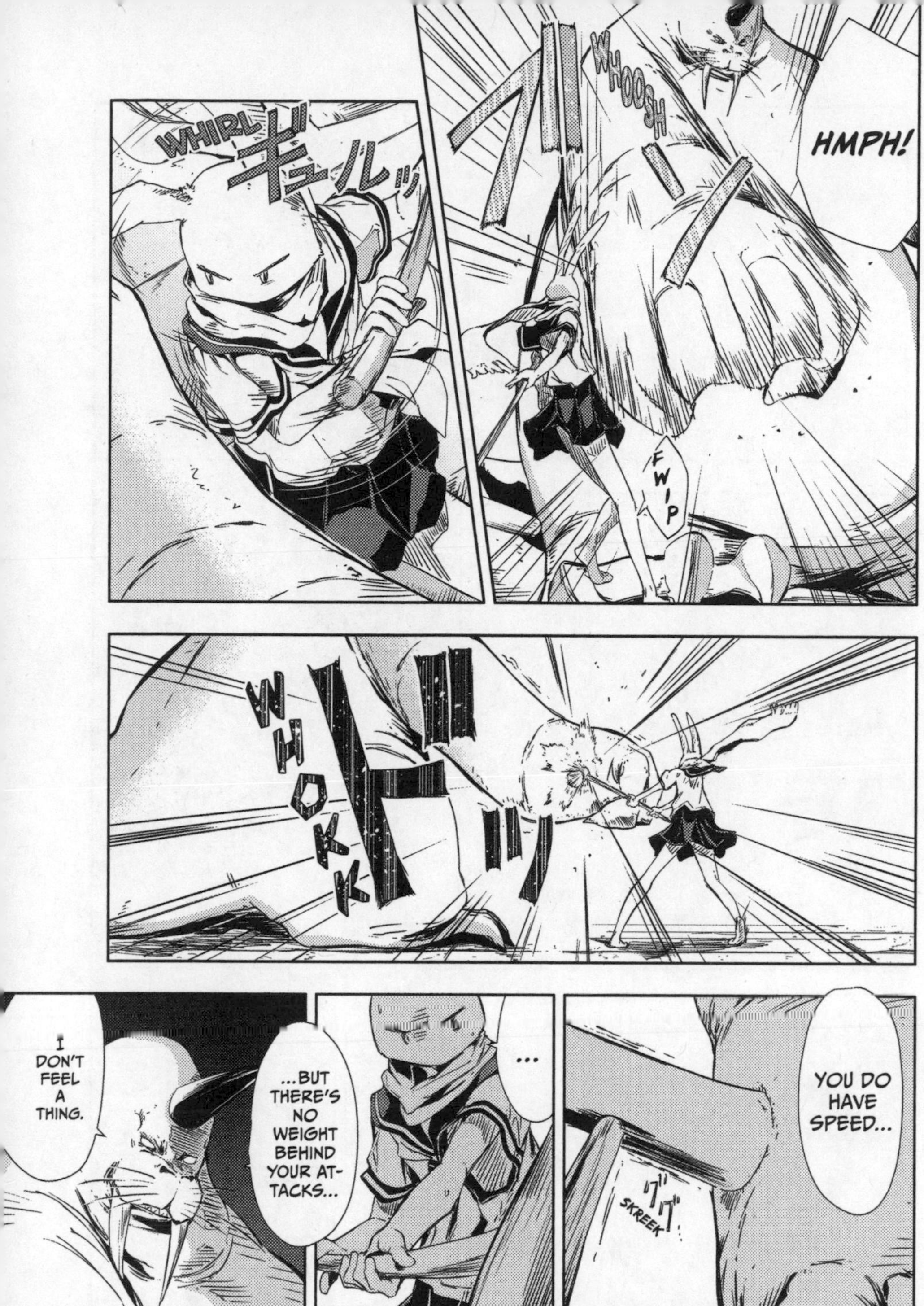
HMPH!
WHOOSH
FWIP
WHIRL
WHOKK
YOU DO HAVE SPEED...
SKREEK
...
...BUT THERE'S NO WEIGHT BEHIND YOUR AT-TACKS...
I DON'T FEEL A THING.

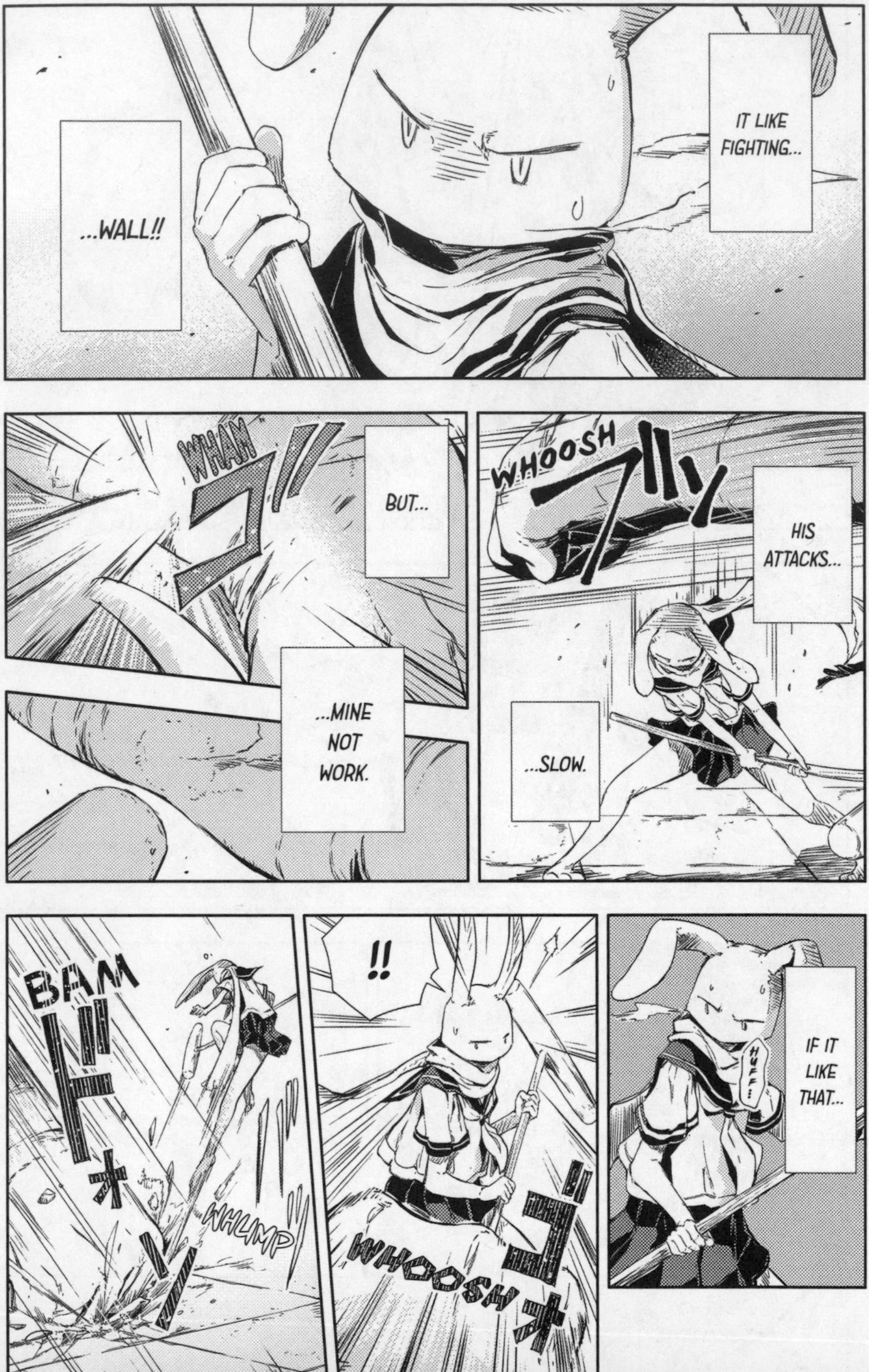
IT LIKE FIGHTING...
...WALL!!
WHOOSH
HIS ATTACKS...
...SLOW.
WHAM
BUT...
...MINE NOT WORK.
HUFF!!
IF IT LIKE THAT...
!!
WHOOSH
BAM
WHUMP

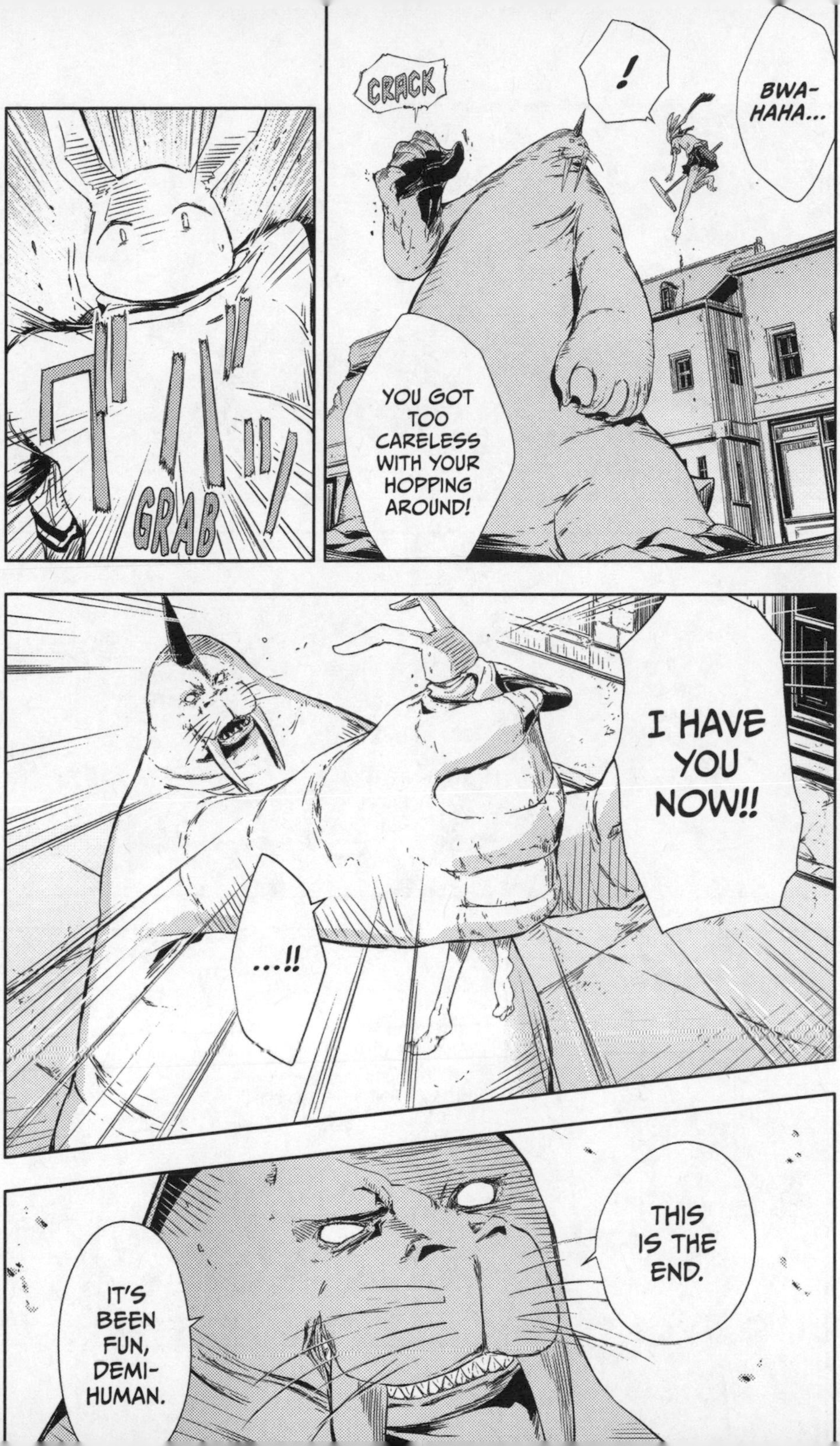
BWA-HAHA...
!
CRACK
YOU GOT TOO CARELESS WITH YOUR HOPPING AROUND!
GRAB
I HAVE YOU NOW!!
...!!
THIS IS THE END.
IT'S BEEN FUN, DEMI-HUMAN.

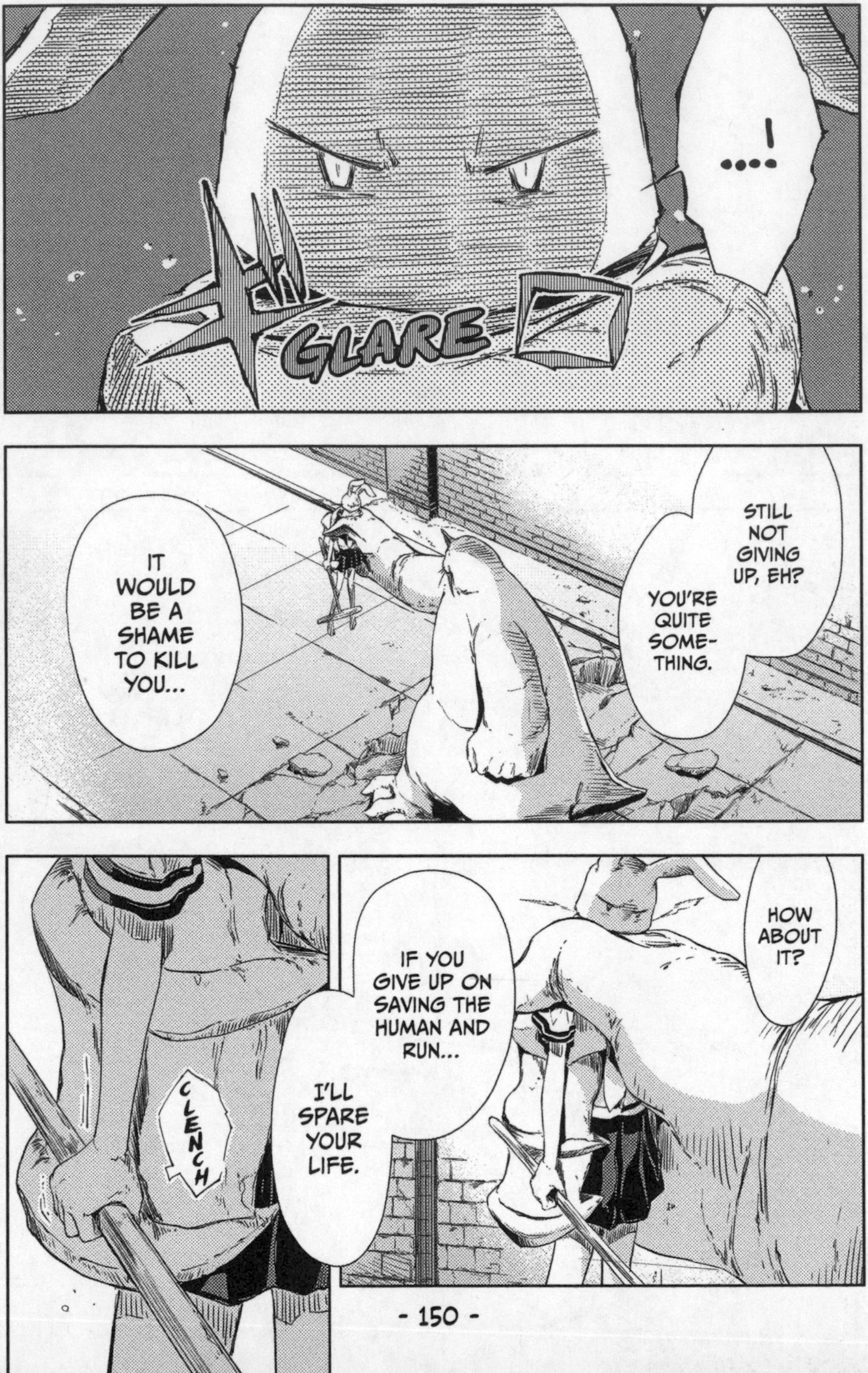
...!
GLARE
STILL NOT GIVING UP, EH?
YOU'RE QUITE SOME-THING.
IT WOULD BE A SHAME TO KILL YOU...
HOW ABOUT IT?
IF YOU GIVE UP ON SAVING THE HUMAN AND RUN...
I'LL SPARE YOUR LIFE.
CLENCH

FRAU!
WHAM
WHAM
PRO-TECT!
SALLY!
WON'T RUN!!
HUFF!
...
THAT'S THE SPIRIT.
VERY WELL.
IN THAT CASE ...!!
WHOOSH
?!

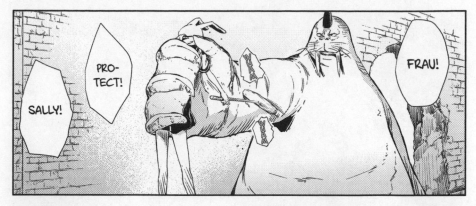

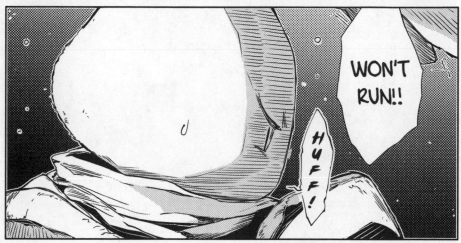

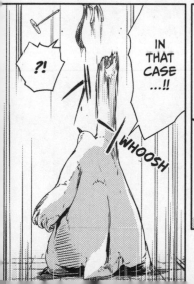

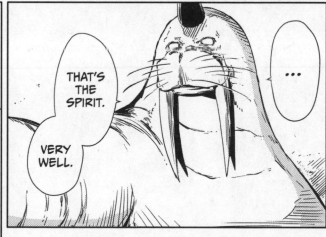

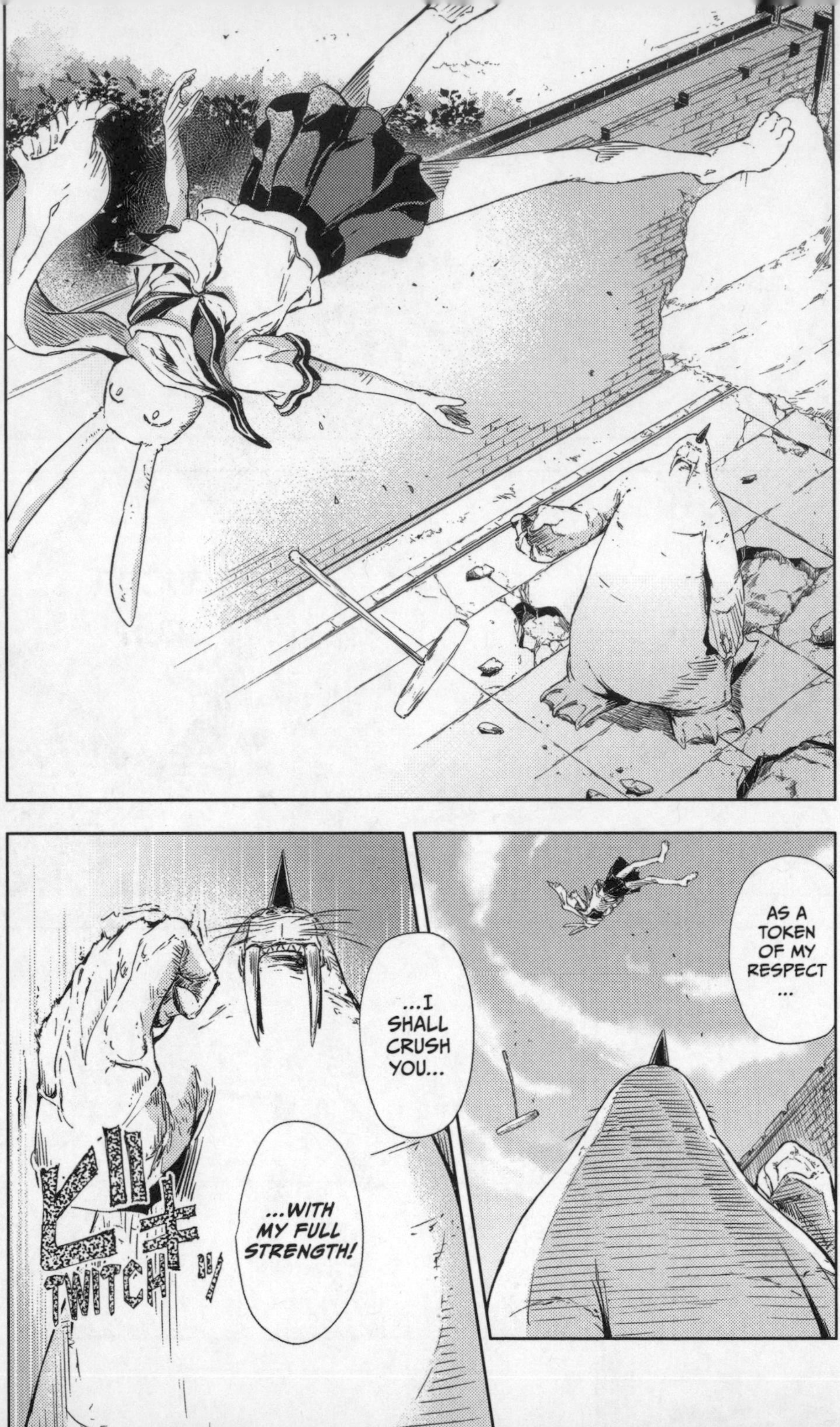
AS A TOKEN OF MY RESPECT...
...I SHALL CRUSH YOU...
...WITH MY FULL STRENGTH!
TWITCH

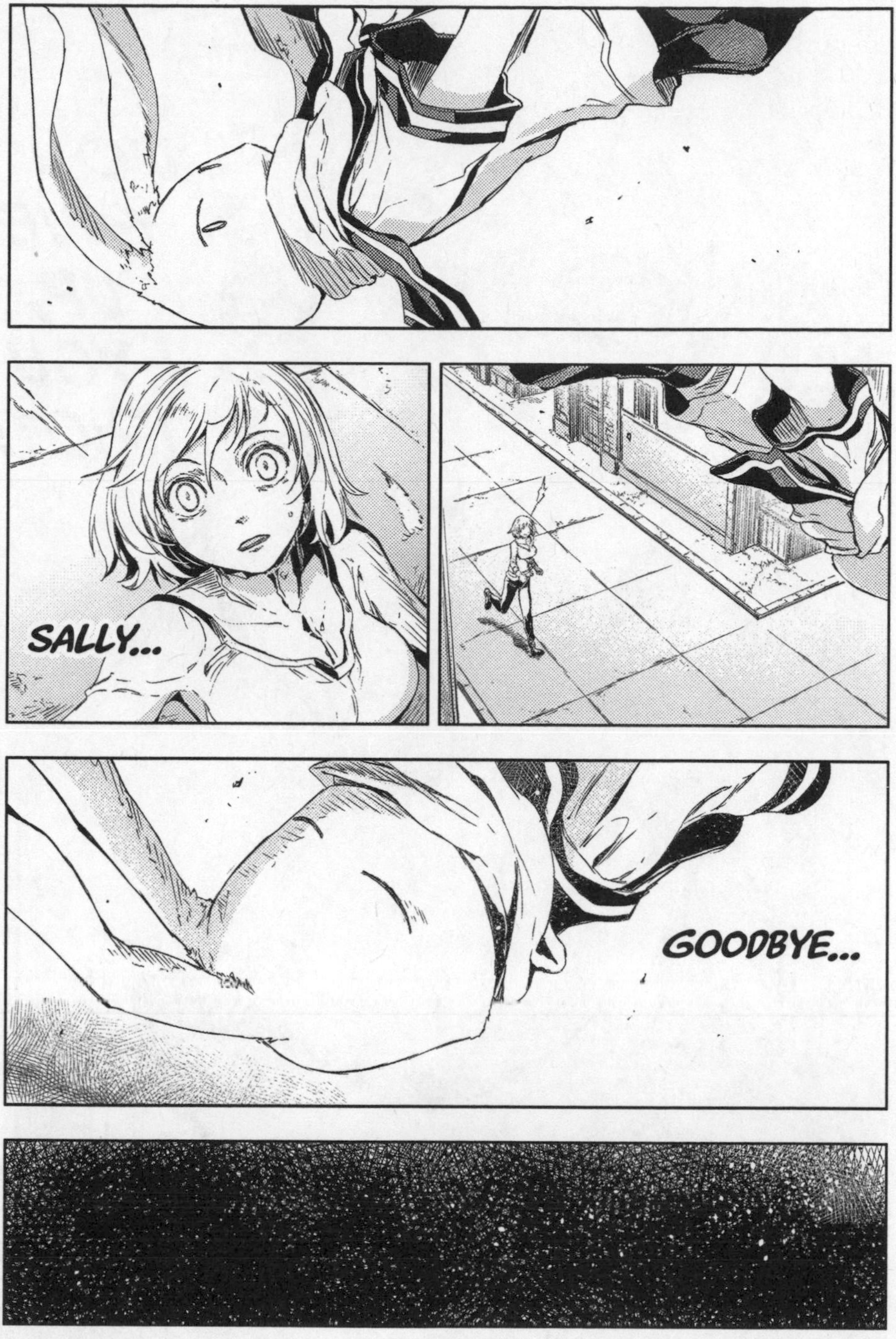
SALLY...
GOODBYE...

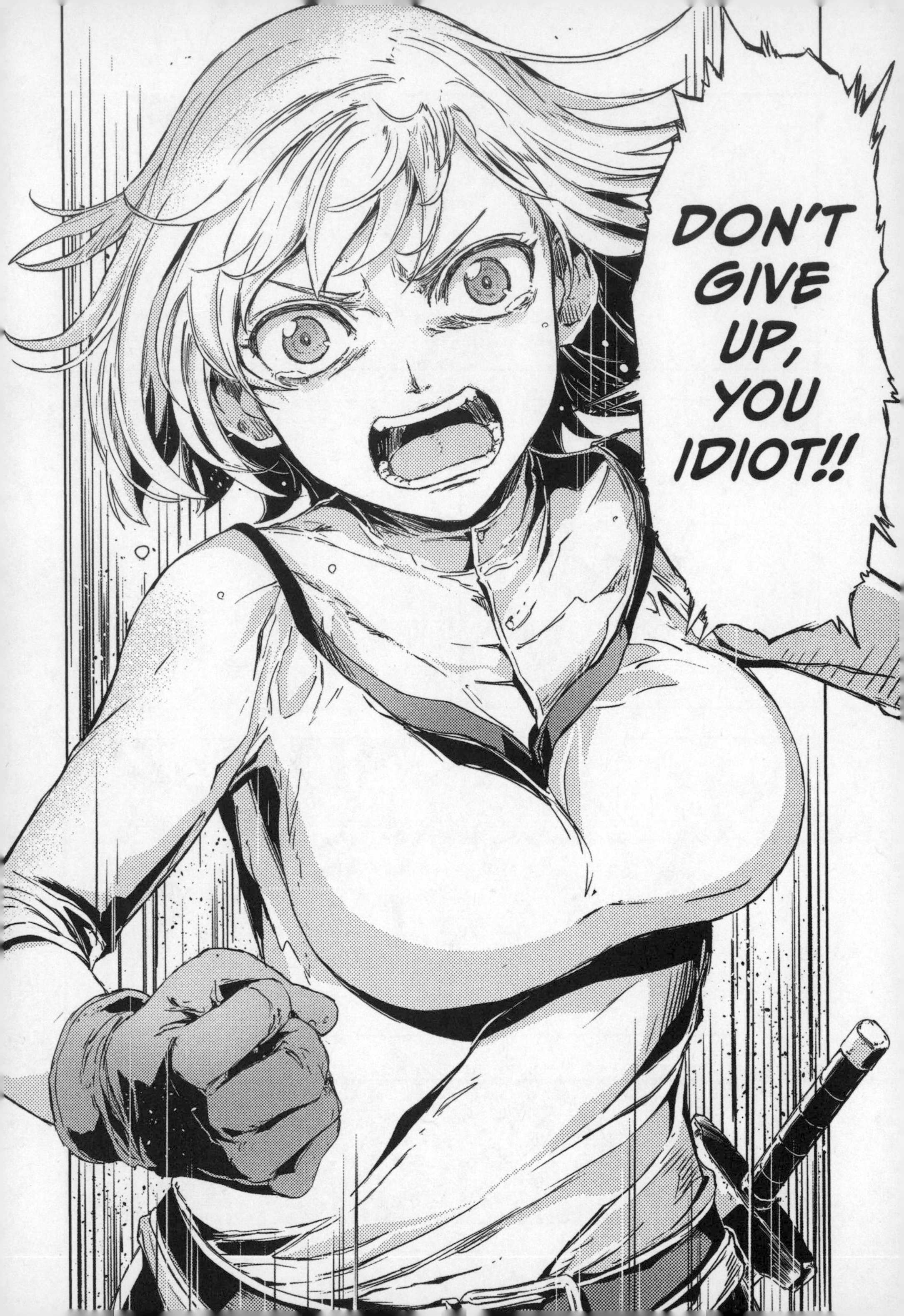
DON'T GIVE UP, YOU IDIOT!!

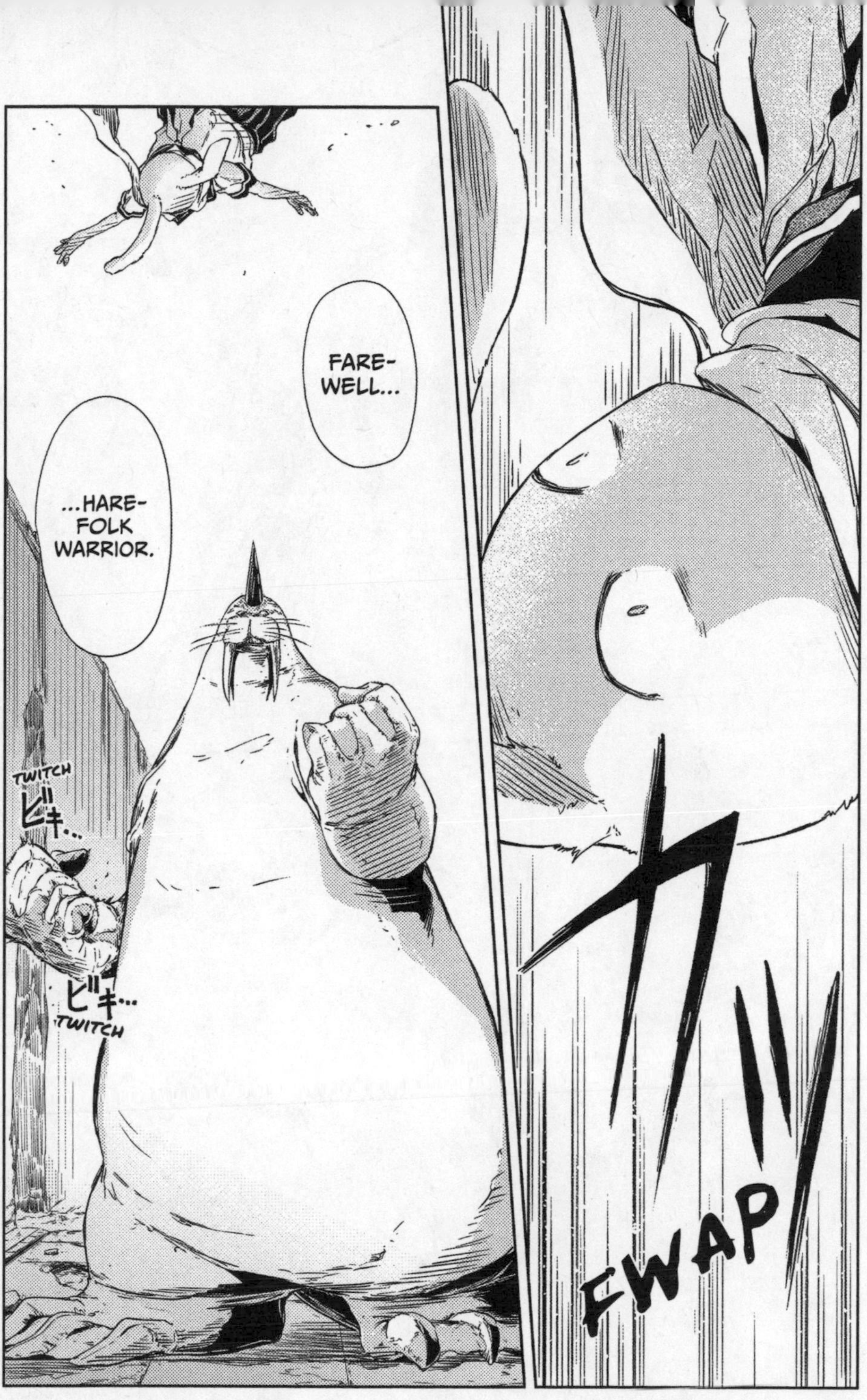
FWAP
FARE-WELL...
...HARE-FOLK WARRIOR.
TWITCH
ビキ...
ビキ...
TWITCH

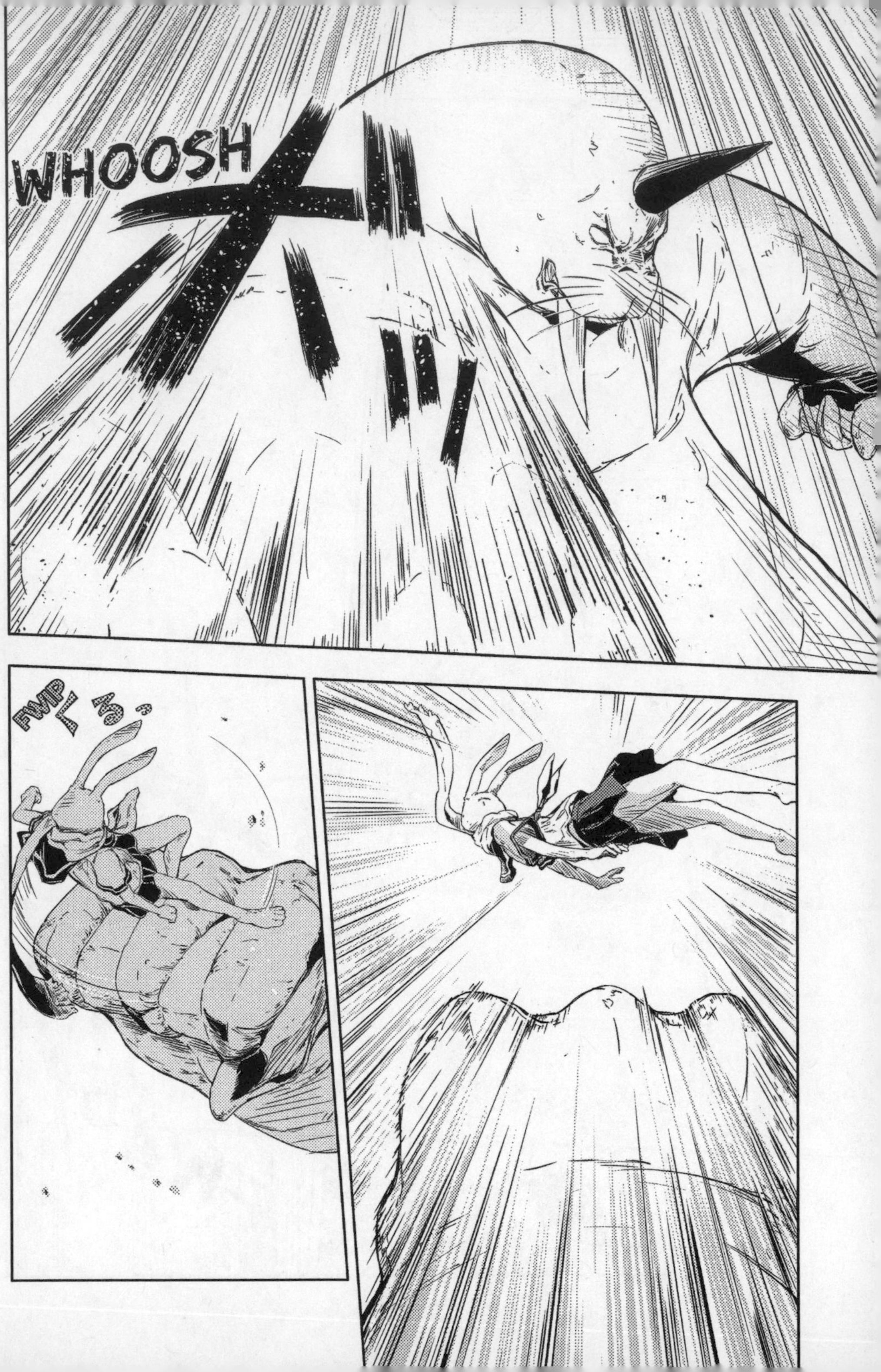
WHOOSH
FWIP

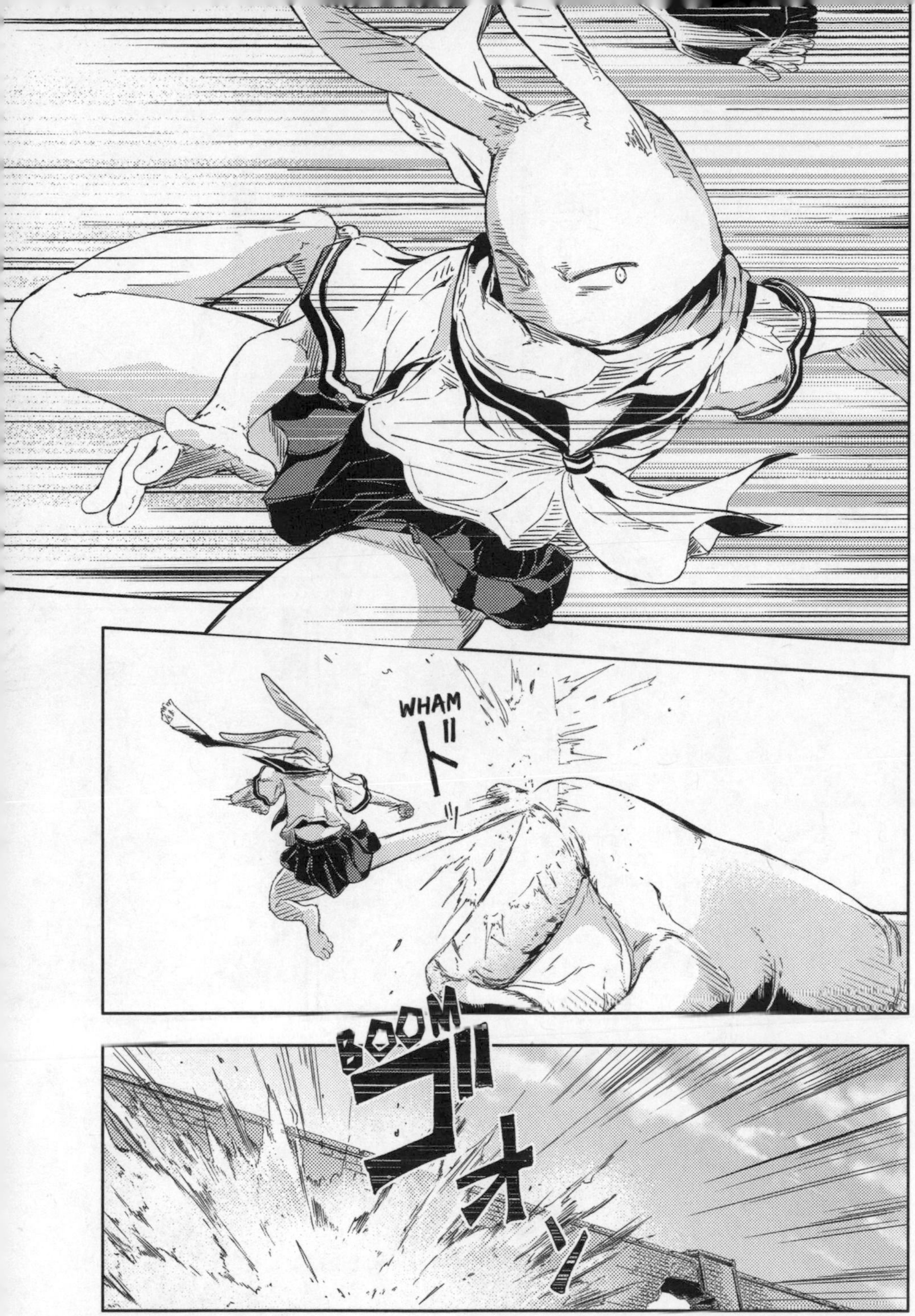
WHAM
ド!!
BOOM
ゴォーン!!

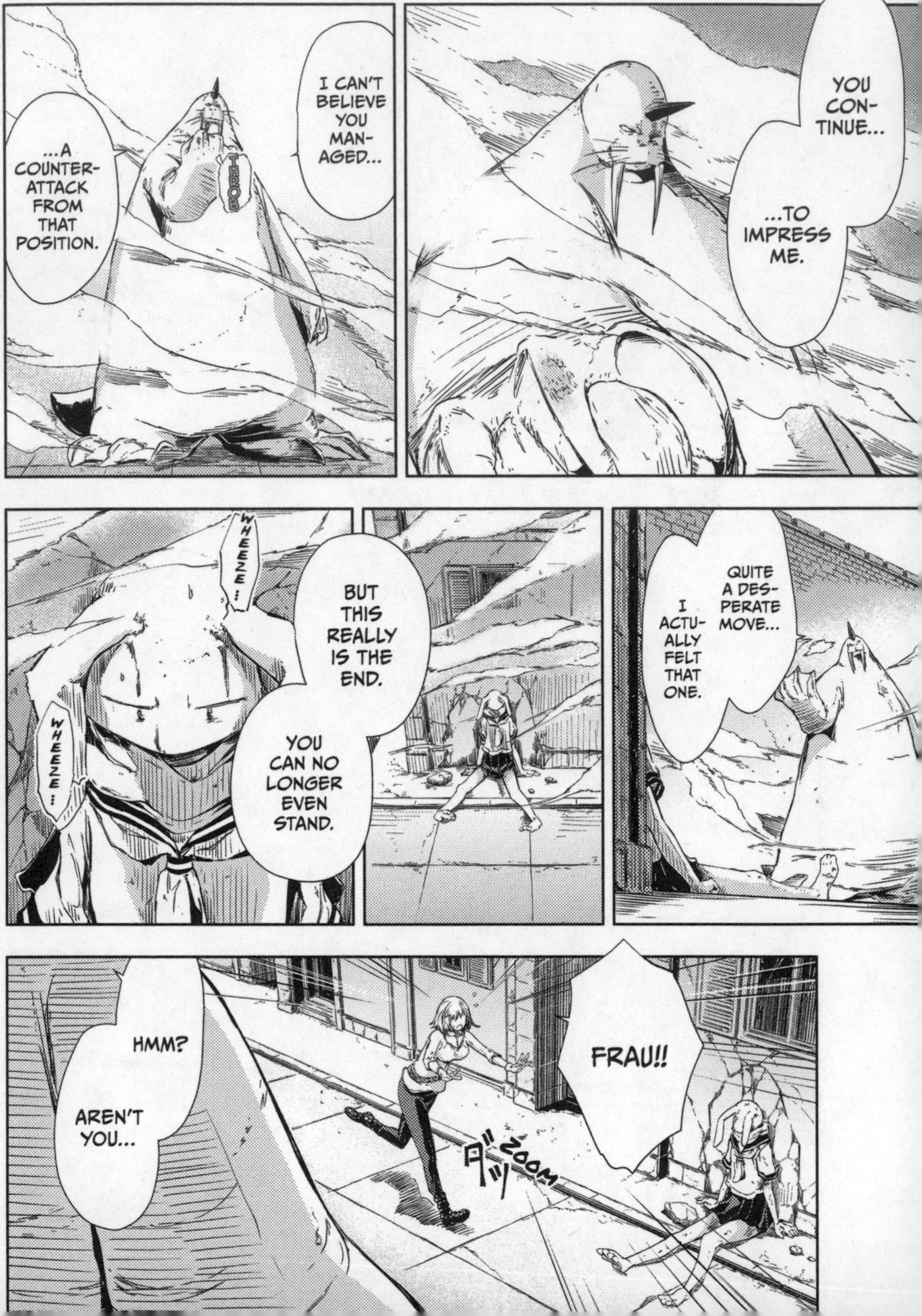
YOU CONTINUE...
...TO IMPRESS ME.
I CAN'T BELIEVE YOU MANAGED...
...A COUNTER-ATTACK FROM THAT POSITION.
THROB
QUITE A DESPERATE MOVE...
I ACTUALLY FELT THAT ONE.
BUT THIS REALLY IS THE END.
YOU CAN NO LONGER EVEN STAND.
WHEEZE...
WHEEZE...
FRAU!!
ZOOM
HMM?
AREN'T YOU...

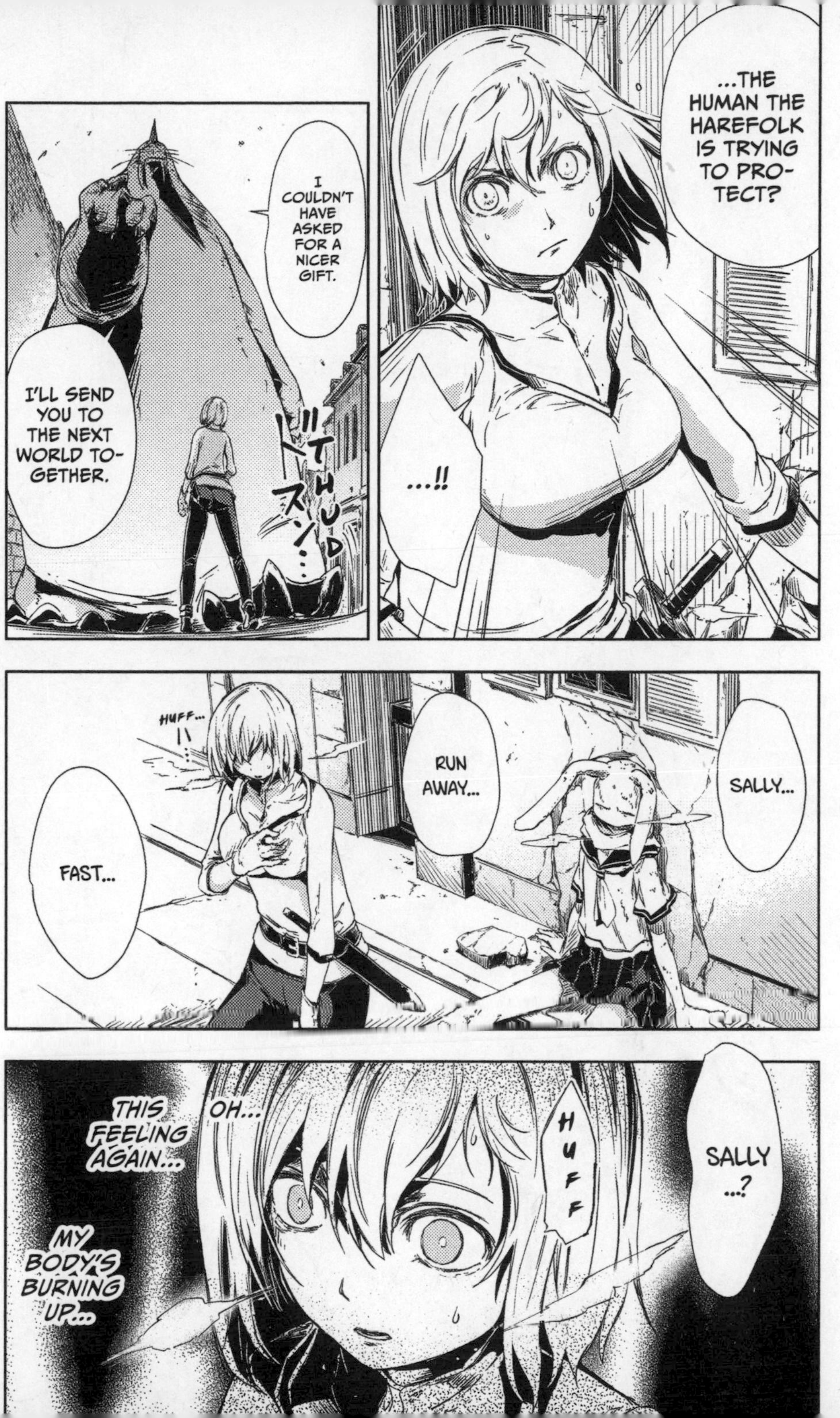
...THE HUMAN THE HAREFOLK IS TRYING TO PROTECT?
...!!
I COULDN'T HAVE ASKED FOR A NICER GIFT.
I'LL SEND YOU TO THE NEXT WORLD TO-GETHER.
THUD
SALLY...
RUN AWAY...
FAST...
HUFF...
SALLY ...?
HUFF
OH...
THIS FEELING AGAIN...
MY BODY'S BURNING UP...

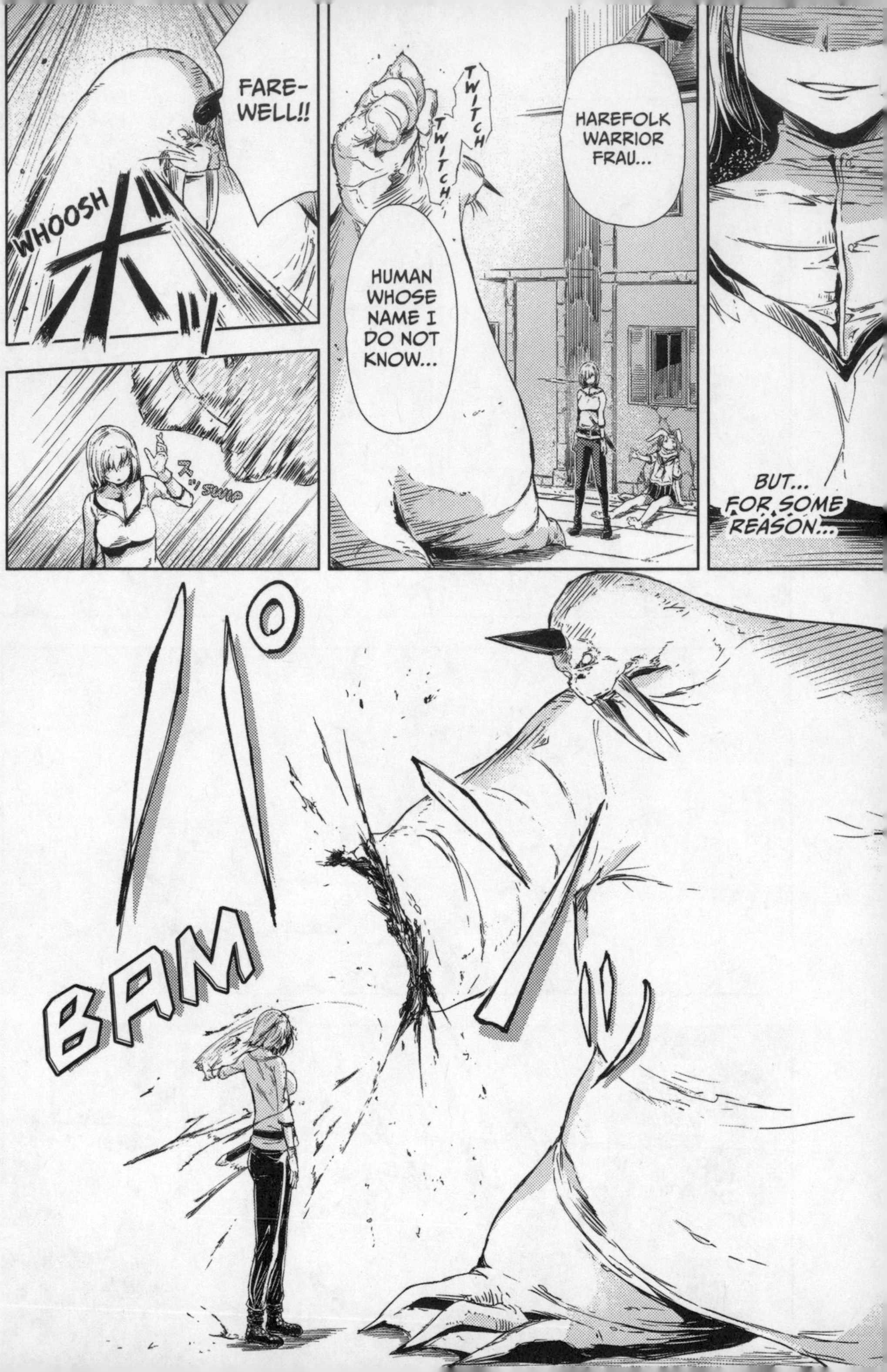
BUT... FOR SOME REASON...
HAREFOLK WARRIOR FRAU...
TWITCH TWITCH
HUMAN WHOSE NAME I DO NOT KNOW...
FARE-WELL!!
WHOOSH
SWIP
BAM

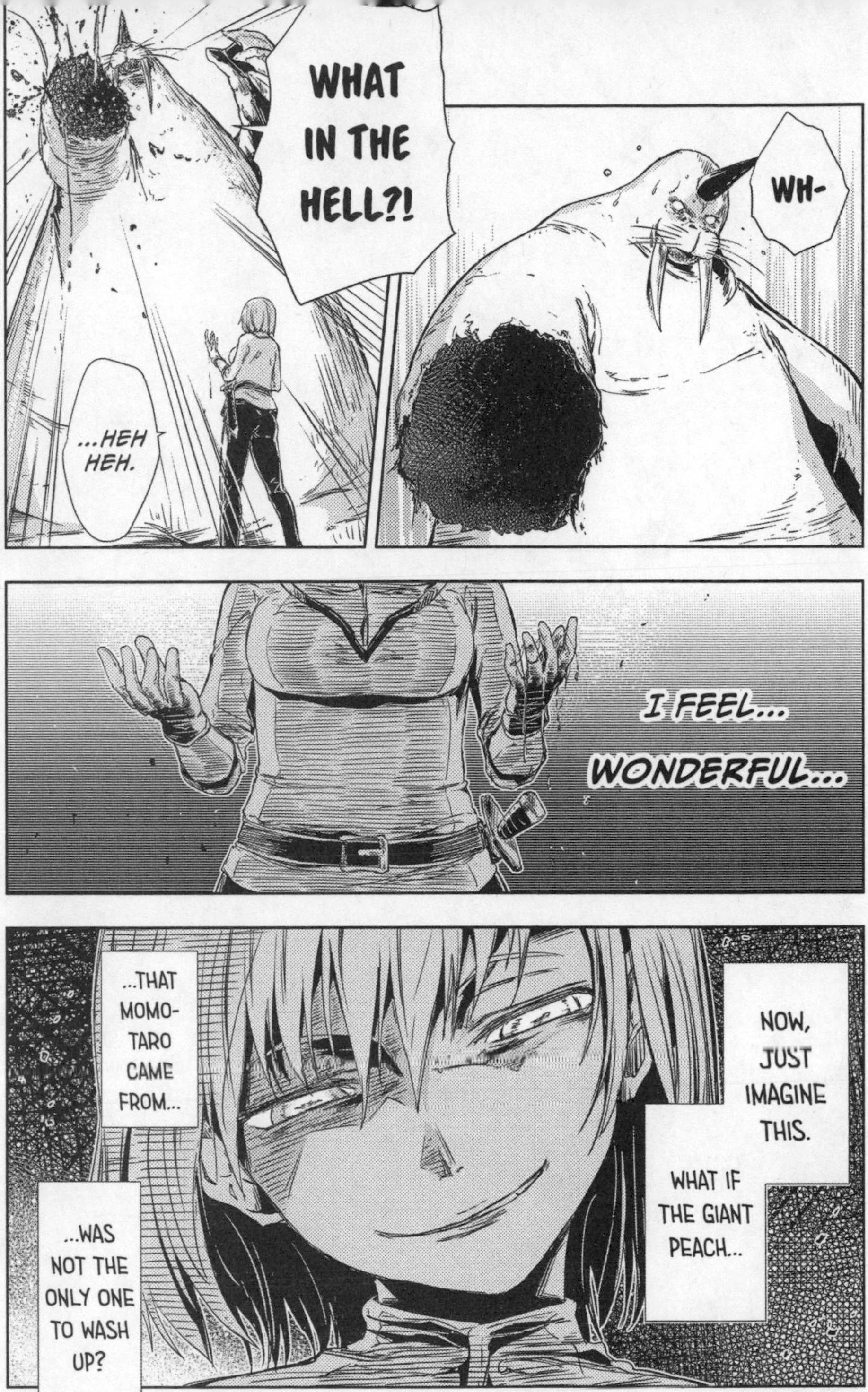
WH-
WHAT IN THE HELL?!
...HEH HEH.
I FEEL... WONDERFUL...
NOW, JUST IMAGINE THIS.
WHAT IF THE GIANT PEACH...
...THAT MOMO-TARO CAME FROM...
...WAS NOT THE ONLY ONE TO WASH UP?

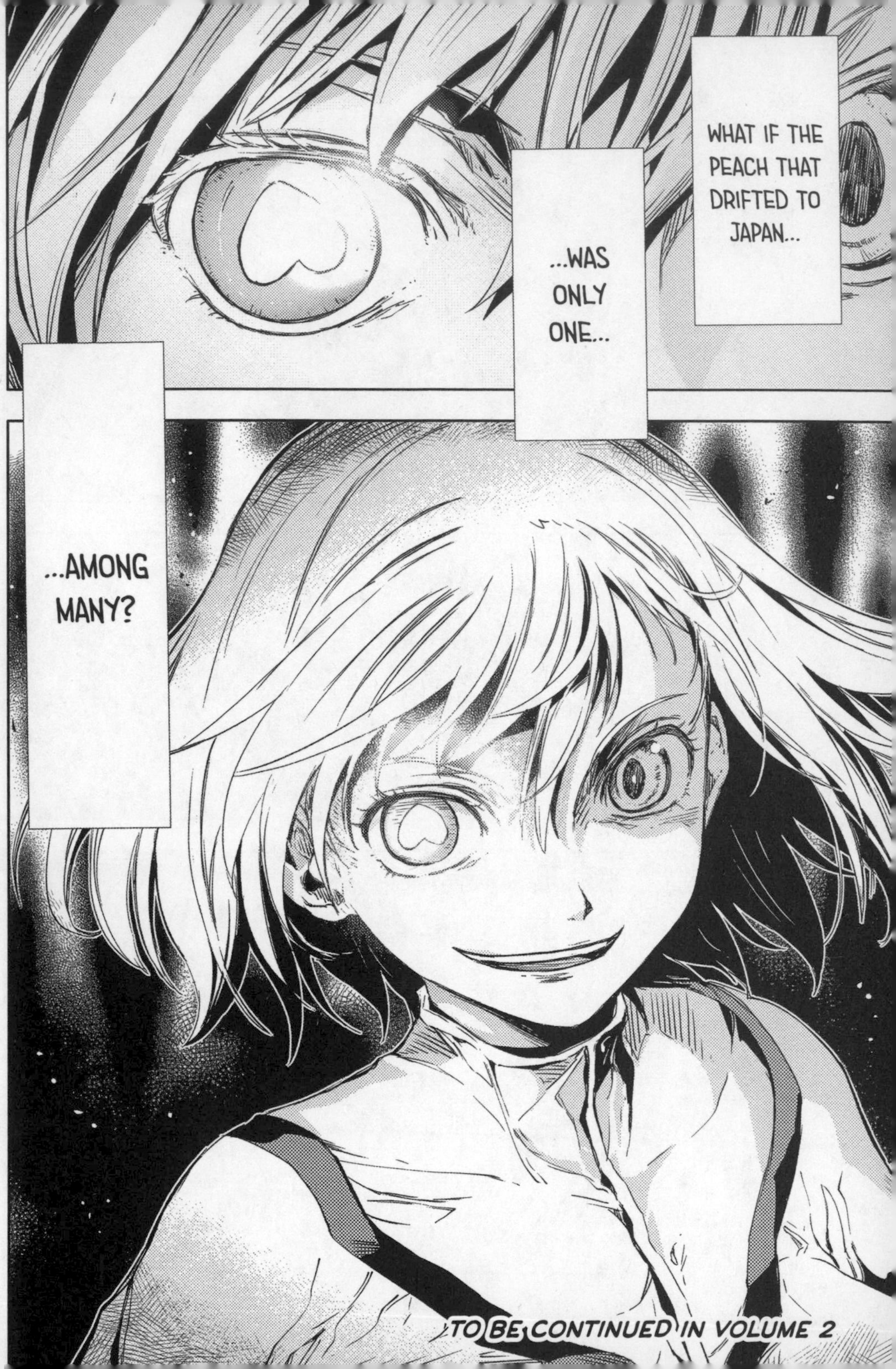
WHAT IF THE PEACH THAT DRIFTED TO JAPAN...
...WAS ONLY ONE...
...AMONG MANY?
TO BE CONTINUED IN VOLUME 2

See you...

...next time.

PEACH BOY
RIVERSIDE

STORY BY: COOLKYOUSINNJYA
BONUS COMIC

EPISODE 0

PEACH BOY
ON THE SEA

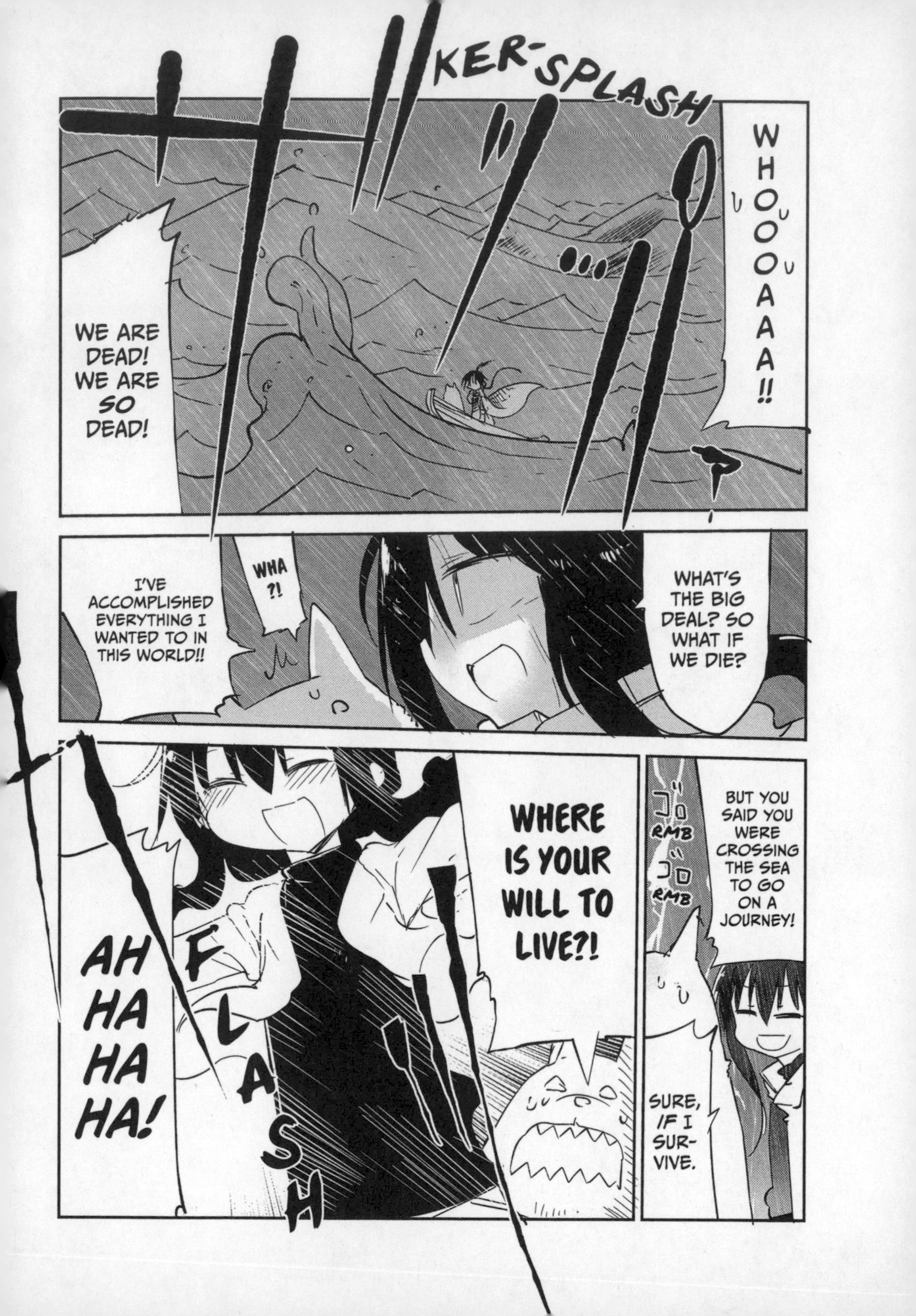
WHOOOAAA!!
KER-SPLASH
WE ARE DEAD! WE ARE SO DEAD!
WHAT'S THE BIG DEAL? SO WHAT IF WE DIE?
WHA?!
I'VE ACCOMPLISHED EVERYTHING I WANTED TO IN THIS WORLD!!
BUT YOU SAID YOU WERE CROSSING THE SEA TO GO ON A JOURNEY!
RMB
RMB
SURE, IF I SUR-VIVE.
WHERE IS YOUR WILL TO LIVE?!
FLASH
AH HA HA HA HA!

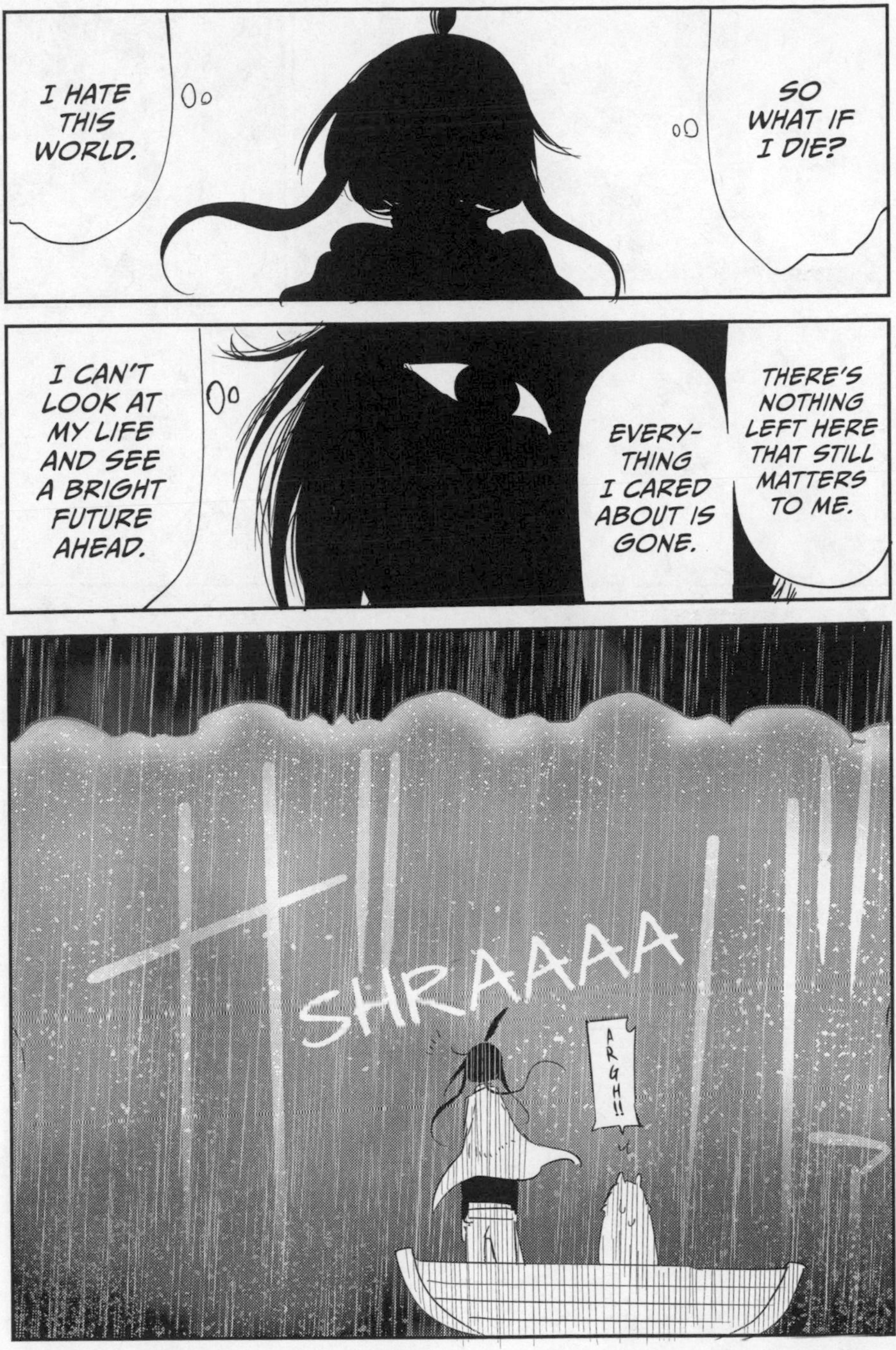
SO WHAT IF I DIE?
I HATE THIS WORLD.
THERE'S NOTHING LEFT HERE THAT STILL MATTERS TO ME.
EVERYTHING I CARED ABOUT IS GONE.
I CAN'T LOOK AT MY LIFE AND SEE A BRIGHT FUTURE AHEAD.
SHRAAAAA
ARGH!!

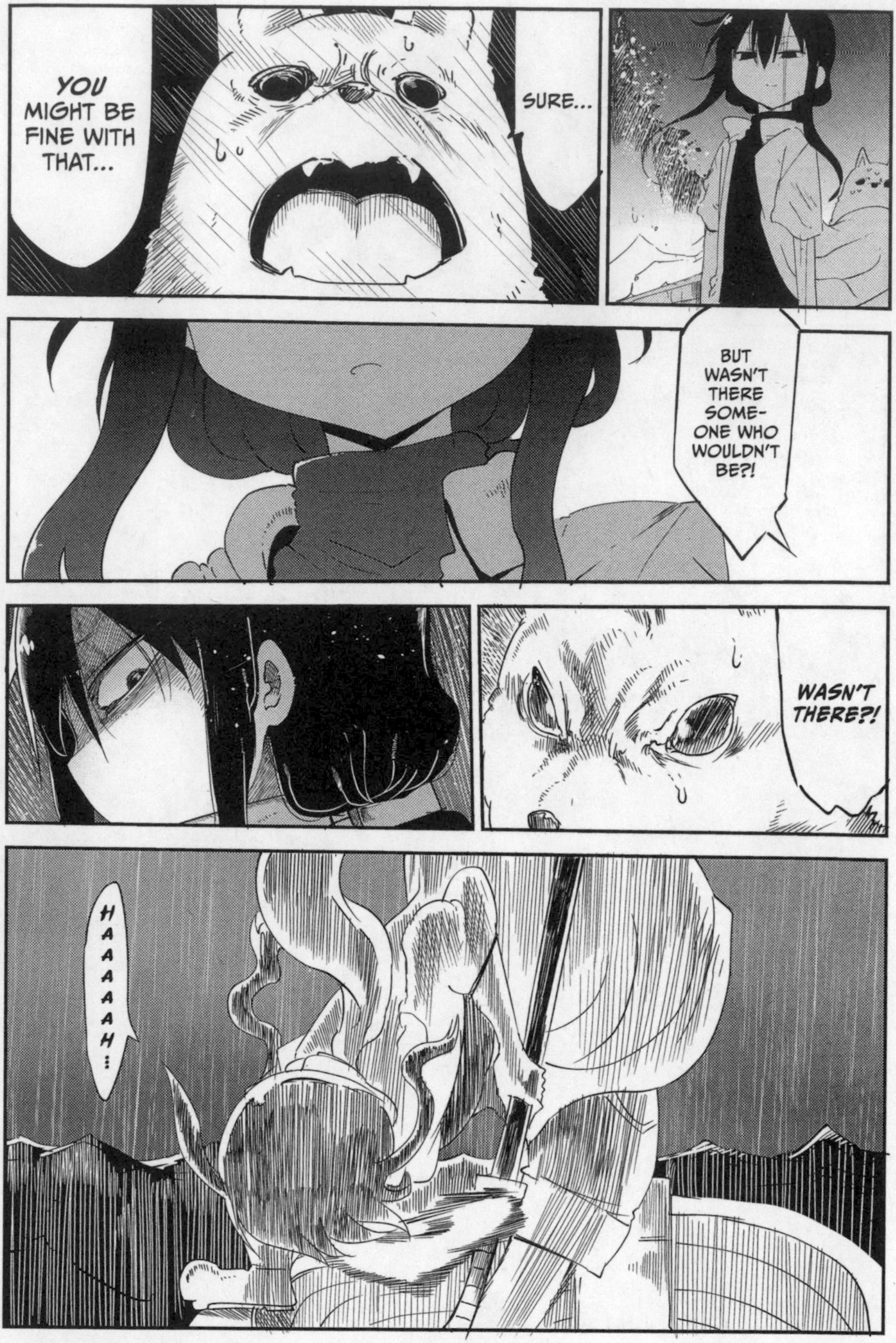
SURE...
YOU MIGHT BE FINE WITH THAT...
BUT WASN'T THERE SOME-ONE WHO WOULDN'T BE?!
WASN'T THERE?!
HAAAAAAH...

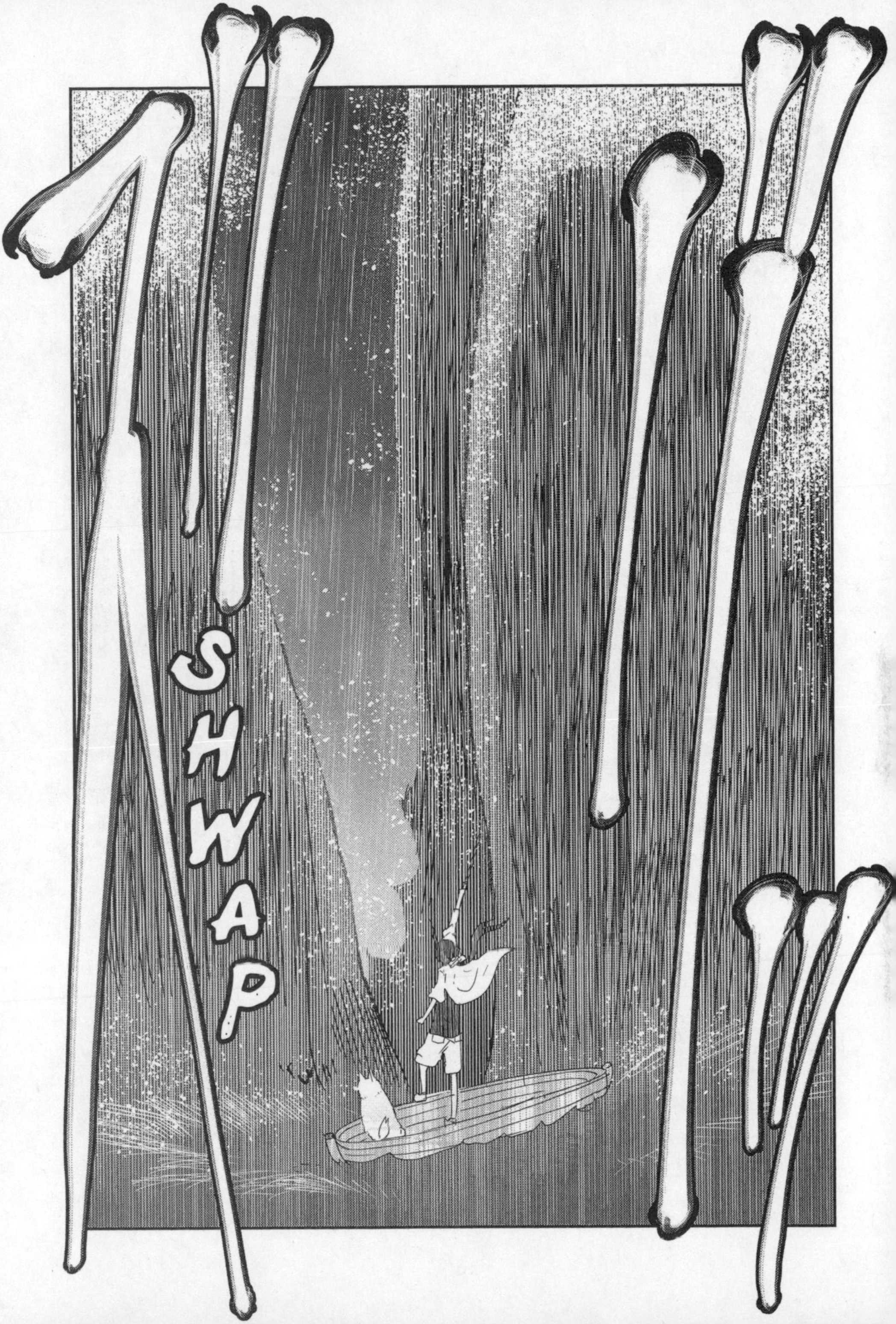
SHWAP

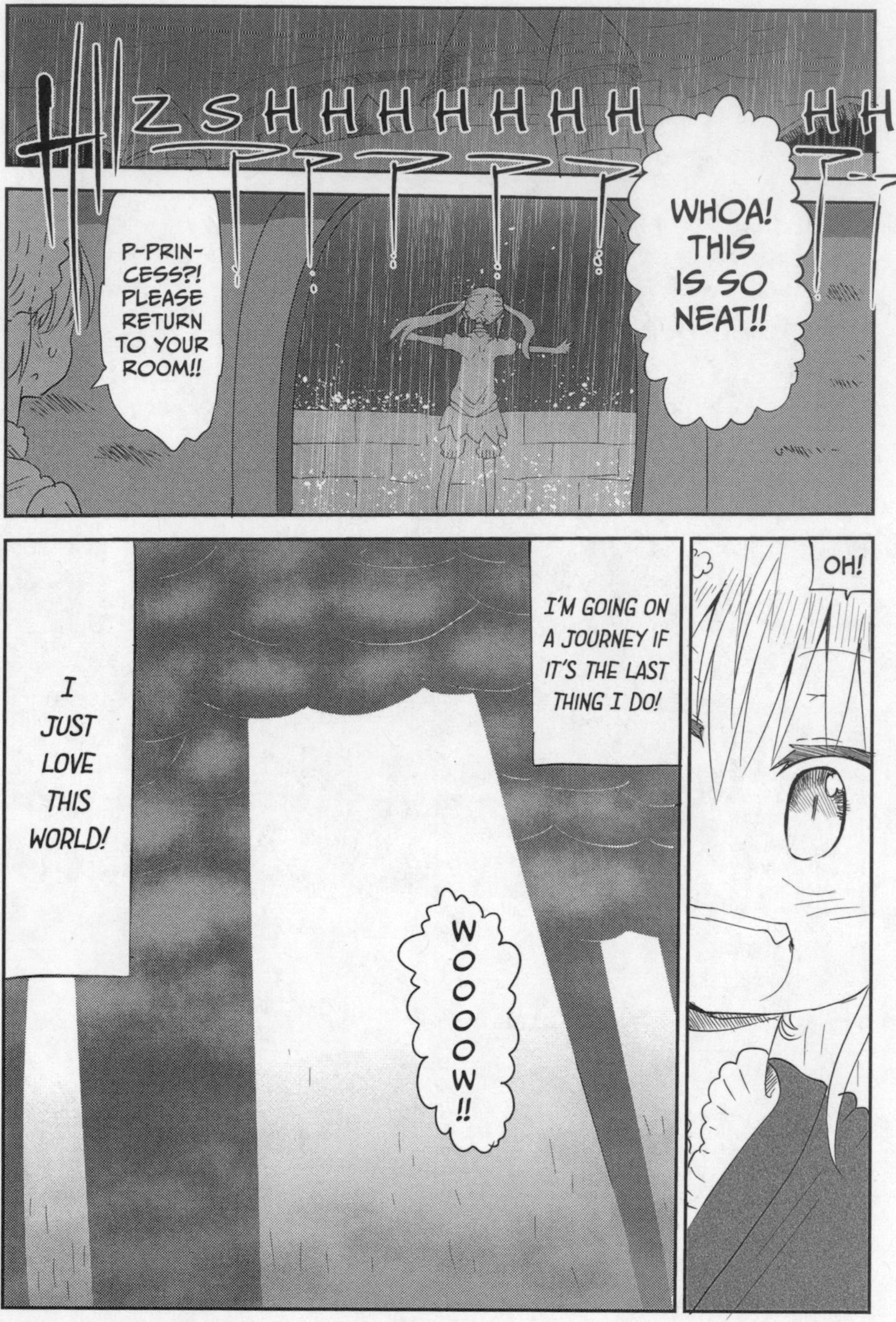
ZSHHHHHHH HH
WHOA! THIS IS SO NEAT!!
P-PRINCESS?! PLEASE RETURN TO YOUR ROOM!!
OH!
I'M GOING ON A JOURNEY IF IT'S THE LAST THING I DO!
I JUST LOVE THIS WORLD!
WOOOOOW!!

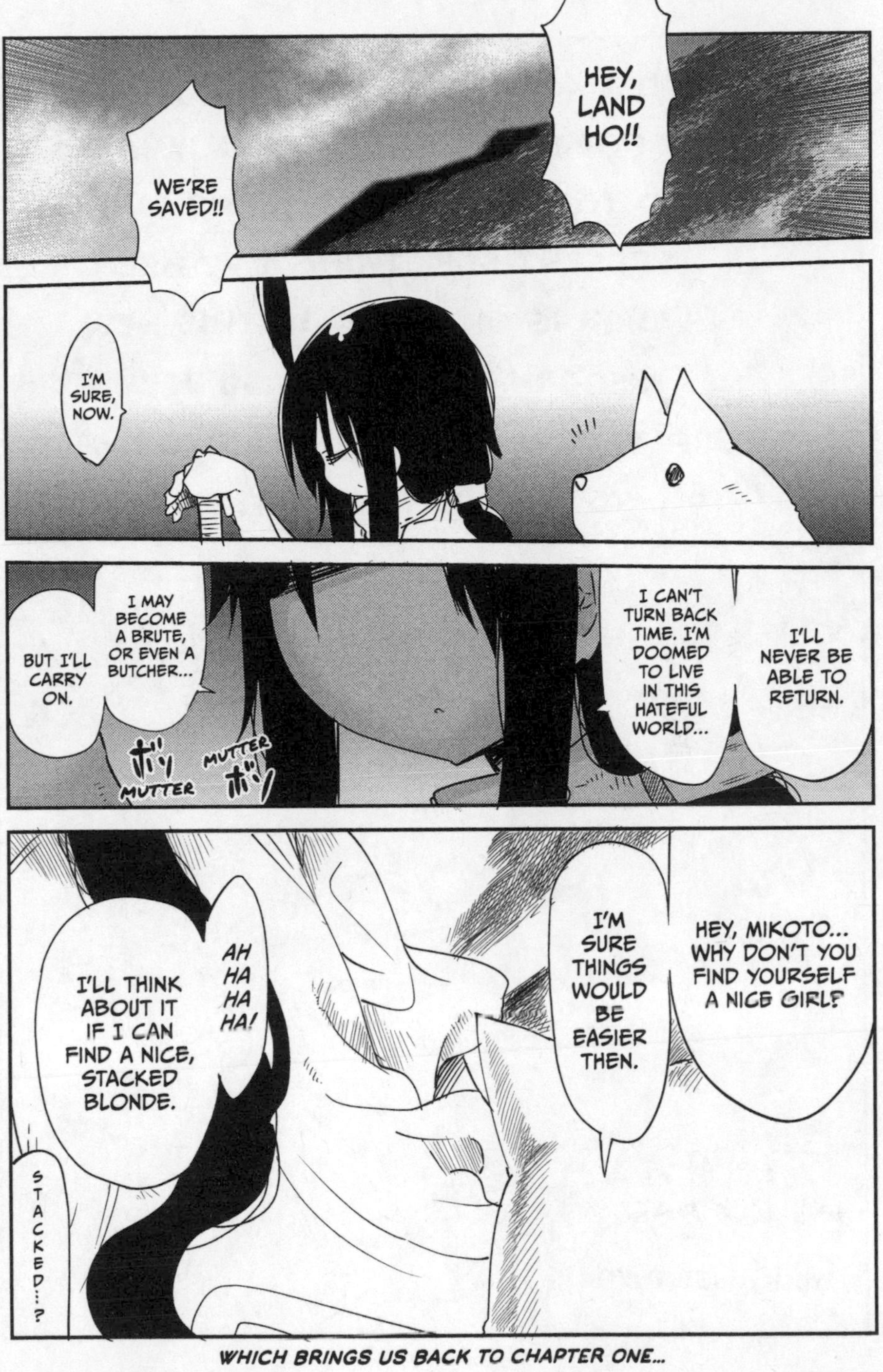
HEY, LAND HO!!
WE'RE SAVED!!
I'M SURE, NOW.
I'LL NEVER BE ABLE TO RETURN.
I CAN'T TURN BACK TIME. I'M DOOMED TO LIVE IN THIS HATEFUL WORLD...
I MAY BECOME A BRUTE, OR EVEN A BUTCHER...
BUT I'LL CARRY ON.
ボソ MUTTER
ボソ MUTTER
HEY, MIKOTO... WHY DON'T YOU FIND YOURSELF A NICE GIRL?
I'M SURE THINGS WOULD BE EASIER THEN.
AH HA HA HA!
I'LL THINK ABOUT IT IF I CAN FIND A NICE, STACKED BLONDE.
STACKED...?

WHICH BRINGS US BACK TO CHAPTER ONE...

Hello and nice to meet you. My name is Coolkyousinnjya. It's hard to believe that I can finally present something I've been working on online in this new, reborn form! I am so very grateful. I hope you look forward to the next volume, too.

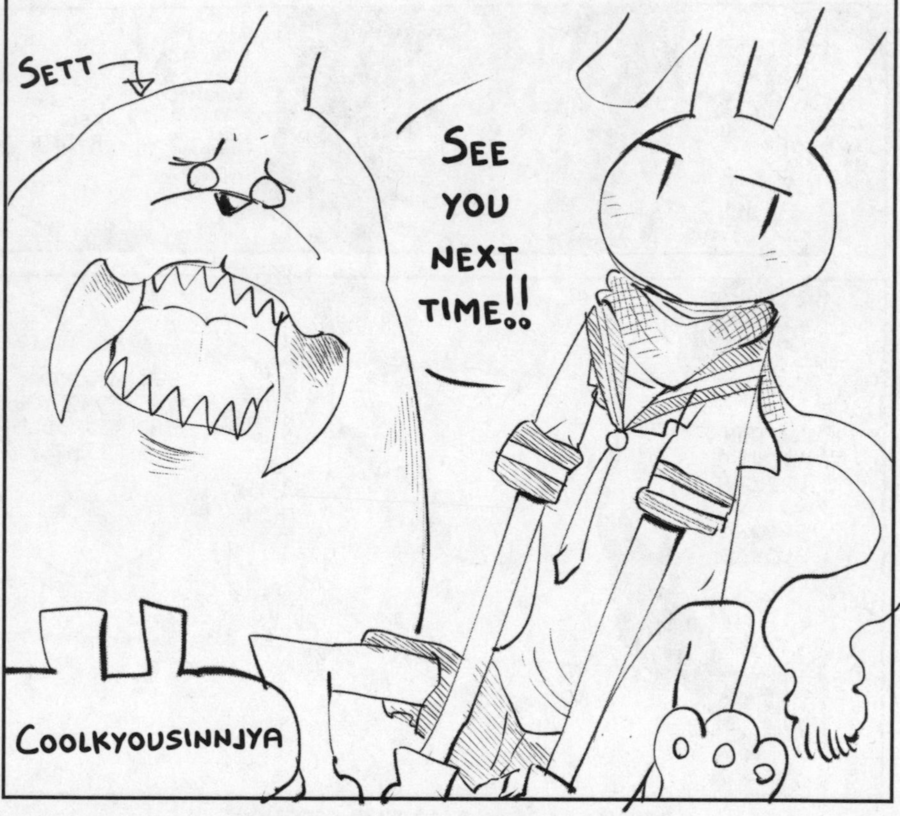

Sett
See you next time!!
Coolkyousinnjya

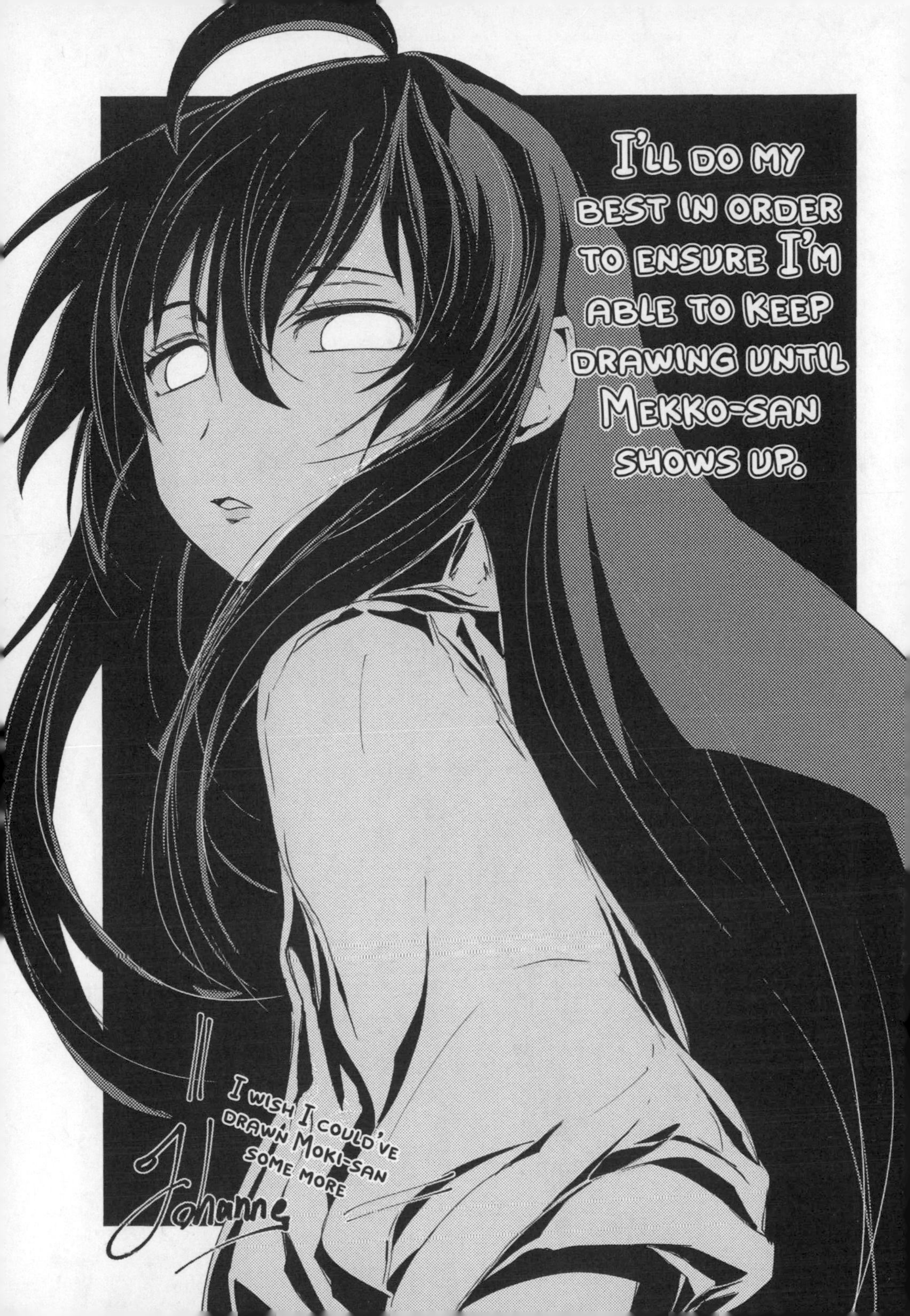
I'll do my best in order to ensure I'm able to keep drawing until Mekko-san shows up.
I wish I could've drawn Moki-san some more
Johanne

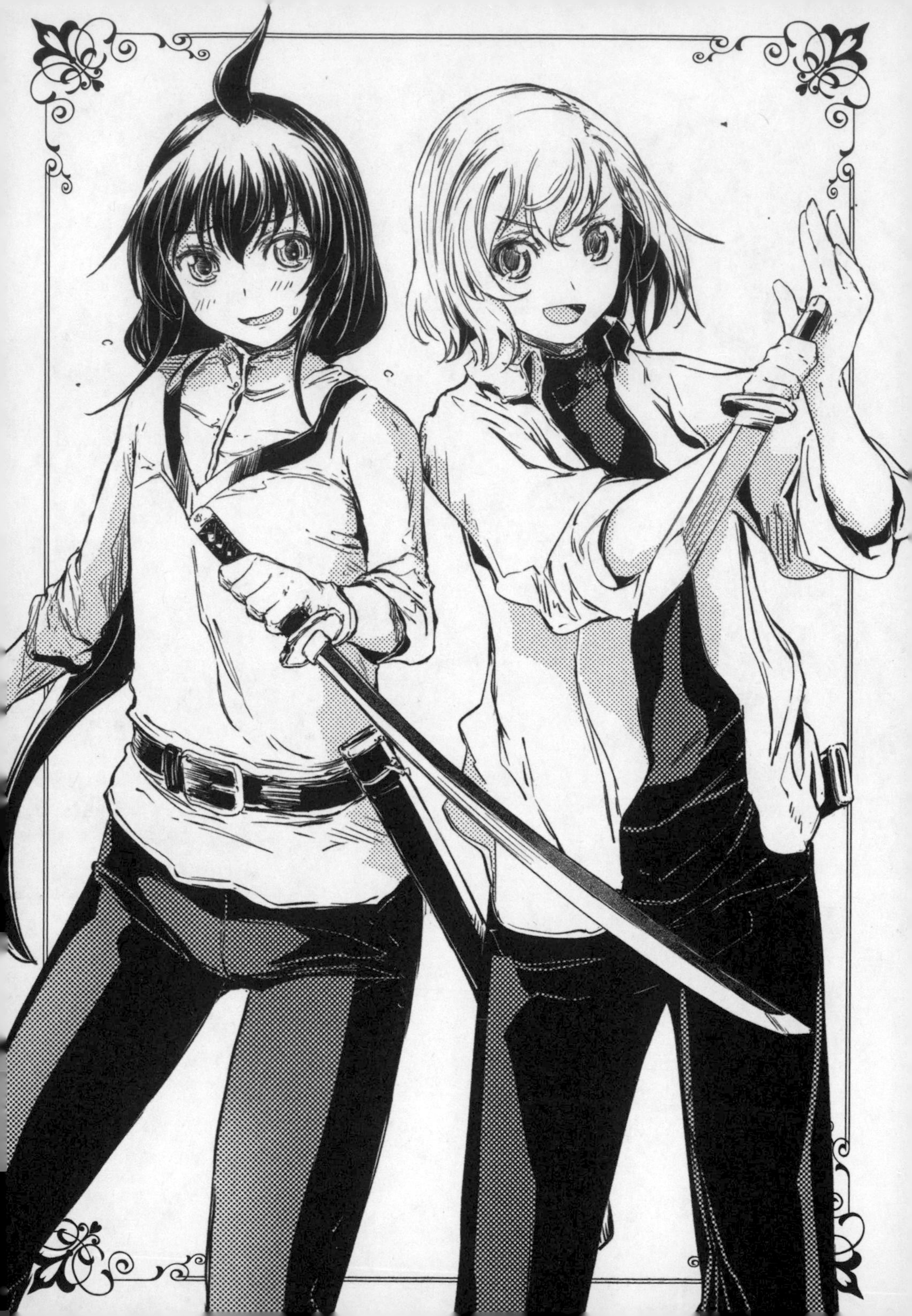

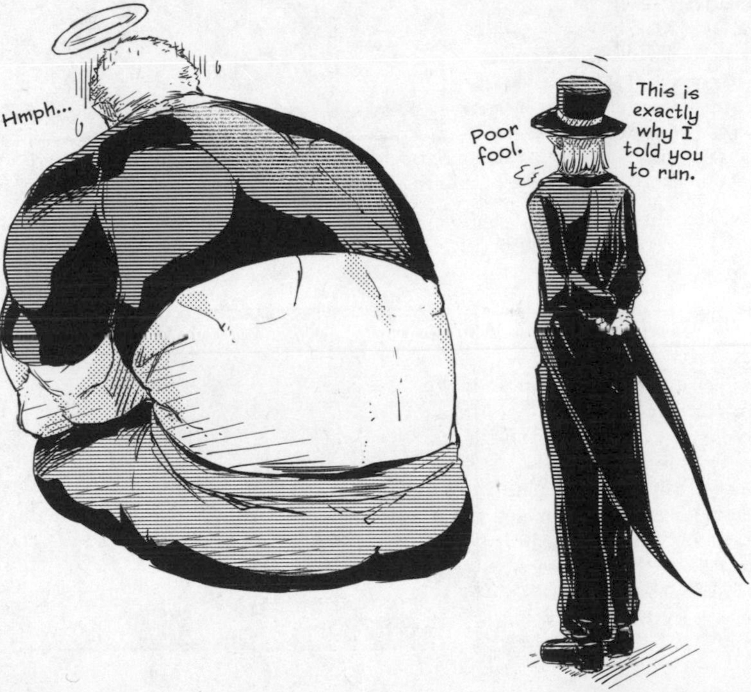
This is exactly why I told you to run.
Poor fool.
Hmph...

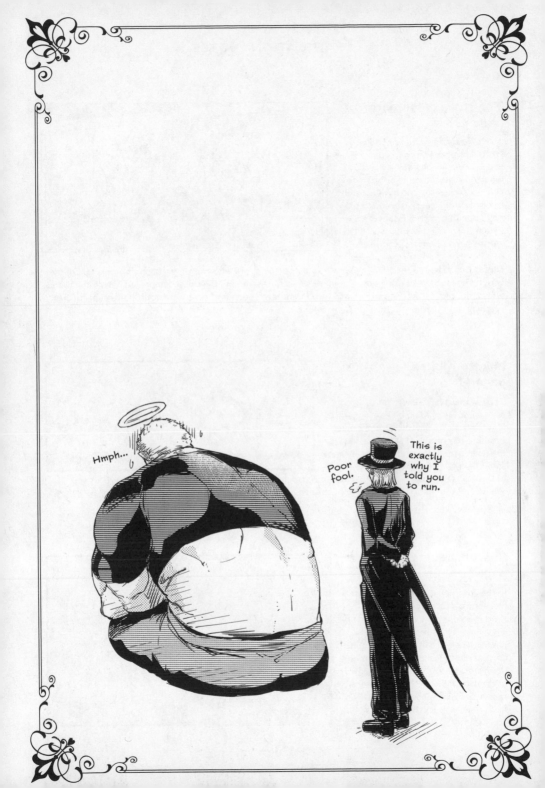

Translation Notes

The story of Momotaro, page 43

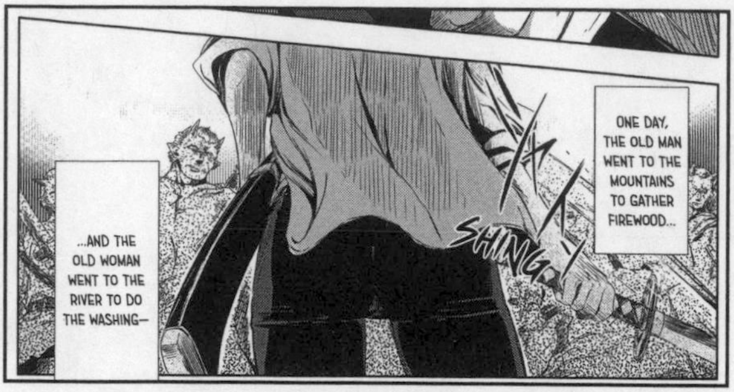
ONE DAY, THE OLD MAN WENT TO THE MOUNTAINS TO GATHER FIREWOOD...
SHING
...AND THE OLD WOMAN WENT TO THE RIVER TO DO THE WASHING—

This folktale, ubiquitously known in Japan, continues on to say that a giant peach came flowing down the river where the old woman was washing clothes. When she and her husband opened up the peach to eat it, a baby boy popped out from inside the fruit, whom they raised as their son. They named him Momotaro, or "peach boy." When Momotaro was in his adolescent years, he set off on a journey to defeat the ogres who were ravaging his homeland. On the way, he befriended a talking dog, a monkey, and a pheasant, and they all accompanied him to the island where the ogres lived. The story ends with Momotaro returning home victorious, but this particular retelling has other ideas.

Mikoto Kibitsu, page 47

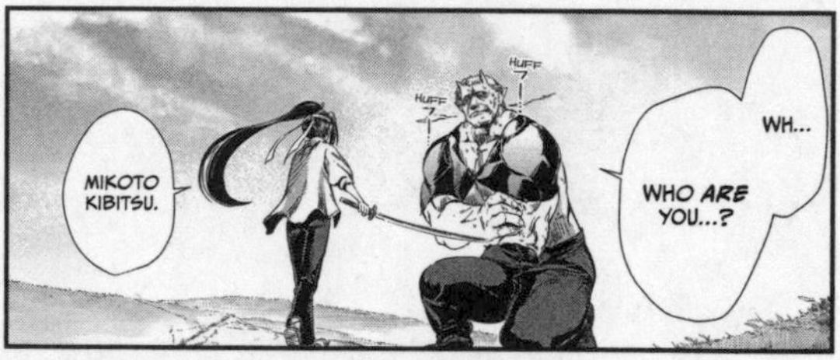
WH...
WHO ARE YOU...?
HUFF
HUFF
MIKOTO KIBITSU.

In Okayama prefecture in Japan, a prince known as Kibitsuhiko-no-mikoto ("-no-mikoto" being a suffix typically added to the names of Shinto deities) is the main deity housed at Kibitsu Shrine, and is likely the inspiration for the name of this manga's protagonist. According to legend, Kibitsuhiko once vanquished an evil ogre named Ura. The tale of Momotaro is believed to have been modeled on that story.

Shared a dumpling, page 53

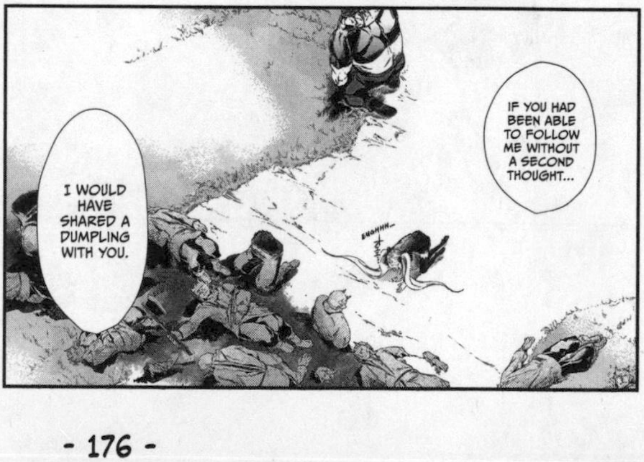
IF YOU HAD BEEN ABLE TO FOLLOW ME WITHOUT A SECOND THOUGHT...
I WOULD HAVE SHARED A DUMPLING WITH YOU.

In the common variant of the folktale, Momotaro's parents packed him rations of kibi dango, or millet dumplings, for his journey. Each time he encountered one of his future animal companions, Momotaro would offer them a dumpling as a sign of goodwill. In essence, Mikoto was prepared to recruit Sally in much the same way he had recruited all his previous companions.

Frau's weapon, page 145

The wooden mallet Frau wields as a weapon bears a close resemblance to those traditionally used to pound rice into mochi, a glutinous rice cake/paste. In Japanese folklore, it is believed that there is a rabbit in the Moon pounding mochi, similar to how a man is believed to be in the Moon in Western cultures.

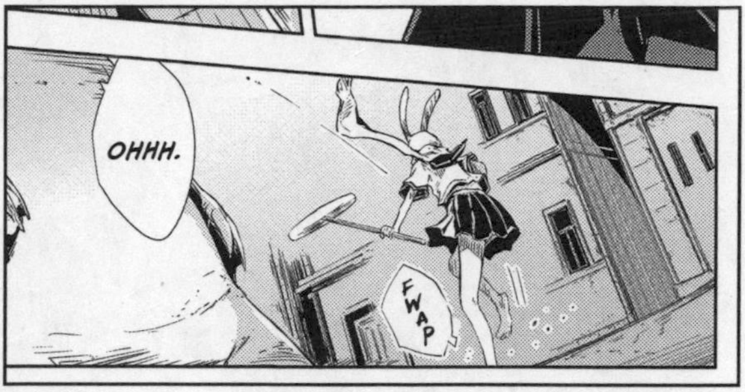
OHHH.
FWAP

Ogre names, pages 36, 37, 126

The names of the humanoid ogres who have appeared thus far all follow the same formula: a Chinese character representing a defining characteristic, followed by the character for "ogre," which is pronounced "ki." The named ogres in this volume were...

Yaki: "Old Man Ogre"
Moki: "Ferocious Ogre"
Meki: "Eye Ogre"

The boys are back, in 400-page hardcovers that are as pretty and badass as they are!

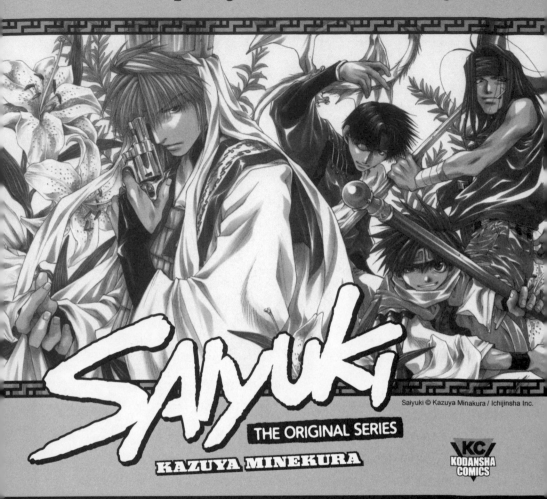

Saiyuki © Kazuya Minekura / Ichijinsha Inc.

SAIYUKI
THE ORIGINAL SERIES
KAZUYA MINEKURA

"AN EDGY COMIC LOOK AT AN ANCIENT CHINESE TALE." —YALSA

Genjo Sanzo is a Buddhist priest in the city of Togenkyo, which is being ravaged by yokai spirits that have fallen out of balance with the natural order. His superiors send him on a journey far to the west to discover why this is happening and how to stop it. His companions are three yokai with human souls. But this is no day trip — the four will encounter many discoveries and horrors on the way.

FEATURES NEW TRANSLATION, COLOR PAGES, AND BEAUTIFUL WRAPAROUND COVER ART!

EDENSZERO
エデンズゼロ

HIRO MASHIMA IS BACK! JOIN THE CREATOR OF *FAIRY TAIL*
AS HE TAKES TO THE STARS FOR ANOTHER THRILLING SAGA!

EDENS ZERO © Hiro Mashima/Kodansha, Ltd.

A high-flying space adventure! All the steadfast friendship
and wild fighting you've been waiting for...IN SPACE!

At Granbell Kingdom, an abandoned amusement park, Shiki has lived his entire
life among machines. But one day, Rebecca and her cat companion Happy appear
at the park's front gates. Little do these newcomers know that this is the first
human contact Granbell has had in a hundred years! As Shiki stumbles his way
into making new friends, his former neighbors stir at an opportunity for a robo-
rebellion... And when his old homeland becomes too dangerous, Shiki must join
Rebecca and Happy on their spaceship and escape into the boundless cosmos.

A dark and sexy body-horror action manga perfect for fans of *Prison School* and *High School of the Dead!*

Shuichi Kagaya is a smart kid, and most smart kids his age would be thinking about college. Shuichi is also a monster, and he's smart enough to know that monsters don't go to college. But after he uses his monstrous form to save his classmate Claire Aoki, it doesn't matter what his plans for the future were, because he's not the one making the decisions anymore. Now that the seductive, sadistic Claire knows Shuichi's secret, she's got her own ideas about what a monster is good for—because he's not the first monster she's met...

GLEIPNIR

"You and me together...we would be unstoppable."

CAN A FARMER SAVE THE WORLD? FIND OUT IN THIS FANTASY MANGA FOR FANS OF *SWORD ART ONLINE* AND *THAT TIME I GOT REINCARNATED AS A SLIME*!

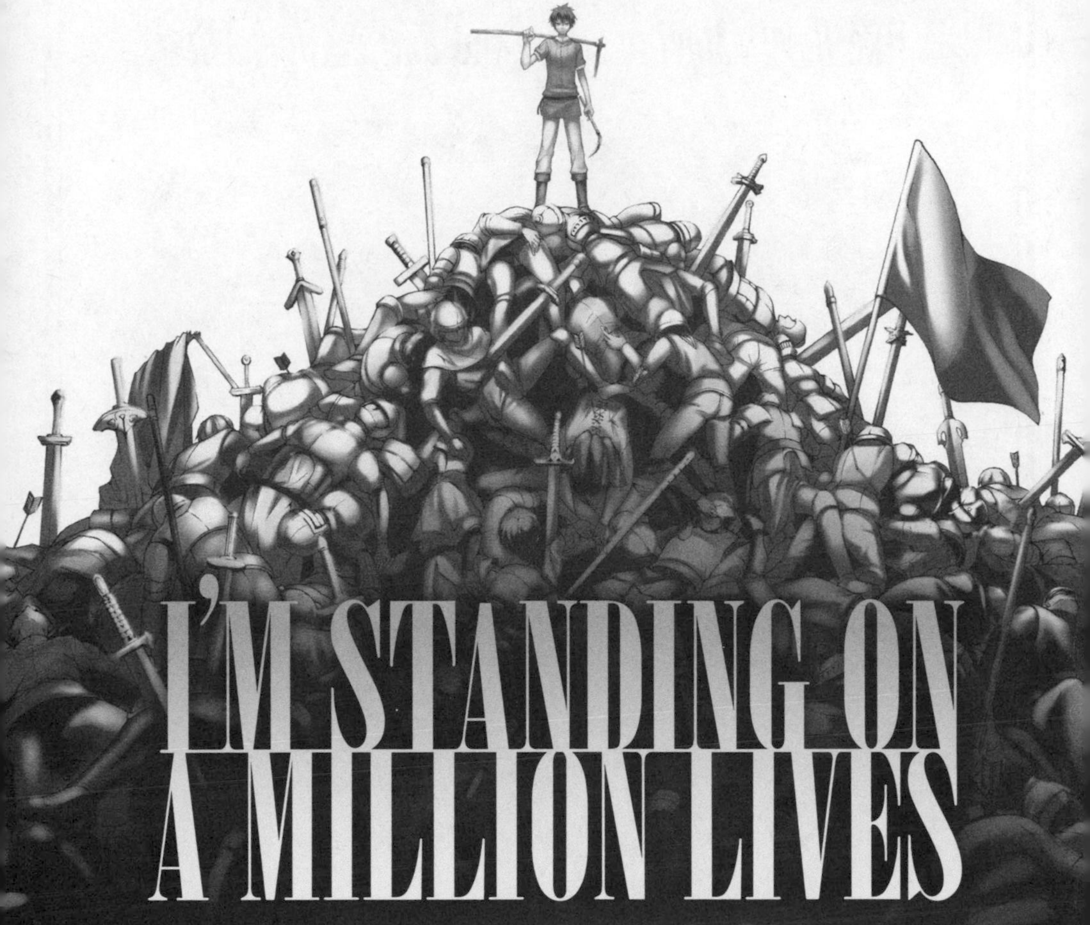

I'M STANDING ON A MILLION LIVES

By
Akinari Nao

Original Story by
Naoki Yamakawa

Yusuke Yotsuya doesn't care about getting into high school—he just wants to get back home to his game and away from other people. But when he suddenly finds himself in a real-life fantasy game alongside his two gorgeous classmates, he discovers a new world of possibility and excitement. Despite a rough start, Yusuke and his friend fight to level up and clear the challenges set before them by a mysterious figure from the future, but before long, they find that they're not just battling for their own lives, but for the lives of millions…

KC KODANSHA COMICS

Young characters and steampunk setting, like *Howl's Moving Castle* and *Battle Angel Alita*

A boy with a talent for machines and a mysterious girl whose wings he's fixed will take you beyond the clouds! In the tradition of the high-flying, resonant adventure stories of Studio Ghibli comes a gorgeous tale about the longing of young hearts for adventure and friendship!

SAINT ☆ YOUNG MEN

A LONG AWAITED ARRIVAL IN PREMIUM 2-IN-1 HARDCOVER

After centuries of hard work, Jesus and Buddha take a break from their heavenly duties to relax among the people of Japan, and their adventures in this lighthearted buddy comedy are sure to bring mirth and merriment to all!

"Brilliant…the physical comedy and facial expressions will make you literally LOL."
—Sam Humphries
(host of *DC Daily*; writer, *Green Lanterns, Legendary Star-Lord*)

PERFECT WORLD

Rie Aruga

A TOUCHING
NEW SERIES
ABOUT LOVE AND
COPING WITH
DISABILITY

An office party reunites Tsugumi with her high school crush Itsuki. He's realized his dream of becoming an architect, but along the way, he experienced a spinal injury that put him in a wheelchair. Now Tsugumi's rekindled feelings will butt up against prejudices she never considered — and Itsuki will have to decide if he's ready to let someone into his heart...

"Depicts with great delicacy and courage the difficulties some with disabilities experience getting involved in romantic relationships... Rie Aruga refuses to romanticize, pushing her heroine to face the reality of disability. She invites her readers to the same tasks of empathy, knowledge and recognition."
—Slate.fr

"An important entry [in manga romance]... The emotional core of both plot and characters indicates thoughtfulness... [Aruga's] research is readily apparent in the text and artwork, making this feel like a real story."
—Anime News Network

KC KODANSHA COMICS

A SMART, NEW ROMANTIC COMEDY FOR FANS OF *SHORTCAKE CAKE* AND *TERRACE HOUSE*!

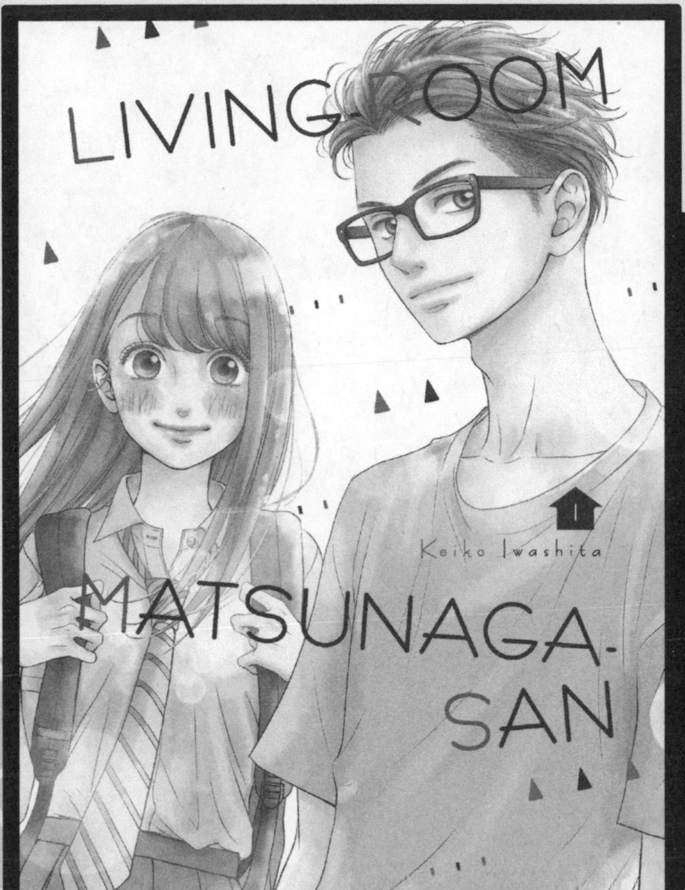
LIVING-ROOM
MATSUNAGA-SAN
1
Keiko Iwashita

KC KODANSHA COMICS

A romance manga starring high school girl Meeko, who learns to live on her own in a boarding house whose living room is home to the odd (but handsome) Matsunaga-san. She begins to adjust to her new life away from her parents, but Meeko soon learns that no matter how far away from home she is, she's still a young girl at heart — especially when she finds herself falling for Matsunaga-san.

Knight of the ICE

Yayoi Ogawa

Knight of the Ice ©Yayoi Ogawa/Kodansha Ltd.

SKATING THRILLS AND ICY CHILLS WITH THIS NEW TINGLY ROMANCE SERIES!

A rom-com on ice, perfect for fans of *Princess Jellyfish* and *Wotakoi*. Kokoro is the talk of the figure-skating world, winning trophies and hearts. But little do they know... he's actually a huge nerd! From the beloved creator of *You're My Pet* (*Tramps Like Us*).

Chitose is a serious young woman, working for the health magazine *SASSO*. Or at least, she would be, if she wasn't constantly getting distracted by her childhood friend, international figure skating star Kokoro Kijinami! In the public eye and on the ice, Kokoro is a gallant, flawless knight, but behind his glittery costumes and breathtaking spins lies a secret: He's actually a hopelessly romantic otaku, who can only land his quad jumps when Chitose is on hand to recite a spell from his favorite magical girl anime!

KC KODANSHA COMICS

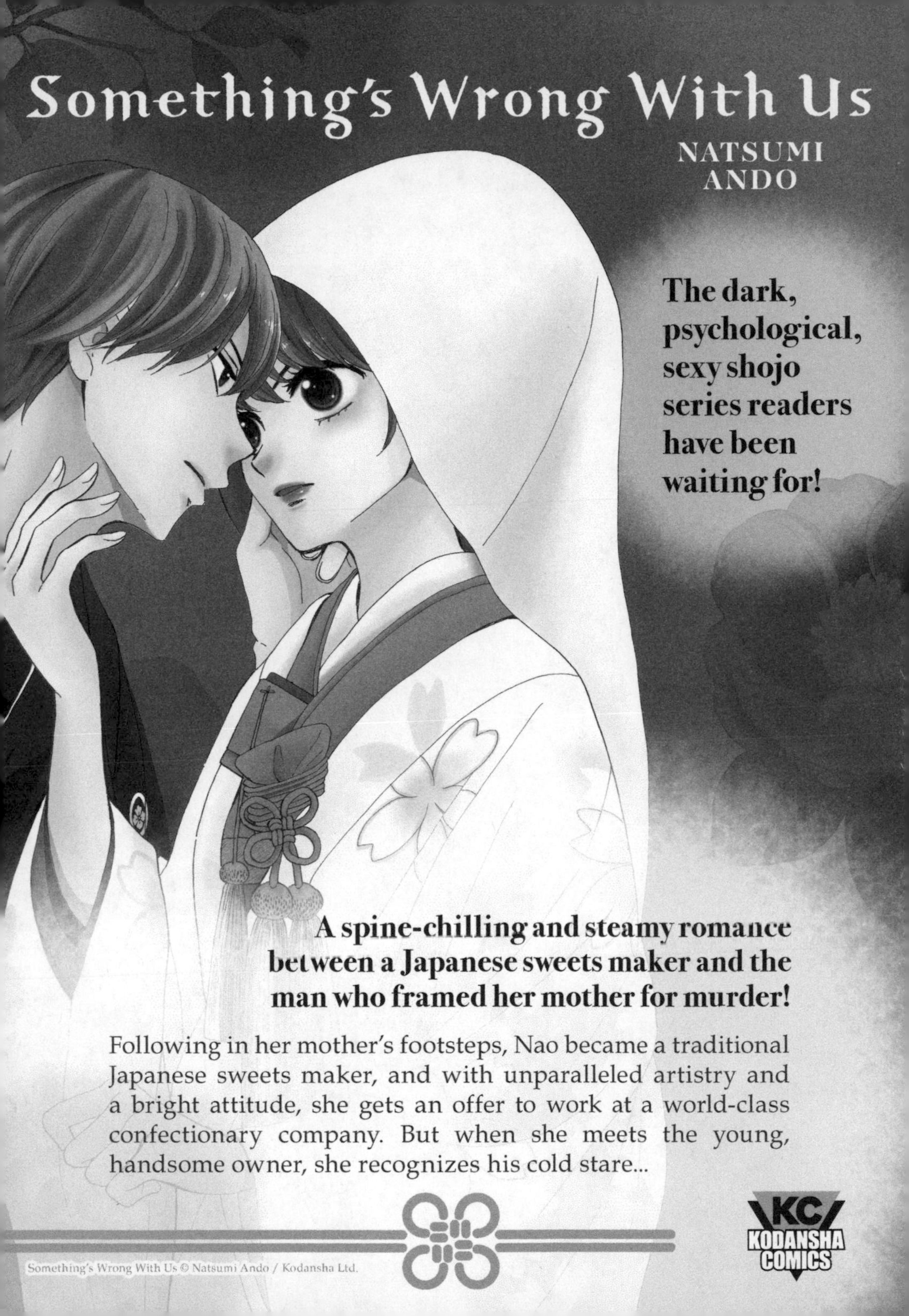

Something's Wrong With Us

NATSUMI
ANDO

The dark, psychological, sexy shojo series readers have been waiting for!

A spine-chilling and steamy romance between a Japanese sweets maker and the man who framed her mother for murder!

Following in her mother's footsteps, Nao became a traditional Japanese sweets maker, and with unparalleled artistry and a bright attitude, she gets an offer to work at a world-class confectionary company. But when she meets the young, handsome owner, she recognizes his cold stare...

Futaro Uesugi is a second-year in high school, scraping to get by and pay off his family's debt. The only thing he can do is study, so when Futaro receives a part-time job offer to tutor the five daughters of a wealthy businessman, he can't pass it up. Little does he know, these five beautiful sisters are quintuplets, but the only thing they have in common...is that they're all terrible at studying!

THE QUINTESSENTIAL QUINTUPLETS

negi haruba

ANIME OUT NOW!

THE SWEET SCENT OF LOVE IS IN THE AIR! FOR FANS OF OFFBEAT ROMANCES LIKE *WOTAKOI*

Sweat and Soap © Kintetsu Yamada / Kodansha Ltd.

In an office romance, there's a fine line between sexy and awkward... and that line is where Asako — a woman who sweats copiously — meets Koutarou — a perfume developer who can't get enough of Asako's, er, scent. Don't miss a romcom manga like no other!

MAGIC ● KNIGHT Rayearth
25TH ANNIVERSARY EDITION
CLAMP

A BELOVED CLASSIC MAKES ITS STUNNING RETURN IN THIS GORGEOUS, LIMITED EDITION BOX SET!

This tale of three Tokyo teenagers who cross through a magical portal and become the champions of another world is a modern manga classic. The box set includes three volumes of manga covering the entire first series of *Magic Knight Rayearth*, plus the series's super-rare full-color art book companion, all printed at a larger size than ever before on premium paper, featuring a newly-revised translation and lettering, and exquisite foil-stamped covers.

A strictly limited edition, this will be gone in a flash!

A Kodansha Comics Trade Paperback Original
Peach Boy Riverside 1 copyright © 2016 Coolkyousinnjya/Johanne
English translation copyright © 2021 Coolkyousinnjya/Johanne

Published in the United States by Kodansha Comics, an imprint of
Kodansha USA Publishing, LLC, New York.

Publication rights for this English edition arranged through
Kodansha Ltd., Tokyo.

First published in Japan in 2016 by Kodansha Ltd., Tokyo.

ISBN 978-1-64651-339-0

Original cover design by Tadashi Hisamochi (hive&co.,ltd.)

Printed in the United States of America.

www.kodansha.us

9 8 7 6 5 4 3 2 1
Translation: Steven LeCroy
Lettering: Andrew Copeland
Additional Lettering: Belynda Ungurath
Editing: Thalia Sutton, Vanessa Tenazas
YKS Services LLC/SKY Japan, Inc.
Kodansha Comics edition cover design by Adam Del Re

Publisher: Kiichiro Sugawara

Director of publishing services: Ben Applegate
Associate director of operations: Stephen Pakula
Publishing services managing editors: Alanna Ruse, Madison Salters
Production managers: Emi Lotto, Angela Zurlo
Logo and character art ©Kodansha USA Publishing, LLC